Spain and EC Membership Evaluated

EC Membership Evaluated Series
Series Editor: Carl-Christoph Schweitzer, The University of Bonn

The Netherlands and EC Membership Evaluated
ed. Menno Wolters and Peter Coffey

Federal Republic of Germany and EC Membership Evaluated
ed. Carl-Christoph Schweitzer and Detlev Karsten

Ireland and EC Membership Evaluated
ed. Patrick Keatinge

The United Kingdom and EC Membership Evaluated
ed. Simon Bulmer, Stephen George and Andrew Scott

Denmark and EC Membership Evaluated
ed. Lise Lyck

Italy and EC Membership Evaluated
ed. Francesco Francioni

Belgium and EC Membership Evaluated
ed. M.A.G. van Meerhaeghe

France and EC Membership Evaluated
ed. François-Georges Dreyfus, Jacques Morizet and Max Peyrard

Spain and EC Membership Evaluated
ed. Amparo Almarcha Barbado

Portugal and EC Membership Evaluated
ed. José da Silva Lopes

Spain and EC Membership Evaluated

Edited by Amparo Almarcha Barbado

Pinter Publishers, London
St. Martin's Press, New York

Pinter Publishers Ltd.
25 Floral Street, London WC2E 9DS, United Kingdom
and **St. Martin's Press**
175 Fifth Avenue, New York, NY 10010, USA

First published in 1993

British Library Cataloguing in Publication Data
A CIP catalogue record for this book is available from the British Library

ISBN 1 86187 899 X (Pinter)
ISBN 0–312–10367–0 (St. Martin's)

Library of Congress Cataloging-in-Publication Data

Spain and EC membership evaluated / edited by Amparo Almarcha Barbado.
p. cm. – (EC membership evaluated series)
Includes index.
ISBN 0–312–10367–0
1. European Economic Community – Spain, 2. Spain – Economic policy. 3. Spain – Social policy. 4. Spain – Politics and government – 1975–. 5. Spain – Cultural policy. 6. Law – Spain. I. Almarcha Barbado, María Amparo. II. Series.
HC241.25.S6S68 1993
341.24'22'0946–dc20

93–21485
CIP

Printed and bound in Great Britain by SRP Ltd.

Contents

List of Contributors

María Pilar Alcobendas Tirado (1941). M A (Universidad Pontificia of Salamanca). She is a graduate of the Complutense University, the Social Institute 'León XIII' and the Diplomatic Training School in Madrid. She currently manages the data bank at the Centro de Investigaciones Sociológicas (Sociological Research Centre). Since 1982, she has been a member of the Expert Group 'Women in Employment' of the Directorate General V of the European Community. Her publications include 'Migrant Women in the Family and Working Life in the EEC' (1986); 'Effects of the Implementation of the International Market over Clothing and Textile Employment in Spain' (1989); and 'Effets de l' Achèvement du Marché Intérieur sur l'Emploi dans le Secteur Bancaire en Espagne' (1990).

Amparo Almarcha Barbado (1945). PhD (Granada), M A (Yale). Professor of Sociological Theory at the Complutense University of Madrid. She has worked with Amando de Miguel, producing – amongst other work, 'Situación Social de España en 1970 y 1975' (Social Situation of Spain in 1970 and 1975) and 'Sociología de la Educación: reforma educativa y comparación a nivel europeo' (Sociology of education: educational reform and a European comparison). She has participated in work on different aspects of social policy in Madrid. She has also published work on authority and privilege in Spanish universities, on health, and on social patterns of change and the birth-rate. She has directed a course on the impact of social change in Europe on women.

Rafaela Alonso Rodríguez (1952). M A. She has worked in the Social Action Department of the Ministry of Work and Social Security, now part of the Ministry of Social Affairs which now deals with personal income taxation and social affairs (children, youth, women, etc.).

Carlos Alvarez Aledo (1962) M A. (Complutense University of Madrid). He also holds further degrees from Escuela de Relaciones Laborales and ICADE, Universidad Pontificia de Comillas. Associate Professor of Economic Policy in the Faculty of Economic Science of the Autonomous University of Madrid.

Antonio Alvarez Sousa (1960). Graduate of the University of Santiago de Compostela and Complutense University of Madrid. Professor at the Department of Sociology, Political and Administration Science of the University of Santiago de Compostela. He has published several articles, among them one on forests in the EC (jointly with J. Pérez Vilariño).

Carlos Bruquetas Galán (1943). Secretary general of the Science and Society Institute; editor of works on citizenship including *Libertades Públicas y Fuerzas Armadas* (1966); *El Derecho al Desarrollo o el Desarrollo de los Derechos* (1991) and *Cambio y seguridad en la Europa de los 90* (1991).

José Luis Buhigas Viqueira (1945). M A (Complutense University of Madrid). Formerly a naval officer and legal consultant in shipbuilding. Former President of the Defence Commission of the Spanish Communist Party (PCE), he has cooperated with the Foreign Affairs Secretary of the Spanish Socialist Workers Party (PSOE) since 1989. He currently is adviser to the Foreign Ministry as well as founding member of the Fundación Europa and the Instituto Ciencia y Sociedad.

Serafín Chimeno Rabanillo (1948). M A (Complutense University of Madrid), M A (Universidad Pontificia of Comillas, Madrid). He is now Associate Professor of Journalism at CUM and head of the press department of the professional magistrates association. He set up the newspaper *Deliberación.*

Alfonso de Esteban Alonso (1943). PhD (Complutense University of Madrid). He is currently Professor of Human Ecology, and Dean of the Faculty of Political Science and Sociology at CUM. He has produced work on the ecology of metropolitan Spain, equipment standards, data for a public business policy and the Social Balance of the National Industry Institute.

Ana González Fernández (1961). M A (Complutense University of Madrid). She is a surgeon with an interest in hepatology, who has specialized in occupational medicine.

Sara González Fernández (1959). PhD (Complutense University of Madrid). She also holds further degrees in European Studies. She is Professor of International Economics and International Economics Organization and General Secretary of the Faculty of Economics and Business Science at CUM. Among other work, she has published articles on the economic effects of integration.

Celia González Jorge (1959). M A (Complutense University of Madrid). She has taken part in research projects on the family and social change; in cooperation with Amparo Almarcha and others, she has published *Pautas de cambio social y natalidad* (1991). She has done research on the effects of gender on the careers of female teachers at CUM.

Benjamín González Rodríguez (1946). M. Phil. (Yale) PhD (University of Granada). He is Professor of Sociology at the Complutense University of Madrid, where he teaches social research methods. His main field of specialization is medical sociology and social psychiatry, and he has published several books and about twenty articles on health and society in Spain. He is now interested in applying complex models to the understanding and analysis of the social impact of AIDS on Spanish society. He is carrying out a research project dealing with multidimensional evaluation of the needs of the elderly.

Antonio Izquierdo Escribano (1950). PhD (Complutense University of Madrid). Professor at the Faculty of Political Science and Sociology in Madrid. He is an expert in immigration topics at the European Parliament and the European Community Commission. He is author of the RIMET Report (Immigration from Third Countries) for the EC (1990, 1991) and of the report on immigrant regularization for the OECD (1989). Between 1989 and 1991 he published three books and some articles in Spanish and foreign magazines, dealing with Spanish migration in Europe and Latin America and immigration into Spain.

María Teresa López (1957). PhD (Complutense University of Madrid). She is Professor of Public Taxation and Fiscal Systems in the Faculty of Economics and Business Science at CUM. Among other publications, she has written an article on international fiscal fraud in the EEC.

Alejandro López López (1940). M.A. (University of Rome); PhD (Complutense University of Madrid). Professor at the Complutense University of Madrid and Joint Director of the University Institute for Environmental Sciences. He has an interest in urban renaissance. Among his works are: *Proceedings of the International Congress for Environmental Education* (1989); *El Espacio Ambiental Europeo* (1990); *La Comunidad Europea y la Conservación de la Naturaleza* (1990).

José Ramón Montero Gibert (1948). PhD (University of Santiago de Compostela). Professor of Political Science at the Autonomous University of Madrid. He has taught political science at the Universities of Granada, Santiago, Saragossa, Cadiz and at Complutense. Formerly the Dean of the Law Faculty at the University of Cadiz and Assistant Director of the Centro de Investigaciones Sociológicas, he has researched in many fields, including political culture, voting behaviour, political parties and processes of democratic transition.

María Luz Morán (1957). PhD (Complutense University of Madrid). Professor of Social Change in the Faculty of Political Science and Sociology. She has published work on Pareto sociological studies, on political culture and democracy in Spain, a sociological analysis of the Spanish Parliament (1977-1986), and a study of the relationship between the European Parliament, the national Parliaments and political parties from the Spanish point of view.

Lorenzo Navarrete Moreno (1947). PhD (Complutense University of Madrid). Professor of Sociology of the Department of Sociological Theory at the Faculty of Political Science and Sociology at CUM. Besides administrative work, he has taken part in various research projects, including comparative studies of Spain and Europe with respect to refugees and cultural affairs.

José Antonio Nieto Solís (1959). PhD (Complutense University of Madrid). Professor of the EEC subjects at CUM. Since 1990, Technical Adviser at the Agencia Española de Cooperación International. He is the author of *Introducción a la economía de la Comunidad Europea* (1990).

Laura de Pablos Escobar (1961). PhD (Complutense University of Madrid). Professor of Public Taxation and Fiscal Systems at CUM. Among other work, she has published *Una Valoración del Impuesto sobre el Patrimonio Neto* (1990); and *Armonización fiscal en la CEE* (1989).

Isabel Ramírez de Mingo (1949). PhD (Complutense University of Madrid). She holds degrees in social work and clinical psychology. Professor of the University School of Social Workers at CUM. She has taken part in the analysis and programming of an action programme against poverty.

Vicente Riesgo Alonso (1952). Holds degrees in theology and sociology from Madrid and Frankfurt. He is in charge of the Department of Migrant Worker On the Job Training in Germany. He edits a monthly publication for Spanish citizens residing in Germany. Associate Professor at the University of Bonn (1984–88) and at the University of Köln (from 1989). Since 1989 he has acted as General Emigration Counsellor for Germany and is a member of the 'Europa-Unión'. Co-author of *Spanien: Laenderkundliche Informationen* (1988).

Manuel J. Rodríguez Caamaño (1953). PhD (Complutense University of Madrid). Professor at CUM. He has published *Gramsci y la Sociología* (1989) and *Sociología disidente* (1991).

Manuel Rodríguez Carrajo (1926). PhD. Former editor of the magazine *Estudios*, he has taught sociology in various Spanish universities. He is currently Professor of Sociology and of Human Rights at the Pontificia University of Salamanca, and of EC Education and Cultural Policy at the Instituto de Estudios Europeos. He has published ten books including *Mella y su pensamiento social* (1972); *El pensamiento sociopolítico de Mella* (1974) and *Cartas inéditas de Concepción Arenal* (1984). He is currently working on several books, among them one on the EC's educational policy.

Emilio Rodríguez Lara (1946). M A (Complutense University of Madrid). Head of the Research Promotion Service at the Centro de Investigaciones Sociológicas, Madrid. Associate Professor of Sociology at the CUM. He has cooperated in the vocational training programme at the University of Granada and the European Social Fund.

Marisa Rodríguez Mojón (1944). M A (Complutense University of Madrid). She also holds a diploma in political psychology from Ohio State University. She is Professor of International Relations and European Political Systems at the Saint Louis University, Madrid Campus. She was Director of Cultural Activities for the Fundación Pablo Iglesias (1982–87) and General Secretary of the Foundation of Studies on Peace and International Relations, Sweden (1984–90). She is also a member of the Instituto de Estudios de Estratégicos of the Ministry of Defence, of the Centre for European Policy Studies and of the Instituto de Ciencia y Sociedad. She has published various articles on the topic of peace, including contributions to, *El Pacifismo Europeo en la Actualidad* (1987) and *Debate europeo sobre paz y seguridad: el pensamiento de Olof Palme*, (1987).

Miguel Angel Ruiz de Azúa Antón (1945). PhD (Complutense University of Madrid). Professor of Political and Administration Science and Sociology at CUM. He is the President of the College of Doctors and Bachelors of Political Science and Sociology. Visiting Professor at Lille University, he is currently responsible for the ERASMUS Programme in Spain. He has participated in research on national and European elections.

Carlos San Juan Mesonada (1954). PhD (Complutense University of Madrid). He has also specialized in Temporal Series Analysis at the Centro de Formación of the Banco de España. Professor of Applied Economy at the Faculty of Economics and Business Science at CUM. Member of the Technical Office of the Experts Commission appointed by the Spanish Government to study unemployment problems. He has written works on efficiency and profitability in Spanish agriculture and the modernization of agriculture between 1956 and 1986.

Manuel Sánchez de Dios (1954). PhD (Complutense University of Madrid). His work focuses on the operation of parliamentary systems. He is currently Professor of Political Science and Administration at the Faculty of Political Science and Sociology, CUM.

Sergio Santillán (1945). M A (University of Tucumán, Argentina). He is director of the UGT technical services and member of the Economic and Social Committee of the European Community.

Mariano Torcal Loriente (1958). M A (Complutense University of Madrid). He is a Professor at the Faculty of Political Science at CUM. He has published several monographs and articles on political behaviour and cultural changes.

Alfonso Utrilla de la Hoz (1961). PhD (Complutense University of Madrid). Among other work, he has published articles on the EC's 'own resources', EC tariffs and trade, Spain's Structural funds and budget relationships with the EC.

Manuel Varela Parache (1927). PhD (Complutense University of Madrid). Professor of Applied Economy at CUM. He has published numerous articles and books, among them some dealing with economic cooperation and integration. He is the editor of journals on applied economics and on the advisory board of *Información Comercial Española* and *Economistas.*

Francisco J. Vanaclocha Bellver (1950). PhD (Complutense University of Madrid). He is the founder and a writer for *Revista de Instituciones Europeas,* edited by the Centro de Estudios Constitucionales (Center of Constitutional Studies). His published work specializes in the study of electoral systems and in the politics of the armed forces. He is currently Professor of Political Science and Administration at the Faculty of Political Science and Sociology, at CUM.

Series introduction

This volume is one in a series entitled *European Community Membership Evaluated.* The series examines the gains and losses of European Community (EC) membership for each of the twelve states.

Over the entire period since the first steps in European integration were taken, with the formation of the European Coal and Steel Community, the impact of membership upon the individual states has been both a matter of importance to, and an issue for evaluation by, the political parties, interest groups, government elites, researchers and, increasingly, the public at large. The renewed dynamism of the EC in the period following the signing of the Single European Act in 1986, and the approach of the completed internal market by the end of 1992, have raised awareness of EC membership to new heights.

It is against this backdrop that the project leading to this series was undertaken. Policy-makers and the European electorate alike require the information to make informed judgements about national gains and losses (or costs and benefits) arising from EC membership.

- How far have the EC's economic policies brought gains?
- Does EC membership impose constraints on the powers of national and regional/local government, or on the legal system?
- What have been the effects of the hitherto somewhat disparate EC activities in the social, cultural and educational policy areas?
- What are the gains and losses of foreign policy co-operation among the member states?
- How pronounced are the specific national interests of the individual member states?

In order to answer questions such as these, each volume brings together a team of specialists from various disciplines. Although the national teams are composed predominantly of academics, the series is aimed at a readership beyond the confines of the education world. Thus each volume seeks to present its findings in a manner accessible to *all* those affected by, or interested in, the EC. Extensive footnoting of academic literature is avoided, although some guidance is offered on the legal bases of EC policies; a bibliography at the end of each study gives guidance on narrower sectoral impact studies and on further reading.

A distinctive feature of the series as a whole is that a common framework has been followed for all eleven studies. This is aimed at facilitating comparison between the national studies. No systematic international comparative study of this kind has been attempted before. Indeed, for some member states there exists no study of the impact of EC membership. The absence of such a series of studies initially seemed rather surprising. However, as the project progressed, the reasons for this became clearer. It is by no means easy to find a common framework acceptable to the academic traditions of all the member states *and* all the policy areas and academic disciplines involved.

The project co-ordinators experienced these tensions in a striking way. Their international 'summit meetings' meant reaching compromises acceptable to all the diverse academic traditions of the countries involved. Then the individual national contributors had to be convinced of the merits of the international compromises. These negotiations brought many insights into precisely the type of problem faced by EC policy-makers themselves. Hence academic perfectionism has been subordinated to some extent to pragmatism and the wish to address a wider readership.

In some countries, for instance the Netherlands, Great Britain, Portugal and Germany, up to thirty scholars of various disciplines make up the national team. In other countries, such as Ireland, a team numbers less than ten authors. In the latter, *one* author deals with several parts of a subject-group or even with the whole of a subject-group. In either case, however, authors have assured comparability by making cross-references to subsections of policies.

The basic principle of the project has been to assess the gains and losses of EC membership for the individual state, with the hypothetical alternative in mind of that state leaving the EC. This alternative may be deemed to be somewhat simplistic but it is far more manageable than making assumptions about where individual states would be, had they not joined the EC in the first place. Such speculation is virtually impossible scientifically and would undermine efforts to make the findings accessible to a wider readership. The terms 'benefits', 'gains' and 'positive effects', and 'costs', 'losses' and 'negative effects', respectively, are used synonymously.

The activities of the EC, together with the foreign policy co-operation process EPC (European Political Co-operation), are grouped under four broad headings in the project (see Table A at the end of this Introduction). *Economic policy* covers a range of EC policies: from the internal market to the Common Agricultural Policy but also including environmental policy. *Foreign relations* comprise not only European Political Co-operation but also the EC's external trade policy and security policy. *Social and educational policy* brings together the rather disparate measures taken in a range of areas, some of which are now coming to be regarded as forming the 'social dimension' of the EC. Finally, the subject area *political and legal system* refers not to EC policies but rather to the EC's impact upon the principles and practices of government.

Each of the EC policy headings is assessed following a common approach. The objectives of the EC policy, and the accomplishments thus far, are assessed against the equivalent set of national policy goals and legislation, many of them common to all countries, some of them obviously specific national ones. The idea, then, is to arrive at a 'balance sheet', both at the level of the individual policy area or sector and, at the macro level, for the member state as a whole. Drawing up the individual sectoral balance sheets has to involve a rather flexible approach. The 'mix' of quantitative and qualitative assessments varies according to the subject matter. There can be no quantitative data on how far foreign policy co-operation has brought gains to national foreign policy; figures may be available, however, on the impact of EC trade policy on national trade patterns. In the case of quantitative data it is important to note that very little, if any, primary statistical research was involved in the project. In consequence, quantitative assessments generally present available evidence from previous studies; they follow no consistent methodological approach while qualitative assessments are often arrived at for the first time. One further point must be made with regard to the common approach of the project: it is clear that the importance of individual EC policy areas varies from one member state to another.

It follows, therefore, that the weighting, and in some cases the categorization, of EC policy areas will vary between the national studies. To assign the same weight to fisheries policy in the British and Luxembourg cases, for instance, would be irrational. Some national policy goals and national interests are related to specific interests of some member countries; for instance, the German question and the problem of Northern Ireland are specific to Germany, Ireland and the United Kingdom respectively.

The whole project has been brought to fruition under the auspices of 'Europe-12 – Research and Action Committee on the EC'. Created in 1986, Europe-12 brings together academics of all disciplines and from all member states, as well as policy-makers and senior politicians. It aims to inform the policy debate through collaborative research and to raise public awareness of the important issues raised by European integration.

As with any such project, a large number of acknowledgements must be made. A number of the participants took on the additional task of horizontal co-ordination, i.e. seeking to ensure consistency of approach across the national studies. For *economic policy* this was undertaken by Detlev Karsten, Bonn, and Peter Coffey, Amsterdam; for *foreign relations* by Carl-Christoph Schweitzer, Bonn, and Rudolf Hrbek, Tübingen; for contributions on *the political and legal system* by Francesco Francioni, Siena, and K. Kellermann, The Hague; finally, for *social and educational policies* by Bernard Henningsen, Munich, and Brigitte Mohr, Bonn. Sadly, Guenther Kloss, a co-ordinator of the British volume, died during the preparation of the series.

Last but by no means least, we are indebted to the Commission of the EC and to those bodies supporting the project: the German foundations, Stifterverband für die Deutsche Wissenschaft, Essen; Bosch GmbH, Stuttgart; Ernst Poensgen-Stiftung, Düsseldorf; as well as the Government of the Saarland and the Federal Ministry for Science and Technology, Bonn. The British and German Studies were made possible by the support of the Anglo-German Foundation for the Study of Industrial Society, London.

Carl-Christoph Schweitzer
Bonn

Table A: Project's categorization of EC policies and structures

I	**Economic policy**	
	Internal market policy	Agricultural policy
	Competition policy	Environmental policy
	Industrial policy	Fiscal/taxation policy
	Technology policy	Monetary policy
	Transport and communications policy	Regional policy
	Energy policy	
II	**Foreign relations**	
	Foreign policy co-operation	Development policy
	Security policy	External trade policy
III	**Political and legal system**	
	Sovereignty	National legal system
	Parliamentary control of the executive	Judicial procedures
	Electoral system	Maintenance of public order
	Political parties	Protection of fundamental rights
	Regional and local government	State organization
	Policy-making process	
IV	**Social, educational and cultural policies**	
	Manpower (employment/unemployment)	Consumer protection
	Movement of labour and migrant workers	Education and training
	Industrial relations	European identity and cultural policies
	Social security and health	
	Equal treatment of men and women	Media policy

Note: This list was a schematic guideline for the project; not every subsection will be dealt with individually and the sequence is purely illustrative.

Europe-12: Action and Research Committee on the EC

Hon. Presidents:
Lord Jenkins of Hillhead
Chancellor of the University of Oxford
H.E. Emilio Colombo,
Minister Rome
Board:
Chairman: Former Minister Dr Ottokar Hahn
Senior Advisor, EC Commission, Brussels
Vice-Chairmen:
Prof Dr Hélène Ahrweiler
Rector and Chancellor, University of Paris
Enrico Baron Crespo, MEP,
President European Parliament Brussels, Madrid
Piet Dankert
Undersecretary, Foreign Office, Den Haag
Dr Garret FitzGerald
former Prime Minister, Dublin
Niels Anker Kofoed, MP
former Minister, Copenhagen
Dr Hans Stercken, MP
Chairman Bundestag Foreign Affairs Committee, Bonn
Franz Ludwig Graf von Stauffenberg, MEP
Representative of the President of the European Parliament
Senior Economic Advisor:
Dr Otto Graf Lambsdorff, MP
former Minister of Economics, National Chairman FDP, Bundestag, Bonn
Co-ordinator of Committees:
Prof Dr C. C. Schweitzer
University of Bonn, Political Science
Steering Committee:
Spokesman: Dr Renate Hellwig, MP
Bundestag, Bonn, Chairman Sub-Committee on Europe
Dr Peter Baehr
Netherlands Scientific Council, The Hague
Prof Dr P. D. Dagtoglou
University of Athens, Law
W. Dondelinger, MP
Chairman Foreign Affairs Committee, Luxembourg
Prof. Dr Francesco Francioni
University of Siena, Law
Fernand Herman, MEP
Chairman Institutional Committee, EP, Brussels
Dr J. de Silva Lopes
Caixa General de Depositos, Lisbon, Economics
Anthony J. Nicholls
Senior Fellow, St Antony's College, Oxford
Dr Hans-J. Seeler
Chairman FVS Foundation, Hamburg
Georges Sutra de Germa, MEP
former Vice-Chairman, Institutional Committee, EP, Pezenas, France
Prof Count L. Ferraris
Council of State, Rome
Jacques Maison Rouge
ex Vice President IBM, Paris
Dr Claude Treyer
Director, European Affairs, IGS, Paris
Research Committee:
Dr Simon Bulmer
University of Manchester, Dept of Government
Gerry Danaher
Secretary, Irish National Economic and Social Council, Dublin
Prof Alfonso Ortega
Political Science, University Pontificia Salamanca, Spain
Prof Dr Grotanelli de Santi
University of Siena, Law and Political Science
Prof Dr R Hrbek
University of Tübingen, Political Science
Prof Dr Detlev Karsten
University of Bonn, Economics
Prof Dr M. A. G. van Meerhaeghe
University of Ghent, Economics
Prof Dr Stavros Theofanides
Panteios School of Pol. Science, Athens
Prof Dr Christian Tomuschat
University of Bonn, International Law
Media Advisers:
Rolf Goll
Chairman, Communications and Marketing, Ansin-Goll, Frankfurt
Prof Dr E. G. Wedell
Chairman, European Media Centre, University of Manchester
Hon. Secretary:
Dr Hartmut Schweitzer, Bonn

Foreword

On 1 January 1986 Spain joined the European Community as a full member. The historic symbolism of this date is worth emphasizing. Spain had finally broken the circle which represented historical isolation and joined the process of modernization shared by the other European countries. Entry meant the confirmation and guarantee of political, social and economic transformation, starting with the transition to democracy. Participation in this EC effort has dynamized Spanish society and had a profound effect on the attitude of Spanish citizens.

Entry and the first stage of accelerated integration in the EC coincided with its relaunching, in the form of an unexpected success for plans for the internal market, of the Single European Act and two intergovernmental conferences that dealt respectively with economic union and political union in Europe. It is likely that the second half of the 1980s will be considered as the time of greatest achievement in the EC's uneven history. After overcoming some of the problems that hindered it for years – such as the British budgetary contribution or the implementation of certain EC policies – and under the banner of the realization of a single internal market, the EC was finally able to create a common goal, capable of binding not only those sectors that had traditionally lent their support, but also entrepreneurs, the new professional classes and, in great measure, the media which influence public opinion. Too long incapacitated by internal struggles and the economic crisis of the 1970s, the EC took on a renewed identity and an economic and political dynamism which caused its more direct world competitors to turn to it as a possible model to follow.

The economic consequences of Spanish participation in the EC have not previously been analysed so exhaustively as in this collective study. Most contributions are the work of professors of the Complutense University of Madrid. Through quantitative and qualitative evaluation of costs and benefits derived from the interrelation of domestic and EC policies, the study examines the potential consequences of *not belonging* to the EC; in other words, the bottom line is the legitimacy of EC policies. So this project is wide-ranging and ambitious, both in the scope of the topics covered, in the number and quality of the contributions from individual authors, and in the difficulties inherent in evaluating results that are often very hard to quantify. I believe that this volume is an excellent example of the manner in which the possible difficulties can be turned into advantages, thanks to the wise use of different methodological resources and to interdisciplinary work. Fine qualitative analysis is presented here. And the use of a matrix to compare the goals of EC policies with the national goals of each sector and subsector turns out to be particularly interesting. It allows us to measure with greater accuracy the impact of EC activities over a specific area – for instance, monetary policy and its relationship with domestic policies, such as price stability, the balance of payments, reduction of unemployment, etc. This permits us to compare the costs and benefits of EC policies in each country.

Under the direction of Professor Amparo Almarcha Barbado, of the Faculty of Political Sciences and Sociology at the Complutense University, the Spanish Group of the Action and Research on the EC Committee has produced this impressive study. Thirty-one different chapters have been prepared, encompassing the main sectors of economic policy, foreign relations, social, educational and cultural policy, as well as the political system.

The first part, coordinated by Professor Sara González Fernández, evaluates economic policy. The first chapters of this section deal with the free movement of capital and financial services, with competition, industrial, technology and energy policies. The evaluation centres on the consequences that EC policies have had, and continue to have, on domestic policies. In some cases, effects relevant to the cost/benefit analysis emerge. Thus, for instance, in relation to energy policy, mention is made of the influence that the European Investment Bank loans will exert on the overall reduction of energy costs. The study in which the advantages of cost/benefit analysis show up most strikingly is the chapter on agricultural policy. Here, analysis of the cost of reform of the Common Agricultural Policy (CAP), with its implications for the internal market and for future CAP planning, form a wonderful frame for the introduction of a later cost/benefit schematic diagram. The same may be said of the chapters on fiscal and monetary policies, where the central question is to determine how monetary or fiscal goals may be modified by the effects of EC policies.

The second part of the book focuses on two aspects of foreign relations: trade policy and development policy. Given the scant EC development in this area, it is obvious that any evaluation of the internal impact of EC initiatives must be general and qualitative in its approach.

The third part, directed by Professor Amparo Almarcha, the general coordinator of the project, deals with social and cultural policies: human capital, industrial relations, social security, equal opportunities, consumer protection, education and training, mass media policy, tourism, social protection and cultural policy. From the results shown in this part of the book, it is interesting to observe how European legislation has served as a catalyst for many legal initiatives developed by the Autonomous

Communities and the central government of Spain. This has been especially noticeable in equal opportunities for men and women, and in consumer protection. The remarks about the redistributive effect of tourism inside the EC also stand out.

The fourth and last part of the book, under the direction of Professor Miguel Angel Ruiz de Azúa Antón, is concerned with aspects of the political and legal system: EC impact on the electoral system, on the formation of transnational parties and, within the Spanish political system, on the process of political decisions, the protection of fundamental rights, administrative law and European identity. The important role that the present and later development of the 'Europe of Citizens' will have for the progressive evolution of the internal protection of citizens' rights and freedoms is also emphasized here.

This volume is the ninth in a series that encompasses the evaluation of EC membership for the twelve member countries. From the very first moment, the Rectorate of the Complutense University has encouraged this initiative. It sponsored the meeting that introduced the project in May 1990 in Madrid. As the current Rector of the Complutense University, I rejoice in the completion of this project. I would also like to thank all thirty-five persons who cooperated in the task, congratulating them on the excellent work they have done. It seems as if, at least once, the well-known Latin tag deserves to be slightly amended: it is a voluminous analysis, *multum*, but its quality is also excellent, *multa*.

Gustavo Villapalos
Rector, Complutense University of Madrid

Preface

This volume has been made possible by the cooperative effort of a team of professionals, most of whom come from the academic world. To start with, half a dozen professors, from the Complutense University of Madrid, approached the idea of this project in accordance with the research guidelines issued by the Action and Research Committee on the EC of the Europe-12 Group in 1985. It was difficult, in 1987, to appreciate the impact of EC membership in terms of cost/benefit, mainly because entry was still so recent; even today, some of the aspects analysed pose the same problem.

To perform this task, we had a team of no less than thirty-five experts, from the following institutions: Faculty of Political Science and Sociology, Faculty of Economic and Management Science, Faculty of Information Science, the School of Social Work and the Instituto Ciencia y Sociedad (Science and Society Institute), all of which belong to the Complutense University of Madrid. Academics from other universities also cooperated in the making of this book: Autonomous University of Madrid, University of Santiago de Compostela (Galicia) and the Universidad Pontificia de Salamanca (Catholic University of Salamanca) and experts from institutions such as the Ministry of Social Affairs, Ministry of Foreign Affairs, Centro de Investigaciones Sociológicas (Centre of Sociological Research), UGT (General Workers Union) and the General Hospital of Asturias.

A task as complex as this required total cooperation from those who prepared the analysis in each of its areas, but its implementation also required financial support. The independence which characterizes our work has not allowed us to receive material help from outside the academic world. We therefore wish to express our gratitude to the Rectorate of the Complutense University of Madrid, which financed the meeting held in May 1990 between the Spanish team and the coordinator of committees, Professor Schweitzer. Translation and secretarial expenses were met by various grants from the Instituto de Estudios Europeos y Derechos Humanos (Institute of European Studies and Human Rights) of the Universidad Pontificia of Salamanca, the Faculty of Political Science and Sociology and the National College of Doctors and Bachelors in Political Science and Sociology. We wish to express our sincere gratitude to all of them. Without their help, this work could never have been finished. We also wish to acknowledge the work of our translators, Ms. Esperanza F. Bustillo, who directed and did most of the actual translation, and Ms. Victoria Hughes.

Amparo Almarcha Barbado
Spanish Coordinator

PART I: ECONOMIC POLICY

Coordinator: Sara González Fernández

Introduction

Manuel Varela Parache

For many countries, membership of the EC has simply meant one step further in their history of economic cooperation, but Spain, for reasons both remote and recent, had lived in isolation from any sort of international cooperation. Inflation, which had financed Spanish economic development since the nineteenth century, was one reason for this; as was protection of the domestic market, for it was not capable of withstanding competition from abroad. Spain's political system may well have been another reason, as this precluded its inclusion in the economic cooperation which was just then starting. Thus, although a certain amount of prior Spanish participation on agricultural schemes should not be ignored, Spain did not become a member of OECE until 1959, hardly two years before it disappeared and the OECD was born. A radical change in its economic policy then made it possible for Spain to join the International Monetary Fund and the World Bank. But, just then, six European countries took a new and decisive step, creating the EEC in the 1957 Treaty of Rome. This excited an extraordinary amount of interest in Spain, and had two clear effects. Firstly, contact was sought, as quickly as possible, with the Community, but without a decision on what type of legal relationship would be best or even possible. Secondly, the idea of some future integration was always behind the economic policy of successive governments. A long and arduous process, whose most important milestones are the Preferential Agreement (1970), the Treaty (1986) and membership in the European Monetary System (1989), followed. The next important step, the Single Market (1993), is the reference point for the chapters in this study. For the first time, Spain will not have to join the bandwagon after it has started moving, and Spain's problems – its previous history notwithstanding – are not different from those of the other committed countries.

This is the framework in which the contributions to Part I fit. Sara González, Professor of International Economy at the Complutense University of Madrid, and coordinator of Part I, has, first of all, approached the free movement of capital and financial services. She reminds us that progressive liberalization, linked to a commitment to exchange stability, may bring down inflation and improve growth, but cause regional or sectoral imbalance. The prevention of social costs and bottlenecks may require the use of development funds. She has also dealt with the energy sector, where EC regulations have had a great influence over Spanish legislation; and with transport and communications policy, which has had to adapt to such regulations. Under monetary policy, finally, she has analysed entry into the European Monetary System, with its advantages – exchange rate stability and consolidation of an anti-inflation policy – and its disadvantages, among which the need for a new approach to the control of the money supply may be mentioned.

Teresa López and Laura de Pablos have dealt with the important topic of competition. Such Spanish regulations as there are on this theme have always taken into account the relevant paragraphs of the Treaty of Rome. The two areas that Carlos Alvarez has discussed are relevant to this. Industrial policy has, in fact, benefited from EC rules on competition – including tariff reductions, which have brought advantages, while, as in other countries, posing some survival problems for specific companies and sectors. Technological policy has improved through EC membership: there is now greater public expenditure on R & D; sectoral scientific policies have been established, as well as concerted programmes; and prospects have improved for Spanish researchers.

Agricultural policy, presented by Carlos San Juan, a professor at the Complutense University, is of great importance for Spain, both because of its structural characteristics and because of the revision and reform it needs. Environmental policy has been presented by Alfonso De Esteban and Alejandro López, both professors at the Complutense University of Madrid. It represents another positive balance for Spain as a consequence of its entrance into the EC. Alfonso Utrilla, who is also a professor at the Complutense University of Madrid, sets out Spanish fiscal and taxation policy as affected by EC membership and policies. Free movement of capital, for instance, makes it necessary to harmonize a whole set of taxes, with a possible increase of fiscal pressure and of prices.

Finally Vicente Riesgo analyses regional policy, of great importance for Spain and, more specifically so, for its regions and Autonomous Communities.

Chapter 1

The free movement of capital and financial services

Sara González Fernández

Characteristics of Spanish external financial operations

All Spanish external investment is regulated by a Royal Decree (November 1986) and by a Ministerial Order (December 1988) which accord with the spirit of the EC regulations about the Single Market. Spanish foreign transactions present the following characteristics:

— Direct investment has been almost completely deregulated since 1979; this process was completed in 1988, when authorization required for investment in holding and real estate companies was eliminated. Since then it has only been subject to prior verification and a thirty-day period during which objections might be raised.
— Portfolio investments have been entirely free since December 1988, although bonds must have an explicit valuation, through a stockmarket listing or trading in an organized market. Additionally, bonds must be registered in a currency listed on the Spanish stock market.
— Real estate investment has also been deregulated, subject to verification as above.

In 1989, following the liberalization, Spanish direct investment abroad grew by 22%, much more than the previous year, when it grew by only 13%. From a structural point of view, it may be concluded that Spanish direct investment had the following aspects:

— The EC countries were the main destination for about two-thirds of exports in the late 1980s. The principal receiving countries were France, Portugal and the Federal Republic of Germany (FRG), which absorbed 56% in 1989. There was no structural continuity, however, about the destination of exports. Marked fluctuations occurred from year to year, as may be observed in the Table 1.1.
— The external activities of Spanish companies centred around a small

Table 1.1 Spanish direct investment in the EC*

Countries	1987 (%)	1988 (%)	1989 (%)
FRG	15.21	3.00	0.82
Belgium	1.32	6.98	3.14
Denmark	—	—	0.18
France	6.65	10.23	2.09
Greece	0.03	0.03	0.02
Netherlands	16.28	3.62	13.10
Ireland	—	—	0.36
Italy	3.16	2.10	7.09
Luxembourg	4.47	8.69	2.36
United Kingdom	5.18	8.14	7.63
Portugal	11.25	6.17	19.81
Total EC	63.57	48.96	57.60

* Percentage of total investment.
Source: BICE, Madrid, March, 1990.

number of highly active firms. Thus, in 1989, 45% of the investment went to thirty-two projects, with a total value of over Pts. 2,000 million.

— As to their sectoral destination, the financial institutions, insurance companies, services to companies and leasings were dominant, with 64% in 1989, 56% in 1988 and 59% in 1987.

The restrictive monetary policy which, especially since 1987, has been concentrated more on interest rates than on amounts, has been an additional stimulus attracting speculative foreign capital. The internal capital market has also been affected, and has channelled funds previously going into traditional financial assets to others more sensitive to market rates of return.

Thus, as a consequence of high Spanish interest rates and of the appreciation of the peseta, short-term capital operations generated a great increase in Spanish short-term external debt, which rose from $476 million to $3,042 million between March 1987 and March 1988. In order to prevent excessive debt, the Bank of Spain decided, in June 1988, to demand a prior permit for any external borrowing with a time limit of under three years. Foreign investment in Spain experienced a stable inflow of autonomous long-term capital. Portfolio investment, however, grew rapidly, reaching 64% in 1988–89, as seen in Table 1.2

Direct investment, which represented approximately 3% of the GNP in 1989, was the highest in the EC, with the exception of Benelux and Portugal. The capital received in Spain came from the United Kingdom, the Netherlands, France, FRG, Switzerland, United States and Japan, in that order. After 1988, the tertiary sector turned out to be the most attractive area

Table 1.2 Foreign investments in Spain

Year	Direct investment (%)	Portfolio investment (%)	Real estate investment (%)	Total in Pts. m.
1984	47.14	11.17	41.68	331,100
1985	40.42	20.36	39.22	406,200
1986	39.86	33.43	26.71	713,058
1987	29.80	50.14	20.33	1,088,799
1988	44.25	32.71	23.00	1,162,119
1989	33.75	50.95	15.30	1,991,779

Source: Registro de Caja, Ministerio de Economía.

Table 1.3 Foreign investment in Spain, by sectors

Sectors	1987 (%)	1988 (%)	1989 (%)
Primary	1.46	1.20	4.40
Secondary	53.15	39.53	40.34
Tertiary	45.39	59.27	55.26

Source: Registro de Caja, Ministerio de Economía.

(see Table 1.3). The main receiving subsectors were (from largest to smallest): financial, real estate, wholesale trade, chemicals, paper industries and insurance. Within direct external investment, greenfield investment experienced growth in 1989, reaching 48% as compared to 44% in 1988. As to the country of origin of direct foreign investment, the highest percentages in 1989 came from EC countries such as France (13%), Holland (15%) and the United Kingdom (11%). German investment did not reach the levels of other countries. It was 4% in 1987, 7% in 1988 and 1989, which indicates that German interest in Eastern European markets might have hindered its investments in Spain, though less than expected.

On the other hand, the external demand for quoted securities experienced a remarkable increase in 1989, with the exception of the private securities market. During 1989, the net currency income for foreign portfolio investment more than doubled. As a result of this cumulative performance, short-term and long-term capital revenue rose from 8% of the GNP in 1978 to 13% in 1988. Short-term and long-term capital payments experienced a more moderate growth, rising from 7% of the GNP in 1978 to 10% in 1988. Under the liberalizing influence of the EC, a new order on foreign investments was published by the Ministry of Economy and Finances in March 1990 which incorporated full liberalization, with no prior administrative verification, for foreign purchases of majority shares in Spanish companies, as long as the investment was under pts. 25 million. This order also deregulated the issue of convertible shares or bonds of Spanish companies in foreign markets, subject to previous auditing; this was established before the time limit set for Spain in the EC Directive of June 1988.

Needless to say, the efficient free movement of capital does not simply require the relevant deregulating legislation in the foreign currency and exchange markets; it also requires two additional factors: freedom for financial services and homogeneous fiscal treatment throughout the EC. As far as this last factor is concerned, budgetary policy showed more restrictive signs in May 1989, when capital revenue withholdings arising from the IRPF (Withholding Tax on Natural Persons) were increased from 20 to 25%. A 17% growth limit was also established for loans to families and companies, through a request for cooperation issued to the banking organizations.

Cost/Benefit Analysis

Three levels of action must be taken into account in preparing a cost/benefit analysis of European financial integration for the Spanish economy: free movement of capital, freedom for financial services and a highly stable exchange rate system.

The free movement of capital implies a reduction of financial costs for companies and a greater possibility of raising resources. Households will also have access to less expensive credit. However, these theoretical benefits may not be put into effect, since the free movement of capital poses problems of a fiscal nature, of exchange rate stability and of possible regional imbalances. Therefore, Spain adopted restrictions on monetary variables so as to achieve the dual purpose of fighting inflation and maintaining a stable rate of exchange. Among the restrictions implemented in February 1989 was the creation of a 30% non-interest bearing deposit on foreign currency financial loans to Spanish residents. However, due to the fact that this restriction was applied after the 24 June 1988 Directive was issued, it is not subject to the safeguards which the Directive mentions for Spain.

The full application of the free movement of capital, together with the commitment to exchange rate stability and to the harmonization of capital taxes – a necessary condition for free movement of capital to be effective – affects the goal of reducing inflation, as it encourages lower rates of interest and the maintenance of a rhythm of economic growth higher than the EC average. This makes it possible for Spanish macroeconomic variables to come close to the EC norms. But direct investment might fuel a greater regional imbalance in our country. This could be partially offset by EC funds to aid regional development, but it seems rather unlikely that these funds would grow sufficiently to cover this need. Unbalanced growth, with strong regional and sectoral differences, would therefore generate bottlenecks affecting economic prosperity and giving rise to undesirable structural and social costs.

Free delivery of financial services

The banking system

The Spanish banking system has started a process of deregulation. Its main characteristics are complete freedom to create new banks and to open foreign financial institutions, deregulation of the applicable interest rates and the development of a process tending towards banking independence. The positive and negative aspects of the Spanish banking system may be outlined as follows:

Positive aspects:

— A high level of solvency;
— A large network of office branches and of product offers;
— A significant level of professionalism, as shown by the prompt adoption of new market analysis and risk management techniques.

Negative aspects:

— The existence of high financial margins and general costs;
— Great dependency in the traditional banking industry, making it very sensitive to the process of change;
— Limited foreign business.

The application of the Second Banking Directive, which guarantees freedom of banking services, means a reduction in costs for these services and an increase in competitivity, no longer limited to the operations of large companies, but will also affect the operations of medium-sized companies and private persons. One step ahead of this, the Spanish banking system started giving very attractive remunerations on some loans, in order to create a customer portfolio with a certain degree of future stability, thus reducing the potential market share which foreign banks might attract. The process of adapting to European competition, however, has only just begun, with questions as important as operating cost reduction and market innovation still pending; these actions are necessary if the previously mentioned effort is not be wasted. In addition, it will also be necessary to reduce the profit margin of banks. It grew during the 1980s and exceeded 4% in 1988.

A study performed by Spain's six largest banks on the composition of banking income forecast stability for income from cheque accounts and loans, and considerable increases for those generated by insurance and pension fund operations. The EC Commission asked the accountants Price Waterhouse to prepare a comparative study quantifying the impact of the

Table 1.4 Savings in the cost of providing financial services

Bank	Belgium	Germany	Spain	France	Italy	Luxembourg	The Netherlands	UK
Commercial credit	−4.6	6.0	18.2	7.3	8.6	6.0	43.0	45.7
Consumer credit	−41.0	135.9	38.5	105.1	121.0	−26.9	30.8	121.7
Mortgage loans	79.0	60.0	25.7	−29.5	88.6	−12.4	42.9	16.2
Secured loans	21.8	−10.0	58.9	−7.2	901.0	27.1	16.5	8.1
Overdrafts	6.2	30.9	196.3	55.6	23.5	33.3	−45.7	16.1
Travellers' cheques	35.2	−7.4	29.6	38.9	22.2	−7.4	33.3	−7.4
Implied price reductions*	16.0	33.0	34.0	25.0	18.0	16.0	10.0	18.0

* The implied price reductions are calculated as the weighted average of prices compared with the averages of the four lowest prices observed.

Table 1.5 The Spanish insurance market

	No. of groups		Funds (Pts. million)		Percentage of funds	
Institution	1982	1987	1982	1987	1982	1987
Saving banks	1	7	3,417	1,315,842	1	53
Independent Spanish insurance companies	49	59	181,489	443,883	63	18
Banks	5	9	39,943	397,130	14	16
Foreign insurance companies	18	36	63,425	318,020	22	13
Total	73	111	288,274	2,474,875	100	100

Single Market on banking services, estimating savings in financial costs in the EC countries. They could reach a 34% saving in the case of Spain. The scenario described in the study is as shown in Table 1.4.

The insurance sector

The gradual entry of the insurance sector into financial markets, going beyond strictly insurance operations, justifies the need to evaluate this sector in analysing the effects of the free movement of capital and bonds. Spanish insurance companies are hardly represented at all abroad, because they mostly belong to banks or saving banks, as seen in Table 1.5. On the other hand, it is significant to record the growing presence of European insurance companies which, year by year, increase their share of the Spanish market. Their number, as reflected in data collected from UNESPA, went up from 30% in 1987 to 50% in 1988. Faced with this situation, any options that Spanish companies might have to increase their participation were limited to two strategies: geographic or product specialization for smaller companies, and mergers or agreements for larger ones. Forty-seven saving banks merged to form the Caja de Seguros Reunidos, CASER (United Insurers Bank), which aims to participate in agreements with European insurance companies.

References

Abella Santamaría, J. (1989) *Inversiones Extranjeras en España*, Madrid, Ed. Banco Exterior de España, Extebank Manuals, 3rd Ed.

Berges, A., *et al.* (1989) *Internacionalización de la Banca. El caso español*, Madrid, Ed. Espasa Calpe.

Fernández, A.I. (1990) *La Banca española de los noventa*, Madrid, Ed. Colegio de Economistas.

Rodríguez Antón, J.M. (1989) *La Banca en España. Un reto para 1992*, Madrid, Ed. Pirámide.

Torrero, A. (1989) *Estudios sobre el sistema financiero*, Madrid, Ed. Espasa Calpe.

Velarde, J. *et al.* (1990) *El sistema financiero de la economía española*, Madrid, Ed. Colegio de Economistas.

Chapter 2

Competition policy

María Teresa López and Laura de Pablos Escobar

It is well-known that the main purpose of the EC is to build a Single Market, formed by its Member States, with free movement of goods, people and capital. Its competition policy is conceived as indissolubly linked to this purpose. The Treaty of Rome approached this aim explicitly, and its Article 3f mentions the establishment of a regime which guarantees that competition would not be adulterated in the Common Market area. The Treaty goes beyond this, however, and specifies in other articles what is to be done to guarantee free competition. The common denominator of Articles 85, 86, 91, 92 and 93, among others, is to draw up a series of rules to suppress and control any practice considered to be incompatible with the existence of a common market.

Thus, Article 85 of the EC Treaty – which will often be referred to in this chapter – establishes that agreements between undertakings, decisions of entrepreneurial associations and practices affecting trade between Member States whose purpose or effects impede, restrict or falsify the interplay of competition within the Common Market are not compatible with the Common Market and are, therefore, prohibited. Relevant among these questions are those which (a) directly or indirectly fix buying or selling prices, or any other trading conditions; (b) limit or control production, marketing, technical development or investment; (c) restrict markets or supply sources to certain groups; (d) apply unequal conditions for equivalent services to third-parties, causing them to be at a competitive disadvantage.

Besides the rules presented in the EC's Treaty, the ECSC Agreement also has some measures against practices considered incompatible with the existence of a coal and steel common market. Specifically, Article 4 lists practices such as discriminatory measures, state subsidies, state aid and restrictive practices. Other ECSC articles, as shall be seen in this chapter, deal further with this issue.

The very complete regulations on competition policy found in EC law are in contrast with the scarcity of Spanish provision on competition; they are covered only by Articles 1 to 5 of Law 110/1963, on Repression of Restrictive Practices in Competition. They establish the following:

(a) Practices originating from consciously parallel agreements, decisions or behaviour, whose purpose is to impede, falsify or limit total or partial competition in the domestic market, or which will cause those effects, are prohibited. In this regard, any agreements between companies, as well as agreements and decisions from any kind of unions, associations or groups that produce or cause any of the practices forbidden in the previous point, are void, being contrary to the law and public order.
(b) Abusive practices by means of which one or several companies exploit their dominant position over a part or the whole of the market in a manner which is unjustifiably harmful to the domestic economy, the interests of the consumers or the actions of the remaining competitors, are also prohibited.
(c) Concerted or abusive practices are particularly prohibited which, if not already included in the previous paragraphs, directly or indirectly fix buying or selling prices, or any other condition for the transaction; which limit production, distribution, technical development or investments in a manner harmful to the national economy; which distribute markets, territorial areas or supply sectors or supply sources; which develop a trade policy which, through unfair competition, tends to eliminate competitors; which apply conditions different from those existing for similar or equivalent services, when trading with third parties, thus creating unequal competitive situations; which subordinate the settlement of a contract to the acceptance of complementary services or commercial operations which, because of their nature and the normal trade customs, bear no relationship with the purpose of these contracts.
(d) The prohibitions under paragraph (a) shall not be applicable to competition restriction situations expressly established by the exercise of legally provided administrative powers. The Competition Defence Court or the Trade Ministry may propose the removal or amendment of restrictive situations for the previously mentioned restriction to competition, and, in every case, the government will decide.
(e) By means of an agreement published in the *Boletín Oficial del Estado* (*BOE*), the Competition Defence Court, following a request from an interested party and after listening to all those who justify a legitimate, personal and direct interest, and, in every case, a trade-union representative, shall authorize agreements and decisions under paragraph (a) which contribute to the improvement of the production or distribution of goods and services, or promote technical or economic progress, as long as consumers or users obtain a suitable part of the benefits resulting from these agreements or decisions and any possible restrictive practice stemming from their application is unavoidable to achieve this end.

Among others, the Court may specially authorize the following agreements and decisions:

(1) Those dealing with the application of common standards and types, of a technical, trade or organizational nature, whose sole purpose is to rationalize economic processes and to increase efficiency or productive levels of the participating undertakings.
(2) Those whose purpose is to adapt supply to demand when the market shows a sustained reduction of this demand, or when the excessive production capacity is clearly uneconomic and as long as these agreements and decisions take into account the general economic situation and public interest.
(3) Those whose purpose is to defend or promote exports, as long as any restriction of competition derived from them is not harmful to the domestic market and they are compatible with duties resulting from international agreements entered into by Spain.
(4) Those dealing with imports from foreign markets where there is no freedom of competition, and as long as any restriction of competition derived from them does not harm the domestic market.
(5) Those, finally, which bring about practices which may cause a sufficiently important increase in the social and economic welfare of depressed national sectors.

In each case, the authorization of the Court will include any conditions whose establishment is deemed necessary by the Court, and whose supervision is its responsibility.

These rules are similar to those under Articles 85 and 86 of the EC Treaty. However, after Spain's entry into the EC, Royal Decree 1882/1986 (29 August) was approved, relevant to the application of the EC's Articles 85 and 86 (*BOE* of 15 September 1986). One of the measures adopted is the recognition of the Competition Defence Court, which was already under consideration in Law 110/63, as the competent Spanish authority to apply Articles 85.1 and 86 of the EC's Rule 1017/68, regulating cooperation between the Commission and the competent authorities of the new Member States.

Distribution

As a consequence of a Court of Law ruling on an appeal from the Italian Government, it was determined that Article 85.1 is applicable both to horizontal and vertical agreements; that is, to agreements between undertakings in different levels of the production and distribution process. These agreements may be seen in the selection of dealers, franchises and exclusive-right sales, price discrimination or resale price maintenance. In accordance with the case law formed by the Commission regarding dealers, the following is to be taken into account:

(a) Selection criteria, where, after passing the selection test, the dealer must fulfil supplementary services, such as, for instance, promotion activities, maintaining minimum stock levels, minimum sale commitment or minimum sales, etc., are not admissible.

(b) Quantitative selection criteria, as well as those based on the number of inhabitants of a specific population centre, or in the number of points of sale, are forbidden under Article 85.1 and are not, therefore, admissible.

(c) Qualitative criteria, however, based on the existence of minimum professional qualifications, minimum service demands at points of sales, or on customer after-sales assistance are admissible. Exception may be applied for under 85.1 in the two first cases, providing it can be shown that the goals pursued by these methods could not be attained without them, or that this seems likely.

The Commission has already forbidden price discrimination on grounds of nationality and the location of the trading partner. The ECSC Treaty prohibits price discrimination (Article 60.1) against any individual seller, while Article 85 of the EC Treaty acts on the previous existence of an agreement. However, the Commission's legal processes have brought the meaning of both rules together. The following legal points may be emphasized:

(a) Discrimination may only be prohibited when equivalent services are offered, although this equivalence is interpreted on the basis of the defence of the free movement of goods.

(b) The Commission has consistently condemned supply discrimination practices.

Finally, and in relation with resale price maintenance, the Commission will tolerate this practice as long as the agreements are not about the price of similar imported products, and the practice does not go beyond national borders.

Business Concentration

In 1981 and in 1984, the Commission proposed a draft Regulation based on Article 235 of the EC Treaty; that is, the power to take measures to allow for the creation of a single market and to foster competition. This draft regulation declares that business concentration is intolerable when it has the power to hinder competition and affect intercommunity trade, because it controls more than a specific percentage of a product or service in the EC total. A later Ruling (November 1988) of the Court of Justice further clarified this point. It states that, to incur prohibition under Article 85 of the Treaty, the purpose of the merger agreement must be to impede, restrict or reduce competition in the Common Market, and, thus, the simple fact that a company purchases a capital share in some other competing company is not, by itself, contrary to competition. As a consequence, merger agreements must be considered within their general economic context, bearing in mind the specific market in question and even economic relationships outside the EC and, especially, whether these agreements are part of a global cooperation policy between the subscribing undertakings.

Spanish commercial legislation went through an important reform process to enable it to adapt its own legislation to those EC Directives relevant to corporation law. The Ley de Sociedades Anónimas (Public Limited Company Law), in particular, deals with the standardization of Spanish legislation in matters of company mergers, to adapt it to the third Directive (78/855/EC), 9 October 1978.

Industrial Property

The main feature of industrial and trade property rights is to confer on their holders the right to exploit a limited monopoly in a specific national territory, since national laws guarantee these rights. Article 36 of the EC Treaty deals with the removal of quantitative restrictions between Member States (reflected under Article 2 of the Treaty, Articles 30 to 34). Article 222 also mentions the topic we are dealing with, stating that 'the Treaty does not in any way prejudice the property regime of the Member States'. Relationships between European national and community regulations are ruled by the following principles: (a) *Territoriality*. Protection of a distinctive trademark is limited to the State territory to which appeal is made for protection. (b) *Autonomy*. Community law is an autonomous process to serve the goals of the Treaty. (c) *Dispossession*. The Commission has no express power in this matter. Solutions to the coexistence of both sets of regulations have been sought through the Court of Justice; a series of basic notions have gradually been established.

The object of a trademark is mentioned first; this is meant to ensure its holder of the exclusive right to use the trademark on launching the product, to protect it against competitors who would otherwise take advantage of the position and reputation of the trademark by selling unsuitable products under it. The Court has also addressed itself to the concept of the trademark's function in guaranteeing the identity of the product's origin to the end consumer or user, allowing it to be differentiated from those with a different origin or source. It has also established the difference between the existence and the exercise of trademark rights. According to the Court, EC law does not affect the attribution of these rights, but limits their exercise in accordance with Article 85.1 forbidding the abusive use of rights derived from national regulations which might impede the application of EC law on concerted practices.

The following provisions or projects may be mentioned as rules leading towards EC harmonization on patents and trademarks:

(a) Munich Convention on European Patents (5 October 1973). This is not

just an EC agreement, but is open to every European country. In fact, both Member and non-Member States have joined this Convention, which establishes a single patent application; it is possible to be granted patents for the same invention in all the Convention Member States that have been named in the application. However, these patents are subject to the legislation of the country for which they have been granted, with the exception of the following: duration (twenty years from the date of presentation, Article 63); protective scope for procedure patents (Article 64.2); the determination of the amount of patent protection, depending on their claims related to description and drawings (Article 69.1), and the only reasons which could cause the patents to be declared void (Article 136).

(b) Luxembourg Convention on Community Patents (15 December 1975). This was strictly a Community Convention and completed any matters relevant to patents for every Member State of the European Community. It created a single regional patent for the Common Market countries, so that when the European patent application names any country among the Member States, all of them are understood to be jointly named. Patents thus granted are EC patents.

(c) Regulation 2349 23 July 1984, on the application of Article 85.3 of the EC Treaty to specific patent licence categories. This may be summarized as follows: patent licence agreements are restricted to negating global exemptions; so, patent licences specify a list of restrictions which may be applied within the global exemption (Article 1), as well as any constraints which do not negate the exemption, since, in general, they do not restrict competition (Article 2).

Different rules (a set of Regulations and a Directive, both compulsory for all Member States) have been chosen for trademarks, taking into account the possibility that the Member States might not ratify patent Conventions. The Draft Regulation on EC trademarks, as introduced to the Council by the Commission in November 1980 based its future Regulations on provisions under Article 235 of the Treaty. Its purpose was to establish a system which by means of an application to a Trademark Office with a single procedure under a single Law, a trademark is achieved for a territory comprising every one of the Member States. An initial Directive to unify the trademark rights of all Member States has also been prepared, along with the Draft Regulation for EC trademarks.

In Spain, these regulations are completed with Protocol no. 8 on Spanish Patents, which establishes the following:

(a) Since joining the EC, Spain has been committed to making its patent legislation compatible with the principles of the free movement of goods and the protection of industrial property in the EC, especially in matters of contractual licences, exclusive compulsory licences, compulsory patent exploitation and introductory patents. Close cooperation is being established between the Commission services and the Spanish authorities to achieve these ends; this cooperation also applies to any transitional problems between the present Spanish legislation and the new legislation.

(b) Spain shall include a provision on reverse proof charges relevant to Article 75 of the Luxembourg Convention of 15 December 1975 on EC Patents. This provision is applicable from the time of membership to any new procedure patent applications filed after that date. This provision applies after 7 October 1992 to all patents filed before membership. Whenever reverse proof charges are not applicable, Spain will continue to make the patent holder liable for proving patent usurpation. In relation to these assumptions, however, Spain would introduce in its legislation, after 7 December 1992, a legal procedure known as a fact verification inquiry. These inquiries are a procedure by means of which any person with a right to act before the Courts in cases of patent usurpation may request a legal resolution.

(c) Spain will join the Munich Convention of 5 October 1973 on European Patents within the established time limits in order to allow chemical and pharmaceutical products to invoke the provisions of Article 167 of the Convention. In this sense, taking into account the fulfilment of Spain's commitment to paragraph 1, the Community Member States, as signatories of the Munich Convention, agree to do everything possible to guarantee an extension of the validity of the reserve foreseen under the previously mentioned Article 167, should Spain so request it, under the terms of this Convention.

(d) After the period of exception is over, Spain will join the Luxembourg Convention on EC Patents, being able to invoke paragraph 4 of Article 95 of the Convention, in order to carry out any technical adjustments needed as a consequence of its entry into this Convention.

By Law II of 30 March 1985, Spain partly fulfilled its duty to adapt its national legislation to the European principles of the free movement of goods.

Anti-Dumping Practices

This is one of the aspects which really did affect Spain from the moment of its entry into the Community. The possible present or future repercussions of EC subsidy regulation in matters of anti-dumping practices unfold in Regulations 2423/88, which establish that any subsidy, directly or indirectly granted for the manufacture, production, export or transport of any product in the country of origin or of export, when it harms intercommunity trade, may give rise to the establishment of a compensatory right.

Among others, the following subsidies may be mentioned:

— Direct subsidies from public authorities to companies or production sectors based on the results of their exports.

— The supply by public authorities or their suppliers of products or services, imported or of domestic origin, destined for the production of export goods, in more favourable conditions than similar or directly competing products or service supplies destined for the production of goods for domestic consumption, if these conditions are more favourable than those exporters may enjoy in the world markets.
— Total or partial exemption, rebate or postponement of direct taxes or social security payments, already paid or pending, from industrial or commercial undertakings.
— Special deductions, directly linked to exports, or to export results, which, when calculating the taxable base for direct taxes, are added to those granted for production destined for domestic consumption.
— Exemption or rebates, based on production or distribution of exported products, of certain amount of taxes received on the basis of the production or distribution of similar products, when they are sold for domestic consumption.
— Exemption, rebate or postponement of pyramiding indirect taxes received in previous stages on goods or services used in the production of exported goods, whose value is higher than that of any similar exemptions, rebates or postponements of pyramiding indirect taxes received in earlier taxes on goods and services used for the production of similar products sold for domestic consumption.

State Aid

In accordance with the provisions of Article 92 of the EC Treaty, the EC unconditionally supports aid of a social nature or to relieve natural disasters. On the other hand, any aid destined to foster economic development must be limited to the specific fostering of economic development in specific, especially depressed regions. In connection with this, the EC approved a Communication on the method to follow in evaluating regional State aid, prior to approval by the EC (88/CS12/02).

With this Communication, the EC seeks to establish several levels for aid relevant to different types of region. Its purpose is to prevent a rise in the level of aid when custom and trade barriers disappear within the Single Market. The ceilings established by the Communication are expressed as the maximum that reflect the nature and seriousness of regional problems in the EC. Within these parameters, the Member States often propose lower regional aid levels to the Commission, which then approves or amends them in its rulings adopted under Articles 92 and 93. The evaluation method contained in this Communication takes into account fundamental socio-economic aspects, such as the level of unemployment, purchasing power, etc. The regions included as possible receivers of aid in Spain and which will, therefore, be subject to the above mentioned evaluation method, are the following: Extremadura, Andalusia, Castile-La Mancha, Galicia, Castile and

León, Murcia, Canary Islands, Teruel, Ceuta and Melilla. Finally, it is important to mention that Spain already has State aid such as: (a) tax credits for investment in new fixed assets; (b) tax credits for job creation; (c) preferential tax treatment for regional development undertakings, venture-capital undertakings and for assets used in research and development programmes.

This brief chapter seems to show the existence of some disagreement between the Spanish fiscal system and the rules established by the EC. Bearing in mind that the EC considers tax allowances as state aid, and that general investment aid is never considered compatible with the existence of a Single Market, Spain is contravening this provision. A trend towards the elimination of this type of incentive is seen in the other EC countries. Thus, for instance, since 1983, France has removed tax credits applicable to general investment. In fact, incentives to investment are only granted in most EC countries in specific, not general, situations. On the other hand, countries such as Ireland, Greece or Spain itself are maintaining fiscal incentives for exports, under one guise or another, and in total opposition to criteria established by the EC.

To sum up, it would seem that State aid through tax allowances is one field where practical harmonization, of extreme importance with regard to the creation of a Single European Market, is still pending. Still, this area has been subject to regulation by the EC, within the general scope of State aid. If the previously mentioned disagreement is taken into consideration, however, it would seem that this regulation has not received sufficient attention from any of the Member States.

References

Carmona Fernández, R. (1986) *La normativa de la CEE sobre la libre competencia*, Madrid, Instituto de la Pequeña y Mediana Empresa Industrial.

Legislación Básica de Derecho Barcelona, de la Politica de Competencia y Propiedad Industrial (1989) Textos Legales Universitarios, Ed. Ariel.

Martín García, P. (1987) *Europa y la Empresa*, Madrid, Fundación Universidad Empresa.

Massaguer Fuentes, J. (1989) *Mercado Común y Patentes Nacionales*, Barcelona, Editorial Bosch.

Pablos Escobar, L. and Valiño Castro, L. (1989) 'El Mercado Común ante las ayudas estatales', *Actualidad Financiera*, No. 39, pp. 2597–603.

Chapter 3

Industrial policy

Carlos Alvarez Aledo

Changes in Spain's industrial policy following EC membership

Any country joining the EC, as did Spain in January 1986, will participate, with all the other Member States, in the search for common strategies aimed at developing and solving goals and problems which affect one of the most important economic areas in the world. From the beginning, the real possibility of achieving economic and monetary union, and finally political integration, was dependent on the successful coordination of national economic interests and the efficient fulfilment of EC goals. There is no doubt that one of the fundamental elements of this economic process is the harmonization of policies and conditions that characterize these countries' industrial production systems.

Even though the first Community institutions (ECSC, EURATOM) were very closely related to the industrial and technological sector of their economies, a Common Industrial Policy of general application for all the EC countries cannot really be imagined without taking account of the seriousness of the problems of the lack of adjustment between supply and demand, or the strong competition from non-European countries in traditional or highly technological sectors (Tamames, 1987). The targets of this EC 'reaction' were noted in the Spinelli Report, approved as the EC's Industrial and Technology Programme in May 1973. It proposed the building of a large internal market, moving production resources within the Community, improving social welfare and harmonizing domestic industrial policies, in order to prevent discrimination between companies in similar sectors.

This industrial policy is being realized, forced by the economic crisis, establishing a series measures for sectoral reconstruction and the reindustrialization of failing industries in Member States, Steel industries and shipbuilding are particularly affected, but others, such as textiles, small and medium-size industries, etc., are also included. It was also necessary to design specific policies for key industrial areas, such as science and technology (whose importance has been reinforced by the special mention it deserves in the Single European Act of 1986) and energy policy. Both of these are important branches, almost independent of the Common Industrial Policy.

Having presented these general remarks on the EC's industrial policies and their meaning in connection with the common European project, we move on to analyse Spain's industry and industrial policy in the years immediately prior to its entry into the EC. We shall also analyse the amendments introduced by the reconstruction and reindustrialization policy as a consequence of entry, which has meant the acceptance of the corpus of EEC law on industry designed in the 1970s, as well as any new strategies that have appeared in the last few years concerning the Single European Market. The special importance of EC technology and energy policies go beyond the limits of this general analysis on industrial policy, although they will be mentioned, whenever necessary.

Spanish industrial policy within the framework of the European economic integration

Main characteristics of Spanish industry at the time of its entry into the EC

In 1986, when the Spanish economy entered the EC, the productive sector was faced with serious structural problems inherited from the past and with conjunctural factors caused by the economic crisis of the 1970s and early 1980s. On the one hand, structural problems were derived from the industrial policies implemented in Spain in previous years, marked by attitudes of isolationism and protection against competition from abroad, disregarding industrial policy development and the strong competition existing between the remaining European countries. In those days, the main concern of Spanish industrial policy was to develop a domestic market.

Meanwhile, the process of Customs integration for some of the main European countries had gradually reinforced competition between their industries, making it necessary to have greater sectoral and subsectoral specialization, in order to achieve the best possible advantage for their national capacities (Myro, 1989a). The almost exclusively domestic nature of Spanish industry, as well as the limited exporting activity present until almost the time of its entry into the EC, were due to its strong custom tariff and administrative protection system.

On the other hand, the priorities of its industrial policy tended towards excessive support for the development of industrial sectors whose demand, after the decade of the 1970s, became weaker (steel, shipbuilding, textiles, shoes etc.) and intermediate (cars, transport materials, food, etc.), while not giving enough attention to sectors with a strong technological content, whose demand was growing (electronics, computers, aeronautics, etc.). With a productive structure as described, the economic crisis of the 1970s and 1980s – which had very negative effects on every European country's industry – was specially bad in the Spanish case (Segura, 1989). Suffice to say, as an example, that during the 1973–84 time-frame one million industrial workers were laid off.

With this brief background, the main industrial reconstruction measures for sectors with greater weight, which started (with a certain delay in comparison with other countries) around 1983–4, were specially traumatic and, in practice, had to accompany the process of adaptation to EC rules which started in 1986 and the common commitment of the Single European Act for 1992. The influence of these circumstances on domestic industrial policy will be analysed in the next section.

Adaptation of Spanish industry to EC rules

Of course every EC rule, among them those concerning production, is directly applicable to Spain as an EC Member State (although, in some cases, an adaptation period is allowed, according to the relevant membership charter). The main general rules affecting industrial policy itself are those which refer to competition policies and to free movement of goods and productive factors.

As far as the *free competition policy* is concerned, the adoption of the EC rules on this subject has had a strong effect on the traditional industrial policy of Spain, since it means an amendment to rules on state subsidies, monopoly and anti-trust laws. EC membership requires the establishment of a controlled and supervised system of subventions to help domestic industries in their structural, financial or labour development and/or write-off. In order to guarantee equal opportunities for every EC company, this aid will have to be really necessary and in proportion with the purposes to be achieved, as well as clearly recognizable and transparent. A large proportion of protectionist aid to national industrial sectors (much of which was lost in compensating their greater production costs above those of other countries) had to be eliminated; and the already implemented reconstruction plans were subject to a new assessment. One of the clearer examples of this may be found in the modification of the control of regional aid and incentives brought about by the prompt approval given by the Spanish government to a new Regional Incentive Law (Law 50, 27 December 1985), whose rules were developed in 1987, and which established:

- A simplification of the number of existing forms of aid.
- Greater transparency in their distribution, as estimation of their amount is now in accordance with the 'Net Equivalent Subvention' Community criterion.
- Greater selectivity, since the number of favoured areas has been limited. They are now established and ordered by the European Commission, taking into account their lesser degree of development.

In connection with the remaining laws that complete the competition policy, the acceptance of monopoly and anti-trust measures has also meant two important modifications in the Spanish economy. The first one is the legal adaptation of oil and tobacco monopolies, which may keep their status as fiscal and production monopolies, but will gradually lose their trade monopolies. This, in turn, means that foreign companies will be allowed access to domestic markets. Second, the approval of the Competition Defence Law, to reform and harden any provisions on this subject. Finally, Spain has started adapting the rules concerning *the free movement of goods and production factors*, with the implementation of the following measures, among others:

(a) A progressive removal of customs duties paid by Spanish industries, on imports from Community countries.
(b) The adoption of technical harmonization principles, as well as of certification and production control as established by the EC (which, unlike in other Community countries, hardly existed previously in Spain). In order to achieve this, the official equalization system initially begun by the Ministry of Industry and Energy is being replaced with another equalization system, under the responsibility of an organization created by industrial companies (AENOR). In future, this system may facilitate compliance with the 'mutual recognition principle' in the industrial production of different countries (Pérez Simarro, 1988).
(c) Modification of its domestic and foreign indirect taxation system, with the establishment (since January 1986) of a Value Added Tax (VAT) to replace other, less transparent, indirect taxes, and the modification of the border tax adjustment.

As an added difficulty, Spain, and all the other countries newly admitted to the EC, must make a contribution, simultaneously with all other Member States, towards achieving the 1992 Single Market, by implementing some of the already accepted adaptation goals, such as the reality of 'A Europe without Borders' for goods and persons, a greater coordination of technical standards, free access of companies from all the EC countries to public purchase contracts, etc. (Ruesga, 1989).

Reconstruction policy

The most relevant aspects of Spain's industrial policy and the influence of EC policies over it, may be focused on three sectors: iron and steel industries, shipbuilding and textiles.

Iron and steel

The reconstruction strategy in this area (legally established in 1981, but not in practice applied until 1983–4), aims to decrease the productive capacity of and modernize the main industries in this sector, where production and employment levels are important for Spain. The specifically affected companies are those of the integrated producers, ENSIDESA, Altos Hornos del Mediterráneo and Altos Hornos de Vizcaya, and those in the special steel sector (ACENOR).

During 1986, these plans, which had already been implemented at the time of entry to the EC, were subject to a series of revisions by representatives of the Spanish Ministry of Industry and by the CECA, due to the fact that this sector was specifically subject to EC control under the Davignon Plan. As a result of this, its approval and final acceptance by the European Commission were conditional on the completion of the already existing plans, with additional measures. The main modifications were those related to the setting up of wider guarantees for the absorption of labour surpluses and to the temporary modification and limitation of these companies' financial write-off plans, which would have to be based on the concession of State subventions and be completed by issue of company shares and by the granting of low-interest credits. These State subventions were only possible for a transition period of three years (1986–8), established by the EC for the Spanish iron and steel sector. In addition, the adoption of EC regulations has affected the Spanish iron and steel industries as follows:

— The establishment of incentives aimed at reducing the productive capacity of the steel sector, to 17.5 million tons/year by the end of 1988.
— The creation in September 1987 of a technical body called 'Gerencia de Siderúrgica' (Iron and Steel Management), to control and follow-up these measures; the minimum viability criteria established by the CECA had to be met after 1989.
— The Spanish government requested in 1986 the effective application of the 'Safeguard Clause' contained in Article 379 of the Membership Treaty to prevent harmful effects on specific subsectors, caused by the deregulation of some of their producers' imports and by the occasionally unfair competition of some EC iron and steel companies as of that year. The Commission finally approved this request at the end of 1986, and extended it to the two subsequent years. Following the end of this transition period, the iron and steel sector was fully subject to EC rules; the reconstruction process was considered formally completed and up to EC standards in 1990.

Shipbuilding

The reconstruction policy for this sector, which, although somewhat delayed, also started in 1984, addressed the modernization and restructuring of the sector and stimulation of new shipbuilding orders after the strong fall in demand experienced in the years immediately following the crisis.

The national aid measures established for this sector were replaced in 1987 – when the Sixth Directive of the Council, dealing with aid applicable to Spain for a transition period between 1987 and 1990, was approved by every EC country. These rules permit the aid to be continued, establishing a maximum ceiling for those destined to continue in operation, and the possibility of reconstruction aid to go beyond those limits, with the Commission's authorization and for as long as this reconstruction maintained the EC plans on reduction of production capacity.

The need to adapt the shipbuilding sector continued through 1989 and 1990, forcing an additional reduction of its work-force and production, and more economic aid. A disagreement arose between the Spanish Ministry of Industry and the European Commission on the limits imposed on this aid to meet the provisions of the 1987 Sixth EC Council Directive.

Textiles

The reconstruction plans for this sector were the least affected by Spain's EC membership, as they had been approved in 1981 and expired in 1986, after compliance with the foreseen goals of labour adjustment, financial write-offs and productivity increase were deemed to have been reached.

A new 'Design and Fashion Promotion Plan: Synthetic Textiles' was implemented in 1986, to reindustrialize, modernize and promote this sector's design and quality. A plan coherent with EC rules has, indeed, been introduced in this sector, for the specific purpose of:

— Prohibiting production increases, especially of synthetic fibres.
— Obtaining additional grants through Community aid for modernization.
— Participating in research projects applied to this sector within the BRITE programme.
— Implementing a textile and clothing research centre, in order to counsel and inform managers in this sector.

New competitivity problems arose, however, in the course of the following years (specially in matters dealing with New Industrialized Countries, NIC), making it necessary to start the adjustment process anew, with a 1991 plan for temporary job suspensions.

On balance job adjustments have been met in most reconstructed sectors, and have sometimes even gone beyond initial forecasts. The goal of achieving a substantial financial cost reduction has also been accomplished. In some cases, the same cannot be said about the new guidelines being applied to the sectors and the real competitivity increase. The reason for this might sometimes be found in a lack of clear strategies suggested by official industrial policy.

Reindustrialization policy and new strategies

We have already seen that EC membership has meant more for Spain than a simple modification of the already existing industrial policies established as a result of the crisis. It has also forced an acceleration of the process of modernizing in the industrial structure and of opening up to EC countries, within the 1993 horizon.

As far as industrial structures are concerned, Spain's particular way of implementing industrial policies had built up an industry of intermediate products, with low competitivity (Buesa, 1989). In 1986, when Spain entered the EC, 85% of this country's industrial production was mainly of low and medium-demand sectors; the only companies involved in high-demand sectors, those 'with a future', were in the remaining percentage.

So Spanish industrial policy has had to give greater attention to these areas and to the progressive disappearance of protection in the traditional sectors, allowing competitive forces in the domestic and EC markets to adjust the productive structure and slowly bring the national industrial structure close to that of other countries. This has had certain social costs. At the same time, and in contrast with the years before 1986, industrial policy started a process of strategic promotion for companies within several sectors, aiming to achieve greater diversification for their industrial products and an improved international competitivity for them. The EC legal framework in this field allows a wide margin of freedom for the implementation of domestic policies of a sectoral nature promoting these aspects.

Following the fast developing industrial policies of other EC countries, Spain is giving special attention to any entrepreneurial strategy aimed at increasing competitivity, not only through the traditional means of cost and price reduction, but also through 'product differentiation' strategies – in other words, increasing the technology element in the products' added value, improving their quality and design by means of suitable marketing and advertising to promote a trademark image that gives products a personality of their own. Financial, training and technical support has mainly been addressed to small and medium-size enterprises, which is the case in other parts of Europe.

To conclude, measures to reconstruct Spanish state industrial undertakings also deserve special mention within the new industrial policy strategies on competition in the Single Market (Fies, 1989). Past errors are once again being corrected, reorienting this new industrial group by means of:

- The reduction of State participation in non-strategic sectors, or their sale to the national or foreign private sector (for example, the 1985 divestment of the Spanish car enterprise, SEAT, in which the German Volkswagen company acquired a majority share).
- The closure of several financially non-viable companies (this solution is seldom used).

— Subdivision into specialized industrial groups, with more independent and competitive management systems, to decentralize decision-making and to come closer to the competitive behaviour of public or private companies in other countries.
— Various enterprise subholdings within the Instituto Nacional de Industria (INI), in sectors such as electronics (INISEL), aluminium (INESPAL) or steel and iron (SIDMED) were also created in 1985.
— Participation in most large European and EC research programmes, such as EUREKA, ESPRIT and BRITE, as well as in international ones like Arianne, Airbus, etc.
— Adapting trade monopoly sectors to new foreign competition situations. In 1987, a new company (REPSOL) was created in the energy sector, within the National Hydrocarbon Institute (INH). It focuses the activity of all enterprises related with oil exploitation and marketing, and is similar in structure to the multinationals in this sector.

Conclusions

The above summary of information allows us to reach several conclusions on the negative and positive effects – general and specific – of EC membership over Spanish industry and its industrial policy. These effects are not exhaustive, nor are they easily quantified. At any rate, they may be considered as an approximation to the ongoing reforms in this sector.

Several of these aspects are very similar to those already present in other European sectors. But there is a difference: many of the changes have already taken place, or are happening, much faster than formerly and deliberately. Also, from the viewpoint of domestic industrial policy, general aid is now controlled by the EC institutions, while it may – and should – have more incentives in aspects where it enjoys greater autonomy, such as those dealing with the modernization of industrial sectors.

Some *beneficial or positive effects* of the process of integration are:

(a) Better rationalization and transparency in the shape and amount of different types of grants and aid to domestic companies. This has contributed to the lowering of an important source of public debt and forces companies to adapt themselves more flexibly to free competition. As a compensation, Spanish industry has now access to EC Structural Funds.
(b) Accelerated internationalization of Spanish companies and the adoption of new strategies on trademarks and design.
(c) The introduction of more rigorous product standardization and equalization rules, which may contribute to the acceptance of Spanish industrial products in other countries and benefit domestic consumers.
(d) Adapting and reducing the excessive public participation in the Spanish

industrial sector, forming more competitive and efficient productive, financial and marketing structures.

(e) The need to modify or replace polluting industrial production processes, in order to adapt them to EC environmental standards. Spanish industry is considerably behind other countries in this matter, due to the previous absence of a national programme of rewards and/or penalties to industry.

Among the *negative or harmful effects* are the following:

(f) Severe problems of growth, or even survival, for sectors which, until a relatively short time ago, were protected against competition by the traditional State customs and aid systems, and whose capability to react is very limited.

(g) Due to the insufficient size of Spanish undertakings, foreign competition and a closer relationship with EC Member States may accelerate or increase the penetration of some multinational companies. If Spanish companies are controlled or taken over by the multinationals, they may have to adopt global strategies, which may go against their own interests.

(h) The existence of adaptation, reconstruction and updating processes for the industrial sector, at a much faster rate than would have been convenient (due to the need to meet EC standards and time limits), may bring about more unemployment than might have been the case under other circumstances. This problem may be partly – although not sufficiently – compensated for by the present guidelines and the Structural Funds destined for less developed regions in the EC, several of which are located in Spain.

Finally, it is necessary to point out that the strong growth of the Spanish economy (4–5% increases in GNP) which was created through a complex set of domestic and international circumstances after 1986, may have given a false impression of the capacity of the Spanish economic system to adapt itself, without serious costs, to EC competition. The growth of domestic demand may be allowing some companies to maintain an uneconomic situation, despite strong external competition.

One of the most recent reports on the repercussions of the 1993 Single Market on Spanish industry (European Commission, 1990) points to the convenience of Spain making good use of its net comparative advantages in certain sectors (in the EC, although not the NIC). In general, these advantages have been seen in labour-intensive sectors with low wage costs (ceramics, shoe-making, textiles, wines, food, shipbuilding, etc.), as well as in some sectors with high capital investment but a low technology content. It is believed, however, that Spain should accept its minimal or nil possibility of competing in other sectors, especially those with a high technology content.

References

Buesa, M. (1989) *Estructura Industrial de España*, Madrid, Ed. Pirámide.

European Commission (1990), *L'impact sectoriel du marché intérieur sur l'industrie: les enjeus pour les Etats membres*, Economie Europeéne, Reviste Europe Sociale, Special Issue.

Fundaciones Fies (1989) *La empresa pública en España, Papeles de Economía Española*, no. 22, Madrid.

Ministerio De Industria Y Energia (1987) *España en Europa. Un futuro industrial: la política industrial en el horizonte 1992*, Madrid.

—— (1988) *Informe Anual sobre la Industria*, Madrid.

Myro, R. (1989a) 'La industria española: expansión, crisis y reconversión', in *España: Economía*, ed. J.L. Delgado, Madrid, Ed. Espasa Calpe, pp. 197–230.

—— (1989b) 'El comportamiento de la industria en 1989', *Economistas*, No. 41, pp. 176–88.

Pérez Simarro, R. (1988) 'La política industrial española ante el mercado único europeo', *Economistas*, No. 29, pp. 137–40. Madrid.

Ruesga, S.M. (ed.) (1989) *1993: España ante el Mercado Unico*, Madrid, Ed. Pirámide.

Sanz De Buruaga, G. (ed.) (1988) *Efectos de la adhesion comunitaria sobre los sectores industriales y las regiones de España y Portugal*, Madrid, Fundación Banco Exterior de España.

Segura, J. (ed.) (1989) *La industria española en la crisis 1978–1984*, Madrid. Ed. Alianza Editorial.

Tamames, R. (1987) *La Comunidad Europea*, Madrid, Alianza Editorial Textos.

Chapter 4

Technology policy

Carlos Alvarez Aledo

Spanish technology policy after 1986

Research and development policy in the EC countries is a particular case within the industrial policy of the EC. This may already be seen in the ECSC and EURATOM Treaties of the 1950s, as well as the PREST working groups and the COST (Cooperation on Science and Technology) actions, at the end of the 1960s. A Common Technology Policy for the Member States, however, did not begin until the FAST Programme was launched, to evaluate and predict the need for R&D projects in the EC. The proposals originating from this programme are the basis for the establishment of the First Community Framework Programme on R&D. The Council approved this First Programme in 1983, and it was implemented between 1984 and 1987, with a total budget of ECU 3,750 million. As was the case with Industrial Policy, the main incentive to achieve a single strategy was the alarming development of other competing countries in this field, especially the United States and Japan (Tamames, 1987).

The First Framework Programme and its followers are really the fundamental instruments for the application of the EC R&D Policy (formally established as such after the signature of the Single European Act in 1986), since it focuses all the scientific and technological goals, priorities and action during the established period of time. From the time of its approval, the Second Framework Programme (1987–91) with a total budget of ECU 5,396, affected every Spanish project. The Programme established eight areas of R&D priority, to be developed through specific cooperation between Member States. Within this area, the most important programmes are:

(1) Quality of life (research programmes on disease prognosis/prevention and on radiation protection).
(2) Information and communications (ESPRIT II, RACE, DELTA and DRIVE Programmes).
(3) Modernization of industrial sectors (BRITE and EURAM programmes).

(4) Optimal exploitation and utilization of biological resources (BAP, FLAIR and ECLAIR programmes).
(5) Energy (JET, NET and JOULE programmes).
(6) Science and technology at the service of development (programmes for agricultural improvement and tropical medicine in developing countries).
(7) Exploitation of marine resources (MAST programme).
(8) Better European cooperation in matters of science and technology (COMMETT, FAST and EUROTRA programmes).

Besides these purely internal research actions, the EC also maintains other forms of cooperation with other institutions and countries, among which the European Space Agency (ESA) and the European Laboratory of Particle Physics (CERN) and the AIRBUS programme deserve mentioning. Any cooperation with other, non-Community, countries is reflected mainly in the EUREKA programme, created as a result of the 1985 Hanover Conference, which was strongly supported in the following years. Until the 1989 Vienna Conference, its budget was of ECU 6,400 million, and it implemented a total of 247 cooperative projects in 160 public and private organizations.

Scientific policy in Spain

The initial situation of R&D activity and policy in Spain

When Spain was admitted into the EC, the deficiency of its R&D activities owed something to the deficiencies in the general situation of Spanish industry:

— Excessive weight on the traditional sectors, where demand has now decreased in most developed countries.
— Scant attention paid to foreign competition and a rigid productive system, insufficiently prepared to adapt itself to new technologies, caused by a strongly protectionist government system.
— Small average size of enterprises (three times lower in technology and strong demand sectors), making it very difficult, for practical purposes, for these companies to have sufficient resources and capacity to invest in high risk areas of R&D.
— Lack of links between the basic research and related sectors, public research centres (especially universities) and private companies.
— An almost non-existent State scientific and technology policy, due to the scant attention granted to public expenditure and aid to the private sector in matters of R&D. The consequence of the protection given to the domestic market against foreign competition was that important investment in R&D was not necessary in this scenario. Industrial needs

were covered by the import of high-technology production goods and by patent and royalty payments for production procedures. In 1980, the total R&D expenditure (both private and public) was of approximately 0.4 per cent of the GNP, while in 1986 this percentage had gone up to around 0.5% (Buesa & Molero, 1989).

The final consequence of all this was that the growing need for technology and production goods demanded by national economic development had to be met through very costly imports, which were not balanced by a high level of exports. This gave rise to a strong technology balance deficit (Sánchez Muñoz, 1984). The proportion of exports to imports fell to its lowest point in recent history in 1988 (it went down to 14% whereas the normal range was about 17–19%). Real payments under the general concept of technology were of Pts. 159.741 million in 1988; around 90% of this sum went to purchase patents and trademarks, and for technical assistance.

Changes in Spanish R&D policy

All this makes it clear that Spain's adjustment and cooperation with the EC R&D goals started late and at a serious disadvantage. Immediately after joining the EC, Spain started trying to catch up. The Law for the Promotion and General Coordination of Scientific and Technology Research (also called the Science Law) was approved in April 1986. It establishes:

(a) The harmonization and simplification of Spanish public research agencies, as well as how to coordinate goals and resources destined for research by the State and the Autonomous Communities (Spain's self-governing dependent regions). Before 1986, there were nine ministries (the Ministry of Education and Science and the Ministry of Industry and Science, most importantly) with responsibility for R&D activities. After the Science Law, an Interministerial Commission for Law and Technology (CICYT) and several councils and commissions of a common nature were created (Martín & Romero, 1988).
(b) The preparation and approval of a National Scientific and Technology Research Plan, as the main instrument of the Spanish scientific policy. The Plan was approved in 1988, for a four-year period (1988–91), with a total budget of Pts. 11,932 million. Above all, it sought to bring total Spanish R&D expenditure in 1991 to 1% of GNP. The Plan established several areas of priority, fitting in with those established in the Second Community Framework Programme. The Spanish research areas are: new materials, computer and telecommunications technology, microcomputers, food technology, biotechnology, space, pharmaceutical R&D, aquaponics, Antarctic research, high energy physics and research

personnel training. Apart from the programmes included in these areas, there also are sectoral and Autonomous Community programmes.

(c) Improved coordination between public research centres and private companies, as well as coordination and follow-up of international R&D programmes with Spanish participation. The main purpose in this latter case, apart from an efficient use of resources, is to achieve the highest possible technological and industrial returns from these programmes.

From the beginning, these functions were assigned to the Technology and Industrial Development Centre (CDTI), which, as it had existed since 1977, had suitable experience in these matters.

In effect, a quantitative and qualitative change in the Spanish R&D system was being sought after, so as to remedy past deficiencies. Although it seems clear that this unequivocal change in the scientific policy of the country was necessary in any case, it also seems clear (though not casual) that these reforms were hastened and promoted by Spain's integration in the EC, as well as by the existence of important EC scientific programmes and by Spain's commitment to meet the provisions established in 1986 by the Single European Act. Without reforms, it would have been extremely hard for the almost non-existent science and technology programme to take advantage of Framework Programmes and to prepare for the challenges of the near future.

The destiny of the available resources, however, seems debatable. According to 1988 data, out of the 691 R&D projects presented in Spain for public financing, the Ministry of Industry finally granted subsidies to 279, for a total of Pts. 3,411 million. Top priority was given to very high technology sectors, whose connection with the main domestic productive sectors was limited. The first area, computer technology, received 15.9% of subsidies. Space technology came second, with 11.4%. In contrast, other sectors – which are very important for the preservation of jobs – such as industrial, electric, textile technologies or metal products, only received about 1%.

In other matters, Spain tried to fit in with the EC; it approved a Patent Law to reinforce legal protection over R&D investment and to enlarge the possibility of using it to spread research and technology (an annual 'Report on the Status of Technology' was planned).

After several decades of regulation, technology transfer was liberalized in 1987. This was not simply done to adapt Spanish rules to those of other EC countries, but also to try to obtain positive effects by lowering the cost of these imports; the real effect, however, has been a strong increase in external payments for technology.

Mention must be made, finally, of the influence of entry to the EC and of the Single Market project on three sectoral technology projects. First, the *Plan Electrónico e Informático Nacional* (National Electronics and Computer Plan, PEIN-II), is not only consolidating the national electronic and computer industry, but has adapted itself to new administrative mechanisms and to the newly-arrived competition from EC enterprises. An important part of its development possibilities lies in its capacity to participate in EC programmes, with leading European companies. Electronic components, microelectronics and computer software are given priority. PEIN-II is shaping as, perhaps, the most important domestic programme, not only because of the importance of subsidies and implemented projects (Pts. 3,018.7 million in 1988, for projects with a value of Pts. 14,278 million), but also for its strong connection with many pertinent sectors in the domestic sector.

The *Research in Pharmaceutical Industries Promotion Plan* deserves to be mentioned in second place; its purpose between 1986 and 1990 was to develop its own technology to produce new drugs, and to manufacture already-known products in a profitable manner, responding to the challenge posed by the introduction in 1992 of product patents and free competitivity in this sector. To achieve this, the Spanish State had to cooperate, within the EC rules for public aid programmes, to raise the total accumulated amounts spent on R&D in this sector from 2.5% of sales in 1985 to 14% in 1990.

Third, an *Energy Research Plan* has also been implemented, in line with the EC's research priorities, to make the use of energy more efficient, as well as to develop technologies for coal, nuclear power, renewable energies and environmental protection.

To conclude, Spain – with the existing EC aid – is actively trying to increase the technology level of small and medium-size industries, whose lagging behind in this field is important enough to cause them a serious competitive disadvantage for the future.

Participation in EC and international R&D Programmes

From the moment of its entry into the EC, Spain started to encourage the participation of private companies and public research institutions in great European programmes, as the most efficient manner to absorb and generate technology within the domestic productive system (Gassol, 1985). Its goals are: (1) to maximize industrial technology profits derived from Spain's economic and human resource contributions to this programme; and (2) to take advantage of the new openings to foreign markets and of the opportunities for cooperation with other European companies fostered by Spanish participation in these programmes. Consequently, Spanish companies are participating in the following programmes:

> *Community Framework Programmes*: In spite of the First Framework Programme's advanced state in 1986, Spain still had the chance to cooperate in some of the main projects, such as BRITE, ESPRIT, RACE, etc., in 1986–7. Profits obtained during this period are estimated around ECU 75.2 million. Spain participated from the beginning in the Second Framework Programme (1988–91), as a full

Member of the EC. Its contribution to the budget established for this period represents approximately 7.5% of the total. The chance to participate – in greater or smaller measure – in most of the projects approved should mean that, at the end of this period, technological returns will be great. The last estimated percentage on returns per share in the Second Framework Programme is around 5% of the funds allocated. *EUREKA Programme*: In 1989, Spain participated in seventy-eight of the 297 projects in this international programme (26% of projects), with a financial participation totalling ECU 448 million (approximately 7% of the total budget, but 24% of the sum specifically assigned to those seventy-eight projects). Some features of Spain's participation in EUREKA explain its present R&D situation:

- 54% of the projects in which Spain participated are relatively small (with a total budget of not more than Pts. 1,000 million), and only 7% of them have investments of more than Pts. 10,000 million.
- Approximately half of the total financial contribution (51%) comes from large companies, 30% from smaller ones, and 18% is contributed by research centres and universities. The remaining 1% is the contribution of other institutions. The participation of small and medium-sized companies (42% of the projects), is in low-budget projects.
- The projects in which Spain has participated belong to the following fields of research: robotics (24.3% of projects); biotechnology (22%); computer science (15%); environment (14%) and laser technology (8%).

After the Rome Conference, the number of projects presented (and approved) by Spain takes fourth place among the participating countries. However, only six of the twenty-five accepted projects (with a budget of Pts. 7,200 million) are headed by Spanish companies.

Other international programmes: It should be pointed out, in conclusion, that Spain completes its international cooperation in R&D activities with financial participation in programmes carried out by various organizations and institutions, such as the COST fund (Spain contributes 5.9%); the European Nuclear Research Organization, CERN (5.8%); the European Space Agency (3.5%); the European Molecular Biology Laboratory (4.5%); the European Sicrotron Radiation Facilities, ESRF (4.0%) and the Airbus Programme (4.2%) etc.

Conclusions

Spain's entry into the EC in 1986 and the Single European Act had a clear and direct influence on the reform of its science and technology system, the implementation of which began that same year; however, other effects, both positive and negative, have also touched upon the R&D sector, as a consequence of this.

Among the positive effects, it seems unquestionable that joining the Common Technology Policy has meant:

(a) A greater official concern for the promotion and development of scientific and technological activities in Spain's economy. The present increase of provision in public expenditure to adapt the organizational structure of the public sector to these concerns has allowed for the design of a general scientific policy in line with that of developed countries.
(b) The establishment of sectoral scientific policies, vital for industries such as electronics, energy or computer science, help to prepare for harsh competition within the Single Market.
(c) The chance for small, newly created Spanish companies, little known at international and EC levels, to cooperate in the high technology research projects of leading companies. This may even lead to unofficial cooperation agreements with these companies.
(d) Greater training possibilities for Spanish researchers in basic technology which is much more developed in other countries, allowing for its later implementation in Spain.

The present process of integration in Community scientific policy may, however, cause certain negative effects and some future risks. They arise from the persistent lack of connection between basic research and technology applications and between universities and enterprises. Excessive participation and massive effort in human and material resources given to many international basic research projects, in order to improve the scientific prestige of Spain, as well as to achieve good returns, may mean that:

(e) The results obtained by some of the larger current basic research programmes will not bring large profits to the domestic productive system.
(f) The relatively scarce human resources available for EC and international research programmes, and especially some of the more advanced research workers, will be overworked. It limits the number of people available to work on Spanish projects and to train new researchers. (The government is partially aware of these problems, and now devotes a high percentage of the National Plan resources to training research personnel.)
(g) As a consequence of all this, technological development opportunities are probably declining, as are resources and researchers in other sectors, which, while more modest, could be those in which Spain has a comparative advantage rather than those that will continue to be dominated in the future by large EC multinationals.

References

Buesa, M. and Molero, J. (1989) 'Política Tecnológica', in *Economistas*, No. 41.

Castells, M. (ed.) (1986) *Nuevas tecnologías: Economía y Sociedad en España* (2 vols.), Madrid, Ed. Alianza Universidad.

Comision Interministerial de Ciencia y Tecnología (1989) *Sistema Español de Ciencia y Tecnología*, Madrid.

Gassol, I. (1985) 'La política científica y tecnológica en España y la CEE', *Economía Industrial*, No. 242.

Martín C. and Romero, L. (1988) *Vías de acceso al cambio técnico*, in J.L. García Delgado (ed.), *España-Economía*, Madrid, Ed. Espasa Calpe.

Ministerio de Industria y Energía (1989) *España en Europa: Un futuro industrial: La política industrial en el horizonte 1992*, Madrid.

Sánchez Muñoz, P. (1984) *La dependencia tecnológica y contratos de transferencia de tecnología entre España y el Exterior*, Madrid, Ministerio de Economía y Hacienda.

Tamames, R. (1987) *La Comunidad Europea*, Madrid, Alianza Editorial Textos.

Chapter 5

The energy sector

Sara González Fernández

The goals established for energy policy were collected in the third Plan Energético Nacional (National Energy Plan or PEN), approved in 1984, whose scope of action covered up to 1992. This Third Plan followed EC guidelines such as energy savings and to replace oil with other types of energy. The specific goals of the Plan were the following:

— To reduce the vulnerability of energy supplies. Given the fact that consumption relied mainly on hydrocarbons, one aim of the energy policy was to reduce the use of oil.
— To improve efficiency in energy consumption and transformation, promoting energy saving and conservation.
— The optimum utilization of resources, in order to meet demand, absorbing any excess capacity in the energy sector.

The oil sector

Although oil is one of the most popular forms of energy used in Spain, this use is now decreasing, because of greater efficiency achieved following the EC's recommendations. These may be summarized as a reduction of 40% of the total, with imports no more than a third of this consumption. Spain has had no difficulty with limiting the use of oil in electric power generation to below 15%. With the exception of the Canary Islands, no electric power station has been built to be fired by fuel oil.

It has been specified that financial support to hydrocarbon research should be for technology, exploration and development, in order to lower the costs of these activities. In these matters, the Spanish Law of Exploration and Research of Hydrocarbons (Law 21, 27 June 1974) covered the initial research stage, with a remarkable increase in drilling and in the area surveyed. A Regulation implying the contribution of an EC subsidy of up to 40% of the total investment was implemented in 1985, and this has encouraged several Spanish companies to submit projects to these programmes.

But in order to have secure supplies and fewer price fluctuations, it is necessary to keep compulsory buffer-stocks. Along these lines, Spain is strictly following the EC rules, since the Spanish oil sector is a member of the buffer-stock safety system known as Euroilstock.

Another important aspect following Spain's entry into the EC is the process of adaptation of the Spanish oil monopoly to the EC rules. Commercial monopolies are not incompatible with the founding Treaties nor with EC-derived law; it is simply required that their legal definition and *modus operandi* must be compatible with the fulfilment of the four great freedoms established under the Treaties, especially free movement of goods.

Special mention should be made here of the anticipation of these measures adopted in Spain. Preparation for this process started in 1981, once membership of the EC was accepted, with the creation of the Instituto Nacional de Hidrocarburos (National Hydrocarbon Institute). The process reached its peak with the Law for the Adaptation of the Oil Monopoly and the Royal Decree regulating the wholesale distribution of oil imported from the EEC.

It then became necessary to draw up a scheme in agreement with EC legislation, whose structure would allow Spanish companies to compete under equal conditions with large EC oil companies, compensating for their greater operational experience and their vertical integration. In addition to this, the scheme should take into account three essential factors of the Spanish system: the economic dimension, the effects on national security and the influence over the territorial organization of the State, as well as on regional development possibilities.

All of these aspects establish the limits and speed of the legal adjustment of the oil monopoly to EC rules. This adjustment is a unique case in the EC records. It was an absolute monopoly, covering all activities with great legal and executive accuracy. It was based on the concept of two parallel systems; one for domestic production, relevant to all refining activities, distribution and final sale, and the other international, relevant to imports and their distribution and sale in a parallel network.

As to the pricing system, its modification has been planned in accordance with EC practices. The new system follows a predetermined time schedule during the period of transition.

Nuclear power

Some of the EC countries have no commitment to a nuclear power programme. Nevertheless, nuclear power is considered a source of energy which will allow the EC to diversify its sources of supply.

Spain's membership of the European Community of Atomic Energy (EURATOM) has had many effects on its nuclear sector. Regarding the supply of raw materials, EURATOM has a common programme for the exploration and research of energy resources. If some of these resources are granted to Spain, this will allow for the promotion of the National Plan for

Uranium Exploration and Research and Spain would also have access to enrichment plants in Great Britain (URENCO) and France (EURODIF). Spain has no plants of this nature, while these countries have installations far exceeding the needs of the Member States, and can guarantee to fulfil Spanish demand. In addition to this, one problem may be solved by the outlet opened for Spanish uranium surpluses through the Supply Agency. Spain has high stocks dating from the time of the ambitious nuclear plan PEN (75), which, when it was reduced, became surplus to requirements.

Community legislation requires compulsory cost/benefit studies before activities can be approved. Bad effects on health and the environment and exploitation costs (these are very large projects) are some of the costs to be taken into account. On the positive side we may place the high energy production level, with decreased dependency on sources in other countries; therefore, job creation.

Access enjoyed by the Spanish energy sector to finance granted by the European Investment Bank on privileged conditions should be mentioned in the cost/benefit analysis, as it will allow a reduction in energy generation costs: these are very large installations, which lock-up investment for long periods of time. In Spain, this is approximately twelve years.

Another way to reduce costs is to recycle irradiated fuel, so as to optimize the use of non-renewable products.

Other sources of energy

Coal has a priority role as a replacement for oil within the EC framework. Many mining shafts were abandoned in Spain because they were unprofitable when oil prices went down. Oil replaced coal, but when oil prices increased, and the enormous external dependency was noticed, the substitution policy was reversed. So the energy crisis and rising prices promoted the recovery of domestic demand for coal, and this, in turn, fostered coal production, which exceeded the supply of oil derivatives by several points. It must be mentioned that national subsidies are necessary for this activity to be profitable.

The Protocol of Intent for the Development of Gas in Spain was signed in 1985, which, among other questions, set up an infrastructure and market regulations for natural gas. The allocation of geographical markets to dealer companies gives rise to their creation of rational and profitable exploitation units, among which we find Serrablo (1984), in the Aragon Pyrenees, and Gravista (1986), close to Bermeo, which together supply 14% of Spain's needs. Besides this exploitation, the import of European natural gas will be achieved by linking Spanish and French gas pipelines.

Finally, the EC goals establish, among other things, the promotion of research and innovation in energy matters and the maintenance, and even increase, of *participation in new and renewable energy sources*. Spain is adapting itself to these goals with its Renewable Energy Plan, introduced in 1986, encompassed by the 1983/92 National Energy Plan. This establishes the need to promote renewable energy in order to reduce our dependence on raw energy supplies.

References

Ballestero, A. (1989) *Buscando Petróleo*, Madrid.
Bice Redacción, (1991) 'La industria eléctrica en 1990', *Bol. Información Comercial Española*, No. 2265, January/February.
Centeno, R. (1988) *El Petróleo y la Crisis Mundial*, Madrid, Alianza Editorial.
Economístas, (1990) 'Sector Eléctrico: Regulación o liberalización?', No. 43, April/May.
Fernandez Cuesta, N. (1986) 'La liberalización del sector petrolero español', *Economía Industrial*, March/April.
Ríos Rodicio, A. A. (1988) *La politica energética española desde 1973 a 1984*, Valladolid.
Salmador, F. (1989) 'Evolución de la industria eléctrica en España', *ENERGIA*, No. 6, November/December.

Chapter 6

Telecommunications and transport policy

Sara González Fernández

The conflict of interest derived from the need to open domestic markets while, at the same time, guaranteeing the viability of the network's public infrastructure has given rise to an important debate in connection with the degree of liberalization that this sector should have and has been translated into slow progress in the practical realization of EC policy. Regulatory measures, however, have already been announced and the Commission is trying to speed up their implementation by means of Directives – which are binding – even though, for the most part, these demand that every one of the Member States adopts some domestic legislation. The debate between the Council, the Member States and the Commission deals with form, rather than with content; the period of time for the effective application of these policies is rather short. However, there seems to be no possibility of going back on the liberalizing process unleashed by the Commission.

All over the world, competitivity and globalization seem to be the current basic goals of the telecommunications sector. In order to be successful on both these counts, the EC has begun various deregulation procedures to define EC policy in this field, through the establishment of rules to permit compatibility of products and services in every Member State. These measures are included in the so-called 'Green Book' and cover the free offer of non-reserved products and the Open Network (ONP) offer. The Directive which regulates these goals does not mention the liberalization of the telecommunications network structures. Thus, each Member State may grant to the existing telecommunications authorities exclusive rights over the traditional telephone lines, optic fibre lines, short-wave radio and satellite links, radiotelephone networks and cable TV. Each State may also grant exclusive rights in the provision of vocal services. This Directive is not applicable to services such as telex, mobile radiotelephones, radio messages, satellite communications and mass-media communications services, such as radio broadcasting or television.

These rules are recent, although their application is expected within a short period of time, which will no doubt require a great effort, if one bears in mind that, at the end of 1989, EC data networks and services were not compatible. Nevertheless, express-post free competition and data base access began in 1990, and basic data communications, which grow at an approximate yearly rate of 25%, were scheduled to begin in 1993.

Telecommunications in Spain

The telephone network is the essential base for telecommunications services, and it is managed in Spain by the National Telephone Company of Spain (CTNE). This chapter now presents some data relevant to this company, to further the cost/benefit analysis of the effects that the application of an EC policy in matters of telecommunications will have in Spain.

In 1986, the Spanish telephone network was ninth in the world in terms of absolute size, and twenty-fifth in terms of telephones per head of population. Since then, the system has been undergoing a process of modernization, so that, for instance, digitalization of exchanges has gone from 13% in 1986 up to 36% in 1990. This process of modernization has been covered under the 1987 Law of Telecommunications Ordinance (LOT), which sets the basis for the liberalization of the value-added service market. Seeking to ensure a position of control in this market, CTNE has introduced, *inter alia*, TS-1, and has signed an agreement with IBM and agreements with telephone service companies in France, Italy, Germany, Portugal and the United Kingdom. CTNE will have to deliver services in a competitive framework. Among those are the SVA, already liberalized in the LOT, as well as services which, under the LOT, are being operated as monopolies. Data switching and circuit leasing may be mentioned here. The purpose of the Directives dealing with open network offer (ONP) and service liberalization is to provide free service delivery throughout the EC for any operator previously authorized by one of the Member States. Thus, Article 7 of the ONP Framework Directive states that, as proposed by the Commission, the Council should guarantee the conditions of mutual recognition of processes for declaration or authorization of service delivery via public telecommunications networks.

This Directive also obliges states to make network access public, objective and non-discriminatory, even though they may have exclusive rights for the establishment and exploitation of public networks. Member States shall also notify the Commission about the authorization procedures; they may not, otherwise, impose any restriction on the free rendering of data transmission services for the public at large. It particularly seeks the liberalization of data transmission services through leased circuits or switched networks. It also makes it compulsory to fulfil the demand for leased circuits within a set period of time, with no restriction on their use (except the previously mentioned conditions dealing with vocal services, and taking account of what the specified ONP Directive determines). Point 6 of the Service Liberalization Directive, of 28 June 1989, on technical, economic and service aspects, deals with the first elements where competition will arise.

Prior to signal transmission through a public network and after its reception, customers are free to treat the signal as they wish with no restrictions. Some resale may be possible, giving access, for instance, to local area networks which could communicate with each other, or with transnational services. Any regulatory powers which CTNE might have had previously would be carried out by an independent organization. When there is a service contract with a client, for a period longer than one year, it may be terminated, with six-months prior notice. This prevents restrictive practices and allows the customer to choose new competitors to deliver services.

Spanish telecommunications: a strategy for the future

Spain, and CTNE particularly, is developing a process that will allow an increase in its competitive capacity. This, however, depends not only on the size of the market, but on the organization of competitors; that is why it is necessary to adapt to the proposed framework without further delay. The strategy followed by CTNE started under the assumptions that the competitive regime for network and service was already in force, and that its network and service provisions were established with an international, or at least European, reference framework. It had to accelerate quality improvement and suitability programmes, on one hand, and cooperate with other network and services providers, on the other; as well as actively participating in the establishment of international specifications and standards, so as to optimize developments or to update them as promptly as possible. An aggressively competitive strategy for large operators does not seem feasible in the short term, given that demand for qualitative improvements puts Spanish investment plans under pressure. So it seems as if the best strategy is to cooperate with other operators, service suppliers and large users. This allows short-term domestic market obligations to be taken care of, and the Spanish position relative to large European operators to be strengthened by processes allowing the optimization of Spanish standards and development, such as joint marketing, single window, market exchange, specialization in specific services and joint ventures in other markets. In view of this, the following recommendations are made:

- Establishment of cooperation agreements with other network and service operators, both public and private (this would also widen our field of action).
- Further participation in EC bodies, where telecommunications policy is discussed.
- To achieve a greater presence for CTNE in EC organizations (Spanish experts to be appointed to the Commission). This would improve knowledge prior to EC actions, saving time later.

— Joint participation, together with other European network operators, in organizations which might develop, such as the Telecommunications Research and Development European Institute, in order to protect CTNE's interests or to compete with third parties in connection with the supply of specific services.
— Progressive adaptation of networks to the ONP requirements.
— Suitability of purchase and supply methods to EC provisions, developing systems that allow more flexibility in the process.
— Increasing Spain's presence in European telecommunications projects, as well as in any debate on the sector, whether fostered by operators, service providers, suppliers or users.
— Establishment of legal or accounting procedures to prevent cross-subsidies between services.

Transport policy

Although Chapter 1 of the Treaty of Rome and Title IV of the Second Part of the Treaty include the design of a common transport policy among their goals, it does not yet exist in a complete form, as full agreement has not been completely reached. Some norms have been implemented on certain aspects of the various modes of transport, and a finished system, implying the removal of contingencies and authorizations, as well as regularization of domestic provisions on fiscal, technical and social matters and the harmonization of State intervention, was due to be realized in 1993.

Rail

In the EC attention has mainly centred on reinforcing investment and making lines profitable. The aim was to make the High Velocity Train (Tren de Alta Velocidad or TAV) viable, and to establish a description of State intervention. So proposals have been made to reorganize the finances of railroad enterprises, and to harmonize the rules regulating financial relationships between private companies and the States. Additionally, the States are taking responsibility for railroad infrastructure, while private companies are responsible for payment for the use of this infrastructure. To create a series of High Speed Train corridors linking all European capitals – according to a Commission study within the Delors Plan – an investment of at least Pts. 12 billion is necessary. The magnitude of this sum has caused the Commission to call for private capital to finance and later manage these lines.

In Spain, railroad services, both for goods and for passengers, are managed by the Spanish Railroad National Network (Red Nacional de Ferrocarriles Españoles, or RENFE), which is a public company.[1] Among the EC countries, Spain makes noticeably less use of this mode of transport, as may

Table 6.1 Railways in the EC

Country	Goods		Passengers	
	Mill. ton./Km	% of total	Mill. pass	% of total
FRG	58.50	21.60	41.66	6.41
France	52.29	26.05	63.29	9.57
Italy	19.57	10.11	43.34	7.42
United Kingdom	18.21	11.64	34.40	6.29
Belgium	7.69	19.15	6.35	7.31
Spain	12.00	8.04	16.38	8.26

be seen in Table 6.1, where the 1988 absolute and relative railroad transport data are presented, for goods and passengers.

Conscious of the need to reform this mode of transport in Spain, various programmes and reports were started in 1984, in order to draw up a railroad transport plan, suited to EC conditions. The 1984 'Commission Report on the Study of Spanish Railroads' (also known as the ROA report), the signature of the first State–RENFE contract for 1984–6, which meant the closing of a total of 882 kilometres of very uneconomic lines, the draft of the Railroad Transport Plan (Plan de Transporte Ferroviario, or PFT) in 1987, the signature of the second State–RENFE contract for 1988-91, new railroad polices and the development of the first stage of the PFT have all been accomplished. Additionally, in December 1988, the Council of Ministers approved the introduction of the international gauge[2] for every line built for the High Velocity Train. It does not seem likely that this modification will be carried out for the whole network (some 15,000 kilometres) in the short term. The estimated cost, including the changes of axles and bogies, would be of more than Pts. 280,000 million. The High Velocity Train track is being built between Madrid and Seville, at an estimated cost of Pts. 300,000 million and a second TAV line, to link Madrid with the French border, costing more than Pts. 600,000 million, is under way.

The cost/benefit analysis of this modernization plan will be developed in two fields: social welfare and private profitability; the ROA report already seems to imply that the second goal has priority.

Shipping

At the time of joining the EC, Spanish discussions on this subject turned mainly around three points: transport reservations for specific goods, limitations on freedom of establishment and free movement of workers.

Spanish shipping services have been going through a process of adaptation to the EC agreements of December 1986; these include:

— Freedom of access to transoceanic shipping.
— Freedom of shipping services within the EC in matters dealing with flag registration, except for any restrictions existing at the time of the agreement, and for gradual adaptation in the case of coastal traffic between specific regions.
— The establishment of a consulting process on EC countries' relationships with third countries and with international organizations.
— The determination of the methods of application of Articles 85 and 86 of the Treaty of Rome to passenger liners, in order to enforce the competition regulations compatible with international practice.
— The regulation of action on unfair tariff practices in connection with international passenger liners, since they are unsettling to Community traffic.

With the exception of liberalization between EC countries, the removal of discrimination between EC countries and third countries, in which any ship with an EC flag may freely participate, was due to come into effect in January 1992. Any type of discrimination from the Member States would end by January 1993. These time limits did not apply to domestic coastal traffic and, thus, in the case of Spain, to the Balearic and Canary Islands. As a consequence of this, Spain is undergoing a series of adaptation periods and so the evaluation of the real effects of EC policy relative to this mode of transport would be extremely inaccurate.

Road

As with shipping, the liberalization of road transport is still in its early stages, total liberalization should have occurred in January 1993 under the terms of the June 1988 Council of Ministers; it means the removal of the quantitative restrictions relative to EC and bilateral traffic, and to in-transit transport, originating in or going to third countries. Customs formalities within the framework of the TIR agreement had already been removed through the application of Council Regulations No. 3690 of 1986. Additionally, there had been advances in the technical field (determination of maximum truck weights and dimensions), in fiscal harmonization, admitting the fuel in automobile fuel tanks without duty and increasing the allowance for commercial vehicles.

Full liberalization of sea and road transport is of particular interest for Spain, since these are the methods of transport for the greatest volume of freight. Evaluation of the effects of a common transport policy, however, is still premature.

Notes

1. Additionally, for short lengths of route, there are some railroad lines partly located in the northern part of Spain, and which are managed by the Narrow Gauge Railroad Company (Compañía Ferrocarriles de Via Estrecha, or FEVE), a public company.
2. This implies going to the European gauge of 1,435mm, instead of the 1,666mm Spanish gauge.

References

Buesa, M. (1989) 'Los servicios de telecomunicaciones en España', *Economía,* No. 2, July/September.
Candido, J. and De Rus, G. (1990) 'Hacia la definición de una política de transporte ferroviario', *Economista,* No. 41, January.

Chapter 7

Agricultural policy

Carlos San Juan Mesonada

The CAP: a Spanish cost-benefit perspective

Spain and Portugal's late entries to the EC, at the outset of 1986, came about when the Common Agricultural Policy (CAP) reform had already made some progress. The transition period agreed upon during the negotiations was twelve years for selected products. Real integration was not scheduled to take place until 1988. The negotiators based their analysis on the differences between Spanish and EC prices, and on the time these would take to disappear.

Spain joined an EC in which the CAP had already been designed to fit the agricultural systems of the founding Member States and, given that Italy's intervention was ineffective and Greece entered late in 1981, it was formulated with the central European countries in mind. But Spain also found a CAP which has been in crisis since 1973. It had joined a game whose rules did not especially favour it, with the exception of the important detail that agricultural prices are, in general, higher in the EC than in Spain. But, in any case, Spain wished to participate from within in the decision making leading to the reform of the CAP, among other issues.

Nevertheless, the main decision of the Agrarian Council was to freeze most agricultural prices, thus drying up the source of hope for all Spanish farmers, in the very year in which they joined the EC. This fact had not yet hit their pocketbooks by 1991, since financial magic (the revaluation of the peseta and the price support system by yearly steps until the EC price is reached) allowed the ECU price to rise, while the peseta price continued to grow for a significant number of products. This, however, gave only temporary relief.

Farmers with problems, therefore, had no choice but to wait and see how far the strengthening of structural policy would go. Efficient farmers, and especially the traditional exporters (citrus fruit, olive oil, table olives and designated wine) hoped that their comparative advantages would prove effective, in a progressively wider manner, as the transition-period obstacles were removed. Other producers, especially those of fruits and vegetables, might improve their exporting position to the rest of the EC under greater freedom of trade. Some processed products, such as pork derivatives, sausages or cooked meats and processed fruit and vegetables might be able to expand into European markets, as was becoming evident.

However, the development of these and other products, such as vegetable oils, was strongly conditioned by the dominance of large food multinationals, whose strategies strongly influenced the market. The multinationals, especially European ones, took positions in smaller Spanish companies, as a part of their strategy for the Single Market. Some non-Community financial groups, for instance KIO (Kuwait Investment Office) also invested heavily in the Spanish agricultural industry, but in this case it was more as part of a financial strategy than an industrial strategy, as it was for the European food multinationals. At any rate, foreign investment in agriculture and food reached a very high level (Soria and Rodríguez-Zúñiga, 1990; Langreo, 1990). Production by the agriculture and food industry represented 5 per cent of the Spanish GNP (INE, 1989).

Structural differences: large-scale Mediterranean agriculture

The deep structural differences between Spanish agriculture and that of the earlier members of the EC (EC-10) must be taken into account in order to establish a starting point for a cost/benefit evaluation. Arable land is mostly dominated by Mediterranean crops (grapes, olives, citrus fruits and vegetables), and to crops such as sunflowers and rye, while the EC-10 specializes in Continental agriculture (soft and hard wheat, tobacco, sugar beet and rape oil). As far as livestock is concerned, Spain specializes in grazing sheep and goats for meat, in contrast with the greater dominance of milk and meat cattle, which need cattle sheds, in the EC-10.

In terms of production value, Spain specializes in Mediterranean crops (except for wine), livestock in mountain and lesser favoured areas (sheep and goats), and intensive stockbreeding (poultry meat and eggs), while the EC-10 specializes in continental agriculture (cereals) and extensive livestock breeding, dependent on cereal crops and meadows (meat and milk cattle) (Barceló and García Alvarez-Coke, 1987). Differences also derive from the structure of agricultural operations, because of the greater polarization of property ownership in Spain, where intermediate-size operations are less common than in the EC-10.

The weight of the agricultural sector in the Spanish economy is noticeably higher than the EC average, both in terms of the percentage of the population working in agriculture (16% as opposed to 7% in the EC-10) and agriculture's contribution to GNP (6% against 3% EC-10) (Eurostat (1990)).

Farmers faced with the CAP reform

In establishing measures to protect family farming, the first difficulty encountered by agricultural policies in general, and by the CAP in particular, is to identify its beneficiaries. This problem may not have been handled with methodological subtlety, and the suspicion exists that a large part of the measures adopted to protect family farming have benefited the more competitive farmers, sometimes in a nearly exclusive manner. The evolution of agricultural trade unions and the united 'farming front' concept for *all* farmers is in the origin of this situation (Moyano, 1989). Another, even larger, part of the legislation deals with protective measures against foreign trade and price maintenance, which, under cover of levelling family incomes, noticeably benefits all farming enterprises. Prices may be the same, but costs differ and so benefits will also be different.

So many crows have arrived to feed from the fields of family farming aid that costs to the EC have eventually become too great. With the arrival of the taxation crisis, family farming now risks being abandoned in future budgetary cut-backs.

The perspective for third countries

From the viewpoint of third countries, European agriculture has become a source of instability in world agricultural markets, because of heavy EC exports. Economic crisis, even though its origin lies in energy price increases and the subsequent need to restructure industry, manifests itself in the appearance of strong macroeconomic imbalances. The main problems in the Spanish economy during the crisis may be summarized as fiscal and balance of payment deficits, inflation and unemployment. With greater or lesser intensity, these features were also prevalent in all other EC countries. Fiscal crisis and 'stagflation', in particular, have raised questions over the CAP model, where contradictions between the policies of various farming subsectors may be solved by increasing the EAGGF expenditure (especially the EAGGF-Guarantee).

Increased VAT income – from 1% to 1.4% – was not sufficient to eliminate the Community budget deficit. Surplus accumulation of several products (butter, cereals and beef meat), together with financial problems in many agricultural operations, in spite of costly price-maintenance programmes, have underlined the weakness of these policies for efficient resource distribution (Tracy, 1989). The most serious accusation levelled against them claimed that the CAP was generating production whose only outlet was to be purchased by the intervention organizations (Barceló and García Alvarez-Coke, 1987).

Monetary instability followed the second energy crisis in 1979, after the mirage of a situation that vanished (high agricultural prices in world markets), an event that caused the practice of dumping surpluses from intervention in these markets to be seriously questioned. Instability of rates of exchange magnified the instability of international agricultural prices, generating violent fluctuations. These negative aspects of supranational agricultural policies in third countries have added to extremely negative indirect effects on income distribution, employment and the growth capacity of the economies which apply these programmes (Miller, 1987).

Japan, with very high protection levels, and the United States with high agricultural protection, also bear heavy responsibility for the effects of this on the economies of less industrialized countries (Kaneda, 1986). No solution may exist to the problem of the external debt of developing countries unless some way is found to diminish their trade deficits (Baker, 1984). The reduction of agricultural protectionism plays an important role in resolving this problem.

From the point of view of Spanish agriculture, the reduction of protectionism may mean greater efficiency in the distribution of resources, if it is replaced by a selective incomes policy, even if adjustment in the agricultural sector has to be performed under less propitious conditions than those enjoyed by the EC-10 countries (García-Delgado and Muñoz, 1989). A regional crop rearrangement accompanied by the introduction of advanced technology, a reorganization of trade structures and support to the agriculture and food industry may allow Spanish agriculture to face with optimism the consequences of gradual trade deregulation within the European framework (Tió, 1989).

In spite of the recent failures to reach agreements experienced by GATT, both the United States and the EC had already started to reform their agricultural policies. In the case of the EC, the general reform policy was collected in the last version of the European Commission (1988) report, which clearly expressed the intention of abandoning the CAP based on a price and market policy in favour of a reformed CAP, founded on political and regional policies:

> From 1984, CAP reform has been accompanied by measures tending to diversify support to farmers (price support and intervention in markets are being partly replaced with more objective measures) and by a greater modification of agricultural support in favour of economically weaker small family farms, and in favour of areas with natural and structural constraints [European Commission, 1988].

This line of action has also been used on forest policy, in search of suitable financial solutions; to this end, the Commission proposed a forest action programme (doc. COM(88) 255). This policy may have an important positive effect from the environmental point of view, since deforestation and desertification are indeed threatening some very large areas.

The shift of policy from considerations of price and markets to a concern for structure, on the other hand, means that wide-ranging reorganization must be faced by the agricultural sector. Its consequences are still difficult to forecast, since they depend on the manner in which the European economies emerge from the present industrial crisis; some of these possible consequences, however, are listed in the rest of this chapter.

Costs and benefits of the CAP reform

Some reports have been pessimistic about the possibilities of compensating purchasing power losses derived from the freezing of agricultural prices through the structure policy (Sumpsi, 1989; Etxezarreta *et al.*, 1989). But others estimate that much of the transformation taking place in Spanish agriculture is related to long-term processes largely independent of the CAP reform, especially those related to intersectoral restructuring and the technical changes induced by economic growth (García Alvarez-Coke 1989; San Juan, 1990). Therefore, although the social costs of these processes are emphasized, including the ecological risks of productivist options, these reports may be in line with the work of Syrquin (1986), who also recognized the trend towards inefficient agricultural infrastructure in his early models of agriculture and the economy.

The final aim of the CAP reform is to narrow once again the differences between world market prices and internal EC prices. Along this same line, it would be necessary to prevent price distortion due to different levels of protection within the EC itself (Koester and Terwitte, 1988). The key objective, however, is to reduce protectionism and to improve resource allocation. It should be remembered that the majority of theoretical models assume the existence of full employment when they deal with optimum resource allocation. This hypothesis is hardly realistic today. The deterioration of farm incomes may create greater pressure on the supply side of the employment market, which, added to demographic factors (San Juan, 1990), may result in higher agricultural unemployment.

If agricultural price growth is frozen or retarded with respect to the growth of the general price level, some realistic ways to safeguard producers' incomes at least partially are:

(1) Improve productivity.
(2) Make the prices of inputs and machinery purchased by the sector change commensurately, thus preventing a deterioration in agricultural price relationships.
(3) Increase direct subsidies (or tax rebates) to family farmers and establish other transfers, especially of a financial nature (New Community Instruments and subsidies to interest rates) to guarantee suitable financing formulas.
(4) Increase the value added contributed by farmers in the total value added of the final food product.
(5) Generate internal economies to improve living conditions in rural areas.

The first option – that is, to improve productivity – is the one which, being more important, will bear the most important part of the reform and of its consequences, if it is done in a rational manner. Nevertheless, as Sumpsi (1989) has observed, the rise in productivity may prevent the disappearance of surpluses, even with fewer farmers, thus returning to the root of the problem.

Spanish family farming is in an ambivalent position on this matter. It is true that its production is very often below the operational level of the rest of the 'old' members of the EC (mostly because their farms were capitalized under the CAP with high prices and protection for all, to promote self-sufficiency in food supply). But it is also true that Spanish agriculture, due to its natural characteristics, is more productive than that of northern countries in a wide range of products (from traditional operations such as olives and citrus fruit to vegetables and horticultural products). In this area, the CAP reform is not compatible with maintaining restrictions on exports of these products, agreed upon for the transition period. These obstacles moderate any general increase in the system's productivity, since they prevent the concentration of production in the areas with a comparative advantage.

For these same reasons, if it becomes necessary to cut wine production, for instance, the areas of the country which are less efficient will be the ones to bear the brunt of these reductions. In this context, the bargaining process of 'historical quotas', which lessen the unfavourable social effects of productivity measures, runs the serious risk of checking the benefits of these policies as far as a better allocation of resources is concerned (Tió, 1989) and of promoting bureaucratic interventionism, which might eventually make the remedy worse than the disease.

It must be remembered that one of the basic goals of the present CAP reform is to eliminate surpluses. However, measures to improve the productivity of EC agriculture may lead to production increases, even with a smaller number of farmers. It is, therefore, fundamental that any measures implemented to stabilize excess production include sufficient corrective factors to prevent family farms from being those mainly hurt by this process.

The fact that family farming contributes significantly to production in Mediterranean countries must also be taken into account, and that the purpose of this production is to satisfy the needs of the local market itself, not for export. Family farming for the local market is not, therefore, the cause of surpluses; we have another problem, namely family farming which focuses on production 'for intervention purposes', which normally co-exists with non-family farming (which, supposedly, produces for the market only), but which, in fact, is producing for intervention purposes and which, no doubt, is an aberration generated by the indiscriminate use of interventionist policy itself.

Structural policy is the appropriate framework to improve productivity in the whole system in an equitable manner. It is necessary to follow this course of action. A single market would not be acceptable unless mechanisms to establish productive structures of Mediterranean countries at competitivity levels similar to those of the rest of the EC had previously been set up.

Before EC membership, Spain's agricultural input price level was, in general terms, higher than the EC average,[1] while the opposite was true for agricultural product prices; for the time being, therefore, there is a margin to prevent a deterioration of the real rate of exchange in the sector. The Fertilizer Reconstruction Plan, among others, has had a positive effect on price adjustment, bringing it closer to the lower levels that exist in the EC.

The third option, that is, to increase direct subsidies (or tax rebates) to family farmers and to establish other direct transfers, may prosper under the present conditions of cost reduction if it shows more efficiency than did the price policy. The main risk in the development of these fiscal policies (as well as structural policies) is that they eventually lead to an inefficient bureaucratic muddle and become too costly. Here, for both efficiency and equity reasons, it would be preferable to have a system based on tax exemptions. It would then be possible to reduce subsidies greatly, but this would demand a high level of harmonization between fiscal systems of the different countries in matters of direct taxation. And this seems a difficult thing to achieve. From an equity point of view, the main advantage of a direct system of income maintenance is that it would be more efficient in preventing public expenditure for benefiting other, non-family, farm operations, especially those in corporate ownership. Politically, however, support for this idea may be more restricted, even though it is less expensive and more equitable. Subsidies on interest paid for specific loans to family farms and on the effective implementation of a sort of NCI (new EC financing instruments) may be one of the most interesting formulae.

The fourth proposal (to increase the proportion added by the farmer to the value of the end product) has, in theory, much potential, especially in Mediterranean countries. In these countries, organization levels have traditionally been low for farmers, and marketing channels are difficult. The greater ease of penetration enjoyed by food and distribution multinationals (with large areas) may improve the efficiency of distribution in this sector. In contrast, the scarce *de facto* effectiveness of legislation protecting competition and the lack of bargaining power by the supply side may cause a loss of equity. It would be worth preparing some measures to promote better and stronger agricultural trade organizations (agricultural producers organizations and family farming trade unions). This is going to become a field where it will be easier to see clearly whether a Single Market really means a 'Europe of the People', or whether, in fact, it will become a 'Europe of Multinationals'.

The fifth proposal, to generate external economies that improve living conditions in rural areas, encompasses both structural and regional policies (and transport policy, especially). Defence measures to protect the natural ecosystem will not be effective without a policy which moderates the system's trend towards rural depopulation and towards the concentration of activities in the economic centres of gravity. In this context, it is important to allow the interests of rural inhabitants to be linked to the preservation of the natural environment around them, and to prevent, whenever possible, a proliferation of intervention by administrative organizations. This way, less costly and more efficient intervention may be achieved, allowing the other members of society to enjoy the benefits generated by the preservation of free natural spaces, which could then be used for tourism, leisure or environmental educational activities; in any case, their value as reserves is essential for industrialized countries.

To sum up, under the present conditions of the EC countries, external economies are generated to benefit rural areas. These, in turn, generate external economies for all other parts of society. In this sense, family farming is strategically important, since the very survival of its environment, as opposed to the alternative of irreversible depopulation, depends in great measure on the survival of a sufficient number of these families (European Commission, 1985; known as the 'Green Book'). The document *L'avenir du monde rural* (European Commission, 1988) already introduces the need to replace the policy of abolishing marginal family farm operations with the promotion of part-time farming,[2] but, in some cases, this may mean a new version of work at home or other variables prevalent in hidden economies. The need to coordinate structural policy with regional development plans is also admitted. The obvious risk of a Single Market generating areas of high industrial congestion as opposed to marginal and depopulated areas lurks in the background of these proposals.

A reformed CAP and the Single Market

The creation of the Single Market implied relocating activities as a consequence of a greater mobility of productive factors. Priorities varied in different EC countries, with regard to growth and resource relocation models, since the starting situations, development levels and productive structures were also different.

In Spain's case, it was the high rate of unemployment (17% in 1989) which determined basic priorities. The base of the population pyramid was very wide for the Spanish population. This meant that the working population was growing rapidly, and created pressure on the labour market on the supply side. This was clearly different from what happened in most of the other Member States, where the ageing of the population produced a narrow base for the population pyramid. Over a quarter of the active population in the latifundist (estate farming) regions, which had a greater number of agrarian workers and high unemployment (Andalusia and Extremadura, in the south-east), were unemployed in 1989. In other regions, where small farms were prevalent (Galicia in the north-west), the relatively low unemployment rates were a function of part-time agriculture. Hidden pockets of unemployment may be suspected, as well as under-employment in rural areas. These peculiar conditions of the labour market in

Spain mean that, just to maintain the present high rate of unemployment, around 130,000 new jobs should be created between 1991 and 1996. The agricultural sector is expected to lose some 570,000 jobs. Only a small portion of them will be the result of the ageing of the population (Escudero, 1988); therefore, even though many young rural people would prefer to find jobs in non-agricultural activities, it is evident that the CAP reform could not be allowed to cause even more stressful situations in the labour market. It is also necessary to remember that a significant part of industrial and service activities in rural areas are linked to agriculture and, therefore, income losses of farmers would have a negative effect on employment in these connected activities. Rural employment is very sensitive to the CAP reform. Between 1986 and 1989, agriculture lost 100,000 people. But the effects of integration were deemed to have been beneficial in the short term.

From this perspective, structural policy has much to achieve, both to protect existing jobs and to generate new activities, complementary to pure agriculture. New EC financing instruments (NCI), which have shown their usefulness in the field of small and medium-sized enterprises, may also have an important part to play in this context.

Prospects

In no way would the re-nationalizing of agricultural policy improve prospects and the CAP reform would, thus, be preferable, since many of its present contradictions may be solved within the framework of the Single Market and of the European Monetary System. In short, the challenge faced by the reformed CAP is to prevent the reduction of the EC's agricultural protection levels from generating depressed regions or sectors of population. These measures, therefore, should have sufficient size and flexibility to counteract those undesirable effects from market mechanisms. The industrial crisis, which has resulted in a period of stable energy prices, is a particularly suitable moment to intensify investment in agriculture. The rural world should be given the chance to fit in with 'green growth'. The failure of food supply policies in eastern European countries as well as in developing countries, opens a door to short-term improvement in global markets, although European export possibilities are very much conditioned by these countries' possibilities of obtaining hard currency. This adds up to a need to find new ways of cooperating with third countries within the framework of the CAP reform.

Benefits

— Regulated prices and food supply security.
— Advantages for exports.
— Funds for structural reform in agriculture.

— A large market for Mediterranean products.
— Increased supply of prepared food.

Costs

— Resource allocation distortions caused by the CAP.
— The possible disappearance of farms in non-Mediterranean agricultural areas (surplus of Continental products).
— Guaranteed price freezing.
— Higher prices for imported livestock fodder.

Notes

1. The most important exception was livestock inputs (fodder) imported by Spain from third countries at a lower price. Pesticides and weedkillers, in general, had prices similar to those in the first nine members of the EC.
2. Part-time farming is no news to Spanish agriculture: 1.34 million agricultural entrepreneurs practise it, as against only one million with a single agricultural activity (INE, 1985).

References

Baker, C.B. (1984) 'Agricultural Effects of Changes in Financial Markets', *American Journal of Agricultural Economics*, Vol. 66, No. 5 December; pp. 541–8.

Barceló, L.V. and García Alvarez-Coke, J.M. (1987) *El futuro de la Política Agrícola Común y la economía española*, Madrid, Mundi-Prensa.

Escudero, G. (1988) 'Requerimientos de empleo agrario: perspectivas de la actividad y ocupación agraria como consecuencia de la integración de España en la CEE', Comisión de Expertos sobre Desempleo, Mimeo, Madrid.

Etxezarreta, M. *et al.* (1989) 'El replanteamiento del proteccionismo agrario y la política de estructuras', *Información Comercial Española*, no. 666, February; pp. 75–100.

European Commission (1985) 'Perspectives de la politique agricole commune' (Green Book), Mimeo, Brussels, (COM (85) 333 end).

—— Commission (1988) *L'avenir du monde rural*, Mimeo, Brussels.

Eurostat (1990) *Agriculture: Statistical Yearbook 1989*, Brussels, Eurostat.

García Alvarez-Coke, J.M. (1989) 'La desprotección agraria y la productividad de la agricultura española en el marco de la Communidad Europea', *Información Comercial Española*, no. 666 February, pp. 131–53.

García-Delgado, J.L. and Muñoz, C. (1989) 'Consideraciones sobre la agricultura española ante la política agraria común de la CEE', *Información Comercial Española*, no. 666, February, pp. 45–50.

INE (1985) Spanish Agrarian Census 1982, INE, Madrid.

—— (1989), *Contabilidad nacional de España 1988: base 1980*, Madrid, INE.

Kaneda, H. (1986) 'Rural Resource Mobility and Intersectorial Balance in Early

Modern Growth', University of California, Davis, Working Papers Series, no. 281.

Koester, L. and Terwitte, M. (1988) 'Las distorsiones de precios en la agricultura de la Comunidad Europea', *Agricultura y Sociedad*, no. 48, pp. 47–79.

Langreo, A. (1990) 'Comparación de las líneas de producción en la alimentación española y comunitaria', *Economistas*, No. 41, pp. 161–5.

Miller, G. (1987) *The Political Economy of International Agricultural Policy Reform*, Australian Government Publishing Service, Canberra.

Ministerio de Economia y Hacienda, Dirección General de Previsión y Coyuntura (1990) Sintesis Mensual de *Indicadores Económicos*, February.

Moyano, E. (1989) 'Una aproximación socio-política al proteccionismo en la agricultura'. *Información Comercial Española*, no. 666. February, pp. 163–74.

San Juan, C. (1990) 'Cambio técnico y empleo', *Agricultura y Sociedad*, No. 54, pp. 15–44.

Soria, R. and Rodríguez-Zú Ñiga, M. (1990) 'Concentración e internacionalización de la industria agroalimentaria española 1977–1987', *Agricultura y Sociedad*, No. 52. July/September, pp. 65–94.

Sumpsi, J.M. (1989) 'Reflexiones en torno a la crisis del proteccionismo y la agricultura española', *Información Comercial Española*, no. 666 February, pp. 153–62.

Syrquin S. (1986) *Industrialization and Growth*, International Economic Association, VIII, W.E.G., New Delhi.

Tió, C. (1989) 'La agricultura española frente a las sucesivas liberalizaciones de la política agraria', *Información Comercial Española*, No. 666, pp. 153–62.

Tracy, M. (1989) *Government and Agriculture in Western Europe, 1880–1988*, Harvester-Wheatsheaf, London.

Chapter 8

Environmental policy

Alfonso de Esteban Alonso and Alejandro López López

In Spain, as in most industrialized countries, 1972 is a key date in environmental matters; in Spain, as in other developed countries, the 'Stockholm Conference syndrome' and the publication of the Club of Rome Report on *The Limits of Growth* were the starting points for environmental policy. The process of equalization finally took off under the democratic regime and entry to the EC.

The environmental decade (1972–82) in Spain

Trends in economic growth which characterized the decade of the 1960s were correlated with positive and negative environmental impacts. The environmental problematique arose during that decade – spreading from universities to public opinion and to the world of business. In Spain, pollution created 'environmental problems' in different sectors and areas: industrialized areas in the north and north-east of the Peninsula, on the Mediterranean shores and in large urban centres, for example.

The decade of the 1970s provoked critical thought, awareness and the drafting of new policies satisfying the needs and demands for a decent quality of life. In order to answer the challenge of this new age, a series of steps was taken in public administration. The first measure was to create the Interministerial Committee for Environmental Conditioning (January 1971); then Decree No. 888/1971 created the CIMA (Comisión Internacional del Medio Ambiente, International Environmental Commission). CIMA functions were to coordinate the activities of every ministry in matters related to the environment; to prepare programmes; to propose projects and legal provisions; to promote public and private research; to coordinate Spanish representation in international organizations and meetings.

Some other laws had been issued prior to the CIMA, among them the Protection of the Atmospheric Environment (1972); creation of the 'Instituto Nacional para la Conservación de la Naturaleza' (National Institute for the Preservation of Nature, ICONA), 1971; Protection of Natural Spaces, 1975; approval of the law of Land Reform and Urban Planning, 1975. The first ecological associations were formed at the same time; the Asociación Española para la Ordenación del Territorio y Medio Ambiente (Spanish Association for Territorial and Environmental Planning, AEORMA) pioneered this movement in 1970. After the first democratic Congress and Senate elections were held in 1977, the Spanish Constitution was changed to include a legal definition of the environment and quality of life.[1]

Between 1979 and 1982, the environmental question concentrated on the need to have a general environmental law, as well as on convening international meetings during the 'European Urban Renaissance' year (a Council of Europe Campaign), the creation of environmental foundations and associations and urban protest movements against nuclear power and urban pollution. A draft of the General Environmental Law was printed in 1982, but was not finally approved.[2]

Stage previous to EEC integration (1983–6)

During 1983–6, environmental management was transferred to the Autonomous Communities; after Spain's access to the EEC, most Spanish legislation was adapted to EC rules. In the international field, apart from relations with the EC and other international organizations, the ratifications of the Bonn, Washington and Bern Conventions deserve to be mentioned, as they are the basis of international law in matters of wildlife conservation. The policy developed by Spain during the London Convention meetings since 1983 strengthened our pragmatic position of opposition to toxic waste contamination of the sea; the Geneva Declaration, issued during the Barcelona Convention, has also brought about a commitment to improve the Mediterranean Sea.

Among the regulations that have been prepared and approved, the environmental contents of the following legislation should be mentioned: Water Law and Hydraulic Public Domain Regulations; Toxic and Hazardous Waste Law; Royal Decree to adjust the lead contents of fuels as established by the EC; Ministerial Order to create a thermal plant supervision network; Royal Decree on restoration of natural spaces in opencast mining works and Development Order; Royal Decree on the creation of ENRESA, Public Company for the management of radioactive waste; Royal Decree on modification of sulphurdioxide and particle emission levels; Royal Decree for the Creation of a National Audit Commission on the Natural Heritage.

Research on the effects of pollution on the environment and public health has been largely ignored until recently; several epidemiological studies have been started, and supervisory networks have been implemented to control atmospheric contamination.

In connection with preventative and educational policies, studies have been set up to evaluate some public works projects prior to their implementation and environmental studies have been made for civil servants who will later be responsible for environmental management. Environmental education and information, as well as public participation, have been deemed to be essential tools for environmental policy; seminars, courses, publications and meetings have been developed, and cooperation with one section of the ecological movement has been institutionalized through the CIMA.

Integration in the EC (1986–90)

Environment and the municipalities

Between 1986 and 1990 the environment has been one of the problems common to every Spanish municipality in its own specific territorial area. The differences between them in size, number of inhabitants and economic activities, however, make it necessary to take their structure into account.[3] Among those environmental problems common to every area, are: water contamination, as a result of urban and industrial spillage; the rapidly growing amount of solid urban waste (10,000 million tons a year, i.e., one kilogram per person per day); atmospheric pollution, especially in towns of more than 20,000 inhabitants, more serious in the large metropolitan areas; degradation of the natural environment, both in suburban areas of cities with more than 10,000 inhabitants and in rural spaces.

According to a survey performed in 1989 by the FEMP (Federación Española de Municipios y Provincias, Spanish Federation of Municipalities and Provinces) and by the State Administration's Dirección General del Medio Ambiente (General Environment Directorate)[4] for cities of more than 20,000 inhabitants, the problems affecting those urban areas could be classified as: waste waters, 37%; solid waste, 23%, beach water treatment, 16%. Problems became more serious in municipalities with more than 100,000 inhabitants, not only because of the larger volume, but also because of increasing of atmospheric pollution and the greater noise level. River and shore degradation began to turn into a serious problem in municipalities with more than 50,000 inhabitants. According to this survey, Spanish environmental problems, as measured in the municipalities,[5] had four broad features:

— Degradation of natural resources caused by industry.
— Insufficient corrective measures.
— A considerable environmental deficit, difficult to restore in the short term.
— Lack of environmental legal regulations.

Public expenditure in environmental matters

Economic development has occurred later in Spain than in those European countries which signed the ECSS, the EEC and EURATOM between 1951 and 1957. The distance between the German Federal Republic or Denmark and Spain on socio-economic matters and the application of environmental policy is very large.

Investment in environmental areas was not significant until 1978, when the amount spent on this subject came close to 0.5% of the GNP, which was one third of the average amount spent on environment in the first nine countries to form the European Community (EC-9). This percentage was only comparable to that of Greece, Ireland and Portugal.

When Spain entered the EC, it also joined in the 'Initial Proposals for the Introduction of Structures for Protective Coding in the Natural Environment in the EC Member States' Programme. In accordance with the information presented under it, Spanish public expenditure in environmental matters was 0.6% and 0.7% of the GNP in 1987 and 1988, respectively.

Complaints and requests in environmental matters

The decade of the 1980s was decisive for the consolidation of environmental concerns among the Spanish population, putting the environment at the core of public opinion, which is increasingly aware of the quality of life and of qualitative and sustained development.

Environmental information and legal guidelines were gradually established. Both Spanish and EC legislation allowed a system of requests, complaints and claims to be implemented. In 1987, twenty-seven complaints and requests were presented, seventy-two in 1988 and 180 in 1989, most of them about damage to the environment, nature and the preservation of the ecosystem. In 1987, there were ten complaints issued to Spain by the EC Commission, forty-six in 1988 and forty-four in 1989; some of them were only requests for information. Sixteen infringement procedures were started. Rulings were obtained concerning the salt water marshes of Santoña (Cantabria); pollution at Bahia de Portman (Murcia), where industrial spillage has since been stopped; spillage in Sabiñánigo (Huesca) by the Inquinosa company.

Ecological organizations

The ecological movement started in Spain after May 1968, as a cry of protest in defence of the natural and cultural environment against the impact of industrial or urban pollution of rivers, seas, industrial areas, excessive use of forests, annihilation of species, etc. By 1984, close to 200 ecological associations had appeared in Spain, distributed throughout the whole State. According to the survey carried out in 1987 by the Madrid AEDENAT association, most Spanish ecological associations concentrated their efforts on the defence of animal species, flora and natural spaces, while only 30% of them focused on urban or industrial themes, and only 3% are concerned with educating citizens about the environment. The lack of interest shown by Spaniards in ecological matters is a historical phenomenon, although this trend seems to be changing.[6]

Analysis of repercussions of and prospects for Spanish EC integration

If a balance of Spain's EC integration over the first few years were to be performed in connection with environmental matters, the results would be positive. Although a Ministry of Environment was not set up at first, there was a General Secretariat, with the rank of Undersecretary, dealing with those matters. Positive action had been carried out to stop environmental deterioration caused by noxious industries, among which the following may be mentioned:

— The wastes flowing to the Porland bay and into the Mediterranean in the province of Murcia have been eliminated.
— Illegal buildings have been removed from the coast of Castellón, following the application of the Ley de Costas (Coast Law).
— Social pressure by citizens and the mass media has succeeded in stopping the installation of a military experimental range in Cabañeros and this area has now been declared a Natural Park.
— Citizens' awareness brought about government awareness, which ended with the closure of the ASCO II nuclear plant at Tarragona, after several accidents and potentially dangerous situations.
— Some city halls, especially in large cities, have started an incentive policy aimed at removing coal-burning heating boilers, replacing them with gas, diesel-oil or electric units.[7]
— Between 10 and 15% of Spanish companies have begun processes of environmental auditing.
— Among the local administration initiatives, an important one is that of Saragossa, on the control on non-domestic waste.[8]
— The banking company BANESTO created in 1989 the Environmental Bank, which has implemented several lines of action: advice, diagnosis and financing, in combination with the EIB (European Investment Bank).
— The fight against forest fires has been intensified, especially in the provision of technical equipment, where Pts. 10,000 million have been invested, and in training programmes for foresters.
— Since 1983, the so-called 'nuclear moratorium' has been introduced in the Plan Energético Nacional (National Energy Plan, or PEN).
— Public and private works.

Within this same framework of positive action in favour of the environment, special mention must be made of the Spanish Programme of Training

Schools (Escuelas Taller and Casas de Oficios), established in 1985[9] for young people under 25 years of age, which focuses on the needs of the environment and the quality of life in urban and rural areas. These institutions work in two ways: the recovery of old traditions in using natural resources or building materials, and specialization in the modern techniques; for instance, computer application to the preparation of maps and measurement of physical data, technology to recover degraded spaces, or cleansing work, etc. This programme is being financed by the INEM (Instituto Nacional de Empleo, National Employment Institute) and the European Social Fund (ESF) and it also tries to solve the serious problem of youth unemployment. To summarize, these Escuelas Taller (School Workshops) are a public employment and training programme, aiming to restore, rehabilitate, recover or maintain the artistic, cultural and historical heritage of the urban environment, as well as artisan techniques and crafts. Their goal is to train unemployed young people, preferably those under 25 years of age, alternating work and vocational training.

Several other initiatives should also be mentioned in the domestic area:

- State aid for private activities in nature preservation, subsidized by the Instituto Nacional para la Conservación de la Naturaleza (National Institute for the Preservation of Nature).[10]
- Public aid for quality-of-life R&D (biotechnology, social and cultural studies, historic heritage, social welfare, toxicology, etc.), financed by Pts. 48,332.1 million for the four-year period between 1988 and 1991.[11]
- The creation in December 1990 of the INI-Medio Ambiente company, with a starting capital of Pts. 125 million, employing a staff of sixty persons and with a yearly turnover estimated around Pts. 3,000 million.

In the private sphere, the CEOE (Spanish Confederation of Entrepreneurial Organizations) has created and developed an Environmental Committee, and the Council of Chambers of Commerce has created its own Environmental Commission. On research efforts, the 'Progama Nacional de Conservacíon del Patrimonio Natural y Procesos de Degradación Ambiental' (National Programme for the Preservation of the Natural Heritage and Environmental Degradation Processes, also known as the CPNYPDA programme) was created in 1989, in the area of the Plan Nacional de Investigación Científica y Desarrollo Tecnológico (National Plan of Scientific Research and Technology Development).[12] Several institutions have been created in the field of university education at post-graduate level, among which the work of the Instituto Universitario de Ciencias Ambientales (University Institute of Environmental Science, IUCA), at the Complutense University of Madrid, deserves special mention.

At international level, finally, and with positive effects on Spain, mention should be made of almost a hundred projects for the European Environmental Year (1987–8), which were stimulating, especially in the fields of training, research and mass media dissemination; awareness among the world of entrepreneurs has also been growing. Approximately fifty of the projects dealing with the European Tourism Year (1990) are linked with environmental matters, an important one being the Spanish–French seminars on Tourism Planning and Development Policies.

Spain has not yet been in the EC long enough to allow for comprehensive statistical information leading to any degree of accuracy in the presentation of the economic and social costs of integration in relationship with the environment. It is hoped that more in-depth research, to be carried out later on, will shed greater light on the matter.

Notes

1. Both of these subjects are mentioned in the Preamble, as well as in Article 45 (1,2 and 3): The right and duty to preserve the environment, the State should have an active policy on the rational use of resources; governing principle of penal and administrative sanctions for violators. And in Article 148 (1–9): The Autonomous Communities (Regions) may assume power in 'environmental management'. In the new administrative organization, management of the environment was accorded the rank of General Directorate, integrated within the Ministry of Public Works and Urbanism (MOPU). The General Environmental Secretariat was created in 1990 (Royal Decree 199/1990), with a high administrative rank.
2. It was too late, since the government had been dissolved and new elections were on the way. The UCD government, which had slowly and shyly prepared a Draft Project, lost the elections. This Draft Project tried to plan the powers of the three public administrations, central, Autonomous and municipal, as well as to establish agreement on the management and design of an environmental organization.
3. It must be taken into account that, in 1986, 73% of municipalities contained some 8% of the total population of Spain, and 20% of this same population was concentrated in the six municipalities of more than 500,000 inhabitants (data from the 1986 Population Census, Madrid, 1988).
4. According to a survey carried out in 1989 by the Spanish Federation of Municipalities and Provinces (FEMP).
5. Only 13% of the municipalities with more than 2,000 inhabitants, and 24% (276 municipalities) of a total of 8,022 in Spain, have specific regulations dealing with this matter. Within the campaigns designed during the 'European Environmental Year' (1987–8), the French Federation of Societies for the Protection of Nature (FFSPN) proposed a programme called '1,000 communes pour l'environment', as a tool to influence municipalities to adopt environmental regulations. Thirty-five Spanish municipalities participated with some kind of activity, approximately 3,125,000 inhabitants. Fifty-six programmes were developed: to promote the protection of nature; to promote environmental education and information; to cleanse or restore the environment; to study environmental impact; miscellaneous one-day meetings, seminars, campaigns to promote public transport.
6. Interest of and action by Spanish ecological groups focus mainly around the areas indicated in the following table:

Activities	Group (%)
Environmental education	2.7
Fight against pollution	9.7
Anti-nuclear action	6.6
Coastal environment	6.1
Rural environment	10.3
Urban environment	7.8
Ornithology	10.6
Pacifist movements	7.6
Protection of natural spaces	18.5
Protection of threatened species	16.0
Others (reafforestation, recycling, etc.)	3.9

Source: AEDENAT Survey, Madrid, 1987.

7. This is the case for Madrid, which has adjusted 12% of boilers, preventing the emission of 1,200 tons of sulphur into the atmosphere.
8. Refer to the Environment Municipal Order of June 1986: 'Zaragoza: zonas verdes y espacios naturales' (Zaragoza, green areas and natural spaces), June 1990. Acoustic Map (Proposals), October 1990.
9. The programme is also being carried out in cooperation with Municipalities and Autonomous Communities. From 1989 onwards, the MOPU (Ministerio de Obras Públicas y Urbanismo, Ministry of Public Works and Urbanism) has also joined in, with the creation of over one dozen new School Workshops. Initially, investment in the programme amounted to Pts. 5,493 million – slightly over ECU 40 million – from the Ministry of Labour. The number of registered pupils was around 5,000. In 1988, more than 700 of these School Workshops had been created, for a total investment of some Pts. 40,000 million (ECU 307 million).
10. The amount is determined as a percentage of the labour cost of the activity, in accordance with the following table:

Activities	Percentage of State subsidy
(a) Land purchase	15
(b) Constitution of recorded rights other than property fees	30
(c) Implementation of a preservation project in land located in a protected natural space	30
(d) Implementation of a preservation project for species, subspecies or populations classified as 'endangered'	55
(e) Implementation of a preservation project for species, subspecies or populations classified as 'sensitive to alterations in their habitat'	40
(f) Implementation of a preservation project for species, subspecies or populations classified as 'vulnerable'	30

Source: *Boletín Oficial del Estado*, No. 164, 10 July 1990.

11. José M. Isaac Gassol 'Las ayudas públicas a la I&D: El caso de España y otros países', *Economía Industrial*, No. 259, January/February, p. 83.
12. According to the Resolution of 6 June 1989 (*BOE*, No. 144, 10 June 1989), the programme encompasses the fields of: desertification, contamination, continental water systems, coastal systems. The estimated cost of the programme, for which the National Fund was responsible, was Pts. 2,375 million, between 1989 and 1991.

References

Asociacíon Juvenil para el Estudio y Recuperación del Medio Físico y Humano, (Seattle), (1990) Madrid, 'I Jornadas Hombre y Medio Ambiente'.

Borja, J.; Castells, M.; Dorado, R.; Quintana, I. (1990) 'Las grandes ciudades de la década de los noventa', Madrid, Editorial Sistema.

De Esteban Alonso, A. (1981) 'Las áreas metropolitan en España. Un análisis ecológico' Madrid. Centro de Investigaciónes Sociológicas.

—— Calderon, E. (1989) 'El papel de las ciudades medias en España: presente y Futuro', *Urbanismo* (COAM), No. 6, pp. 6–16.

Secretaría General del Medio Ambiente, (1990) 'Medio Ambiente en España, 1989', Madrid. Ed. Centro de Publicaciones de la SGT, del Ministerio de Obras Públicas y Urbanismo.

Fuentes Bodelon, F. (1990) 'La incidencia del ingreso de España en la C.E.E. en el derecho ambiental español', Santos López, A.: 'Introducción a la Sociología Ambiental y del Consumo', Madrid, Ed. Instituto Nacional del Consumo.

López López, A. (1989a) 'Actas del Congreso Internacional sobre Educación Ambiental, 1988', (Coord. Ed.) Madrid, Instituo Nacional para la Conservación de la Naturaleza.

—— (1989b) 'La política del medio ambiente en la C.E.E.', *Estudios Internacionales*, pp. 93–121, Madrid, Ed. Sociedad de Estudios Internacionales.

—— (1990a) 'La Política de Protección del Medio Ambiente', *Jornadas sobre el Acta Unica*, pp. 121–32, Sevilla, Ed. Junta de Andalucía. Consejería de Fomento y Trabajo.

—— (1990b) 'El Espacio Ambiental Europeo', Foreword C. Ripa Dimeana, Madrid, Edit. Universidad Complutense de Madrid, Instituto Nacional del Consumo.

—— (1990c) 'Organización administrativa del Medio Ambiente en el ámbito local', *Gestión Municipal del Medio Ambiente*, León 1990; pp. 1–22.

Chapter 9

Fiscal and tax policy

Alfonso Utrilla de la Hoz

This chapter is organized in four sections. The first deals with the more relevant aspects of Spain's fiscal policy and taxation system, including the political and economic context in which it developed and its adaptation to the European environment, as a consequence of Spain's entry into the EC. The second section analyses the effects of fiscal harmonization originating from the application of the Single Act to the Spanish tax system. The implications of harmonization on the fiscal structure are set out from the dynamic perspective of the EC's successive proposals on this matter. The third section takes into account the successive stages proposed to achieve an economic and monetary union, in order to analyse the repercussions on Spanish economic policy of the convergence of the fiscal policies of the EC's Member States. It will also take into account the most significant elements of budgetary policy and its effects on the Spanish economy, through greater integration in the EC. Finally, the last section evaluates and synthesizes the overall losses and gains which the EC fiscal policy and tax harmonization may mean for the Spanish economic policy.

The general framework of the Spanish fiscal policy and tax system

An analysis of the more characteristic fiscal and taxation features of the Spanish economy could not be performed without taking into account the double framework, both political and economic, which has conditioned its recent development. There are two relevant political facts that have specially affected the design and implementation of economic policy. First, the changeover from an authoritarian political system to a democracy. This fact has had a double repercussion on the budget: a prompt absorption of the social demand for public services and goods within the public expenditure programmes, giving greater coverage to community needs. At the same time, the financing of this greater demand from the expenditure programmes has made it necessary to establish a modern taxation system, based on a tax structure in accordance with the greater participation and responsibility of citizens. It also guarantees a high degree of financial efficiency for the public sector. Second, the double process of regional decentralization and European integration, which was implemented simultaneously in Spain, was linked to the complexity of the changing political system.

Building the State of Autonomies has meant changing from a centralistic State to a regional system, close to a federal model in its responsibilities and financial means. There is no doubt that this fact has had, and still has, repercussions on the implementation of economic policy and on taxation, both through the system of local finance agreed upon and through the responsibilities and functions taken up by each level of the government and its materialization in public expenditure programmes. On the other hand, the process of Spain's entry into the EC has meant opening its economy to the outside. Consequently, it needs to be efficient and dynamic enough to allow for its development within a competitive framework. The implication for a traditionally protected economy is a fast process of adjustment to the EC structures within an area – fiscal and tax policy – which, even in the EC environment, is in permanent evolution.

The framework of Spanish economic policy in the last few years has been affected in various ways by the economic crisis. This crisis particularly affects Spanish industry, both because of the characteristics of its economic structure and because of the delay in the adoption of a suitable economic policy. This initial vagueness about economic policy was the reason why the necessary adjustments and reorganization came later and required a greater sacrifice from society. The Spanish economy's potential and dynamism, however, allowed for considerable economic growth, though there is some maladjustment.

Table 9.1 briefly presents the main economic trends from 1961 to 1990, both in Spain and in the EC as a whole. These figures demonstrate the gradual convergence of the Spanish economy towards the EC average, although important differences remained, especially in unemployment rates and the balance of payments on current account and, to a lesser degree, in the level of inflation.

The size of the Spanish public sector, measured as a percentage of the gross national product, grew in the twenty years up to 1990, during which time it practically doubled, to come close to the EC average. After 1985, this happened within a context of deceleration and public expenditure reduction, in which the Spanish economy has participated, though to a lesser extent. This relative reduction, given the trend in national income, has allowed for a significant decrease of public deficit levels. Thus, the imbalance between Spain's public expenses and revenues, which had caused a 7 per cent public deficit in relation to 1985's GNP, was reduced to an estimated 2.8 per cent for 1990. These figures are seen in Table 9.2.

As the Spanish public sector experienced fast growth, its expense and revenue structure gradually adapted to the EC average, with a few differences. Table 9.3 shows the composition of more significant public expenses and revenues, as estimated for Spain and for the EC in 1990. Spain's public expenditure structure shows the investment activity of these financial periods, the increase in interest due to more orthodox financing of the public

Table 9.1 Main economic indicators: percentage change per annum

	Spain					EEC				
	1961–73	1974–81	1985	1989	1990	1961–73	1974–81	1985	1989	1990
GNP	7.2	1.8	2.3	4.7	3.5	4.8	2.0	2.5	3.5	2.9
Gross Fixed Asset Formation/GNP	24.2	23.9	18.9	22.7	25.0	23.3	22.1	19.2	20.1	20.8
Inflation	6.6	17.5	8.3	6.7	6.8	4.6	12.3	5.9	4.7	5.1
Productivity	6.5	3.3	3.7	1.8	2.1	4.5	2.1	1.8	2.0	1.6
Employment	0.7	−1.5	−1.4	3.5	2.7	0.3	−0.1	−0.6	1.5	1.7
Unemployment	0.4	6.3	21.4	17.5	15.8	2.2	5.1	11.9	9.0	8.5
Current Account Balance/GNP Financing	−0.2	−2.0	1.6	−3.0	−3.8	0.4	−0.6	0.7	0.0	0.3
Capacity or Necessity/GNP	—	−1.3	−7.0	−2.5	−3.0	—	−3.7	−5.2	−3.0	−3.9
Public Administration's Gross Debt/GNP	—	15.5	46.4	48.7	42.8	—	39.4	56.6	60.7	57.6
Interest paid by Public Administration/GNP	—	0.6	3.2	3.3	3.5	—	2.8	5.0	4.8	4.9

Source: Comisión de las Comunidades Europeas, *Informes Económicos Anuales* (several years).

Table 9.2 Public administration income and expenditure as percentage of GNP

	1970		1982		1986		1988		1990*	
	EEC	Spain	EEC	Spain	EEC	Spain	EEC	Spain	EEC	Spain
Public administration expenditure	37.2	21.7	48.2	37.5	48.4	41.7	47.1	40.5	46.0	40.2
Public administration incomes	36.1	22.5	42.7	31.9	43.6	35.6	43.5	37.3	42.8	37.4
Financing necessity	−1.1	0.7	−5.5	−5.6	−4.8	−6.1	−3.6	−3.2	−3.2	−2.8

* Estimated forecasts for 1990.

Source: *Economie Européene*, 41 (1989).

Table 9.3 Estimated public expenditure and revenue as percentage of 1990 GNP

	EEC	Spain
Structure of public expenditure		
Current transfers	20.2	17.3
Public consumption	17.7	14.2
Interest	4.8	3.3
Public investment	2.7	4.3
Capital transfers	0.6	1.0
Structure of public income		
Indirect taxes	13.0	10.1
Direct taxes	12.2	10.7
Social Security contributions	14.3	12.6
Other income	3.2	4.0

Source: *Economie Européene*, 41 (1989).

deficit and the differences in current transfers and, especially, in public consumption relative to the EC average, with their corresponding reflection in public allowances and in quality of public services.

The Spanish public revenue structure is very similar to that of the EC, following the gradual reduction of the impact of social security contributions and the strong increase in indirect taxation brought about by the implementation of VAT in 1986, and in direct taxation as a consequence of the economic recovery and of improved management. This fiscal structure, a consequence of the taxation framework designed in 1977, which implemented a modern fiscal system in Spain, is again immersed in a process of reform, in order to adapt it to constitutional requirements and to bring it in line with the rest of Europe.

The effects of fiscal harmonization on the Spanish taxation system

When the Single Act was signed, with the aim of achieving a barrier-free internal market within the EC, the EC established a clear purpose within a specific time frame. In order to achieve it, the Commission put forward a set of measures to remove physical, technical and fiscal barriers. As far as fiscal matters were concerned, all of the Commission's initial proposals, contained in the twenty-first White Book, were still waiting – on 31 December 1989 – to receive final ratification from the Council. This situation emphasizes both the difficulties experienced by the Member States in adopting harmonizing proposals and the different strategies – of competence, coordination and 'status quo' defence – available.

For indirect taxation, the only actions considered in the White Book were the isolated ones adopted to foster cooperation among companies, and to harmonize taxation of savings, in order to prevent fiscal distortions arising from the deregulation of capital movements. Differences between net rates of interest and dividend withholdings may influence the location of direct investment for fiscal reasons and not strictly for economic efficiency. Within this context, the risk of movement of savings and investment may stimulate reform in some areas of direct taxation, such as taxation of capital income, the degree of fiscal progressiveness, the treatment of capital gains, the system of source withholdings, loss compensation and inflation adjustment for companies, as well as the information and control models needed to reduce the risk of fiscal evasion.

To sum up, the free movement of capital questions the existence of different fiscal treatment of income from capital in different Member States. This may accelerate the process of fiscal harmonization in some aspects of taxation. In other aspects, the final degree of harmonization will depend on the predominance of a framework of general political agreement and on the flexibility of common approaches. In any case, the repercussions on Spanish taxation seem to point towards a reduction of capital revenue assessment, in order to favour a more competitive fiscal system. This gives rise to a double consideration: on one hand, the arrival of external investment would foreseeably be favoured; on the other, the degree of capital revenue concealment and evasion will increasingly depend on the exchange of taxation information between the different administrations.

The initial proposals pertinent to the harmonization of indirect taxation have been much more ambitious. The need to remove fiscal barriers hindering the formation of the internal market makes it mandatory to adopt measures that prevent the appearance of distortion after the abolition of the different indirect taxation systems.

In August 1987 Lord Cockfield presented proposals on VAT/excise harmonization. The initial project on VAT harmonization was based upon two main points: payment of tax in the country of origin, so that it would assess production, and the existence of a European clearing house to guarantee the correct adjustment between accrued and carried taxes. But this approach, used to define a free space for consumer decisions, presented several problems. First of all, the differences between the currently existing taxation rates in the different countries would upset the tax's neutrality, since it would affect fiscal variations in entrepreneurial competitivity. In this sense, the harmonization of the taxation rates by means of a series of minimums would only minimize the problems caused by a lack of a neutral taxation system. Second, the need to establish an EC clearing house would require the setting up of a complex bureaucratic system. Unless a sufficiently transparent and efficient administrative mechanism for invoice checking were established, this would lead to an increase in the already existing levels of fraud connected with this tax. In addition to this, for those countries which, like Spain, are net importers of consumer or investment goods, this system would imply a permanent creditor status with the clearing house, with all the subsequent financial problems incurred in this situation.

Commissioner Scrivener put forward a new proposal and the successive agreements reached by the Council of Economy and Finance have modified the initial draft, establishing a broad transition period during which the VAT collection system in the country of origin would continue to be applied, in accordance with its rates and conditions. Divergences in taxation rates still exist and, thus, it seems that the determination of the proposed collars (4–9% for the reduced rate and 14–20% for normal rates) in the negotiating strategies, is oriented towards the establishment of minimum rates. On the other hand, it seems that the proposal of a macroeconomic clearing house for a portion of the trade exchanges is gaining acceptance as a means of guaranteeing a balance between the Member States.

The application of this tax in Spain, fully adapted to EC rules, as well as the adoption of taxation rates comparatively lower than those existing in other countries, seems to forecast a rising approximation of the minimum and normal rates to the EC average rates. This will no doubt lead to an increase in tax collected, with some risk of inflation at the time of its adaptation and a tax decrease over those goods subject at present to the maximum rate of 33%.

Any kind of agreement on the harmonization of special taxes or, in EC parlance, excises, which generically are concentrated on fuel, tobacco, spirits, beer and wines, has experienced great difficulties. Its levying importance in several countries, the differences between the taxed products and the existing special taxes in each country, as well as the difference between the existing tax rates are the main causes of the lack of agreement between the Member States. The initial harmonization proposals revolved around the excises to be maintained and the approach to tax rates, through a calculation which was sometimes based on the arithmetic average of the existing rates and, in others, on its weighted average. The link between these taxes and the consideration of desirable and undesirable goods, as well as pressure from producers in different countries, the substantial effects of a rapid harmonization over large productive sectors in specific countries, and over tax collection, gives rise to problems of a political nature for some EC governments.

The possible effects of this harmonization in Spain point to a substantial increase of tax revenue, because of the low assessment previously imposed over the most important products. This may have consequences for price levels and, by its very nature, cause changes in consumer patterns and habits.

Repercussions of Economic and Monetary Union on Spanish fiscal policy

Following the Hanover European Council in June 1988, European integration progressed with the relaunching of economic and monetary union. This new impetus was embodied in the Delors Report on economic and monetary union, issued on 17 April 1989. The Delors proposal, which was grounded in the 1970 Werner Report, is based on the need to achieve greater convergence in economic management, to take advantage of the opportunities for economic advancement to be had from the greater degree of integration and interdependency of the national economies, as a consequence of the application of the Single Act.

Economic and monetary union took shape as the result of a progressive process of economic integration, in which the aims of price stability, balanced growth, convergence of living conditions, full employment and balance of payments must be achieved within a framework of full freedom of movement of people, goods, services and capital inside the EC, of irreversible fixed rates of exchange between the different national currencies and of a single currency. This design demands a common monetary policy and a high degree of fiscal policy coordination within a consensual macroeconomic framework, with compulsory procedures and rules as to the size and shape of budgets.

The Delors Report focuses on four characteristics of economic union:

— The Single Market, with free movement of people, goods, services and capital.
— A policy strengthening market mechanisms.
— Common policies to address structural and regional development changes.
— Coordination of macroeconomic policy, including compulsory rules for budget issues.

To establish such a system implies a mid-term framework for budgetary policy, balancing between binding rules and discretional coordination adapted to each situation. As to rules, the Report points to the establishment of maximum limits for the public deficits of Member States, the exclusion of central banks and other financial institutions from access to direct credit, the establishment of limits to loans in non-EC currencies and a definition of the overall orientation for mid-term budget policy, including size and financing of the added budget balance, both for national and EC budgets.

Yet the foreseeable unequal impact of economic advantages generated by this whole process of integration on the different regions makes it necessary to reinforce common policies through structural and regional developments. The reform of the Structural Funds could contribute to the reduction of the spatial impact of the internal market and of economic and monetary union, by emphasizing its coordination, doubling its resources and centring its action on the more problematic regions and areas.

The consequences of economic and monetary union for Spanish fiscal and budgetary policies have to be taken into account within the need to make a sound macro-economic budgetary policy compatible with the effort of the Spanish public sector to close the gap between its levels of public provision and basic structures and those of the new Europe. The limitations of some of the fundamental instruments of national governments' economic policies

Table 9.4 Cost/benefit analysis

National goals	Community policies: Fiscal policy	Community policies: Fiscal harmonisation
Macroeconomic goals		
Growth	++	+
Full employment	+	+
Inflation	+	−/+
Balance of payments	+	+/−
Sectoral structure	+	+/−
Socioeconomic goals		
Spatial structure	+/−	+/−
Distribution of rent	−/+	−
Quality of life	+	+
Income from taxation		
Fund adequacy	+	++
Economic efficiency	+	++
Personal incidence	−/+	−
Spatial incidence	+/−	+/−

may condition the degree of achievement and the speed of implementation, unless the various structural characteristics of the EC economies and their development needs are suitably weighted. On the other hand, the progressive convergence of the main Spanish economic budgets with the EC average minimizes the problems derived from the convergence of economic policies and encourages the Spanish economy to take advantage of the present phase of economic development. The reinforcement of structural action throughout the EC allows it to share in the economic and social modernization of the Spanish productive structure.

Evaluation of costs and benefits for Spain

Aside from the general advantages that Spain derives from its belonging to the EC as far as its political, social, economic or strategic interests are concerned, and from the practically irreversible process of European integration, which was accelerated by the changes in Eastern Europe, the evaluation of costs and benefits of Spain's entry to the EC poses numerous problems from the fiscal and taxation point of view. One of them, certainly, is how to determine the goals which might be affected by EC fiscal and budgetary policies.

Table 9.4 emphasizes the most significant national goals, differentiating between macroeconomic ones (growth, full employment, inflation and balance of payments), those of a socioeconomic nature (sectoral productive structure, spatial structure, degree of income distribution, quality of life) and strictly fiscal aims (financial adequacy, personal and spatial incidence of taxation). The evaluation of each of the goals as a cost or benefit depends on fiscal harmonization and the convergence measures within the scope of fiscal and budgetary policies on these goals, without taking into account the repercussions of EC actions as a whole – outside the ones mentioned – over them. The results are conditional on the final evolution of the harmonization strategies and the compensatory policies which may be adopted along the process of integration which the Community has initiated.

References

Albi Ibañez, E., ed. (1990) *La Hacienda Pública en la Democracia*, Madrid, Ed. Ariel.

Carbajo, D. (1990) 'La política de ingresos públicos en la década de los noventa', mimeo, *Universidad Complutense*, Madrid.

Fuentes Quintana, E. (1990) 'Los deberes económicos de los noventa: el arte del acercamiento y de la convergencia', *Economistas*, 41.

Gómez Aviles-Casco, F. (1990) 'Qué nos espera en la CEE?' *Información Comercial Española*, 676.

González-Paramo, J.M. (1990) 'The role of the public sector in Spain: structural characteristics and policy adjustment on the road to the EEC Internal Market' in Bliss and Braga de Macedo (eds) *Union with Diversity in the European Economy*, Cambridge University Press.

Smith, S. (1990) 'The European Community's priorities in Tax Policy', *Institute for Fiscal Studies*, London.

Utrilla de la Hoz, A. (1990) 'Los Fondos Estructurales y las relaciones presupuestarias de España con la CEE', *Economistas*, 41.

VV. AA (1990) *La política fiscal en España ante la libre circulación de capitales*, Madrid Instituto de Estudios Fiscales.

Zabalza, A. (1990a) 'La Política Fiscal española en la perspectiva del Mercado Interior Europeo', *Doc. D-90001* Ministerio de Economía y Hacienda.

—— (1990b) 'Las líneas básicas de la política fiscal para el futuro inmediato', *Cuadernos de Actualidad*, 1. Instituto de Estudios Fiscales.

Chapter 10

Monetary policy

Sara González Fernández

Since 1985 the Spanish economy has undergone a process of recovery in its rate of growth of GNP at constant prices and Gross Capital Formation (GCF), and experienced a fall in its rate of inflation. Using Purchasing Power Parities (PPP), it can be seen that the corrected Spanish per capita GNP only fell two points between 1980 and 1988, to 46 per cent. This is equal to the decline experienced by the Federal Republic of Germany, which went from 75 to 73 per cent, and lower than that of France, which was 74 per cent and went down to 70 per cent, during the same period of time. The unemployment rate fell slightly between 1985 and 1989.

Table 10.1 Trends in Spanish economic variables, annual percentage changes

Variables	1982	1983	1984	1985	1986	1987	1988	1989
GNP (Const. price)	1.2	1.8	1.8	2.3	3.3	5.2	4.7	3.9
GCF (Const. price)	0.5	−2.5	−5.8	3.8	7.9	13.8	13.0	10.00
Inflation rate	14.5	12.3	9.5	8.3	8.7	5.2	4.8	6.8
Unempl. rate*	16.2	17.7	20.1	21.4	21.0	20.5	20.0	19.6

* Unemployment rate as a percentage of the active population.

Source: EUROSTAT, 1990

The characteristics of Spanish monetary policy and its implications

The Spanish economy presented two basic imbalances: inflation and a deficit on current account in the balance of payments. The solution to both of these was to be found in increased competitivity and greater flexibility in the factor market. A 1989 study by the World Economic Forum showed that the competitivity and dynamism of the Spanish market ranked eighteenth in a list of twenty-two countries.

During the late 1980s, Spanish monetary policy has centred mainly on

Table 10.2 Consumer price index yearly variations: percentage of mean yearly rate

Countries	1987	1988	1989
FRG	0.2	1.3	1.8
France	3.1	2.7	3.5
Italy	4.8	5.0	6.3
UK	4.2	4.9	7.8
Spain	5.2	4.8	6.8
EC Average	3.2	3.5	5.2

Source: Junta Superior de Precios.

Table 10.3 Spanish interest rates in real terms, 1980–8

Variable	1980	1981	1982	1983	1984	1985	1986	1987	1988
(1)	0.8	1.4	2.0	4.7	7.5	5.3	3.1	8.2	5.9
(2)	1.6	3.0	3.5	5.6	9.1	8.6	7.1	11.3	9.4

Note: (1) Interest on the National Debt in real terms. (2) One to three-year credits for new operations. The Consumer Price Index (CPI) has been used to calculate real rates.

Source: Banco de España.

measures to control inflation and to define an environment favourable to economic growth, so that it exceeded the EC average by a minimum of 1%. With regard to inflation, the goal is not only to control the Spanish rate, but also to reduce its differential with respect to the other EC countries, as anything else would mean a loss of foreign competitivity, with serious effects on the level of unemployment and on the trade balance. In 1987–9 the rate of inflation exceeded the EC average by 1.3–2.0% (see Table 10.2).

A restrictive monetary policy has been applied as a consequence of this gap, resulting in high interest rates; thus, in 1986, when Spain joined the EC, interest rate differentials were 4 to 6 points with respect to the FRG or the United States. During the decade of the 1980s, the trend in Spanish interest rates, therefore, was as shown in Table 10.3.

Restrictive monetary policies in 1989 encouraged wide interest rate differentials among EC Member States (see Table 10.4).

In 1989 a restrictive monetary policy was put into effect with a 1.5 point increase (from 16.5% to 18%) of banking institutions' cash ratios and by the redefinition of their computation, as well as by a one point increase in the banking base rate, which then stood at 13.4%. An obligation to keep certain non-interest-bearing deposits was imposed on the lenders until the end of 1989 or, in some cases, until March 1991.

Table 10.4 Long-term interest rates in January 1989*

Country	%
Spain	13.43
United Kingdom	9.05
France	8.66
FRG	6.90

* Rates on Government long-term bonds.

Source: Banco de España.

Table 10.5 Changes in Peseta spot rates*

Year	US$	ECU	DM	FFr	£
1986	140.05	137.45	64.61	20.23	205.35
1987	123.48	142.26	68.69	20.54	201.88
1988	116.49	137.60	66.32	19.56	207.07

* Monthly averages

Source: Banco de España.

Sterilization of the expansion of reserves was carried out during 1989, by three methods:

(a) Higher reserves in the banking system, through the increase of the obligatory percentage or the enlargement of computable resources in the coefficient denominator (Banco de España Memorandum, 13/89, 7 July).
(b) Injection or drainage intervention by the Banco de España.
(c) Having obtained additional Public Treasury financing, the government's appeal to the Banco de España was postponed until the month of October. Methods (b) and (c) prevented interest rates from falling.

The conflict between domestic monetary control and exchange rate stability was solved with a moderate rise of the interest differential in favour of Spain, which encouraged the entry of foreign capital (see Chapter 1, 'The free movement of capital'), particularly speculative money. This, in turn, increased the inflow of foreign currency and reserves reached levels far above those of previous years. In January 1990, they stood at $44,242 million, whereas they had only reached $40,303 million in January 1989.

On the other hand, and especially after 1987, the peseta started to rise, which stimulated a greater trade deficit. In relation to the EC, for instance, the peseta index during 1989 rose 5.5% or 7.8% in real terms, from January to November. The upwards pressure was also noticeable on the ECU rate, so that, at the end of 1989, the quotation was of Pts. 130.3/ECU, a rise of 1.3% over the central parity (see Table 10.5). This factor contributed to the increase in private consumption, which OECD forecast would reach a cumulative value of 20.5% in 1988–93, as opposed to 11.6% in 1982–7. So, the real change in private consumption during 1988 was around 5.8%, while public consumption was set at 4.6%.

As a whole, savings as a percentage of GNP started to show an upward trend from 1985 onwards. A disaggregated analysis, however, would show that business and public sector savings acted as a compensating factor to household savings.

Monetary policy and exchange rates

Situation previous to membership in the European Monetary System

For a considerable length of time, exchange rates were allowed to be a reflection of the consequences of domestic policy, to prevent adverse effects on the balance of payments, although the Banco de España has been practising a policy of correcting large exchange rate deviations since 1974. This was noticeably modified by Spain's entry in the European Monetary System (EMS), and by the progressive liberalization of capital markets, which hindered the manipulation of the exchange rate and caused it to be considered as a parameter.

Membership of the 'peseta' in the European Monetary System

The process of EMS membership was started in May 1987, with the contribution of 20% of gold and dollar reserves to FECOM and the listing of the ECU in the foreign currency market after July 1987. It reached its peak in 1989, when the peseta joined in the fixed rate system and became a component of the ECU.

Following a favourable recommendation from the Monetary Committee on 16 June the peseta unexpectedly joined the European Monetary System on 19 June 1989. A central rate of exchange of Pts. 133.804/ECU was defined, and a bilateral central rate of exchange of Pts. 65/DM, with a temporary fluctuation range of ±6%. The chosen rate of exchange was close to that of the market, as a consequence of the attitude of monetary authorities following the inflationary outburst during the summer of 1988. Thus, in December 1987 the market rate of exchange was of 68.5 Pts./DM, and of 64.15Pts./DM in April 1989.

Expert opinion, however, considered the chosen parity as excessively high, especially bearing in mind that, at the time of joining, the forecast deficit on current account was more than $11,000 million, around 3% of GNP. The Banco de España estimated that the deficit would reach 4.5% of GNP in 1990. It was generally believed that the modification of the composition of the ECU in September 1989, as a consequence of the inclusion of the peseta and the escudo in the money basket, would be accompanied by a revision of exchange rates. This, however, did not happen, and the peseta was included in the ECU with a 5.4% weighting, keeping the initially agreed rate of exchange. The weight of the peseta in the ECU averaged from 6.75% of GNP to 4.2%, according to the volume of Spain's trade with the EC.

At the end of May 1989, the real rate of exchange of the peseta with respect to the remaining EC Member States was 15% over the average of the 1983–7 period. Even at the beginning of its membership in the EMS, a growing trend was evident, so that, at the end of the first week, quotation closed at 63.81 Pts./DM, with the Banco de España starting a series of purchasing interventions. This initial behaviour continued, so that the rate of exchange of the peseta against the Deutschmark went from 64.69 in December 1989 to 63.5 in April 1990. This trend has been reinforced more than once by the attitude of the Banco de España, for example, the squeeze it exerted on the interbanking market in July 1989.

Cost/benefit analysis

Membership of the peseta in the European exchange discipline has generated several stands of opinion. Almost generally, membership has been considered to be positive. The suitability of the moment chosen to join has, however, been questioned. The more significant arguments on advantages and disadvantages of this membership of the European exchange system will now be briefly presented:

The following may be considered as advantages:
- A more effective integration of the Spanish production sectors in the EC, due to the greater stability of the exchange rate.
- Strengthening of the political process of economic union.
- Consolidation of economic policy after 1982, with an anti-inflationary bias.

Some restrictions imposed by membership:

- The exchange discipline imposed by the EMS meant a change in priorities, emphasizing exchange rate stability rather than control of the money supply and interest rates, decreasing therefore scope for monetary policy. So this policy ceased to be centred on the maintenance of high interest rates, because this would be translated into a substantial influx of foreign capital, trying to obtain greater profits. The arrival of capital would press the peseta exchange rate upwards, which would make it difficult to keep the initially acquired commitment. As a consequence, the exchange priority, linked to the free movement of capital, noticeably limited the use of cash ratios and informal credit control as instruments of restrictive monetary policy in Spain. Thus, in January 1990, a bearish adjustment of the cash ratio happened, because excessively high borrowing was taking place. So, in order to make Spanish cash ratios conform to those in the EC, it was decided in March 1990 to reform the system by establishing two segments, one based on the current accounts of issuing banks, and the other covered by certificates issued by the Banco de España. A reduction in legal obstacles affecting the Spanish financial system also became necessary. The first measure, at the beginning of 1989, was a decrease in the compulsory investment coefficient, scheduled to be discontinued completely after 1993. This all required change from the practice of earlier years.

— Because of these conditions and in order to reinforce the anti-inflationary monetary policy, some supporting fiscal and income policies became necessary. A restrictive budgetary policy seemed to be required, with restrictions on real public expenditure, accompanied by selective taxation affecting consumption rather than investment, if the goal of job creation was to be sustained. An economic policy like this would generate important social costs, whose evaluation would lead us into a level of argument beyond the strictly economic scope.

— This greater exchange rate discipline implies less opportunity for growth for the Spanish economy. This thesis is supported by the fact that the rate of growth of the Spanish economy, measured in terms of the Gross National Product at constant prices, decreased in 1989 as compared to previous years. It is fair to point out that this trend had already begun in 1988, prior to Spain's entry into the EMS. Besides, the rate of growth of the Spanish economy has remained above the EC average.

— Additionally, after joining the EMS, inflation continued to fall, as it had been before entry, when frequent intervention was required to sustain the exchange rate and no competitive advantage was obtained.

Membership in the EMS has been marked by cooperation in the battle against inflation and in the reduction of exchange rate stress, but does not have a determinant nature, as may be derived from the reasonable success already achieved in both goals.

Private use of the ECU in Spain

Spanish residents need prior authorization from the monetary authorities to purchase issues of ECU securities in foreign markets. This circumstance, however, does not seem to have hindered the development of a small private ECU market in Spain. ECU financing has been undertaken in Spain since the end of 1983. The first organizations to use this currency were Insituto de Crédito Oficial, the public corporation RENFE, 'Hidroeléctrica' of Catalonia and the Spanish Airline IBERIA. They are mainly public enterprises. On average the loans raised have an average maturity of 8 to 9 years and a variable rate of interest, based on the interbanking interest rate in ECU or the LIBOR.

Additionally, as a result of a Resolution of the Ministry of Economy and Finances, Spanish residents were generally authorized as of September 1989 to open ECU accounts in banking undertakings operating in Spain. So far, this general field of application has been granted solely for ECUs, and not for other foreign currencies.

In April 1990, the first issue of ECU debt was launched in Spain. Its total value was of ECU 500 million and its five-year bonds are listed in the four Spanish stock markets. The Barcelona Corporation issued an ECU five-year bond. To make this issue more attractive, a 95 per cent tax rebate was offered to non-residents. This reveals the importance of fiscal conditions in increasing effective profitability.

References

Banco de España (1989) *Boletín Económico*, Madrid.

Ceca (Confederación Española de Cajas de Ahorros) (1990) *Boletín de Coyuntura Económica*, several issues, Madrid, January/June.

Fernández Manera, R. (1989) 'Los beneficios del mercado único europeo. ¿Se cumplirán las expectativas?' *Aduanas*, No. 30, October.

Ferré, F. (1989) 'Sobre el tipo de cambio del DM y el Sistema Monetario Europeo', *BICE*, No. 2207, November, p. 4409; 'El diferencial de inflación', No. 2205, November; p. 4198.

—— (1990) 'OCDE: Perspectivas económicas', No. 2215, January, p. 101.

Moneda y Credito (1989) No. 188.

Rodríguez Quiros, J.L. (1989) 'Los flujos de inversión entre España y la CEE', *Aduanas*, No. 30, October.

Rojo, L.A. (1989) *El sistema monetario europeo y el futuro de la cooperación en la CEE*, Madrid, Ed. Instituto España-Espasa Calpe.

Ruesga Benito, S.M. (1989) '1993: España ante el mercado único', Madrid, Ed. Pirámide.

Chapter 11

Regional policy

Vicente Riesgo Alonso

Regional Policy (RP) is acquiring a growing importance in the conception and performance of the EC's sectoral policies. After the enforcement of the Single European Act, which states its purpose of 'reducing differences between the various regions, and backwardness in the less favoured territories' in order to enhance the EC's economic and social cohesion (Article 130a, EEC Treaty), it became apparent that RP might already be considered as an isolated field of action within the EC, capable of being identified with the ERDF and its activities. Article 130b of the enlarged EEC Treaty determines that the performance of Community policies and the establishment of the Single Market must take into account the goals of Article 130 and the normal tasks of the Regional Fund, contributing to their achievement. Thus, under Article 130b, different Structural Funds are mentioned (EAGGF-orientation, ESF, ERDF) as being of equal importance, and as instruments to help meet those objectives. Structural Funds must be harmonized in order to achieve the goals which were previously assigned to the Regional Fund (Article 130c, 130d).

RP goals should thus become the shaping and coordinating principle for all remaining Community sectoral policies; in other words, it is not so much the immediate 'material' RP goal (i.e., regional development) or its instrumental shaping that defines the European Community's RP, but rather, and above all, its aims, its 'formal' aspects (the adjustment of regional imbalance and the strengthening of the Community's social and regional cohesion). The EC's RP, therefore, is not only directly 'promotional', which was for years the main feature of the Regional Fund, but takes over shaping and coordination of EC policies as well as the activities of the existing Structural Funds and all other financing instruments. In addition, its 'compensatory' function (the compensation of undesirable effects of other sectoral policies) has a growing importance in the conception and performance of RP. The new rules on the use of the Structural Funds clearly underline this compensating RP component.

The Single European Act gives high priority to the Community's RP, and prescribes the strengthening of the EC's economic and social cohesion, through adjustment of regional imbalances. This means that any sectoral measure – agricultural, social, industrial, etc. – which exerts a positive or negative influence over the balance and on EC cohesion, may also be subject to consideration and to eventual action from RP.

The application of political measures, solely agricultural in theory (such as abandoning cultivated land or agricultural price stagnation), could, from the viewpoint of RP, have noticeably higher effects on regions such as Galicia or western Asturias, whose main characteristics are small farms and a high rate of working population in the agricultural sector, than many conventional infrastructure projects. Similarly, the effects of industrial policies in regions such as the central area of Asturias, extremely dependent on its heavy industry (iron and steel works, mining, etc.), may have RP implications.

Generally speaking, it may be stated that the more unbalanced the economic structure of a region or the various regions of a country among themselves, the greater the regional significance acquired by the development of sectoral policies. In countries like Spain, with extreme regional imbalance[1] in matters of income, in infrastructure equipment, in production and employment structures, in the productivity and profitability levels of different economic sectors, especially that of farming, the classic sectoral EC policies (agriculture or industry, for example) give new guidelines. Simply adopting EC regulations (free competitivity and movement of goods, common external tariff and so on) and a suprasectoral and spatial/regional realization breaks the framework of any RP in its strictly conventional sense.[2] The specific mechanisms of regional compensation, introduced for instance during the CAP reforms, take account of these effects, although they are often insufficient to neutralize them.

Some consequences may be derived from the Community RP's double goal: to adjust regional imbalances and to achieve social cohesion in the EC.

(1) Consideration of spatial/regional effects of sectoral policies belongs to the RP's field of problems and actions (Article 130b of the EEC Treaty).
(2) In order to be able to determine the consequences of Community RP, it is necessary to register the economic and social position of each Member State and of each region within its own State and within the EC.
(3) In countries marked by regional imbalances, as is the case of Spain, the Community's RP audit or cost/benefit analysis must be performed early and more firmly than in those countries whose social structure is more homogeneous. It must be performed *in each and every one of the regions*, classified if possible in accordance with some regional typology.[3] At a later stage the level of reduction in regional disparities *at State and EC levels* may be measured.
(4) The goal of 'regional balance' is not simply one more among other goals for countries whose regional differences are large, but implies, among other aspects, a balanced spatial realization of the other economic priorities. Thus, for instance, higher economic growth as a consequence of economic policy could create more damage (of a political, social,

ecological, etc. nature) than benefits in Spain, if it should remain concentrated in a couple of regions (for example, Madrid or Barcelona), coexisting with the economic decline of other parts of the country (such as Asturias, Galicia, Castile). From the perspective of an RP, this phenomenon would be categorically considered as a failure. From the same perspective, other effects, positive for the State as a whole, would be considered as negative (for instance, on the balance of payments through resource transference). This means that RP must not only contribute to the domestic and global fulfilment of economic goals, but to the balance of these goals in each region (domestic goals are also regional goals).

(5) Due to the great regional imbalances within the EC and within some of its Member States, RP as presented here could lead to problematic situations: as a shaping principle and critical example of other sectoral policies, and for social and regional reasons, it could delay structural reforms which would eventually be urgent (i.e., in agriculture or heavy industry); or it could have to raise any compensatory mechanisms (Structural Funds) considerably to buffer the resulting problems, thus increasing the financial load on the EC budget. This is the dilemma stemming from stresses between two principles of the RP which are hard to reconcile: equity and efficiency.

(6) Owing to the scarcity of available funds, or even in order to achieve greater efficiency, RP must maintain its complementary characteristics to the regional policies of the Member States and of the regions themselves.

The effects of Community sectoral policies considered as problems and the field of action for RP

The regional effects of the EC agricultural policy

Because of the highly agricultural nature of many regional centres of production and employment, the CAP has an exceptional regional importance in Spain. The Third Periodic Report on socio-economic status and development of the EC regions (1987) states that in nine Spanish regions over 18% of the working population were in the agricultural sector, twice the EC average. In 1987, that percentage was even higher than 20% in five of those regions, and two of them (Extremadura and Galicia) had over 30%. Leaving aside the serious structural problems of Spanish farming operations (smallholdings, latifundism, low productivity and profits, etc.), 62% of the country's arable surface is land termed 'unfavoured' by the EC.

In Chapter 7 of this book, devoted to the CAP, reference is made to specific agricultural problems raised by Spain's EC membership. This chapter will now develop a regional typology that permits an approach to cost/benefit analysis, taking especially into account the degree of regional development in relation to the national average, as well as the positive or negative effects which the CAP market and price components and the different compensation mechanisms might bring to bear over each type of region:

(1) Backward regions, whose occupational and productive structure have a high agricultural component, and which suffer negative effects from the CAP (Extremadura, Galicia, Castile-Leon and some parts of Aragon). These regions' basic products (cereals, sugar-beet, milk, cattle, potatoes) contribute to the EC surplus. The situation of cereal producers is especially serious, due to the EC restrictions imposed on this sector and to the low productivity of the soil, especially in Castile-Leon, where even irrigated land does not reach two thirds of the average EC yield. These regions may obtain a maximum benefit from the compensation mechanisms: subsidies to improve farm structures and compensation in less-favoured and mountain regions, EAGGF-O aids of up to 50% of investment for agricultural industries and marketing, regional ERDF subsidies of up to 55% of farm infrastructure improvement projects, EAGGF-O subsidies of 30–50% for specific farm development regional measures.
(2) Regions developed below the national average, but on which the CAP has had positive effects. Castile-La Mancha, Andalusia and Murcia are among them. The primary sector is important in all three of these regions, both in its predominance in employment (over 18% in the first two regions, 1987) and through its contribution to the gross added value (over 10% in 1982). Olive oil production, important in large areas of these regions, may benefit from subsidies to production greater than these given before entry into the EC. Andalusia also enjoys a favourable position for sunflower and cereal crops, with yields similar to those in the EC. Other crops with good prospects are those in irrigation areas (corn, cotton and tobacco), fruit, vegetables and rice. In La Mancha, wine can be expected to continue being able to compete within the EC. These regions, capable of making a less extensive use of the compensation mechanisms described in (1) above, are nevertheless subject to serious problems, some of a structural nature (large land holdings (latifundism)), poor industrialization, while others are economic and social (unemployment and underemployment).
(3) In some regions whose development level is slightly higher than, or equal to, the national average, the negative effects of the CAP are added to a sharp crisis in the industrial sector (Asturias, Basque Country, Cantabria and some parts of Aragon). Even though the natural conditions for milk production are favourable, agricultural production in the Cantabrian region is still below that of the EC, due to unsuitable farming structures, especially those of very small farms (smallholdings). The severe price policy made compulsory in the last few years leaves these regions with very little margin for the essential investment that

would allow them to reach European competitivity levels. Rural areas are undergoing a demographic desertification process whose economic, social and ecological consequences are unforeseeable. It is questionable whether the regional policy mechanisms will be able to compensate for what is destroyed by sectoral policies.

(4) Those Spanish regions whose development level is already above the national average will be those which will obtain greater benefits from EC membership, and the positive CAP effects over their agriculture coincide with positive evolution in other economic sectors. So-called 'Mediterranean' Spain (Valencia, Rioja, Murcia, Catalonia and Navarre) offers clear comparative advantages for the production of numerous agricultural crops, especially fruits, vegetables and wine. This part of the world has optimum prospects in the race for leading positions in European markets.

The effects of Common Market integration on the industrial development of Spanish regions

Taking as a base the structures of the industrial sector and their participation in Spanish foreign trade, a regional typology may also be achieved from the standpoint of industrial policy:

(1) Regions in the north-eastern quarter of Spain (Catalonia, Navarre, Rioja, Aragon and, partially, the Basque Country) are the first group with good short-term prospects, owing to their favourable geographic location, to the high degree of infrastructure development and to the wide diversification of their production structures.

(2) The remarkable structural dependency of the Basque industry on steel and iron manufacture and metal manufacture links it rather more to the other two Cantabrian regions, Asturias and Cantabria, which are also seriously affected by the iron and steel crisis. Over one third of all jobs that have been lost in Spain through industrial reconversion were located in these regions. In some sectors (mining, iron and steel etc.) this process has not yet touched bottom.

(3) Madrid forms a great industrial island in the centre of Spain, with good development prospects, which will probably radiate to the neighbouring regions and towards Portugal. Madrid is the favourite location for high-technology investments. From the beginning of the 1980s, Mediterranean regions to the south of Catalonia – especially Valencia, but Murcia and Balearic Islands as well – are showing a growing dynamism, greater than the national average, in industrial sector investments. Together with some coastal provinces of Andalusia, which are similar, and with those regions mentioned in group (1), these form the so-called 'Mediterranean industrial arc'.

(4) For regions in the centre of Spain (both Castiles and Extremadura, as

well as some parts of Andalusia), and for Galicia, prospects are not particularly positive. They would even appear negative for industrial development in Extremadura and in the Castile-Leon provinces bordering Portugal. An ideal goal for the efforts of EC's Regional Policy would be to foster development of these territories, as well as of the Cantabrian coast and Galicia, within the framework of supraregional and supranational development programmes. Larger urban centres within Castile have more positive prospects and could also enjoy long-term benefits radiating from Madrid.

ERDF aid to Spanish regions

Territorial distribution

During 1986, the first year of Spanish EC membership, this country received a total of ECU 640.88 million from the ERDF. Eight regions and one province – the equivalent of 74% of Spanish territory, and with 48% of its population – benefited from Community aid that year. Subsidies per inhabitant in those Spanish regions subject to Community aid was similar in 1986 to that of Italy: ECU 35. This indicator reached higher values in Greece and Portugal (ECU 48 in both of them) and in Ireland (ECU 36). Almost 40% (ECU 249.53 million) of the total ERDF aid to Spain flowed towards Andalusia, which became the region most favoured by the Community regional subsidies.

The second position was taken by the interior area of Castile-Leon which was granted ECU 146.84 million (22% of the funds assigned to Spain). During 1986, Andalusia and Castile-Leon also took second and third place (after La Campania) among the regions receiving greater ERDF subsidies in absolute numbers: 7.8% and 4.6% respectively of the total aid. In relative values, however, the situation is rather different. Thus, while subsidies per inhabitant were raised to ECU 168 in Basilicata, to 146 in Alentejo and to 75 in Campania, Andalusia and Castile-Leon had to make do with ECU 38 and 57 respectively.

The remaining financial resources assigned to Spain by the ERDF were distributed among the following regions – internal regions: Extremadura (11%) and Castile-La Mancha (9%), Atlantic regions: Galicia (7%) and Asturias (6%), Mediterranean regions: Murcia (4%) and the Canary Islands (2%). Over 85% of the subsidies were thus concentrated in the central and southern regions of the Spanish State. If these regions' development status and structural problems are taken into account, this concentration of means seems plausible. In 1986, the ERDF aid to Spain amounted to 0.3% of the GNP, and 1.4% of gross investment in production goods.

The Autonomous Communities were able to have direct access to the ERDF in 1987. Of the ECU 633.34 million destined to Spain by the Fund, 69% was used in central government projects, and the remaining 31% was used for projects presented and implemented by the autonomous administrations. That same year, Andalusia consolidated and improved its position as the first Spanish beneficiary of EC regional aid, with 43% (ECU 269.4 million) of these subsidies. Andalusia, with 9% of all ERDF aid destined to project co-financing in European regions, also maintained this same position after Campania, as the second most favoured European region, in absolute values, by the Fund's resources. Nevertheless, that year Andalusia did not appear among the top ten regions receiving subsidies per inhabitant. Castile-La Mancha, with ECU 65.3 per inhabitant (Basilicata, ECU 151.1; Algarve, ECU 93.6; Campania, ECU 89.2) is the only Spanish region among the top ten on the list. Castile-La Mancha also benefited from an increase in its receipt of aid, which that year reached ECU 107.68 million (17% of that received by Spain), taking the second position which Castile-Leon had been occupying. The share of Murcia (ECU 38.41 million, 6%) and Asturias (ECU 48.74 million, 8%) in ERDF aid destined to regional development projects also improved in comparison with the previous year. By contrast, Galicia (ECU 39.45 million, 6%), Castile-Leon (ECU 84.9 million, 13%) and Extremadura (ECU 24.6 million, 4%) experienced an important setback, both in absolute and in relative terms. These three regions, located on the frontier with Portugal, are rather backward.

In 1987, Spain also received ECU 27.34 million from the ERDF, for its participation in the EC programmes STAR (ECU 11.93 million) and VALOREN (ECU 11.09 million), as well as for the Asturias PNIC (ECU 4.32 million). The STAR and VALOREN programmes finance development projects in fifteen Spanish regions. The macroeconomic aspects of ERDF aid to Spain were maintained during 1987 at a slightly lower level than those of the previous fiscal year, representing 0.27% of the GNP and 1.33% of gross investment in capital goods. The total amount of subsidies per inhabitant received in Spanish regions subject to ERDF experienced an important drop in comparison with the previous year; it was of approximately ECU 26.4 per inhabitant, considerably below Greece (ECU 47.1 per inhabitant), Ireland (ECU 46.3), Italy (ECU 42.4), Portugal (ECU 39.4) and even the United Kingdom (ECU 29.5).

In 1988, Spain received 20% of the total aid granted by the ERDF (20% in 1986; 19% in 1987), or ECU 732.84 million. That year, the subsidy granted to the Autonomous Community projects went up to ECU 302 million, approximately 45% of financial means destined to Spain.

The area covered by regions benefiting from ERDF aid was extended to 85% of Spanish territory in 1988 and included 56% of the total Spanish population. This meant a considerable change in territorial distribution, both in absolute and relative amounts of funds received for regional development. Thus, for instance aid to Andalusia fell drastically to ECU 124.63 million (17% of the total sum received by Spain) and it ceded to Castile-La Mancha (with ECU 132.02 million, 18%) the first place it formerly held as the region receiving the highest ERDF aid in Spain. The third position went to the Valencia Community, a region which was entitled to regional funds for the first time (ECU 77.61 million, 11%) and which now received more than one of the most depressed Spanish regions, Castile-Leon with ECU 70.72 million (10%). Galicia still received ECU 46.59 million (6%), holding its previous position; the sixth position was occupied by a region which certainly does not belong among the less developed ones in Spain, Catalonia, with ECU 38.46 million (5%).

Besides Valencia and Catalonia, Madrid, Navarre, Cantabria and the Basque Country also received ERDF funds for the first time in 1988. This group of 'new' subsidized regions also achieved over a quarter (27%) of the whole of ERDF aid to Spain. Three regions included in the 'Spanish Regional Development Plan' (1989–93) among those regions 'capable of self-sustained growth' (Navarre, Catalonia and Madrid) received ECU 66.05 million, that is 9% of ERDF subsidies. In 1988 Castile-La Mancha and Andalusia were the two Spanish regions among the ten most subsidized European regions, receiving 4% and 3% respectively of the total ERDF aid.

In 1988, Spain continued to participate in the EC STAR and VALOREN programmes, for which the ERDF committed to Spain a total amount of ECU 210 and 105 million respectively, for the period 1987–91. Besides this, a new PNIC for the building of motorways for which the ERDF has committed around ECU 492.85 million, was added to the one already being implemented for Asturias since 1987, for which the ERDF granted ECU 18.92 million in 1988. This region, one of those most affected by sectoral crisis and reconstruction (agricultural, livestock and industrial), received in 1988 a total of ECU 31.18 million (4%) from ERDF aid; this amount, both in absolute and relative numbers, is considerably lower than the one received in previous exercises. In macroeconomic terms, the ERDF aid for Spain took a slightly downwards trend in 1988 and amounted to 0.26% of the GNP and 1.16% of gross investments in production goods.[4]

Measures subsidized by the ERDF

The great weight granted to projects as opposed to programmes seems to stand out from the list of financed measures. The financed projects, in turn, in a huge majority of cases, were for infrastructure. These received 98% (1986), 96% (1987) and 93% (1988) of the total amount that the ERDF had assigned to Spain. Among subsidized infrastructure measures, the first place is taken by transport and communications projects (roads, railroads, ports and airports, etc.). In 1987, for instance, almost half of the resources (48%) – or even 72% in the case of projects sponsored by Savings Banks – went to road building, especially in Andalusia, in both Castiles, Asturias, Canary Islands and Galicia.

In the railroad and airport sector, 29% of total ERDF funds were spent during that same year. These investments amounted to 42% of the resources assigned to the central government, since they were their responsibility. Andalusia and Castile-La Mancha benefited especially from these railroad and airport projects (HVT from Madrid to Seville). Hydraulic works are another block of infrastructure measures which received a considerable amount of resources. In 1987, for instance, they were assigned 21% of all ERDF aid.

In 1988, projects for the development of endogenous regional potential started receiving ERDF funds in Spain. A total of ECU 2.29 million was destined to this type of project (0.3% of the ERDF aid to Spain), allowing them to participate in the financing of business centres and innovations in Bilbao, Cadiz and Madrid. Also in that year, some other new projects were financed by the ERDF for the creation of technological and industrial parks in the Basque Country, Catalonia and Navarre, for applied research centres in Navarre and Catalonia, or for vocational and technical training centres in Valencia.[5]

We have already mentioned the importance of Spanish participation in EC programmes, as well as that of both PNICs (Asturias and motorways). However, the ERDF resources granted for the subsidy of PNICs were less than 3% of all aid received during 1987 and 1988. Within the total ERDF aid and in contrast to aid destined to individual projects, the percentage of resources destined to programmes has been especially low in Spain compared with other EC countries. For instance, Spain received in 1988 7% of resources for programmes, against 68% in Germany, 52% in Ireland, 41% in Greece, 38% in Belgium, 31% in the United Kingdom, or 11% in Italy.[6]

Final considerations: the effects of the EC's Regional Policy on the economic goals of Spanish regions

The fundamental question remains whether the EC's Regional Policy can contribute, in the long term and in a decisive manner, by means of its promotion and compensation instruments, to the reduction of inequalities in development levels, both for Spanish regions among themselves and in relation to the EC region as a whole. The purpose here is not only to overcome backwardness in some specific territories, but also to reverse the decline in other regions, which has deepened since joining the EC, within the framework of intersectoral restructuring and international competition. On the other hand, certain positive aspects of the application of the EC's Regional Policy instruments have been noticed in Spain, in connection with nearly all economic aspects and certainly in the short term.

Growth and employment

It is certain that the ERDF funds that are used in Spain do contribute to the creation of new jobs, thus benefiting the regions with structural problems. But the infrastructure measures financed with these funds may cause contrary effects connected with growth and employment: they may facilitate new investment, but they may also increase imports in the future. On the other hand, to supply these infrastructure measures (i.e., railroad building), production goods are being imported (i.e., machinery and installations) from the large industrial and technological centres of the EC, which strengthens the unequal distribution of work in the EC, sometimes harming Spanish industry itself. So infrastructure development measures are often subject to external direction, increasing the degree of external dependency and control over the regions.

Technological capacity

The means directly granted to companies for technological capacity – and to aid competitivity as a consequence – are very few. In this sense, a higher participation of less favoured companies in programmes such as STAR and VALOREN would be desirable, as they facilitate access to modern technology; a greater volume of projects to develop endogenous potential, preferably aimed at small and medium-size companies would also be very useful.

External balance

In both the short and long term, measures implemented with the help of ERDF funds may contribute to increased imports of production goods in a first stage and of consumer goods later on and, therefore, to a negative trade balance. Just as the ERDF subsidies result in an improvement of infrastructure and technological equipment of Spanish companies in the less favoured regions, so the foreseeable increase in competitivity will contribute, in the long term, to an improvement of the country's position and of each of its regions through foreign trade. It may also be true that infrastructure measures will attract new investment in the productions sector.

The relatively short period of Spanish EC membership prevents us making any definite, long-term evaluation of the efficiency of the EC Regional Policy as applied to Spanish regions, both in this context and in connection with other points in these final paragraphs.

Regional balance

By itself, the limited ERDF aid will not be able to achieve this goal of regional balance. The future development of regional differences will depend in a greater measure on the effects that other community sectoral policies may have on the Spanish regions, and from the international economic and political factors (competition from third countries, economic and political stability in regions adjacent to the EC, such as the Maghreb, etc.).

The present situation of progressive deterioration threatening large rural regions of Spain is of special concern. The implementation of the regional development projects has not been able to slow this process down, far less to stop it. These regions urgently need integral development programmes (for instance, in the shape of PNICs, with several subprogrammes specific to each region), in order to withstand their demographic, social and ecological desertification. Another factor that also seems especially serious from the point of view of regional balance, is the marginalization of a large part of the Atlantic shore regions (Cantabria, Asturias, Galicia, Castile-Leon, Extremadura), as opposed to the predominance of the Mediterranean area. The Atlantic regions are being partially excluded from projects (motor-way communications with central Europe, HVT, etc.) that are decisive in the future planning of a European economic space and for the competitive advantage of each region within this space.

The enormous foreign investment that came into Spain after it joined the EC re-emphasized the previously existing regional imbalance, as most of this investment was concentrated in very few regions (Madrid and Catalonia, especially).

Environmental protection

Some projects and programme measures financed by the ERDF are directly addressed to environmental improvement and preservation: sewage treatment and rivers, treatment of industrial waste and refuse dumps, etc. RP, however, may concentrate on ecological goals more strongly in two ways: first, by fighting congestion in the existing demographic and industrial aglomerations (Madrid, Barcelona, Bilbao, etc.); and secondly, by struggling against and, if possible, reversing depopulation, erosion and desertification processes in rural areas (Extremadura, both Castiles, Aragon, the Cantabrian corner, etc.).

Budgetary aspects

The resources of the Regional Fund take some of the load off the Spanish government, especially in the infrastructure sector, which became even more pressing after EC entry; thus, the government has greater leeway for other projects. At the level of regional budgets, the ERDF aid represents a considerable volume. In 1987, it amounted to 6% of Andalusia's budget, or 20% of that of Castile-La Mancha. The different levels of Autonomous Community responsibilities – and budgets, as a consequence – must be taken into account here. The ERDF aid makes an important contribution to the financial autonomy of the regions themselves, and thus, of their political field of action (policy regionalization).

Notes

1. In connection with Spanish regional imbalances, see *Papeles de la Economía Española* 'Economía Regional: Hechos y Tendencias', (34), 1988, pp. 17–172.
2. As an example of this strict RP compression, we quote its definition by Claus Schoendube: 'An assembly of every measure for the development and promotion of economic regions in accordance with the existing conditions' (Claus Schoendube, *Europa-Taschenbuch*, Bonn, 1981, p. 324, translated by the author of this chapter). The definition does not take into account, for instance, external RP limitations imposed by domestic or European sectoral policies, etc.
3. The 1989–93 Spanish Regional Development Plan contains a regional typological classification which distinguishes five different types of region and which, in great measure, coincides with those that, with partially different criteria, are presented in this chapter. The Regional Development Plan (PDR) makes a distinction between: (a) regions capable of self-sustained growth (Madrid, the Ebro basin and Mediterranean arc, especially Catalonia and the Balearic Islands); (b) declining industrial regions (Cantabrian mountains, especially the Basque Country and Cantabria); (c) intermediate development regions (Asturias and Valencia); (e) other backward regions (Extremadura, Castile-La Mancha, Castile-Leon, Galicia and the Canary Islands).
4. The 1989–93 Spanish PDR estimated that, during this period of time, the regions of top priority would request from the ERDF total financing of Pts. 1,218,867 million, to be distributed as follows: 1989, Pts. 186,238 million; 1992, Pts. 270,725 million; 1993, Pts. 305,747 million. The demands estimated for this same period of 1989–93 from the remaining Structural Funds should be added to the above; they would be of Pts. 122,124.1 million from the ESF and Pts. 420,660.3 million from the EAGGF-Orientation. For second-priority regions, the PDR estimated for 1989–93 a total demand of Pts. 156,460 million from the EAGGF and of Pts. 53,535.2 million from the ESF.
5. A clear preference is still granted in the 1989–93 Spanish PDR (pp. 43–71) to development measures leading to the provision of the so-called 'hard' infrastructures of the top priority regions (they receive approximately 40% of the total public investment estimated for these regions); such infrastructure would cover transport networks, hydraulic works, etc. However, larger amounts (of approximately 25% of the total investment estimated in the Plan) are estimated for providing these regions with social equipment and the so-called 'soft' infrastructures (housing, health, education, tourism, environment, research, etc.) and for agricultural structures (approximately 7% of investment). Besides action on infrastructure and equipment, the PDR defines other regional development 'instrumental priorities': regional incentives, development of endogenous potential, urban planning and environmental policy.
6. In connection with this, the 1989–93 Spanish PDR states 'It is the will of the Spanish government to progressively grant greater relative weight to operative programmes, as experience grows'.

References

Kommission der Europaeischen Gemeinschaften (1987a) *Die Regionen der erweiterten*

Gemeinschaft, Dritter Periodischer Bericht ber die sozio-oekonomische Lage und Entwicklung der Regionen der Gemeinschaft, Brussels/Luxembourg.

—— (1987b, 1988, 1989) *Europaeischer Fonds fuer Regionale Entwicklund Jahresberichte der Kommission (1986, 1987, 1988)*, Brussels.

Ministerio de Economía y Hacienda, Secretaría de Estado de Hacienda (1989a) *Plan de reconversión regional y social de España 1989–1993.*

—— (1989b): *Plan de desarrollo regional de España 1989–1993.*

—— (1989c): *Política regional de la Europa de los años 90.*

Molle, W. and Cappellin, B. (1988) *Regional Impact of Community Policies in Europe*, Aldershot.

Papeles de la Economía Española (1988a) 'Economía regional: Hechos y tendencias'.

—— (1988b) 'Economia Regional: Ideas y politicas'.

SPRI (Sociedad para la promoción y reconversión industrial, S.A.) (1989) *Regiones europeas de antigua industrialización. Propuestas frente al reto tecnológico*, Bilbao.

PART II: FOREIGN RELATIONS

Coordinator: José Antonio Nieto Solís

The impact of EC membership on Spanish foreign policy

Marisa Rodríguez Mojón

When Spain became a member of the EC in January 1986, its political system had just emerged from an authoritarian regime. It had held its first democratic elections, after forty-one years of dictatorship, in June 1977. As a result, Spanish politics were undergoing a period of readjustment. No country's foreign policy can be divorced from its internal politics, so the reorganization of Spanish political interests in the world system were not just a consequence but a major factor interacting with the redefinition of its domestic political interests and structure.

It is generally accepted that Spain had not introduced basic changes in its diplomatic behaviour since the end of World War II. Spain remained a neutral country in both World Wars, and in the early 1970s the Spanish government still hung on to the idea that neutrality could be considered as a possible source of influence. In addition it had a clear Third World policy, basically oriented towards Latin America and the Arab and Maghreb countries.

In spite of Spain's evident sympathies towards the Axis countries during World War II, and the continuation of an authoritarian, pro-fascist dictatorship, the changing nature of the international system and the necessities posed by the cold war had brought along, in the mid-1950s, privileged relations with the United States. Spain had been considered important for the strategic interests of the United States, and a Mutual Defence Pact was signed between the two countries in 1953, which implied the establishment of US military bases in Spain.

Military dependence was enhanced by an increasing penetration of US interests at various levels: in the economic field, investment and loans soon became significant in food manufacturing, metals, agricultural products, banking, finance, the car industry, pharmaceuticals, insurance, transport, electronics, electricity. At a cultural and educational level, it took the form of several bilateral agreements, which also covered Spanish technological capacity.

This combination of neutrality, defence dependence, Third Worldism, and a growing technological and economic dependence on the United States, seriously augmented the vulnerability of the Spanish situation at the international level (Pollack, 1987).

However, Spain retained its independent action in several foreign policy issues, sometimes even in open contradiction with the desires and recommendations of the US governments. This was clear in its policy towards Latin America, where it always held relations, both political and economic, with Castro's Cuba, and Allende's and Pinochet's Chile, considering that Spain had to be regarded by Latin America as a trustworthy friend, irrespective of political regimes. Loyalty was based on historic, cultural and language ties, rather than on political ones.

Another area towards which the attitude of the Spanish authorities has shown consistency through decades has been the Middle East. The Arab and Maghreb countries had long been considered as 'good neighbours' by the Spanish dictatorial regime. The Spanish representatives in the United Nations consistently supported Arab and Palestinian interests in the United Nations in respect to the Arab–Israeli conflict and rejected the opening of diplomatic relations with Israel.

Soon after democracy was legally established, a redefinition of Spain's international interests was undertaken. Three areas were considered especially relevant: Europe, Latin America and the Mediterranean region.

As far as Western Europe was concerned, the new Spanish democratically elected authorities showed a clear interest in tightening relations. Once its political system was in accordance with that of the European democracies, Spain did not want to continue being absent from the economic and political project of European integration. Entering the EC became a major goal in the Spanish global political project.

Becoming a member of the EC in January 1986 had two major impacts on Spanish political development. First, the necessary adjustment to long-tested democratic administrations has had a positive influence on the capacity of Spanish institutions to develop flexible democratic habits, and contributed to the erosion of tendencies that could have posed obstacles to the desired evolution of the administration. Dealing with the democratic performance of the EC is probably one of the most important events for the Spanish bureaucratic institutions in the last decades. And, second, there has evidently been an important rise in prestige and influence in our relations with other countries.

European integration is still in progress. One of the latest moves has been in European political cooperation – the collective organization of information, mutual consultation and common action among the twelve Member States of the EC on issues of foreign policy. Its purpose is to ensure a common attitude among EC members on political affairs that will complement their collective rules and norms in the economic field. Decisions are taken by consensus. Although the final outcome may be made public, the process of agreement is kept secret. This political cooperation has become especially relevant since the end of the cold war, as new answers have to be devised to confront events that have little to do with the old post-war situation. Western Europe now has the chance to become a qualified counterpart in the formation of Western policy in response to the economic and political changes that are taking place in Eastern Europe. And Spain's membership of this group can only improve its ability to influence decisions. The same is true in other areas. The debate that is currently taking place inside the EC, concerning the possibility of building a unified Western European defence system, with the proposal made on 11 October 1991 by the foreign ministers of Spain, France and Germany, shows how Spain has managed to introduce itself into the EC's decision-making bodies.

Concerning the Mediterranean, the foreign policy of Spain has undergone a very important change. After decades, Spain finally recognized the State of Israel and established diplomatic relations with it in January 1986. Israel has a comprehensive trade agreement with the EC, which includes special treatment for its agricultural products, some of them in clear competition with Spanish products. European political decisions concerning the Middle East would have been even more problematic for Spain if it had remained the only EC country that did not have diplomatic relations with Israel.

The new political situation facilitated the Spanish government during its presidency of the EC. In this period:

— An EC delegation visited the Middle East on four different occasions (a group made up the presidencies of Spain, France, Ireland and Italy).
— A decision was made to double the aid to the Occupied Territories (Declaration of Strasbourg).
— Statements were made concerning the illegality of Israel's planned colonization of the Occupied Territories by Russian Jews (20 February 1990).
— And the Declaration of the European Council in Madrid has completed the Declaration of Venice, recognizing the right of the Palestinians to participate in peace negotiations, which in the opinion of the EC, should take place in an international conference organized by the UN (Benavides, 1991).

In Europe, Spanish politicians have also pressed for the establishment of a kind of Conference on Security and Cooperation for the Mediterranean, following the model of the European CSCE.

With regard to Latin America, the Spanish democratic authorities have enhanced their ability to influence events in this subcontinent. The idea that Spain can be a link between Latin American countries and Europe is reinforced with membership of the EC. Efforts to raise EC's concern towards their problems have resulted in the San José Process, the dialogue with the Rio Group, and the contacts between the EC and the Andean Pact. However, Spain knows that it still has a long way to go in order to achieve its main purposes: that declarations from the EC are complemented by cooperation programmes and a different approach to the debt problem.

The importance of EC membership for Spanish relations with the countries of Eastern Europe must be emphasized. In the Commission set up at The Hague with regards to peace-keeping in former Yugoslavia, one of the two vice-presidents is Spanish. Involvement with other practical measures that will bring the EC closer to designing the new Europe is also of great interest for Spain, as is its participation in the programme for humanitarian and technical assistance to the former Soviet Union, which will cost the EC ECU 750,000,000.

Trying to sum up costs and benefits of EC membership for Spanish foreign policy, we would say that gains have largely outstripped costs, as the scope of influence of any Spanish activity is now so much wider and deeper. This owes much to the increase in legitimacy derived from decisions taken within a group with the capacity to implement them.

References

Benavides, Pablo (1991) 'Política Exterior Española y Cooperación Política Europea', *CEE NEWS*, no. 75, April.

Pollack, Benny (1987) *The Paradox of Spanish Foreign Policy*, London, Pinter, p. 30.

Chapter 12

Trade and development policies during the process of EC integration

José Antonio Nieto Solís

The basis for a common trade policy

This chapter presents some thoughts about the characteristics and operation of the EC's foreign policy, with emphasis on the common trade policy and the policy for aid to development. It starts from an analysis of the EC's foreign policy system as a whole, develops three basic ideas and mentions another three additional points, more directly related to Spain's integration in the EC.

First, there is a difference between common policies of the EC and other means of community action which, in spite of their designation, do not achieve the rank of common policies. The EC trade policy is a common policy in the strict sense of the word, since the Member States have transferred sovereignty to the EC institutions which now have full powers in this matter. That is why the Member States may not apply a common policy on their own, apart from the principles and practices that shape EC laws on trade matters. In this sense, trade policy would be part of a group of common policies (as, for instance, those dealing with agriculture, iron and steel industries, nuclear power or fisheries), and it would be different from other EC action where the main approach is based on the legislation of the Member States (such as social, environmental or research policies and technological development). The difference between the former and the latter is not merely formal, since it starts from a rather precise concept of economic integration in which priority is given to certain aspects of economic activity, pertinent to trade among others, and leaving for later stages other aspects less related with market integration.

It is well known that the so-called 'Founding Fathers' of the EC assigned to trade the main role as the stimulus of economic development; that is why they liberalized it as much as possible between the Member States and why, simultaneously, they established a common protection system in relation to external trade, so that no individual Member State could set up a trade policy different from the others. This obviously implies a series of restrictions, stemming mainly from a loss of sovereignty on trade matters; it may, however, also imply advantages. As might be expected, growth in inter-community trade was, from the quantitative point of view, much higher than the EC's external trade and world trade; it may be inferred that this greatly contributed to the economic growth of the EC. From a harder to specify qualitative point of view, there are various theoretical and empirical studies which point out the advantages of commercial and productive specialization, fostered by a reduction – even if it is partial – in the level of protection against foreign trade.

The development of trade between industries and other phenomena of economic integration are at the centre of the advantages offered by a process of economic integration in general, and certainly by the EC's in particular, independently of the answer later given to another, no less important, question: how to share the advantages or profits of economic integration. Particularly relevant to this is the reallocation of resources derived from changes in trade policy adopted by the Member States that participate in the process of integration. It may be that the existence of these advantages is enough to justify the choice of the trade policy as a common policy for the EC, and, perhaps, the very existence of these advantages has allowed the Member States to transfer important shares of national sovereignty to the EC institutions, which may not be the case in less commercial areas of economic activity.

The role of the common trade policy

Secondly, the central role of the common trade policy in the EC's system of foreign relations must be emphasized, though it is obvious that the common trade policy is not the only means of action on foreign relations. Later in this chapter we shall classify the different areas into which the EC's foreign policies may be divided, for analytical purposes. It should be remembered here that the third part of the Single Act is devoted to the establishment of a series of provisions on European cooperation in matters of foreign policy, enlarging the framework of the EC's external action. This will become more important in future.

Thirdly, we note the peculiar configuration of EC trade policy, from a theoretical point of view and in its technical organization and operation. It is not a general policy, but rather discriminatory, applied with different intensity to third countries or to groups of non-community countries.

In reviewing the first of these points, remember the distinction which arises from the first articles of the Treaty of Rome, the distinction between EC policies and Member States' legislation. In order to do this, however, it may also be interesting to bear in mind the general purposes of the EC and its instrumental aims, as reflected in its founding texts, since this clarifies their basis as well as the debates over EC foreign relations. The Treaty of Rome, for instance, dwells on the need to contribute to the balanced growth of world trade, but it also mentions the association of the EC with overseas countries. These are two points that really seem to contradict each other. In accordance with the first of them, the Community has chosen liberalism in matters of trade as a general acting principle. Under the second point, the EC has decided to favour some countries: its colonies, to be specific. This apparently double standard is the origin of the preferential trade system that the EC has been adopting and developing for over 30 years. This preferential trade agreement, together with common protection against external countries, shapes EC trade policy, which is the first of four areas of action for EC foreign relations.

The EC's four areas of foreign relations

The four areas of action for EC foreign relations might be described as follows: the institutional area, the strictly commercial area (trade policy), cooperation with developing countries (EC development policy) and the mutual implications of the EC's domestic and foreign policies. These four areas (the second and third ones fundamentally, but not exclusively) are closely related.

With respect to the first area, the EC institutions jointly represent the EC's interests to the rest of the world. Fundamentally, this is a diplomatic task (the third-party countries have representatives in Brussels, while the EC has accredited delegates in some countries outside the EC); but this, in turn, implies the presence of the EC institutions in the main forums where the problems of the world economy are debated, from the GATT and the OECD to the summit meetings of the more industrialized countries (attended by the Chairman of the EC Commission).

This first institutional area will undergo important modification in the course of the coming years, as the political cooperation instruments established in Title III of the Single European Act come into force. One of the central purposes of this political cooperation established under the Single Act consists of the progressive application of a common or single foreign policy. In this context, some decisions on Central America, the Middle East and South Africa have drawn on the community spirit of consensus.

The other side of the coin, however, and because, in matters of foreign relations, political cooperation has to be adopted unanimously, is that such events as the invasion of Panama by the United States army must be, at the very least, mentioned. The British government acted in advance of the remaining Member States, showing a position favourable to the United States, thus pre-empting the adoption of a common European position different from its own. Faced with such action, we might wonder whether political cooperation established by the Single Act is not in serious danger of turning into a gag or a corset that prevents the EC as a whole from adopting common positions on matters of fundamental international importance. It would even be possible to add that if Europe, both the EC and Eastern

Europe, does not define its own position, the position of the world as a whole will continue to be dictated – with no opposition – from the United States, while the EC, imprisoned in its need to adopt unanimous positions, will be unable to argue with its main Western ally. The second and third of the areas of the EC's foreign relations, that is, trade and cooperation for development, will be considered later in the chapter.

The fourth area into which the EC's system of foreign relations has been divided for analytical purposes, is complex, due to the fact that it deals with the links between the domestic policies of the EC and its foreign policies. In connection with this, it should be remembered that the EC may accept commitments that are legally binding on the Member States in matters of foreign policy and that, due to the common legal regulations of the EC, its institutions have implicit responsibility for all those areas for which they already have internal responsibility. It is this perhaps, which, together with the problems arising in or magnified by the economic crisis, will give us a better understanding of the dual purpose which governs the EC's foreign policies, combining, on one hand, a liberal trade philosophy and, on the other, a series of protectionist and often restrictive measures for its own trade. More often than not, trade policy is used to protect sensitive products or those for which competition might cause serious trouble in some depressed or failing regions of the EC. But it is also a question of discriminating between third countries when these restrictions are established, to cause less damage to the developing countries considered 'preferred' (or 'associated', in the old terminology). These considerations may also be seen when reviewing, no matter how briefly, those elements that form the common trade policy.

The components of the common trade policy

The EC's trade policy includes, on one hand, a segment known as autonomous trade policy, formed by:

- a customs law;
- a variable protection system within the national borders;
- a general set of import and export rules;
- a set of trade defence measures; and
- the generalized preference system (which the EC itself prioritizes among its instruments to aid development).

It also includes, on the other hand, a second segment known as conventional trade policy, which incorporates a series of multilateral and bilateral agreements, as well as several agreements on trade in specific products (fundamentally a textiles or multifibre agreement and agreements on trade in basic products). The multilateral agreements include the Lomé Agreement, linking the European Community with sixty-nine countries in Africa, the Caribbean and the Pacific (ACP). Among the bilateral agreements are those signed with the various countries in the Mediterranean basin, but also those with nations in Asia and Latin America. There are also agreements with developed countries, most importantly those signed with EFTA.

The EC's trade policy may also be analysed from a geographical perspective. In this case the agreement binding the EC to the EFTA countries might be mentioned first. It is a set of preferential and reciprocal trade agreements, establishing an area of free trade for industrial production between the twelve countries of the EC and the six countries which form EFTA. The remaining developed countries (members of OECD) have not entered into similar agreements with the EC and are thus lower in the hierarchy regulating the external trade of the EC.

The EC maintains a continuous trade war with the other two great commercial powers in the world, that is, the USA and Japan, some of whose episodes make the front pages of the newspapers where, as may be easily understood, journalists often give them much more importance than they really have if they are compared with the complete picture of trade between the EC and the United States or Japan.

The countries of Eastern Europe, the COMECON countries, are in a very special situation. Until recently, there was little more than a set of rules that partially deregulated trade of some specific products. In 1988 the EC and the trading countries of Eastern Europe entered a new stage which, at last, started with the mutual recognition of both groups of countries. The German Democratic Republic had a particular position among these nations, different to that of the other COMECON partners, since it was relatively free to exchange products with the FRG. It appears that the GDR had an occasional 'back-door' access to the EC, as if it were another Member State, because of its customs relationship with FRG. The reunification of Germany finally solved this question. It is evident that the course taken by the Eastern European economies will have decisive influence on the shaping of a new framework of relations between the EC and the non-OECD European countries.

Relations with developing countries

Having broadly dealt with relations between the developed countries and those which, until recently, might have been termed 'socialist', 'centrally planned' or, simply, of 'Statal trading', we next examine the EC's relations with the developing countries. Organized as pyramid of EC trading preferences, these countries would be ranked as follows: ACP countries first, the Mediterranean countries next, and, forming the base of the pyramid, all other countries that benefit from the generalized preference system (in Asia and Latin America fundamentally).

As is known, the ACP countries, which signed the Lomé IV Agreement, are mostly former colonies of European countries, and enjoy three types of measures for economic and social development, as mentioned in the Treaty of Rome itself. Trading measures will be mentioned first, as most of their products enjoy duty-free access to the EC. There are also some instruments, called STABEX and SYSMIN, used to stabilize their income from exports, which enable the transference of resources from EC funds to those developing countries when their export income falls below a certain level, based on income in previous years. Specific resources, secondly, are channelled by the European Development Fund and by the European Investment Bank, which grant the ACP countries credits at better-than-market terms and foster the development of the economic infrastructure of these nations. These are, therefore, measures specifically aimed to help development, which are complemented by bilateral cooperation measures individually undertaken at will by each Member State. The third measure to be mentioned consists of joint ACP–EC institutions, whose responsibility is to supervise the application of the agreements signed by the parties.

The privileged situation of those countries signing the Lomé Agreement does not only arise from an altruistic EC spirit. There is also a wish to keep and, perhaps, to enlarge a set of markets which are not very significant as yet from the point of view of demand (although they could become so in the future), but whose greater importance lies in the fact that they may offer important raw materials to some EC industries. Privileged links with these countries are encouraged, to define positions relative to the other two great world trade powers.

The countries which lie along the Mediterranean benefit from the measures included in the so-called EC Mediterranean policy launched in 1972 to give coherence to the different agreements signed with each of the Mediterranean countries (with the exceptions of Libya and Albania). Even though there are some differences between the Mediterranean countries themselves, generally they enjoy a series of trade advantages less important than those applied to the ACP countries (customs duty ceiling and quantitative contingents are stricter) and a set of measures leading to cooperation for development less significant than those taken into account in the Lomé Agreements.

There is no doubt that the Mediterranean is a strategic area for Europe; most Europeans are very aware of this, as are the other great powers. If, however, EC policy in the Mediterranean area is analysed in detail from its origin in the 1960s, the conclusion may be that the EC does not seem always to have been guided by the same basic guidelines. It seems as if the EC has been carried away periodically by its need to renew the existing agreements with each one of its Mediterranean partners, always having to be very careful that the others would not feel discriminated against and demand to be treated in the same manner as the most privileged Mediterranean country. All of this has led to a rather complex situation which will, nevertheless, continue to be applied as long as the Mediterranean countries and the EC are interested in fostering bilateral trade.

However, in the short term it does not seem possible to think of deepening EC relations with the Mediterranean countries. On one hand, because the EC's main focus of attention is now addressed towards the building of its own internal market and, later, towards the rest of the countries on the continent of Europe. On the other hand, because a deepening of these relations should be based on the progressive constitution of a free trade area between the EC and its Mediterranean partners, which does not seem feasible as long as the Mediterranean countries do not agree among themselves. The recent agreements between the Maghreb countries are, no doubt, an element to be kept very much in mind for mid-term purposes, as long, of course, as the political, social and religious evolution of the Arab world is not a hindrance to closer EC links with these countries.

Relationship with non-preferential countries

It would seem, finally, that most Asiatic and Latin American countries form the base of the pyramid. They are the poor relations, the forgotten ones in the EC's programme of foreign relations, benefiting only from the general trade preferences offered by the Generalized Preference System, receiving also a lesser amount of resources to promote development. And, as may be more important with respect to the future, it does not appear that this situation will change easily in the coming years. On one hand, because the EC's system of preferential relations is already too consolidated to admit new countries. And on the other, because these preferential relations are aimed at countries with a very different level of economic development, which already maintain important economic and political relations with other industrial powers.

The EC, however, urged perhaps by the Iberian countries, might consider the merits of reducing the differences between these nations and the previously mentioned group – even if, for the time being, it were only more *de facto* than *de iure*.

Some remarks on the incidence of the EC system of foreign relations

This brief presentation of a wide problem ends with three thoughts for debate or reflection relevant to possible modifications to the EC system of foreign relations and to their role in a country like Spain. On one hand, there is a new spirit introduced by the Single Act in the EC system of foreign relations. On the other, we find the influence which the adoption of EC law might have on Spanish external trade. Finally, Spanish policy on cooperation with developing countries might have to undergo modifications as a consequence of the new EC framework to which it will have to adapt itself in an increasingly uncompromising manner.

Bearing in mind the peculiar drafting of Title III of the Single Act, which could also be reviewed after the conclusion of the intergovernmental conferences between the EC countries – convened in December 1990 – it might be concluded that, up to a point, the first important step in the EC integration process has, in fact, been taken in matters of foreign relations. The final purpose is that the EC increasingly expresses itself with a single voice to the rest of the world and defends its political, strategic and economic (even military) interests 'as if it were one single land'. This is a decisive step, which should logically be adopted with the remaining provisions of the Single Act. What is, perhaps, curious – and this may lead to reflection – is the fact that foreign policy has been so decisively chosen as the first area in which the EC is beginning to step from economic to political integration. This stems not only from a need to define its own identity in terms of the external space. It is also a necessary step resulting from the process of EC integration. This may be a controversial opinion and one may even disagree with the geopolitical and military implications of this decision, given that, as is also well known, the Single Act mentions NATO and the WEU (Western European Union) for the first time in the history of EC documents, reminding readers that European political union cannot ignore the commitments signed by the developed Western countries within the framework of these defence organizations.

Some considerations on the possible evolution of Spanish external trade

In order to analyse the hypothetical future evolution of Spanish external trade yet further, one might start from a basic assumption. If Spain were to apply the EC rules in trade matters, Spanish external trade might resemble the rest of the EC partners more closely. This may seem a simplistic assumption, but there is no doubt that, taken with certain precautions, it may be an efficient way of changing Spain with regard to the probable behaviour of external trade. It may be especially efficient if one considers that there is no reason why the harmonization of Spanish and EC trade structures should be total, much less mechanical, although certainly some approximation – hard to specify – will have to take place between countries that are about to shape a common market and which apply the same commercial laws in their relations with the rest of the world.

We cannot dwell here on the complete data for Spanish trade. Nor can we consider a complete sectoral breakdown (let us simply remember the peculiar configuration of the Spanish trade deficit, at least in connection with energy and high technology products). Lastly, we cannot analyse the geographical breakdown of the Spanish economy (direction of trade flows) with sufficient detail. But two points are relevant here. For instance, the six EFTA countries hardly represent 4% of the Spanish external trade, while the corresponding figure is greater than 10% for the EC. By contrast, at the end of the 1980s, Latin America represented around 3% of the EC external trade, but a much higher figure of Spanish external trade (over 6% of exports and almost twice of imports, although among the latter, practically half was accounted for by Mexican oil).

In the course of the last few years, the two chosen areas have shown different trends in this area. While the importance of EFTA's trade with Spain and the EC has increased, Spanish and EC trade with Latin America – for a variety of reasons – has shown a frankly unsatisfactory trend. The future is unpredictable, but it seems likely that Spain will increase its trading links with EFTA, as well as with those countries located at the top of the EC's preferential pyramid, in other words, with those of the ACP and the Mediterranean, because it will have to apply trade rules that favour those nations over the others. Simultaneously, and since the combination of these groups may supply Spain with some products which, until now, were purchased from other countries – Latin America, for instance – it does not seem illogical to think that the Spanish–Latin American trade may be negatively affected, even though the significance of this damage cannot be measured strictly.

Another, harder to specify, matter is whether this hypothetical decrease of trade with Latin America will only affect Spanish external trade. Until now, Spain has not been too open to the outside world. As the degree of external exposure is increasing, imports from all over the world – including Latin America – may also increase, although the percentage of increase for this part of the world may be smaller. Because of this, it may happen that the overall figures of trade with Latin America are not affected, even though they may lose relative to Spanish total trade.

If the problem is approached from a wider and, no doubt, less pessimistic point of view, Latin America could increase its sales to the rest of Europe, which would amply compensate for the hypothetical relative reduction of trade with Spain.

Final remarks on Spain's options about the new definition of some elements of the EC's development policy

We conclude with a very brief mention of the Spanish policy of cooperation with developing countries. It is evident that the EC policy on this topic is conditioned, to say the least, by historical and political considerations. It is also clear, although perhaps not quite so obvious, that the EC development policy is often used as a compensatory tool for the imbalance generated by EC trade with its associated developing countries. Is there anything that Spain could do in this area?

As a first option, Spain could increase its aid to developing countries which, as is the case of Latin America, might be harmed by Spain's entry into the EC, if the importance of these previously mentioned hypothetical biases is, indeed, confirmed. As a second option, Spain could simply take over the EC area dealing with trade and aid to development matters. In principle, this possibility does not seem to be harmful for Spain, since it would give comparative benefits to countries with a very large trade volume with Spain, both from the qualitative and quantitative sides. Spain may, for instance, have markets of fundamental importance in the Mediterranean basin (in North Africa, to be specific – although the Persian Gulf also has a relevant role), which might well be consolidated and enlarged if the Spanish authorities would add their weight to the EC's Mediterranean policy, instead of hampering it. A third option for Spain would be (along with Portugal and, perhaps, some other EC countries) to try to achieve a gradual reduction of the EC's levels of formal discrimination existing nowadays between Latin America and Asia and the ACP and Mediterranean countries. This option seems to be the most coherent with the non-discrimination principle found in the commitments signed by GATT; it could, however, find serious opposition within GATT itself, fundamentally from the United States. There are other problems as well (briefly mentioned already) that seem to hinder the development of EC – Latin America relations. They may be summed up under these three points.

- First of all, the level of consolidation of the EC's system of foreign relations, which makes it difficult to admit new preferential countries.
- Second, the strong links between Latin America and the USA.
- Third, the different economies and levels of development existing between the Latin American countries themselves, which makes a global approach to their problems practically impossible.

Central America – the isthmus – may be the exception here, as the EC seems to have become especially interested in this area over the last few years, from the beginning of this decade, to be specific. In this case, the fundamental problem lies in keeping peace in the area, which does not strictly depend on the EC, but which is a basic condition for the development of a more efficient policy of cooperation.

Needless to say, there may well be other options; it is, of course, hard to show clear support for any of them, even though some basic ideas may be expressed about them. On one hand, Spain must make an effort to enlarge its aid to development, while at the same time giving it greater scope, seeking to achieve an optimal level of economic and social efficiency in the receiving countries; it should not, however, limit its aid to development to an exclusively economic approach. The connection between the EC's trade and development policies is to be taken into account on this issue and may be taken, above all, as a point of reference when Spain designs and implements a genuine policy to aid development. On the other hand, Spain already has historical, cultural, political and economic commitments with Latin America, and these cannot be ignored; it seems therefore mandatory to make a serious effort within the EC institutions so that Latin America's exports may, *de facto* if not *de iure*, reach the European countries under the best possible conditions. It is obvious that this will not solve the problems of some countries, but it will at least allow them a better use of the possible advantages of international trade itself, and of the cooperation between developed and developing countries, through the use of international trade as the cornerstone for this cooperation.

References

Alonso, J.A. and V. Donoso (1989) 'Características y Estrategias de la Empresa Exportadora Española', Madrid. Instituto Español de Comercio Exterior.

Alvarez Gómez, J.M. (1985) *La Aduana en el Mercado Común*, Madrid, Banco Exterior de España.

Benavides, P. (1986) *La Política Comercial Común*, Madrid, Trivium.

Comunidad Europea (1990) 'Trece Años de Cooperación al Desarrollo con los PVD de Asia y América Latina', 10 May.

El Agraa, A.M. (1990) *The Economics of the European Community*, Philip Allan.

ICE, (1985) 'La Nueva CEE', *Información Comercial Española.* No. 626–8.

Nieto Solís, J.A. (1989) 'España y América Latina ante las Políticas Exteriores de la CE', *Pensamiento Iberoaméricano*, No. 15.

—— (1990) *Introducción a la Economía de la Comunidad Europea*, Madrid, Siglo XXI.

OECD, 1990: *Coopération pour le Développement*, Paris.

Parlamento Europeo (1988): *Fichas Técnicas sobre el P.E. y las Actividades de la Comunidad*, Luxembourg.

PEE (1985) 'La Nueva CE', *Papeles de la Economía Española*, No. 25.

Ruesga, S.M. (1989) *1993: España ante el Mercado Unico*, Pirámide, Madrid.

Chapter 13

Spanish security policy

José Luis Buhigas Viqueira

Because EC Security Law is at an incipient and controversial stage, a cause and effect relationship which would allow us to determine any advantages or disadvantages of Spanish entry does not as yet exist. But by indirect means a fairly reliable evaluation may be made; Spain's admittance to the Atlantic Alliance, for instance, or the Western European Union (WEU), neither of which could really have taken place if Spain had not become a partner in the EC. At any rate, the peculiarities of the Spanish model and its late entry into European democratic institutions make it necessary to refer to modern Spanish history as the only means of understanding the present Spanish security policy.

Background

In the last two centuries, Spain has eschewed democratic traditions, with the exception of short and confused periods such as the Second Republic. But now the country is living through the longest period of peaceful democratic coexistence in its modern history. The last two centuries of Spain's history have been dotted with civil strife and with a complete absence of external relationships, once the last colonies were definitely lost. Spain's non-participation in the two World Wars shaped a complete heritage of international isolation and coined an erroneous concept of Spanish neutrality. The fact is that Franco's Spain did not ally itself with the Axis powers, as would have been its wish, thanks to the Regime's foresight. Nor was there any real neutrality in the years following the war, since Franco, in order to break Spain's isolation, aligned himself unconditionally with the United States. This for long caused a feeling rejection in Spain's left wing, which could not understand how an American regime which had contributed in such a decisive manner to freeing Europe from neo-fascist totalitarianism could allow the consolidation of an authoritarian government. And herein lay one of the elements which differentiated Spanish and European public opinion towards the United States when, having recovered democracy after Franco's death, membership in the Atlantic Alliance was proposed.

The main characteristic of the onset of the *democratic transition* in Spain was the idea of a consensus between all political forces, which set all divergences aside in order to give priority to a peaceful and stable transition into democracy. Among the implicitly set-aside topics was membership in the Atlantic Alliance, which was delayed until the process of reforms had consolidated. In exchange for this, the forces which in 1975 were against NATO did not question the continuity of the bilateral relationship with the United States with some minor changes. What was sought was to preserve the existing balance, in favour of the stability of emerging democracy.

In February 1981, the then President J. Calvo Sotelo, announced the proposed entry to the Atlantic Alliance, believing that democracy had already become consolidated. Two days later, the failed coup of 23 February wholly denied such a statement. In September of that same year, the Parliament gave the green light to membership of NATO, but one month later, the Socialist victory in the elections froze the whole process of entry. President Gonzalez' government adopted a new approach to Spanish NATO membership, on the basis of a series of political priorities, whose common denominator was, and still is, Spain's clearly European vocation.

The government produced a statement about security policy in Spain in 1984. It contained a new approach which, initially, had been contrary to permanent membership of NATO and does not contain a censure against the Treaty of Washington, as this was a point of consensus among the parliamentary political forces, with the exception of the Spanish Communist Party (PCE). However, the wish not to become integrated into the NATO Military Structure was still maintained. In connection with the United States, the bilateral relationship option continued, oriented towards a progressive reduction of the US Armed Forces on Spanish territory and of their support facilities. The principle of a non-nuclear Spain was also kept and, for the time being, signing the Non-Proliferation Treaty (NPT) was not deemed to be necessary, although its future realization was not excluded. The wish to participate in the Western European Union was then expressed, although the expected results of Spanish integration in the EEC had yet to be evaluated.

Spain entered the EC on 1 January 1986, with a consultative referendum about Spanish permanence in NATO, called for 12 March 1986 hanging over its head like the sword of Damocles.

The link between these two topics was implicit in the discussion. Although it was true that no legal or causal tie existed between these events, it was obvious that things would have been extremely difficult, not to say untenable, if the 'noes' had won. The government's argument was, in fact, based on the necessary solidarity with the other allied countries, with which Spain shared a democratic system, a growing economic integration and a vision of European union. The referendum, although of a consultive character and not binding as far as the government was concerned, was indeed morally binding and, as such, entailed great risks which seem hard for a foreign observer to understand. It was the first time that a key foreign policy decision had been subject to a referendum, and there was a risk of a chain reaction in Europe if the result had been negative. Seen in perspective and given the historical background, there is no doubt that the referendum was a risky, albeit unavoidable, decision. With public opinion totally divided only a referendum was able to close this page of history in a non-traumatic manner. The referendum, with 52% of votes in favour and 39% against, gave a green light to the participation model proposed by the government. It may be stated that, without a doubt, the Spanish democratic transition ended on 12 March 1986; after this date, it entered a stage of normality and harmony with the remainder of the European partners.

Once the double membership – in the EC and in the Atlantic Alliance – was consolidated, the government set out on a new stage in the definition of its security policy, and new priorities were established in April 1987, when, starting with the double premise of its membership of the EC and of NATO, it started along the road which will, someday, make it feasible for Spain to have a positive role in European security. In this context, Spain decided to make a significant defensive contribution within the Atlantic Alliance, without participation in its integrated military structure. Inside the framework of relations with the United States, a substantial reduction of the North American military presence in Spain was planned. The government announced the process of joining the NPT, renouncing any manufacture of nuclear weapons and maintaining the prohibition of installing, storing or introducing such weapons into Spanish territory. Finally, the government insisted on its wish to enter the WEU if this organization revitalized itself, so as to develop a European security policy.

To carry this programme out, Spain joined the NPT in 1987 and renegotiated the bilateral treaty with the United States, under conditions which were approved by the Congress in 1989 with the foreseen terms of reduction (30% reduction of human resources and a stepped exit of 72 F-16 aircraft from the Torrejon Air Base). It also negotiated Spain's level of participation in the Alliance, by means of the relevant cooperation agreements which exclude membership of the Integrated Military Structure. On 14 December 1988, Spain signed the Protocol of Membership in the Western European Union, thus completing the process which might be called the constituent element of the Spanish security policy as designed in the famous 1984 statement. Since that moment, having normalized its participation in every Western security forum, Spain has been actively participating and cooperating in international security and *détente* within new security patterns at lower levels and with a climate of loyalty towards its partners and allies.

Spain's incorporation in the process of European integration and its firm vision for Europe could serve to modify the delegitimatizing perception held by an important group of young people with respect to the role of the armed forces. There are two different traditions in Europe: the British and French tradition, where, aside from the political consensus, there exists a social consensus around the role of the armed forces, granting them an important legitimacy; and the German and Spanish tradition, where there is a recent and growing trend towards 'pacifism', perceived as an increase in conscientious objection, in which political consensus has no correlation with social consensus.

In Europe, Spanish public opinion is the most favourable towards ceding sovereignty on the birth of a supranational structure; it is logical, therefore, that if the legitimacy of the new emerging model is accepted, the legitimacy of a new defence model, resulting from the former, must also be accepted. It is then foreseeable that, parallel with the process of consolidation of the new State, a system of defence will be born, separated from the delegitimatized models of the state-nation, which will receive the benefits of the new EC legitimacy; as a consequence, the emerging defence system would have to be as complex as the state structure to which it would be subordinated.

This transition stage presented the chance of carrying out two key purposes within a new EC defence policy: first, to recover the civic values of military service, giving greater emphasis to its positive aspect, the right to do it, than to its negative value, duty. A common European programme, aiming at greater social support for the new defence model, would be a useful measure intellectually to isolate the opponents. Second, to prevent at any cost the rebirth of national defence policies which would have had disastrous consequences in a historical period which witnessed the emergence of problems that had been frozen since the Treaty of Yalta and which had already been the cause of two World Wars. Another important milestone in Spanish security policy was its participation, under the safeguard of the United Nations mandate, in the multinational forces in the Gulf War. This was the first time Spain had broken its historical isolationism.

One of the lessons that Spain learned at European level during the Gulf War was the need to reinforce the path towards political union. As Jacques Delors stated, 'Europe is an economic giant, a political dwarf and a military larva'. The war has shown that there is a close link between those three elements, so that, without a suitable military back-up, diplomatic action is highly deficient in times of crisis. The ideal instrument for this European goal could well be the WEU, which, in order to be able to serve its European political vocation efficiently, will have to undergo a process of militarization, in the positive sense of the word. It is not a good thing to militarize civil societies, but it is absurd that a European alliance with defence goals should lack any suitable military means to perform its functions. It is therefore urgent to create a European identity in matters of security and defence, in order to complement and rebalance relationships across the Atlantic, reinforcing the stability of the new world order and enlarging the voice of Europe in the concert of nations.

To achieve this, it is essential to join in the common goal of a common defence policy within the Treaty of Political Union. Until 1996, the WEU should be responsible for the management of common defence, at the Union's expense. That date, two years before the deferment of the Brussels Modified Treaty, would be appropriate to take stock and to review the different viewpoints on the basis of the accumulated experience. The

European defence identity should evolve in a gradual manner, not subsidiary to the Atlantic Alliance, but complementing it, maintaining a relationship of coherence and transparency and taking into account that its final purpose is globality.

To conclude, it is possible to state that Spain's membership in the EC has served the purpose of firmly anchoring our country on the side of democratic countries, of abandoning our falsely neutral secular attitude of isolation, which seems to be the common denominator of the inward-looking sector of the right wing and of certain nostalgic elements of the left wing. Membership has firmly settled our political stability and has established a democratic framework of consensus along the larger lines of our foreign and security policy.

On the other hand, membership has had the virtue of strengthening the Spanish position in its bilateral relations with North Africa, making it easier to hold initiatives such as a Security and Cooperation in the Mediterranean Conference, whose goals are to prevent political, economic and social lack of stability in the South degenerating into lack of stability for the whole of Europe; this requires a preventative policy, able to correct the foreseeable effects of such instability before it develops.

From the security point of view, there is no doubt that entry into the EC, with everything this means, has noticeably improved Spain's position in this matter, without any weighty counterbalance. The balance, thus, is frankly positive. The only possible objection would be that there still remains a long way to go before this European identity of security and defence becomes a reality.

PART III: SOCIAL AND CULTURAL POLICY

Cooordinator: Amparo Almarcha Barbado

Social policy

Rafaela Alonso Rodríguez

A brief analysis of Spain's social policy shows that, given the range of sectors that would be favoured, two goals to take into account are the following:

(1) Improving equal opportunities and policies leading to social equality.
(2) The development of social protection policies and compensatory policies in connection with every group affected by deficiencies or shortages, whether they are of an economic, social or cultural nature.

Equal opportunities

Children

Let us now consider this group's social reality. Children are a relatively small social group but the state and public attention is increasingly focused on them. In 1988, the Spanish population was of 38,891,313 inhabitants, out of which 22.25% were children. In 1990, this age group numbered 8,106,000, only 20.65% of the total population. Spain ranks second in demographic growth in the EC, with a young population whose rate of growth is moderate (in comparison with other EC countries).

Andalusia, The Canary Islands, Ceuta, Melilla, Murcia-Valencia and Madrid have the highest population of children in Spain. The majority of the child population lives in urban areas (65.3%). This is the reason why child poverty is important, given the fact that it is far greater in urban areas, due to the importance of this group in ordinary life, both in the processes of urbanization and the redistribution of physical and social spaces.

Parliament has promoted campaigns and programmes to stop, treat and prevent child abuse and begging. The International Youth and Childhood Commission has been created and an Integral Children's Plan has been implemented to collect contributions from every State administration and to grant special attention to the needier social sectors and children's groups. Campaigns aimed at equality for children have the following goals:

- To develop civil rights for children, giving them more importance and responsibility in deciding their own identity and future.
- To focus social rights on the needier groups, to improve the quality of life and social status of children, and to demand greater quality in social services of every kind.

Youth

In this field, the main goal is social and labour integration, training and preparation for work, improvement of the quality of life and association among young people, as well as developing the positive aspects of youth.

The number of young people living on their own has gone down since 1984, while those who stay with their families or share living quarters with others are relatively more numerous. A tenth of unmarried young people live outside their parents' home, and a fifth of married couples have not yet established an independent home.

Various administrative departments foster job promotion, vocational training, reform of the educational system and, above all, an increase in school scholarship numbers and funding. The Instituto de la Juventud (Youth Institute) has granted priority to the following:

- Exchanges within Europe and international cooperation.
- Youth clubs.
- Establishing a service network for young people.

Women

In Spain, the status of women is going through a process of profound change within the social structure, due to the fact that more and more women are entering the employment market. Women's employment in paid jobs is changing; they no longer have to leave their jobs to take care of children, since the Statute of Workers and the Law of Public Servcies now grants them the right to maintain their job seniority. It is also true that, as the level of education increases, employment and job-holding increase and unemployment decreases. Cultural and social changes, essential to achieve women's adaptation to the requirements of a modern economy, have affected the relationship between the sexes, families and demographic patterns.

On the other hand, battered women, prostitutes and women in prison now have less protection. The Instituto de la Mujer (Institute of Women) is working to create direct programmes and services for women, especially these marginalised women. As a result of this line of action, a network of centres for advice and information to women has been created for battered women. Vocational training programmes have also been created, and a campaign held to promote jobs for women who are alone or have family responsibilities.

A plan for equal treatment for men and women has been approved. A network of about eighty women's associations was created throughout the whole country, which, through a consultant commission, works on the implementation of the equal opportunities plan. This principle of equality is part of the Spanish Constitution, allowing Spanish women to have the same rights as all other women in the more advanced States of the EC. The Spanish legal system has been adapted to take account of this in matters relevant to employment and to the penal code.

Social protection and integration

The elderly

The policy to be followed is one of protection, but it is also hoped to give greater participation and importance of this group of citizens. It has been estimated that there will be between five and six million people over 65 years of age in the year 2000, 15.1% of the total population. In 1988, to take care of the increased needs, there were 2.04 places in old people's homes for each 100 older citizens, while sheltered accommodation had risen from two in 1982 to ten in 1989. Geriatric care programmes are now being implemented, to improve the general health and welfare of those using these centres. They offer assistance and preventative medicine, rehabilitation, etc.

As to home care, conventional links are being maintained, guaranteeing domestic help (cooking, personal hygiene, etc.), as well as psycho-social and other support. Extra help could be provided in the form of family assistance, day care homes or centres, technical and economic aids, and spas.

The handicapped

The State is expected to develop a policy of prevention, treatment, rehabilitation and integration for the physically, mentally and sensorially handicapped, who will receive all the specialized care they require and will be specially protected in the enjoyment of every right granted to all citizens.

Refugees and those granted political asylum

In 1978, Spain joined the 1951 Convention on the Statute of Refugees, as well as the 1967 Protocol, and became one of the democratic States of the international community offering asylum. The programme for refugees and for persons granted political asylum was established under Law 5/84, which regulates the right to asylum and the status of refugees, R.D. 511/85, and approves the regulations for its application. The services granted relate to emergency and reception work, health care, periodic aid, legal advice and other assistance. In 1986, 9,273 people received help through the programme, and this number went up to 11,651 in 1989. The main purpose of this programme is to develop State policy for this group of persons, granting them the assistance they may need until their request for the status of refugees or of being granted asylum has been resolved and their status has been recognized.

Conclusion

A family policy has been followed since 1988, with special attention to single-parent homes. Family policy in Europe is oriented towards a growing recognition of the role of women and family in society and in employment. The present demographic tendencies and the evolution of the family structure have created certain vulnerable groups. In 1989, legislation connected with the status of children, dealing with violence within families was passed (Protection of Children's Rights). In 1991, a synthesis of all the above topics was carried out, giving special attention to the problems of poverty and marginalization.

Chapter 14

The working population

María Pilar Alcobendas Tirado

Human resources and the labour movement

This chapter presents an evaluation of Spain's membership in the EC with respect to social policy, and especially of its effect on the working population. The following items will be taken into account:

— the adaptation of Spanish legislation to the main social policy Directives,
— the trends in the working population, both employed and unemployed,
— developments in labour contracts,
— subsidies from the European Social Fund for training and contracts,
— the Community Programme for Equal Opportunities for Women and its influence on Spanish equal opportunities policy.

Adapting Spanish legislation to EC Directives on free movement of labour and social policy

As Spain's policy on the free movement of labour and social policies is broadly in agreement with the main EC Directives, Spanish legislation has only undergone minor modification and enhancement since 1986, in order to adapt itself to EC demands.

As a consequence of Spain's admission to the EC, and in order to fulfil Directives 68/360 and 72/194, pertaining to movement of Member States' workers and to the right to work abroad, provisions have been adopted which were previously unnecessary. These provisions are Royal Decree 1099/86, on entry, permanence and work in Spain for EC citizens, as well as Royal Decrees 119/86 and 116/88, to approve and amend the implementing Regulations of the Ley Orgánica (Organic Law) 7/85, on Rights and Freedoms of Foreigners in Spain.

Adapting Spanish legislation to the main social policy Directives has meant complementing the already existing legislation relative to Directives 76/207 on equal opportunities for men and women on access to employment and 79/007, on equal opportunities for men and women in matters of social security; this has been accomplished by means of the Ministerial Order 1105/88 and Law 3/89. This law extends maternity leave to six weeks and establishes a set of measures to promote equal treatment for working women.

In order to adjust the Spanish legislation to Directive 88/108, for the protection of workers against risks arising from a noisy environment and to Directive 88/364 banning the use of specific agents, Royal Decrees 1316/89 and 88/90 have also been adopted. The first deals with measures to protect workers against noisy environments and the second bans some agents or some activities to ensure the protection of workers against carcinogens. There have not been any new provisions issued in relation to Directive 75/129, which deals with collective dismissals, to Directive 77/187 on workers' rights in the event of transfer of a company's ownership, to Directive 78/117 on equal wages, or to Directive 89/987 on workers' protection in the case of an employer's insolvency, since the legislation existing in Spain before its entry to the EC was already in agreement with those Directives. Directive 89/048 on recognition of academic degrees and Directive 89/391 on improvement in safety and health of workers in their place of work need legislative adjustment.

To summarize, it may be pointed out that Spain's entry to the EC has meant the adoption of new provisions to complement Spanish labour legislation; this may be positively evaluated, as it increases workers' protection and labour rights.

Trends in the working population, both employed and unemployed

Between 1985 and 1990, the Spanish working population maintained a steady annual growth. While in 1985 the total number of the working population represented a total of 13,541,500, by 1990 this group had gone up to 14,992,400, which meant an increase from 47.4% to 49.4% of the total population over 16 years of age. A similar increase may be seen in the employed population. The redundancies that had occurred from the middle of the 1970s stopped in 1985. As of 1986, the number of people employed increased, from 10,822,400 in that year to 12,481,900 in 1990. The number of jobs created during that period was 1,661,500. The rate of employment went from 37.0% to 41.1%, and this increase affected men and women equally, although the latter had a much lower rate of employment than men. Thus, while the rate of employment was 58.6% for men, it was only 24.9% for women. See Tables 14.1 and 14.2.

The growth shown in the employed population was not the same in different economic sectors. While the agricultural sector lost nearly 351,300 jobs between 1985 and 1990, the service sector increased by 1,470,900. The industrial and construction sectors also experienced job creation (see Table 14.3).

It is obvious, however, that Spain's entry into the EC has meant the

Table 14.1 Trends in working population; persons in employment and unemployed persons ('000s)

	Working population	Employed	Unemployed
1985	13,541.5	10,570.7	2,970.8
1986	13,781.2	10,820.4	2,960.8
1987	14,297.8	11,355.4	2,942.5
1988	14,620.5	11,772.7	2,847.9
1989	14,819.1	12,258.3	2,560.8
1990*	14,992.4	12,481.9	2,510.4

* First quarter

Source: Ministerio de Trabajo y Seguridad Social, *Boletín de Estadísticas Laborales*, No. 73, July 1990.

Table 14.2 Trends in activity, employment and unemployment rates

	Activity rate	Employment rate	Unemployment rate
1985	47.4	37.0	21.9
1986	47.7	37.4	21.5
1987	48.8	38.7	20.6
1988	49.1	39.5	19.5
1989	49.1	40.6	17.3
1990*	49.4	41.1	16.7

* First quarter

Source: As in Table 14.1.

Table 14.3 Distribution of persons in employment by sector ('000s)

	Agricultural	Industry	Construction	Services
1985	1,925.9	2,589.0	769.9	5,285.9
1986	1,740.6	2,631.9	827.0	5,621.0
1987	1,718.2	2,746.2	925.1	5,965.9
1988	1,694.2	2,803.9	1,020.3	6,254.2
1989	1,597.9	2,898.0	1,133.9	6,628.5
1990*	1,574.6	2,981.4	1,174.2	6,751.8

* First quarter

Source: As in Table 14.1.

Table 14.4 Activities whose rates of employment have increased ('000s)

	1986	1987	1988	1989
Agriculture	1,344.4	1,247.8	1,117.2	1,036.8
Fishing	102.1	105.9	102.8	101.7
Coal Mining	48.5	44.4	41.8	42.3
Mineral Mining	37.0	33.5	36.1	32.3
Textile Industry	175.7	171.2	172.4	162.5
Leather Industry	31.2	30.6	30.6	30.0

Source: As in Table 14.1.

restructuring of certain economic activities, with a decrease in the level of employment connected with them. Agriculture, fishing, coal mining, mineral mining, textile and leather industries are the fields of activity where numbers of jobs have decreased, meaning that Spain's admission to the EC has been negative for employment levels in these activities (see Table 14.4).

The number of unemployed persons in Spain gradually grew from the middle of the 1970s; it reached 2,970,800 by the year 1985, which meant a rate of unemployment of 21.9%. Registered unemployment gradually decreased since that date to a total of 2,510,400 in the first quarter of 1990, or a rate of 16.7%. (see Table 14.2). This decrease in the rate of unemployment benefited men more than women. In 1985 the rate of unemployment for men was 20.5% and 25.5% for women, while in 1990 these rates were 12.5% and 24.8% respectively.

Although it may be said that unemployment is slowly decreasing, it nevertheless has a tendency to remain the same or to worsen for some specific groups. In 1985, 34.4% of the unemployed had been in that situation for a period of over two years, and this group rose to 40.2% in 1989. These figures are worse where women are concerned: in 1989, 46.5% of the female unemployed population had been jobless for more than two years.

Development of labour contracts

In the course of the period under consideration, the creation of new jobs has been enhanced by different programmes to encourage employment, implemented by the government since 1985 in order to control the high unemployment rates. These programmes have meant a remarkable increase in temporary labour contracts, part-time contracts and contracts for in-job training and practice. In 1985, the total of contracts filed under employment-fostering programmes was 1,056,039, while in 1989 this figure rose to 2,290,448. It may be stated that the cost of this rise in the number of jobs has been an increase in precarious contracts and employment, as the various trade unions have been quick to point out. In 1987, the Active Population Survey for the first time makes a distinction between permanent and short-

Table 14.5 Employees by type of contract ('000s)

	Permanent	Short-term	Total	Percentage on short-term contracts
1987	6,377.4	2,139.8	8,517.2	25.1
1988	6,527.3	1,613.0	8,140.3	19.8
1989	6,478.6	2,545.2	9,023.8	28.2
1990	6,458.1	2,667.2	9,125.3	29.2

Source: Author's own elaboration on the *Encuesta de Población Activa.* Data from 1987, 1988 and 1989 are relevant to the 4th quarter, while those from 1990 are for the 1st quarter.

term contracts; the wage-earning employed population on short-term contracts was only 25.1%. This proportion rose to 28.2% during the same period – the fourth quarter – in 1989, and it reached 29.2% during the first quarter of 1990 (see Table 14.5). This new flexibility in contracts may be considered to have ambivalent effects, since it has brought about a decrease in unemployment, while simultaneously generating an uncertainty in the situation of workers.

Subsidies from the European Social Fund for training and contracts

Between 1986 and 1989, Spain received subsidies of ECU 1,861 million from the European Social Fund. When Spain was admitted to the EC in 1986, the subsidy was ECU 358 million; this amount increased in successive years, reaching in 1989 a total of ECU 556 million.

As to where and how subsidies have been applied, it must be emphasized that training activities have taken priority over contracts. In 1986 and 1987 68% and 69% of the subsidies were for training, rising to 79% and 75% respectively for the years of 1988 and 1989. For each of the four years under consideration, the number of beneficiaries was about 500,000.

In evaluating the effects of Spain's entry in the EC, it is clear that the subsidies from the European Social Fund have been very positive, assisting 2,109,404 beneficiaries (Domínguez, 1989).

EC programme for equal opportunities for women and its influence on Spanish policy of equal opportunities

The purpose of the Plan for Equal Opportunities for Women, approved by the Spanish Government for 1987–90, was the constitutional development of non-discrimination by gender, to increase women's access to education and culture, to protect their health, to incorporate them into the labour market without discrimination, to reallocate family responsibilities and to improve the protection of especially needy women's groups (Instituto de la Mujer, 1990). This Plan drew on the mid-term (1986–90) EC Programme for Equal Opportunities for Women; it was the subject of special congratulations from the European Parliament on work situation resolution for women of Spain and Portugal.

In the course of implementing this Plan for Equal Opportunities for Women, some other legislative measures pertinent to employment and social policy were adopted, including the following:

- Extension of maternity/paternity leave to sixteen weeks and one year unpaid leave of absence to take care of children (Law 3/89, 3 March 1989).
- Classification of sexual harassment at work as a misdemeanour and, as such, the availability of legal redress (Law 3/89, 3 March 1989).
- In claims of discrimination at work, the employer, and not the employee, will have the burden of proof of non-discrimination (Law 7/89, 12 April 1989).
- Classification of employer's discrimination offences, terming them as very serious both in relation to access to the job and to working conditions (Law 8/88, 7 April, 1988).

These and other achievements of the Plan, coordinated by the Instituto de la Mujer, are the effective crystallization of some of the measures and actions proposed in the EC Programme, whose existence should be considered as a positive encouragement to action by the different Member States.

Conclusion

It would be a dangerous simplification to consider the entry of Spain into the EC as the sole cause of the trends in its working population and social policy. It may be, however, inferred from this brief study that, in general, Spain's entry to the EC should be considered positive, although the precarious conditions of employment and the loss of jobs in specific fields of activity are the negative counterparts of a process whose acid test will come with the working out of the Single Market.

References

European Community Commission (1986) 'Equal Opportunities for Women: Mid-term (1986–90) Community Programme', *European Community Bulletin*, Supplement 3/86.

Domínguez, Aurora (1989) 'El Fondo Social Europeo y España', *Revista de Economía y Sociología del Trabajo*, No. 4/5, pp. 59–72.

Instituto de la Mujer (1990) *Plan para la Igualdad de Oportunidades para las Mujeres* (follow-up report).
Instituto Español de Estadística, *Encuesta de Población Activa*, detailed results, 4th quarter, years 1987, 1988, 1989; 1st quarter for 1990.
Ministerio de Trabajo y Seguridad Social (1990) *Boletín de Estadísticas Laborales*, No. 73, July 1990.

Chapter 15

Industrial relations and trade unions

Sergio Santillán

Spanish trade unions always wholeheartedly supported Spain's entry into the EC, knowing that this would cause problems and meant taking risks, but fully convinced that it was the right course to take. It meant that Spanish society and its institutions would have to undergo a profound process of change, which, naturally, would also affect trade unions. Within an integrated and strongly competitive market economy, the transference of State sovereignty has given trade union action a new dimension. Before some conclusions can be reached about this new scenario, the characteristics of the current state of European integration, as well as its effects on industrial relations, must be mentioned.

The challenge of the Single Market

In one of his recent works, José María Zufiaur, leader of the Spanish UGT trade union, stated that 'the challenge posed to trade unions by the Single Market is emerging with well-defined contours', and pointed to some specific effects of this; in summary, he mentions the following:

The centre of decisions is moving further away and companies are acquiring supra-national dimensions.

The implementation, on one hand, of the 279 White Book proposals addressing free movement of capital, people, goods and services, will give Brussels a great deal of decision-making power. On the other hand, the process of company concentration, mergers and take-overs, which is already under way (among the largest 1,000 companies, these operations have gone up from 29 in 1983–4 to 197 in 1988–9), means that more and more of them will be transnational, that decisions and strategies will be defined at European level, and that workers' rights, unless the present situation is modified, will only be controlled by domestic laws and agreements.

Market logic imposes industrial re-structuring, whose social consequences will be deeply felt, and which will not be balanced by trade union power or EC control.

The growth of international markets will unavoidably be accompanied by a large amount of sector and company restructuring. The enlarged market will be competitive in the international arena, but will also affect the country itself, unleashing a ruthless battle among companies (European or otherwise) seeking to ensure their own market quotas. There is no doubt that this process will affect employment, the professions and regional development. It may also be accompanied by a progressive dismantling of so-called offensive EC policies, oriented towards steel and iron manufacture, shipbuilding or agriculture. Quota liberalization and the reinforcement of control over national aid to steel and iron industries, for instance, were two of those policies. As a countermeasure, trade unions have been insistently demanding social, industrial and regional development measures, to prevent, accompany and govern those processes.

Community integration is being carried out simultaneously with monetary union, which, in the absence of other policies, will mean greater damage to economic and social cohesion.

EC integration policy pivots on Economic and Monetary Union (EMU), which has been given the role of driving the other policies. Without the effective coordination of the economic policies of the Member States, without guidelines for common policies (CAP, transport integration, environment, research and development) towards regional development and the correction of regional imbalance, without a suitable fiscal policy, one which is harmonized and just, EMU will tend to exaggerate regional differences and the more degrading and socially evil forms of competition.

The rebuilding of an EC 'social space' is being given a secondary, even residual place, without guaranteeing that its implantation will be simultaneous with the introduction of the Single Market.

In the course of a third of a century of Community life, social matters have always been given residual importance, even in the text of the Treaties themselves. In respect of social rules and policies, the balance of those years has been a very disappointing one indeed.

Although trade unions did not feel excessively enthusiastic about it, the Community Charter on Fundamental Rights, approved by the Strasbourg Summit in 1989, was a step forward. But the implementation of its forty-seven measures, sharply opposed to the White Book, is encountering great difficulties. The Commission's 1990 Action Plan, in fact, did not fulfil its deadline, and 1991 seemed to go the same way. Firm entrepreneurial opposition, lack of political will on the part of some governments and the legal weakness of the Treaties themselves shaped the obstacles that prevented the establishment of a social dimension in the Community.

The political will to build a 'common economic and social space' in the Community, an expectation backed by the trade union movement and by the majority of social and political forces continuously trips over a decision-taking institutional system vitiated by the requirement for a unanimous vote and by the lack of democratic institutions to govern the European integration process from the standpoint of collective interests.

The limits of a single-dimension Community project, the economic-monetary one, are increasingly evident. Whether it is a question of adopting a balanced development policy, of establishing a set of social rules, of answering new demands from those Eastern European countries entering into democracy, or of playing a distinct role in the world, the exclusive suit of clothes that the Single Market is wearing is turning out to be too close-fitting for wear in the 'Common House' for Europeans, even Community Europeans.

If social stresses, economic imbalances and untenable protectionist reactions are to be prevented, the very progress of this enlarged market is demanding advances into other fronts, particularly that of economic policy coordination (starting with budget policies) and that of reform of democratic institutions.

A great effort needs to be made

Within this framework, what is the possible outcome of Spain's entry into the EC in 1986? Even though it is still too early for definite evaluation, some unquestionably positive aspects can certainly be mentioned, beginning with the break up of the isolationism which dominated Spanish society for such a long time, and whose consequences were so negative.

The legislative *aggiornamento* which began at the end of the 1970s has been accelerated. Since entry, the economy has registered high rates of growth – 4.7% annual cumulative growth between 1985 and 1989. The production system has experienced much modernization and renewal, and a slight reduction has occurred in the gap between Spanish income and the Community partners' average.

Problems, however, have also been perceived. As a consequence of having to face a gradual process of customs tariff reduction without a sufficiently competitive industry, the commercial balance of trade has suffered. Regional differences remain, and the various indicators show that the distance from more developed countries is still the same.

With Ireland and other regions in the south of Europe, Spain shares a series of features among which unequal social structures, old-fashioned economic structures and low levels of per capita income may be mentioned. A low activity rate may also be perceived (especially in the case of women) and an important differential in matters of social protection. An unemployment rate that affects 15% of the working population should be added to all the above, as well as an educational and professional training system still not suited to the needs of the enlarged internal market.

In order to face this situation in a resolute manner, there is no doubt that a great effort is required, focussing on the next few years and revolving around several fields of action. First, it is necessary to increase the level of *social protection* (Spanish expenditure on this, around 17% of the GNP, is 10 points below the Community average), and in order to do this we should increase pension coverage, increase unemployment insurance and family protection, universalize the right to receive a minimum income and improve health care. As a second step, priority should be granted to the *improvement of every level in the educational system*, and greater attention given to basic *vocational training* and on-the-job adult training. Thirdly, the rights of *workers to participate in companies* should also be increased through measures such as those that ensure the presence of control organizations to monitor the existence of information, consulting and bargaining powers for workers' committees, staff representatives and trade-union sections. A fourth point would deal with *taxation*, since Spain is still far from the Community standard, both in connection with the design of its tax system (unfair and regressive, since it is mainly levied on income from work), and with the taxing power itself, subject to a great disregard for rules, that is, to fraud. Finally, let us touch on *social legislation*, where common European regulations are imperative in matters of labour contracts, of equal treatment to men and women, working hours, minimum wages, on-the-job safety and health, the status of foreign workers, environmental conservation, etc. This is the goal of the Action Plan of the European Confederation of Trade Unions, based on fifteen groups of measures. The establishment of social regulations that take into account the highest levels of protection is a *sine qua non* condition to ensure harmonious Community development and to prevent the always latent possibility of less-developed countries using the practice of social dumping in order to try to increase their competitivity.

Let us now remember that Spanish trade unions are proposing action in every one of those fields. Their strategy is centred around the will to 'level upwards'. To do this, they demand a change in the guidelines for economic and social policies. All this explains the stress experienced in labour relations at this time. Although some of the agreements signed between trade unions and the government after the great general strike of 14 December 1988 brought about a certain amount of relaxation in a relationship that had broken down and was marked by serious confrontations, discrepancies still remained at the root of the matter.

On one hand, the Socialist government which came to power in 1982, in the midst of a serious economic crisis, applied a policy of adjustment to which the demands of social matters were subordinated. The fight against inflation and a reduction in the public deficit were given priority over the need to create jobs and to improve the status of less-favoured sectors. As a consequence of this, economic growth was not translated into a decrease in the gap between social indicators or, at least, not in the measure that might be required.

We find, on the other hand, a debate about the competitivity of the economy. After more than a decade of wage moderation, trade unions felt that possibilities had run out in this field, and that competitivity should be fostered through ways that respect European social culture: improvement of infrastructure, investment in technology, higher quality in goods and services, better qualified workers and employers, etc. Trade unions would no longer accept that competitivity be raised through a further lowering of already sufficiently competitive wage costs, or through the maintenance of a legal framework of labour contracts that has resulted in 31.5% of workers being employed on a casual basis.

Repercussions for trade unions

At a time when the international practice was veering towards day-to-day trade-union action, the situation described above gave Spanish trade unions the will to support the establishment of an overall European Trade Union strongly. Faced with the process of EC integration, trade union power is limited or non-existent if union activities are restricted to the national territory. In industrial democracies, trade unions use collective bargaining procedures to exert their influence on decisions between workers and employers, as well as exerting pressure on government to have social measures issued and implemented. None of these things could happen in the EC, where no framework existed to make collective bargaining possible, where a minimum social regulation, applicable to every one of its Member States did not exist, and where only little influence might be exerted because the EC institutions (Parliament, Commission) did not have real political power.

Meanwhile we do not have a real European Trade Union, capable of taking strike action or of bargaining for fair collective agreements. Thus, and as a matter of priority, it is essential to establish the conditions for a true European Trade Union, by means of:

- Strengthening the European Confederation of Trade Unions; in order to do this, national trade unions must transfer an important part of their competences.
- Achieving political union.
- Reforming the constitutive Treaties in order to clarify or enlarge the Commission's competence and to remove the rule of unanimous agreement on every social question.
- In opposition to the almost exclusively monetary dimension being given to European integration, implementing the simultaneous establishment of the social dimension.

— Establishing a legal framework to make it possible to have sectoral collective bargaining in the European sphere.
— Requiring the existence of European Workers' Committees in multinational companies operating in the EC.
— Preparing common trade union policies.

Secondly, relations between trade unions must be improved. A reinforcement of the movement towards unity, fundamentally between the two largest Spanish trade unions, Unión General de Trabajadores (General Workers' Union, or UGT) and Comisiones Obreras (Workers Commissions, or CCOO) is quite likely, because it is clearly impossible for a trade union acting independently to undertake the tasks listed above. Furthermore, the very fact of wishing for a common European Trade Union movement makes it compulsory to be coherent and maintain the same criteria within the national borders. It must be also taken into account, when dealing with this matter, that the status of Spanish trade unions has undergone a great evolution in the course of the last few years. Trade union behaviour is no longer influenced by political strategies (this being the main cause for past divisions), but by trade-union needs for efficiency. Finally, both trade unions are perfectly conscious that they will hardly be able to increase their low rate of membership in a climate of confrontation.

Thirdly, in the field of collective bargaining when the country's economic policy is, and will become even more, strongly conditioned by economic and monetary union, wage agreements no longer are the central component of collective bargaining. A deep qualitative change in the contents of agreements, with much greater emphasis on questions such as on-the-job health and safety, the protection of casual workers, the reunification of the labour market, vocational training, the participation of workers in the introduction of new technology, is already beginning to manifest itself.

References

European Community Commission (1990) 'Las regiones de la década de los 90'. *Fourth Periodic Report on the Socioeconomic Status and Evolution of the Community Regions*, COM (90), 609 end, Brussels, 9 January.

European Trade Union Confederation (1988) *VI Congress Resolutions*, Stockholm.

Instituto Sindical de Estudios, (1977–87, 1988 and 1984). 'Informes sobre evolución social en España'.

Ministerio de Trabajo y Seguridad Social (1990a) 'La Política Social Comunitaria', *Revista de Economía y Sociología del Trabajo*, Nos. 4/5.

—— (1990b) *Política Social de la Comunidad Europea* (3 volumes).

Zufiaur, José Maria (1993) 'Mercado Unico y Acción Sindical' *Revista de Economía y Sociología del Trabajo*, (forthcoming).

Chapter 16

Health and social welfare policies

Benjamín González Rodríguez and Ana González Fernández

In 1989 the Spanish population was some 39 million inhabitants, distributed over 504,450 sq. km. In numbers, the Spanish population was fifth among the EC countries. Its total fertility rate was 1.38, second to last on this indicator. The birth rate per thousand inhabitants was 10.7, one of the lowest figures in the EC, and net migration was negative.

Spain's entry into the EC meant a sort of 'injection' of youth, although it must be taken into account that natural growth trends were strongly downwards in Spain (from 13.1 per thousand in 1960 to 2.5 in 1988). Young people, aged from 0 to 14 years, form 21% of the population, with only Ireland and Portugal having higher numbers.

Life expectancy at birth is 73.1 years for males and 79.6 for females. This situation, favourable to Spain, is, among other factors, due to the fact that the infant mortality rate has decreased considerably and furthermore that the survival rate for the aged has increased. This life expectancy is the highest in the EC, except that of French women, which is slightly higher. The infant mortality rate is of 8.1 per thousand, which puts Spain in the fifth lowest place in the Community.

As far as causes of mortality are concerned, Spain follows the guidelines of the other EC countries; slightly over two thirds of deaths result from cardiovascular diseases and cancer (46 and 21%, respectively). Other causes for death are respiratory diseases (9%), digestive system diseases (5%) and external causes (5%). Traffic and industrial accidents are of special importance in Spain, as well as occupational diseases. Infectious diseases, following the pattern elsewhere in the EC, have been replaced by chronic and degenerative processes, in accordance with growing life expectancy and the progressive ageing of the population.

Habits and life styles offer the following profile: (1) 54% of males and 20% of females are smokers; (2) 32% lead sedentary lives and 62% are totally inactive during their leisure time; (3) alcohol consumption leads to a high rate of cirrhosis of the liver and traffic accidents, and this habit has a greater incidence among poorer persons and those with a lower level of education and occupation. The percentage of heavy drinkers was almost 4% of the total of persons interviewed in the Encuesta Nacional de la Salud (National Health Survey).

From the point of view of health resources, the first thing that should be mentioned is that Spain, together with Italy and France, was in 1988 the EC country that had least inhabitants per physician. But the inhabitants per nurse ratio was 260, which was one of the lowest figures in Europe. The number of persons per hospital bed was 185; only Portugal, with 195, had a higher number. Thus, Spain had an excess of physicians and not enough nursing staff or hospital beds. Total health expenditure for 1988 was only higher than that of Greece and Portugal.

Health policy

Spain is undergoing a process of health decentralization, which implies a re-organization of the Spanish national health system. Our country has joined the WHO European Regional Office programmes, 'Health for All in the Year 2000'. As in other EC countries, a document has been prepared in connection with this, *Strategies of Health for All in Spain.* The key elements of Spanish health policy are oriented towards (1) an increasingly equitable distribution of services; (2) intersectoral cooperation and community participation; and (3) service re-orientation towards primary health care. The operational schematic of health planning may be seen in Figure 16.1:

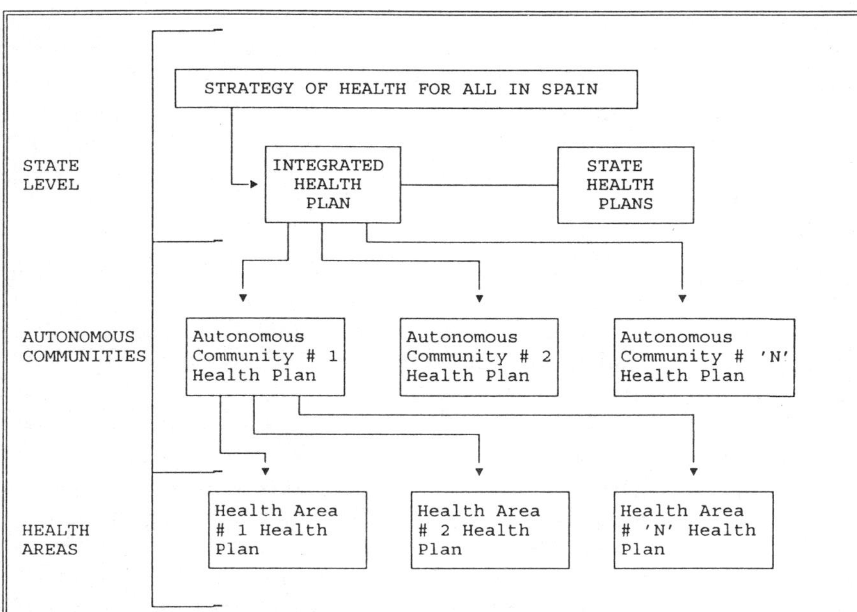

Figure 16.1 State health planning

Legal foundations

The Spanish health system is governed by the General Health Law 14/1986, of 25 April 1986 (*BOE* 29 April 1986), which follows these general principles, established under the Spanish Constitution (Article 43): (1) integral health; (2) health for all; (3) citizen's participation; (4) health education; and (5) patient's rights. In accordance with this Health Law, the Spanish health system is formed by all the health structures and services in existence at State and Autonomous Community level. On the other hand, each Autonomous Community has its own health service, which includes all facilities, services and centres in that Community, including all the county authorities, town councils and any other existing territorial administration.

The basic units that form the health system of the Autonomous Communities are the health areas, and the management of centres and programmes is implemented around them. Their average population is 200,000 to 250,000 inhabitants. Each of these areas, in turn, is made up of basic health areas, which are the territorial units for primary care, starting from the health centres, which are staffed by multidisciplinary teams.

Functional structure of the health system

In accordance with the Health Law (Article 46) the National Health Service features the following: (1) services may be used by every member of the population; (2) the system will be responsible for organizing integral health care (promotion, prevention, treatment and rehabilitation); (3) all health resources must be coordinated and integrated; (4) costs of the services will be paid by the government, by the users' contributions and by payment for specific services; (5) the State will warrant the quality of integral care, which will be evaluated and controlled.

Following the administrative decentralization process, responsibility for health matters is shared by the State, the Autonomous Communities and the local authorities. State responsibilities focus on foreign relations' aspects of health, high-level inspection, environmental health, and food and drug control. The responsibilities of the Autonomous Communities are determined by their respective statutes of autonomy. Every one of the Communities already has full competence over health promotion, prevention and education. Full control of health services management and administration, however, has only been transferred to Catalonia, Andalusia, Valencia and the Basque Country. Full transference is being prepared for the remaining Communities. Although the General Health Law has decreased the responsibilities of the local authorities, they still have important roles to fulfil, such as environmental health control, public health protection with respect to industry, commerce and services, transport, noise and vibration levels, buildings, hotels, schools, leisure and sports areas, food and beverage distribution and transport, cemeteries and funeral parlours, etc.

As a whole, health care is given to the population through four main networks: (1) Instituto Nacional de la Salud (Social Security), INSALUD; (2) Territorial Administration Network (Autonomous Communities, Deputations, Island Councils and Town Councils); (3) Military Health Services (Ministry of Defence); (4) Muface, Mumpal and Isfas, health insurance agencies for civil servants in central administration, municipal councils and the armed forces, respectively.

Approximately 99% of the population is covered by the public health system, thus fulfilling the Constitutional principle of the right of all the population to health. The 1% not included are those in the highest socio-economic levels of society, who can afford private health services.

Regarding health and social security financing, the following may be mentioned. (1) social security spending amounts to more than 70% of the total; (2) in 1988, total health care expenditure in Spain represented 6.34% of the GNP; (3) 79% of the total amount spent on health care was through the public sector, and about 21% through the private sector.

Gains and losses

As for any other Member State, Spain's entry into the EC will mean certain costs and a set of benefits. We shall now mention some of the most important ones.

Costs

1. If the health system's inputs and outputs are taken into account, the balance may be negative from the point of view of outputs, if measured in terms of indicators such as life expectancy and infant mortality. In both indicators, Spain occupies one of the best positions. Possibly, with EC membership, a change in life-style in the medium and long term will mean a change in eating habits. The adoption of European eating habits would mean a cost in that it would probably have negative health consequences, derived from the loss of the Mediterranean diet. From that perspective, the Spanish case emphasizes the hypothesis that higher health expenditure is not necessarily accompanied by better health, as reflected in the imbalance between inputs (low physical, human and financial resources) and outputs (relatively high level of population health).
2. Bearing in mind the harmonization required by EC membership, it is to be expected that Spain's expenditure on health will noticeably increase, especially as a result of drug prices.
3. Thus, Spain will have to divert a large increase in its GNP percentage to health matters, in order to become comparable to the EC average.

4. The establishment of free movement of professionals will allow health professionals from the EC to work in Spain, thus increasing the relatively high rate of medical unemployment that already exists in our country.

Benefits

1. Spain's entry into the EC may promote greater control of environmental and labour health policies, following the application of Community regulations.
2. When carried out, harmonization of medical specialties will be useful.
3. Spain's entry into the EC has meant a remarkable upsurge in R&D activities. Spain is already participating in various European programmes: cancer, AIDS and drug addiction, for instance. Other initiatives have been started, such as a campaign against cardiovascular diseases, consumer protection, regulation of pharmaceutical products and biomedical research.
4. Spain is maintaining bilateral relations with several European countries on matters of scientific and technical cooperation in the field of health.

To conclude, in terms of cost/benefit, the global evaluation of Spain's EC membership must be considered as positive, from the point of view of the health system, although repercussions will be possibly greater in other sectors.

Social protection

In matters of social security and of social protection in general, Spain's entry into the EC has not brought about any significant changes, nor could it cause them, since Community provisions in this area are simply intended to coordinate the concurrent application of the legislation of different Member State applying to migrant workers, and have not, as yet, tried to unify this legislation.[1]

Protective action and its scope

The idea underlying every social protection system is that the day-to-day needs of individuals should be covered:

— By each household using the income that one or several of its members obtain, primarily from their work, and, secondarily, from their savings; and
— When households are not capable of satisfying their needs, whether due

to excessive burden or a lack of income, society as a whole should step in, through the State or specialized institutions.

Protective action materializes as services, which may take three forms: (a) social relief; (b) social services; and (c) tax relief granted to individuals, with the same purpose as social relief. The same situations are protected in each EC country, with slight variations: ill health, family burdens, housing, psychiatric and physical handicaps, disabilities, unemployment, old age and poverty.

The social protection effort

Table 16.1 presents the main figures for: (a) Gross National Product at market prices (GNP mp) per inhabitant, in ECUs; (b) the total social protection expenditure per inhabitant in ECUs and as a percentage of GNP

Table 16.1 Social protection expenses in the EC countries per inhabitant (1985)

Countries	GNP mp* (ECUs)	Effective social protection expenditure (ECUs)	Effective social protection expenditure As % of GNPmp	Inferred social protection expenditure† As % of GNPmp	Inferred social protection expenditure† At PPP‡
Belgium§	9,862.7	2,894.9	29.4	28.2	3,351
Denmark	15,002.5	4,130.2	27.5	31.1	3,966
France§	10,812.3	3,076.9	28.5	28.9	3,271
German FR	13,483.1	3,785.8	28.1	30.5	3,944
Greece	4,392.3	—	—	17.9	—
Ireland	6,839.7	1,637.0	23.9	24.4	1,867
Italy	9,738.4	2,279.0	23.4	28.1	2,803
Luxembourg	12,795.4	3,183.2	24.9	30.1	3,781
Netherlands	11,447.8	3,577.4	31.2	29.4	4,078
Portugal§	2,388.8	374.9	15.7	—	735
Spain	5,611.0	1,222.2	20.0	21.8	1,764
UK§	9,565.0	2,318.0	24.2	27.9	2,805

* 'GNP mp' = Gross National Product at market prices.

† Linear correlation between GNP mp per inhabitant and social protection revenue expenditure per inhabitant is determined in ECUs, according to SEEPROS.

‡ PPP = Purchasing Power Parity, equivalent to a weighted ECU in relation to purchasing power in each country's currency.

§ For Belgium and the UK, data are from 1984; for Portugal, 1982; and for France, 1983.

Source: Eurostat, 'Système Européen de statistiques integrées'.

per head and (c) social protection expenses per inhabitant at purchasing power parity (PPP).

In 1985, the GNP mp per inhabitant was ECU 2,655.5 in Portugal and ECU 5,611.0 in Spain; that is, 17% – in the case of Portugal – and 37.4% – in the case of Spain – of Denmark's. In the same way, Greece's GNP mp was 29.3% and Ireland's 45.6% of Denmark's. These four countries are noticeably poorer than the remaining EC countries.[2] Under these circumstances, even if the poorer countries should assign to social protection the same portion of their GNP mp as the wealthier countries, the results, as far as the level of protection is concerned, would be lower.

Apart from that, however, the poorer the country, the smaller is the percentage of its GNP mp that it can give to social protection. Thus, the column headed 'Inferred social protection expenditure' (Table 16.1), explains this phenomenon. In fact, only the most prosperous countries may devote important sums to social protection or, in other words, only the most prosperous countries can allow themselves the luxury of being fairer. If this hypothesis is well defined, it turns out that in 1985 Denmark, with the largest sum for social protection per inhabitant (ECU 4,130.2 and 27.5% of its GNP mp) would be below its capacity (31.1% of its GNP mp), while Portugal, in 1982, would have made a comparatively larger effort, given its GNP mp per inhabitant, to achieve its modest social protection expenditure of ECU 374.9 per inhabitant.

There are two versions in Spain: the first gives computed social protection figures, which do not include the expenditure of Autonomous Communities, local authorities, social protection organizations, and companies or non-profit making private organizations; and second, which adds estimates for these missing data. According to the second version, in 1985 Spain spent a figure equivalent to 20% of its GNP mp (as opposed to the computed 17.7%), which is a slightly lower percentage than the 'inferred' one: 21.8%. Only two EC countries were above their capacity that year: the Netherlands and Belgium.

Because social protection, especially that granted in money, should be measured in accordance with its purchasing power, it is essential to translate its amount to a common Purchasing Power Parity (PPP) fraction. Thus it is possible to see that, in 1985, the total Spanish social protection expenditure per inhabitant,[3] when expressed in ECUs, was the equivalent of 27.2% of the Danish expenditure, while that same year the amount of its social protection expenditure per inhabitant, expressed in PPP, was approximately 44.5% of that of Denmark, also in PPP.

Level of social protection

Apart from the overall amount seen in Table 16.1, some indicators show that the differences between EC countries in levels of social protection are very noticeable, as well as their allocation being very different. In Spain, expenditure per inhabitant, as classified by SEEPROS, for illness, disability, maternity, industrial accidents and industrial diseases[4] may be taken as indicators of the level of protection in health matters; the extreme difference here is of 4.9 to 1 between Germany and Portugal. Using the weighted average of the countries under consideration, the level of social protection in Spain is 65.5% of this average for money allocated in unemployment benefits to registered unemployed persons, 60.3% in money allocated to old age pensions for people 65 years of age or over; 47.2% for various health services per inhabitant and of 9.4% in family benefits per children under 15 years of age. The total amount destined to social protection per inhabitant is 58.8% of the EC weighted average (Eurostat, 1988).

The difference in social protection

When social protection amounts were first included with the rest of the EC countries' statistics and made public, it was discovered that Spain had the second lowest social cover (17.4% of the GNP) in the EC. Spanish social protection differs from the EC average: (1) in terms of resources: (2) in terms of loans. In terms of resources, this difference, measured in relation to GNP, is indicated in Table 16.2. Incomes also, although they have increased, are lower in 1990 than the EC average.

Table 16.2 Social protection in terms of percentage of GNP, 1980 and 1990

	Incomes		Expenditure	
	1980	1990	1980	1990
Spain	15.7	18.4	15.6	18.0
EC average	26.9	27.2	24.9	25.6
Difference	−11.2	−8.8	−9.3	−7.6

Source: COM (88), 655. Eurostat, 1984–90.

As far as social allocation is concerned, in 1990, the benefits were distributed as indicated in Table 16.3, and although their growth has been higher than that of the Community, the total is still lower than the EC's.

For Spain, these data make the following clear:

— The social differential between Spain and the EC is still significant as far as allocation is concerned.
— Family benefits are noteworthy: in 1990 in Spain they were only 5.2% of the European average, and were the lowest in the Community.
— The EC trend in social protection expenditure is decreasing (−1.5) instead of increasing, as is happening in the cases of Spain (0.6) or

Table 16.3 How benefits were allocated in 1990

	Health loans	Retirement pensions (old-age and subsistence)	Family aid (maternity and family benefits)	Unemployment benefit	Others
Spain	33.4	48.5	1.5	16.3	0.2
EC average	37.5	44.3	7.7	7.4	3.1
Difference	−4.1	+4.2	−6.2	+11.1	−2.9

Source: Eurostat, 1990.

Greece (0.1); this is doubtless due to an endeavour to compensate for the perceived deficits.

— It should be finally mentioned that INEM funds[5] have significantly increased in Spain, and they are already higher than Pts. 1 billion since 1987, although the unemployment loans still do not reach the European average; in 1990, they amounted to Pts. 3,445 per person in Spain, while the EC average was of Pts. 4,669 for the same year.

Notes

1. The data on protection were drawn from the EC statistical office for 1985, but a statistic is still missing which inhibits comparison; limitations of space and the short time of EC membership mean that only a general scenario can be presented.
2. In six of the twelve EC Member States, the social protection expenditure per inhabitant, expressed in ECUs, is higher than the Portuguese GNP per inhabitant.
3. The social protection expenditure is the sum of the allocated expenses plus administrative expenses and other revenue expenditures.
4. These refer to reimbursements for health care expenses; preventive medicine; various grants (for private schooling; house rentals; transport for the handicapped; migrant workers; telephone expenses, or help to the destitute and drug addicts), free food distribution (Eurostat, 1989).
5. Data from the Consejo General del INEM (Instituto Nacional de Empleo, National Employment Institute), on 6 December 1990.

References

Banco Mundial, (1990) *Informe sobre el desarrollo mundial 1990 La pobreza, Indicadores del desarrollo mundial*, Washington, DC, IBRD.

Bosch Domenech, A. and C. Escribano Saez (1989) *La Seguridad Social Española: Un Debate Inaplazable*, Madrid, Eudema.

Comision de la Comunidad Europea (1988) *Proyecciones a medio plazo de los gastos de proteccción social y de su financiación. Proyecciones con el horizonte de 1990. Informe de Síntesis*, Brussels, COM (88) 655.

Eurostat (1988) *Basic Statistics of the Community*, Luxembourg.

—— (1986) 'Système Européen des Statistiques Integrées de la Protection Sociale (SEEPROS). Récettes et dépenses courrants, 1970–1984', *Statistiques Rapides: Population et Conditions Sociales: 1986–2*, Luxembourg.

—— (1989), 'Système Européen des Statistiques Integrées de la Protection Sociale (SEEPROS). Récettes et dépenses courrants, 1970–1984' *Statistiques Rapides: Population et Conditions Sociales: 1989–2*, Luxembourg.

Gonzalez Rabanal, M.C. (1990) *Los problemas de la Seguridad Social Española*. Madrid, Tecnos.

Ministerio de Sanidad y Consumo, Secretaría General Técnica (1990) *Las instituciones sanitarias de ámbito europeo y su política*, Madrid.

—— Secretaría General Técnica (1990) *Indicadores de Salud*, Madrid.

—— Dirección General de Planificación Sanitaria, (1989) *The Spanish Health System: Highlights*, Madrid.

Ministerio de Trabajo y Seguridad Social (1989) *Anuario de Estadísticas Laborales, 1988*, Madrid.

OECD, (1985) *Measuring Health Care 1960–1983*, Paris.

—— (1987) *Financing and Delivering Health Care: A Comparative Analysis of OECD Countries*, Paris.

Oficina de Publicaciones Oficiales de las Comunidades Europeas (1990) *Eurostat, Estadísticas Demográficas 1990*, Luxembourg.

OIT (1984), *La Seguridad Social en la Perspectiva del año 2000*, Geneva.

Chapter 17

Equal treatment of women

Celia González Jorge and Amparo Almarcha Barbado

The coming of democracy and the 1978 Constitution brought important progress in the recognition of equality between men and women. These achievements became more noticeable in 1985–90, coinciding with Spain's access to the EC, which reinforced the progress of the policy to achieve the principle of equality between men and women. The great majority of specific claims for the rights of women by social movements and groups in 1976 have become a reality by 1990.

It is worth underlining that the main problem that concerns Spanish women, both then and now, is the discrimination to which they are subject in their work, and which is especially noticeable in their access to jobs, working conditions, promotion and vocational training. Women have a clear disadvantage in their participation in the work market and, when compared to men, they have to exert a greater effort in their careers.

If working women agree on anything, it is on the double workday they have to perform, for their families and for their jobs: household tasks are estimated to take three hours a day for working women, when they come home from work, whereas men are estimated to spend around half an hour a day in this way.

Public policies in favour of women

The promotion of policies whose goal is to achieve equality between the sexes, in accordance with Article 14 of the current Spanish Constitution of 1978, began with the ratification of the United Nations Convention of 18 December 1978 by the Spanish Parliament.[1] The development of this Convention, and of the Constitution itself, meant a series of legislative measures in civil, penal, labour and administrative matters, giving practically identical legal positions to both sexes, with the still current exception of succession to the throne.

Though formal equality of rights has been achieved, practical and concrete equality is still being sought. In order to do this, the United Nations and the Council of Europe recommended the creation of national organizations for the promotion of equality between men and women.[2] These national organizations should present so called 'positive action' policies, based in the philosophy that the mere removal of legal obstacles is not sufficient, but, rather, that active support to individuals and institutions whose clear aim is to achieve real equality of opportunities is required. The Spanish organization in charge of positive action in favour of women is the Institute for Women, part of the Ministry of Social Affairs. There are also some complementary organizations, under the responsibility of various Autonomous Communities.

Development of EC legislation for equal treatment of men and women

In its Article 119, the Treaty of Rome points out that all Member States should guarantee the application of the principle of equal pay for equal work for men and women. Until 1975, the so-called 'International Women's Year', however, the EC did not adopt a more active position. During the last few years, the EC has developed an important normative activity, and the principle of equal treatment of men and women has been placed as one of the basic principles governing the social policy of the Community. The role as interpreter of this process developed by the EC Court of Justice deserves to be mentioned, as well as the work of the Economic and Social Committee as a consultative body (Ministerio de Asuntos Sociales, Instituto de la Mujer, 1990b).

All approved Directives, Resolutions and Recommendations make it compulsory for all Member States to comply with the principle of equal treatment of men and women. These principles are summarized as follows:

(a) Directives (binding rules for all Member States):
   - Council Directive 75/117, concerning the principle of 'equal pay for equal work'.
   - Directive 76/207, concerning equal treatment by reason of civil or family status.
   - Directives 79/7 and 86/378, concerning equal treatment in social security regimes.
   - Directive 86/613, concerning equality in the exercise of autonomous activities, including agriculture.

(b) Other, lesser rules (non-binding) from different organizations of the EC, which confer supervisory and promotion powers on the national organizations, in education and access to vocational training and employment, especially in those sectors where women have little representation.

The influence of EC legislation over equal treatment in Spain

The EC Commission has established two plans for equality, the first of which covers the period of time between 1982 and 1985, and the second one from 1986 to 1990. In the course of the Second Plan, and in accordance with the Council of Ministers of 25 September 1987, Plan I of Equal Opportunities for Men and Women was applied in Spain from 1988 to 1990. The governing council of the Institute for Women was the body in charge of coordinating the implementation of the Plan, through an interministerial policy which encouraged its development and the performance of public awareness programmes and campaigns to achieve real equality between men and women.

The goals of Plan I for Equal Opportunities for Women (1988–90) were the following:

— To develop the Constitutional principle of non-discrimination for reasons of sex.
— To increase women's access to education and culture.
— To improve health protection among women.
— To achieve equality in access to employment and in working conditions.
— To promote fair distribution of family responsibilities.
— To increase social protection to especially needy women's groups.
— To encourage women's associations.
— To foster international solidarity with women of the Southern countries.

The Plan has laws, programmes and action in six areas: legal planning, family and social protection, education and employment, health, association and international cooperation.

In 1988–90, 96% of the action taken came to completion.[3] It contributed to the creation of a basic structure for the implementation of ministerial policies aimed at the development of the social role of women.

Areas of influence of the policy of equal treatment for men and women, both in the EC and in Spain

Employment and labour relations: The influence of EC regulations on matters of employment and labour relations in Spain, through Directives in 1975 (75/117/EC) and 1976 (76/207/EC)

In a short period of time, Spain has carried out important legislative amendments in matters of labour regulations, in order to develop the Constitution, and to bring Spanish law up to the same level as Community laws. The amendments to the Statute of Workers deserve special mention.

— Law 8/88, of 7 April, which classified employers' infringements through discrimination, which are qualified as very serious, both as regards to access to jobs and to working conditions, and established penalties between Pts. 500,000 and 15,000,000.

— Law 3/89, of 3 March, which extended maternity/paternity leave to sixteen weeks, and established measures which favour equal treatment at work. It regulates leaves of absence of at least one year from jobs in companies or public administration, to take care of children, without losing the job; and gives legal protection against sexual harassment.
— Law 7/1989, of 12 April, about Labour Procedure Basis, which reverses the burden of proof in cases of sex discrimination, so that the employer now has to present proof of the absence of discrimination.
— Royal Decree-Law 1/88, of 22 February, which regulates the recruitment of women to the armed forces.

Besides Directives, the Council of Europe ordained a series of Resolutions and Recommendations:

— Council Resolution on the promotion of equal opportunities for women (July 1982).
— Resolution on action leading to fight women's unemployment (June 1984).
— Recommendation to promote positive action in favour of women (December 1984).
— Resolution to promote equal opportunities for women (July 1986).
— Commission Recommendation on vocational training for women.

The EC Equality Plan (1986–90) has much influence on Plan I for Equal Opportunities for Women (1988–90), in Spain. This Plan I meant the development of legal measures and training programmes, especially aimed at women, to fight discrimination in access to jobs and in labour relations. Apart from the above legal advances, several other actions carried out in connection with these matters, with excellent results, should be mentioned (Ministerio de Asuntos Sociales, Instituto de la Mujer, 1990b).

— Agreement between the National Employment Institute and the Institute for Women, to prepare programmes for women with family responsibilities, for computer science training, pre-training for back-to-work programmes, self-employment and business creation.
— Training programme and hiring of women in professions with a low proportion of women.
— Agreements between the Ministry of Education and Science and the Ministry of Culture, Fisheries and Food, to teach vocational training courses.
— Professional guidance programmes in the Institute for Women.
— Programme to promote positive action in industry. In connection with the existing wage discrimination, it is estimated that in Spain women receive 20% less wages than men, for the same job (INE, 1990).

One third of this country's workers are women. This is nine points below the Community average, only better than that of Ireland. Women's unemployment rate has also experienced gradual increases, with youth as the most numerous group of sufferers. In 1982, the rate of female unemployment was around 19%, while in 1990 it had risen to 24%, the total being 16% (INE, 1990). Eurostat's last two statistics show that, although the unemployment rate is of 9.3% for the totality of the Community, women are more affected by it, with 12.2% against the 7.3% rate for the total working population. The Spanish rate of unemployment is the highest in the EC, significantly higher than the rest of the Member States (Eurostat, 1989). The reason for this increase in unemployment rates is bound up with the massive increase of women in the working population, especially young women looking for their first job, and older women going back to work, after taking care of their children.

A fact that has caused great concern is that most women who have entered the labour market in the last few years have done so on a casual basis. Women have the highest proportion of temporary workers, somewhat above 34% of the total wage-earners, while men have no more than 27%.

By sector of activity (agriculture, industry and services), Spanish women are especially centred around services (where they are 72.1% of workers), followed by industry (16.7%) and agriculture (10.1%). Within the service sector, the fields of activity are still those traditionally assigned to women: health, teaching, cleaning, dressmaking and catering.[4]

The National Plan for Vocational Training and Employment is the most important vocational training programme in Spain. In 1989, the number of pupils trained under this programme reached 349,229, 51% of whom were women, while in 1984 they did not even reach 30% of the total number. This strong increase of women's participation in vocational courses means that 35.5% of every 1,000 working women have had training, whereas for men the figure is only of 17.8%. This difference is an answer to the new policy of favouring women's entry into the labour market, especially in those professions where their presence is low, and in those sectors where future growth is expected to be highest (Ministerio de Asuntos Sociales, Instituto de la Mujer, 1990a). Several Occupational Training Programmes have been implemented through the National Training Plan; these programmes have been addressed to professions in which women are poorly represented, as well as to the return of women to the labour market and the promotion of women's participation in cooperative control and organization.[5] The population of trained women has gone from 72,614 in 1986 to 143,165 in 1989 (FIP Plan, 1984–9). The number of women trained in business schools has shot up; they were 9.6% of students in 1982, and in 1989 this percentage had risen to 48.9%. On the other hand, the proportion of women training in office and administrative work, textiles, nursing and beauty-care has fallen heavily, from 54.4% in 1985 to 29.27% in 1989.

One of the goals of the Equality Plan (1988–90) is to improve the situation of women in rural areas. The percentage of Spanish women working in agriculture was 10.1% of employed women in 1990. In 1984 this figure had been 16.2%. Spanish membership in the EC benefited this sector which, in a very short space of time, underwent a process of adaptation, especially in structural matters, in production and market orientation, as mentioned in the Equality Plan (1986–90).[6] The participation of rural women in the National Plan for Vocational Training and Employment is 45% of the total group.

Social security: EC influence over the legislation of the Spanish social security system, through Directives on Social Security, 1978 (79/7/EC), and 1986 (86/378/EC)

The amendments to the Spanish system of social security coverage are the following:

— Article 7.2 of the General Social Security Law, which allows an employee's spouse to be an independent member of the system.
— Assessment of old-age pensions for domestic servants.
— Equal compensation for men and women in case of occupational injuries.
— Revaluation of the minimum widow's pension, in a proportion far above that of the remaining pensions within the social security system (Analysis of the Equality Plan, 1990).

Taxes: EC influence on Spanish taxation law through Directives (75/117/EC) and (76/207/EC)

The amendments of the Spanish Tax Law in connection with this report have been:

— Removal of the obligation of separated spouses to add to their own income those sums received as alimony for their children for income tax purposes.
— The possibility of filing independent income tax returns when both spouses receive taxable incomes. (Analysis of the Equality Plan, 1990).

Education

The Equal Opportunity Plans (1982–85) and (1986–90) of the European Commission have direct influence in matters of education in the Equality Plan I (1988–90). The action foreseen on education and culture in the Plan of Equal Opportunities for Men and Women may be summarized in the following agreements:

— Removal of gender stereotypes from teaching material and school curricula.
— Making the teaching staff aware of these topics, in order to promote change in attitudes through initial and on-the-job training and specific campaigns.
— Promotion of equal opportunities for boys and girls in all modes of teaching.
— Adaptation of permanent education to the specific needs of adult women.
— Promotion of a non-stereotyped image of women in mass media.

These advances have resulted in an increase in female pupils as compared to males, the former now surpassing the latter at practically every level of education. There is now a balanced choice between the arts and science as a career for women. As a whole, a larger proportion of women in secondary education choose science (Ministerio de Asuntos Sociales, Instituto de la Mujer, 1990a).

The proportion of female students on business courses has grown strongly; in 1982 the percentage was of 9.6% and by 1989 it had gone up to 48.9%. The most spectacular increase has been that of female university students (see Table 17.1).

Table 17.1 University students

	Women		Men	
Year	Total	%	Year	%
1976–77	214,441	36.3	331,637	60.7
1986–87	452,400	50.1	449,900	49.8
1987–88	490,033	50.5	479,475	49.4

Source: Ministerio de Asuntos Sociales, *Análisis Gráfico del Plan de Igualdad (1988–90)*, Madrid, 1990.

The main purpose of these actions in the educational field is to have the whole teaching system respecting the principles of non-discrimination by gender; in order to achieve this, an interministerial agreement has been established, which promotes several actions. The following are emphasized here:

— Introduction in the LOGSE[7] of the principle of non-discrimination for gender reasons.
— Curricula reforms, to include the LOGSE principle of equal opportunities (Agreement between the Autonomous University of Barcelona and the Institute for Women).

— Programmes with the purpose of preparing non-gender-specific teaching material.
— Creation of a Provincial Coordination network of the Equality Plan and training courses for provincial coordinators, in Teaching Centres (in 27 provinces).
— Seminars on initial training for teachers.
— Seminars on co-education, for regional, provincial and local teachers.
— European research and action by the Ministry of Education, on initial and on-the-job training for teachers.
— Fostering the participation of the young in the new technologies.
— Seminars for careers advisers and for school inspection.
— Support for the activities of the university seminars on Women's Studies.
— Support for the Spanish Confederation of Parents' Associations (CEAPA), in order to promote the disappearance of sexism in education (Agreement between the CEAPA and the Institute for Women) (Ministerio de Asuntos Sociales, Instituto de la Mujer, 1990a).

Cost/benefit analysis

An evaluation performed by the Ministry of Social Affairs has estimated that the results obtained from the implementation of the Plan I for Equal Opportunities for Women (1988–90), three years ago, have been significantly positive. The Plan, whose implementation and development was entrusted to the Institute for Women, has achieved 96% of its goals. Five hundred and fifteen 'positive' actions in favour of women were carried out. Five are still pending completion, of which three depend on the coming reforms in civil law (choice of the order of family names) and of the penal law (reform of the laws affecting rape, and an increase in penalties for it). One of the two remaining actions deals with the signing of an agreement with Spanish Radio and Television, to increase the presence of women in executive positions, and give women greater responsibility in this governmental body. The other is pending parliamentary approval, and deals with the Agreement entered by Spain in one part of the European Social Charter to prevent women performing 'dangerous and unhealthy' underground jobs. The proposal would remove this amendment. In employment, labour relations and education more positive benefits have been experienced. These are the areas on which the EC Equality Plans (1982–5) and (1986–90) have placed greater emphasis. The agreements signed with the Ministry of Work and Social Security and the Ministry of Education deserve special mention in this context.

One of the most valuable contributions of Equality Plan I was the consolidation of the infrastructure needed in Spain to allow greater scope for any work relating to equal treatment. Action structures and programmes have been developed by the various administrations. Eight Autonomous Communities have already given shape to their own Equality Plans. Agreements have been signed with different ministries and organizations, both public and private. Special mention should also be made of the joint Congress–Senate Commission, the special Commission on women's affairs and the Spanish Federation of Municipalities and Provinces. The Plan has given special attention to non-governmental associations and organizations, which have received important support. Courses have been organized on the different areas covered by the Equality Plan, and these organizations have been helped with premises and infrastructure; 176 of them have received subsidies (Pts. 135 million) from the Institute for Women, the Ministry of Social Affairs and 0.5% from personal income tax. Much remains to be done in this field, however; these associations should be strengthened, to enable them to take up their essential role in the defence of women.

The Plan has fostered the development of specific programmes in different areas, among them the following: police assistance to women; improvement of living conditions of female prisoners; improvement of health care for women; programmes to give information and education on sex, pregnancy and birth; health information and education programmes; international cooperation programmes, etc. Special attention has been given to groups of women suffering from greater discrimination, and those in more unfavourable conditions.

There is no doubt that the most outstanding achievement of this Equality Plan I is the adjustment of legislation to the Constitutional principle of non-discrimination, *putting it on the same level as every Community rule*. Bearing in mind that Spanish democracy is hardly over a decade old, and that Spanish entry into the EC is relatively recent, the global evaluation is significantly positive; the results obtained have meant an important step forward towards equal treatment for men and women. *Spanish membership in the EC has been an undoubted benefit for women of this country, as well as for society as a whole.* Progress has become more evident in the last five years, coinciding with the length of Spanish membership in the Community. The speed of progress has been really surprising; the expectation of achieving all the goals established under Equality Plan I has gone well beyond its initial forecast: practically every one of the goals has been met. Equality Plan II is already under way, centring around four areas: education, employment and vocational training, distribution of family responsibilities and, finally, action for socially marginalized women.

We could say, in conclusion, that Spain's admittance to the EC has been *substantially beneficial* as far as matters of equal treatment are concerned. It has promoted faster and more active policies leading to the achievement of real equality between men and women, while reinforcing improvement measures which started coming into effect in 1978, after the introduction of the Spanish Constitution. Although great progress has come about in the development of regulations, both in the EC and in Spain, some important factors – such as habits, stereotypes, social structures, etc. – where change is important to achieve equality – are still far behind the regulations.

Notes

1. In connection with this, see the Decennial World Conference of Nations on Women, Madrid, Ministry of Culture, 1990; and the Report presented by Spain at the Decennial World Conference of the United Nations on Women. Madrid, Institute for Women, 1985.
2. See the Council of Europe's Comparative Study of National Organizations to promote Equality between Men and Women. Madrid, Institute for Women, 1984; and *The European Community and Spanish Women*, No. 1, Madrid, Institute for Women, 1983.
3. See *Graphic Analysis of the Equal Opportunities for Women Plan*, Madrid, Ministry of Social Affairs, Institute for Women, 1990.
4. According to the most recent data from the Working Population Survey (1990), occupational groups in which over half of the female working population participate are in services: hairdressing (85.4%); dressmakers (82%); health personnel (80.9%); cleaning personnel (78.5%); domestic and shop service (70.69%); office personnel (61.2%); sales assistants (60.3%); and teachers (59.9%).
5. In 1989, steps were taken to create 833 cooperatives.
6. The most outstanding actions have been:
   - Specific vocational training courses for farm women, through the Services of the Agricultural Extension of the Autonomous Communities (Aragon, Asturias, Cantabria, Catalonia, Valencia and Galicia).
   - Training on new accounting, administrative and business management techniques, technologies applied to agricultural production and naval/fishery training.
   - Studies on the legal treatment of women in the agricultural environment.
   - Comparative study of European farm women.
   - Support to female employment in rural areas, through the promotion and support of companies – in associated work cooperatives – in the rural environment (310 cooperatives have been created).
   - Information and guiding campaigns and programmes in rural areas.
   - Courses on Rural Women and Policies of Equal Opportunities for Men and Women.
7. LOGSE: Law of General Planning of the Educative System (Plenary Session of the Congress and Senate, 13 September 1990).

References

European Community Commission, Directorate General for Employment, Industrial Relations and Social Affairs (1990) *Unemployment in Europe*, Luxembourg.

Council of Europe (1984) *Comparative Study of National Organizations to Promote Equality between Men and Women*, Madrid, Instituto de la Mujer.

Eurostat (1989) *Employment Statistics*, Luxembourg.

INE (1990), *Encuesta de población activa (EPA). Resultados definitivos. Tercer trimestre, 1990*, Madrid.

Instituto de la Mujer, (1991) *Análisis Gráfico del Plan de igualdad 1990*, Madrid.

Ministere des Affaires Sociales de L'Emploi (1988) *Les Femmes au 2000; Quel project pour les Femmes dans la Societé du Troisième Millénaire?* Paris, La Documentation Française.

Ministerío de Asuntos Sociales (1989) *Plan de Igualdad de Oportunidades para las Mujeres, 1988–1990*, Madrid.

—— Instituto de la Mujer (1990a), *La Mujer en España-Situación Social: Educación*, Madrid.

—— Instituto de la Mujer (1990b), *Igualdad de Oportunidades: Un reto para el 93: Mujeres en Europa*, Madrid.

Ministerío de Cultura, Instituto de la Mujer (1987) *Efectos de la crisis económica sobre el trabajo de las mujeres*, Madrid.

OCDE (1985) *La Integración de la mujer en la economía*, Madrid, Ministerio de Trabajo y Seguridad Social.

Chapter 18

Demographic and family policies

*Manuel J. Rodríguez Caamaño and Alfonso de Esteban Alonso**

One of the most important changes that Spanish society has experienced in recent decades is the qualitative transformation that has taken place in man–woman relationships. These alterations have specifically affected women's quantitative reproduction rates. In other words, the family, as a dependent organization which institutionalizes the ties between men and women, has again been affected by this abatement in reproduction, which is now one of its lesser basic functions (there has been a drastic reduction of the number of children per family), and by the fluctuations that have appeared for various reasons in the social fabric of which it is part.

In the course of its 'updating' process, the Spanish social system has experienced alterations in the different elements that shape it, and their repercussions have been so great that they allow us to point out, both in theory and in the practice, the notorious and obvious differences that exist between the 'pre-modern' system and the present social system, which conforms with 'modernity'.

This chapter deals only with demographic and family matters; but the causes – economic, political, psychological and socieconomic – that have generated the present demographic and family situation were, and still are, many. It may be argued briefly, reducing the matter to economic terms, that the new models of the general system cause it to *supply* 'other' realities and, therefore, *demand* from individuals 'new' means of adapting to contemporary times: the optimum operation of this relationship (supply–demand; system–individual) increases the freedom of those subject to this correspondence. In other words, the satisfaction of needs in the social system and of those individuals that compose it brings about benefits to the former and to the latter. Spain, in just over a decade, has become a political democracy. While dictatorship encouraged reproduction by means of a transparently 'pro-birth'

* A first version of this chapter was given as a lecture in the postgraduate course, 'Social Changes in Europe: Their Effects on Women', directed by Professor Amparo Almarcha in the Instituto de Investigaciones Feministas of the Complutense University of Madrid, in January 1990.

demographic policy, democracy, in the absence of a precise demographic policy, is operating on a *laissez faire* basis.

The aim of this chapter is to clarify, in an approximate and probabilistic manner, the reason for the following situation: in the presence or absence of a coherent and firm demographic and family policy, why has Spanish society behaved, and why does it continue to behave in a manner similar to the rest of societies belonging to the EC? Our social reality obviously reveals that the birth rate has gone down, and the perceivable trend allows us to deduce that this descent is stabilizing, or going even lower, the population is progressively ageing and emigration is declining. This report will try to answer when, how and where this fall in the birth rate has happened and, at the same time, reflect what has happened to so-called 'senior citizens' and emigration.

Demographic changes

To explain the possible causes of these changes, we have used the assumptions which social scientists have formulated on the theme as a whole. These assumptions clearly show the methodological perspective that has been adopted and also help us not to brood for too long over a portion of social reality which is obvious *per se*.

These assumptions are:

— 'Human social life is a reaction to the practical problems of life on earth'.[1]

— 'The elementary unit of social life is the individual human act. To explain institutions and social change is to demonstrate the manner in which they emerge as the result of individual acts and interactions'.[2]

— 'Capitalism has drastically changed every material, social, political and cultural aspect of any society it has reached'.[3]

— 'Policies which are not strictly demographic, but of a fiscal, health, housing, etc., nature, may have repercussions on the size and characteristics of populations'.[4]

In reality, recent statistics show that there are some very specific causes giving rise to the fall in birth rates and to the subsequent changes in the pyramid-like age structure of society. In this sense, the following statistical information is now presented, which refers significantly to the above-mentioned topics; 'the perception of the influence of a series of reasons for the fall in birth rates, according to sex and age' [5] was as shown in Table 18.1.

The data in Table 18.1, among other things, confirm the theoretical approaches (the consistency is remarkable). This chapter now presents an analysis of results as a possible explanation of the relationship which exists, in this specific case, between theory and reality, bearing in mind that:

Table 18.1 Percentage indicating causes of the fall in birth rates

		Age group and sex									
		18–25		26–40		41–50		51–60		Over 60	
	Total	M	F	M	F	M	F	M	F	M	F
Use of contraceptives	78	78	89	80	82	85	81	77	77	69	68
Legalization of abortion	37	36	44	32	31	38	38	36	40	40	41
Greater independence of women	71	67	76	72	73	76	74	71	69	66	64
Insufficient economic aid to families	68	66	71	67	70	73	67	69	72	63	61
Parents' wish not to get tied down by children	63	60	67	56	62	66	61	66	65	64	68
Easier divorce	33	25	31	25	30	35	41	36	37	36	39
Women joining the work-force	77	71	83	75	82	77	78	76	78	73	71
Children are too expensive	76	75	74	77	77	82	79	79	78	73	71
(*N*)	(2,498)		(489)		(654)		(404)		(398)		(539)

Source: CIS, (1989/90).

- We are only concerned with societies integrated in the EC, which, in greater or lesser measure, may be considered as developed social organizations.
- All these societies may be termed 'capitalist societies'.
- It is obvious that important and significant differences exist in these societies – economic, social, cultural and political differences – among the 'social classes' that form them and give them shape. In other words, a divergence still exists and is maintained between 'formal' aspects and reality; paradoxically, it tends to increase.
- Although the analysis refers to society as a whole, it must be stated that the observed trends especially affect those sectors of the population which are somehow comparatively well located in terms of so-called 'welfare'.
- We fully accept that 'the Western world is losing its revolutionary model, in the same manner as it is losing its model of progress in the old fashioned sense. These were models of such a great importance that losing them is, therefore, a sign that a very deep transformation is taking place in Western mentality'.[6]
- Conservatism – to preserve the superior welfare we have – has lost its individual nature. It is a *de facto* conservatism which supports itself mainly in cohabitation in which behaviour must become homogeneous.[7]

Social and individual adaptation

The analysis of results, besides the previously mentioned factors and a solid statistical basis, insists on a series of questions that contribute to the understanding of the changes that have happened in Spanish society as far as the family, the birth rate, senior citizens and emigration are concerned. In this sense, our research has allowed us to deduce that it is probably true that 'rational choice'[8] of individuals, in whatever freedom they have, is the key to answering the questions we are dealing with: from the moment in which, in the presence or absence of demographic and family policies, the resulting manifestations reveal that the behaviour of individuals tends to be similar under the same conditions.

From the premise that human circumstances tend to be social and the changes people make are answers to the realities in which they live, it may be concluded that people are the result of their socioexistential realities; that is, rational adaptation of individuals somehow responds to the logic that the capitalist economy imposes over the social system. Without descending to crude economics, we uphold the point of view that the most ruthless and efficient policy is the one which – as ever – the socioeconomic sphere imposes: a realist policy whose basic demand is individual adaptation to the requirements of the economic system if the individual wishes to satisfy needs and wishes derived from socialization. Within this framework, it would be

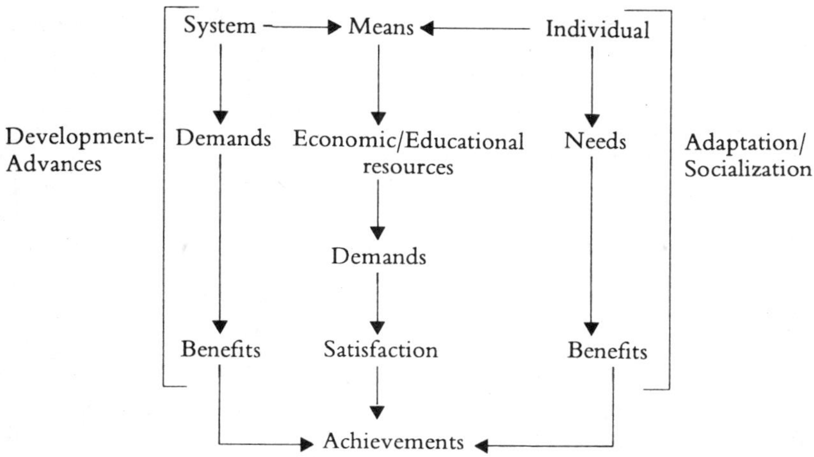

Figure 18.1 Development of the system and the individual

good to point out the differences that may be observed between the recent past and the present, or between those who have not adapted and those who have. A manifestation of this is the transition that has happened from 'quantitative reproduction' to 'qualitative reproduction'. In short, individual and group planning or rationalizing is increasingly important and tends to consolidate itself.

From this perspective, the answer to the 'how?' question is to be found in the progressive adaptation of individuals to the demands of the system of which they are part. These shifts have effects that are linked to the changes experienced by the family. We are specifically referring to its reproductive function and, thus, to birth rates. It is, however, necessary to specify and to insist that the adaptation to new 'material' and 'sociocultural' demands requires that individuals have modern information and resources, rather than an anachronistic set of values which might hinder the process of adaptation. See the schematic diagram in Figure 18.1.

This graphic diagram, whose nature is apparently functional and utilitarian, is also *life-like* and denotes a greater individual control over reality: the design implies a response to the needs of individuals, materially and socioculturally conditioned to the demands offered by the system's development: out of optimum correspondence between one and the other (individual–system), when interdependent, there arise possibilities for personal achievement (what is known as 'individualism') and advances of the system (called 'development') which enable them (welfare).

From all the above, it is fair to admit that those sectors of society that have more economic and educative means or resources are those in which transformations (new adaptations) have taken place. When dealing with this, statistics are transparent and allow us to deduce, in general terms, that in these societies we are analysing, what does happen is that:

— For married or unmarried couples, more children mean less possibilities for personal achievement.
— For married or unmarried couples, less children mean, on the contrary, more possibilities.
— For children, whether of married or unmarried couples, more siblings mean less possibilities.
— For children, whether of married or unmarried couples, less siblings mean more possibilities.

That is probably the reason why families with more or better adapted resources tend to reduce the number of children in order to increase the possibilities for every one of their members. Thus, the projects of the couple increasingly tend to take into account other goals, of higher priority than progeny, and, furthermore, each person's existential project tends to shape itself in a more individual manner.

As to 'when?', we refer to the demographic realities of the last decades which, in their process, explicitly tell of diminishing birth rates, the progressive ageing of population, the reduction in emigration rates and, as a consequence, the increase in immigration rates.

We may thus deduce, once the relevant comparisons with the remaining EC societies have been established, that Spanish society has experienced a series of transformations in the course of its evolutive adaptation to modernity, whose tendencies and results tend to equate it with the other societies with which comparisons have been established. Table 18.2 shows an obvious proof of this.

Our point of view is supported by, among others, Mackensen, who maintains the convincing opinion that:

> For the last twenty years, the demographic development of nearly every European country has been marked by a strong reduction in fertility. This is obviously a sign of the growing adaptation of the reproductive behaviour of families to the living conditions of the industrialized and socially oriented modern societies. It is, therefore, a rational change in behaviour; this change has been caused by the developments that have been happening in these countries, and with which we all agree: higher living levels, an increase in social services, health, work and consumption.[9]

This acquires importance in the judgement formulated by Carlos Moya, when he stated that 'capitalist development is the economic development typical of the Western world, which, at the same time, represents the historical process which shapes society'.[10] This explains the fact that EC societies are tending to become homogeneous and their individuals, thus, present similar features.

Since this chapter began by referring to man–woman relationships, we

Table 18.2 Percentage distribution of the total population by age groups in the EC countries, 1985 and 2000

	1985			2000 (Projections)		
EC countries	0–14	15–64	+65	0–14	15–64	+65
Belgium	18.9	67.4	13.8	18.3	64.9	16.8
Denmark	18.4	66.5	15.1	17.4	67.1	15.1
Spain	23.1	64.9	12.0	19.0	66.0	15.0
France	21.2	65.9	13.0	19.0	65.3	15.7
Greece	21.3	65.4	13.3	23.1	62.5	14.4
Netherlands	19.5	68.5	12.1	17.4	68.3	14.3
Ireland	24.5	59.7	10.7	n/a	n/a	n/a
Italy	19.3	67.8	12.9	16.0	67.4	16.6
Luxembourg	17.3	69.3	13.2	18.9	67.3	13.8
Portugal	23.5	64.5	12.0	21.0	67.9	12.0
United Kingdom	19.2	65.7	15.1	20.5	64.4	15.1
FRG	15.6	69.7	14.7	14.9	68.1	17.0
Total	20.0	66.6	13.4	18.6	66.3	15.1

Source: Eurostat, *Demographic Statistics, 1989*, Luxembourg, 1990.

shall continue using this relationship to show that the changes in behaviours and attitudes (re-adaptations or adaptations) of individuals also answer to another conception of the bonds that should exist between men and women and, no doubt, to the new possibilities for women. As Lluis Flaquer points out: 'It is impossible to understand the dynamics of couples today, without taking into account the increase in individualism and the growth of feminism, two phenomena that are characteristic signs of our era'.[11]

The contemporary nature of capitalism and democracy starts from a socialization/adaptation that has suppressed any pre-modern feature which might limit the freedom of individuals of both sexes. This is the cause of the permanence of social relations with a strong content of 'pragmatism', 'individualism', 'hedonism', 'narcissism', 'consumerism', and with 'rationalism' rooted in its infrastructure. All this is settled through relationships whose frame of reference is 'competition', which tends to exclude anyone less well adapted. Thus, 'nowadays, certain family behaviour bears witness to radical mutations of values and institutions. It is not that families are coming to an end; it is, simply, that they are changing in double quick time'.[12]

Cost/benefit analysis

Benefits

It must be stated in principle that, during the last few years, Spain has considerably enlarged its social welfare policies, a sample of which is, for instance, the care received by so-called 'senior citizens'. However, and although no explanation exists for it, there still remain certain deficiencies in the general services, when compared with most of the other societies considered here.

We here admit as benefits all those achievements and expectations derived from integration in the EC; as a whole, the social policies of this organization are more developed than Spain's own and, as such, they mean an increase in the services received by citizens in the relevant groups. A rough list follows of the sectors of society that have been favoured by integration and its relevant benefits:

— *Emigrants*: Although emigration has gone down, due to the improvement of working conditions and salaries, and to the economic crisis that affects all countries, it is possible that the social group that has benefited most from Spain's adhesion to the EC are Spanish citizens working in any of the other Member States.
— *Senior citizens*: This is the most protected and cared for group under present Spanish social policies, but it is still possible that joining the EC has meant the consolidation of trends favouring them in every social field.
— *Marginal groups*: Although it is not yet possible to quantify their numbers, it is necessary to mention that, due to changes in people's attitudes and behaviour, it is possible that some groups have been positively affected, because membership of the EC, which they can now argue, gives validity to their demands. We are particularly referring to women and young people seeking more specific, equalitarian and realistic remedies for their respective problems.

Provisionally, in this sense, it is feasible that family protection policies in the EC Member States may work as correctives, given the notorious differences seen in comparing them with the Spanish family protection policy. Thus, it would be possible to compare the situation of Spanish families and those of families in the remaining EC countries in matters of services received.[13]

To summarize, we conform to the belief (generalized and maintained throughout Spanish public opinion) that being an active member of some organization, such as the EC, whose scientific, economic, human and cultural resources make it possible to go forward in matters of equality and freedom for its members, is always beneficial.

Costs

As to costs, by which we understand any detraction from the benefits of integration, in our opinion, none exist at the moment, since the relevant policies in force in the EC are not deficient in beneficial matters, if compared with those held by and still maintained by Spain.

Objectively, however, and based on factors that seem to make them evident, it is necessary to argue that Spanish society is achieving many of its real social demands, which were ignored only a few years ago and which, as a consequence, were totally abandoned. There is no doubt, however, that the State tends to invest more in social policies, and a prompt and full equality with the EC will soon be more than a mere hope. This is slow to arrive, and means that most of the population which is expecting these changes experiences some frustration between the goals to be achieved and those that have already been met.

Notes

1. Harris, 1982, p. 11.
2. Elster, 1990, p. 23.
3. Berger, 1989, p. 7.
4. García Ballesteros, 1984, p. 18.
5. CIS, 1989, p. 24.
6. Tierno Galván, *Tradición* . . ., p. 186.
7. Idem., p. 175.
8. Elster, 1990, p. 31.
9. Mackensen, 1986, p. 507.
10. Moya, 1978, p. 501.
11. Flaquer, *El País* (28 December 1990).
12. Idem.
13. De Esteban collected and pointed to three types of demographic policies, which directly influence fertility: pro-life, 'laissez-faire', and those in favour of abortion. A. de Esteban, 1990, p. 12.

References

Berger, P.L. (1989) *La Revolución Capitalista*, Barcelona, Península.

Centro de Investigaciones Sociologicas (1989) '*Problemas Sociales: Actitudes y Opiniones de los Españoles ante la Natalidad, el Aborto y la Eutanasia*', Estudios y Encuestas, No. 16, Madrid.

Commission of the European Communities (1989) *Family Policy in EEC Countries*, Luxembourg.

Elster, J. (1990) *Tuercas y Tornillos*, Barcelona, Gedisa.

De Esteban, A. (1990) 'Politicas Demográficas y de Familia en los Países de la CEE', in *Cambios Sociales en Europa: su Impacto sobre las Mujeres* (ed. Amparo Almarcha), Madrid.

Flaquer, L.L. (1990) 'La Familia Alternativa', *El País*, 28 December 1990.

Garcia Ballesteros, A. (1984) *Crecimiento y Problemas de la Población Mundial*, Barcelona, Salvat.

Harris, M. (1982), *El Materialismo Cultural*, Madrid, Alianza.

Mackensen, R. (1986) 'Políticas de Población en Europa', in A. Olano (ed.), *Tendencias Demográficas y Planificación Económica* Madrid, Ministerio de Economía y Hacienda.

Moya, C. (1978) 'Argumentos para otra Ciencia Social', in J.Jiménez Blanco and C. Moya, *Teoría Sociológica Contemporánea*, Madrid, Tecnos.

Tierno Galván, E. (1962), *Tradición y modernismo*, Madrid, Tecnos.

Chapter 19

Consumer protection

Serafín Chimeno Rabanillo

Europeanization, a phenomenon of economic, political and social scope, has unleashed in Spain a serious process of change, oriented towards the confrontation between the demands of duties and the claims of rights inherent in the condition of citizens, as consumers and users of services or products.

Protection of users and consumers within the framework of European social policy

John F. Kennedy was the first politician to commit himself on this topic, with a public statement on consumer rights; since then, the movement for citizens' protection has expanded very quickly – albeit unequally – throughout the industrial world.[1] The movement for consumer protection and consumer protection policy, in which the United States is a pioneer, may be presented in two well-defined and differentiated models:

The Western Model – consumer defence is conducted by two bodies: the administration, which creates public organizations to this end, and private associations, which anyone may join and which, generally, are self-financed. This model includes, among others, the United States, Canada, Great Britain, France, Spain, Holland, Belgium, Switzerland, Australia, Japan and Germany. This group of countries, however, presents marked differences; Spain, although it is included under the sub-block of the less advanced countries, is beginning to go forward and approach the more developed countries in the area of consumer matters.

The Scandinavian Model – no private associations exist in this model, and the task of protecting consumers is totally taken by the public administration. Sweden, Norway, Finland and Iceland are the countries implementing this model, whose efficiency has already been proved.

In parallel with these, other countries have their own particular policy, which does not fit into either of the above. Such is the case of Denmark, half-way between the Western and Scandinavian models, or Italy, where responsibility is shared by the public administration and workers' trade unions, and where private organizations do exist, but not as an institutional organization specific to that area, as is the case of the Spanish National Consumer Institute (INC).

The movement to protect consumers was first started in Europe at the beginning of the 1970s,[2] when the EEC authorities were already aware of it, as shown by the Communication issued on the meeting of all Heads of Member States, held in Paris in 1972. Article 100 of the Single European Act proposes the harmonization of the legislative process in matters of consumer protection, placing it, besides, 'in a high level of protection'. The imminent arrival of the Single Market will, no doubt, hasten this process, especially on areas as important as consumer health, safety and economic interests.[3] The EC policy Directives in this area, and on the Single Market itself, state that consumer protection must necessarily stem from educational programmes on consumption themes, as well as from the setting up of legal mechanisms which guarantee nimble and efficient repair of damage arising from the use or consumption of goods and services.

Organizations responsible for consumer protection

The International Consumer Directory, published in the United Kingdom by the IOCU, in 1989, has a list of all the organizations in the world whose aim is to protect consumers' interests. Out of all these organizations, only twelve are of an international nature, the rest being domestic. Needless to say, most of these organizations or institutions, whether public or private, belong to the industrialized world, some of which are active within Member States of the EC. Spain is one of those with a great number of organizations (31), in comparison with the rest of the world; their efficiency, however, due to their short life-span, has not yet been tested.

In Spain, the first association (UNAE) was created in 1967, but most associations date from the 1980s. Over half of the existing organizations were created in 1978. The real increase in membership came after 1982. An example of this may be the fact that, in 1982, the number of members was 295,497, while by 1986 it had already reached 608,000.

It is undeniable that the southern part of the EC has been behind the northern countries in matters of consumer protection, and that, in the south, Spain is effectively leading Portugal, Italy and Greece. Representation has already been achieved for those countries in the pertinent EC organizations, where, only a few years ago, the criteria of the older Member States, such as Belgium, the UK, the Netherlands or Germany, were imposed. The creation of an international organization, with headquarters in Brussels, which would integrate the southern EC countries, is currently being studied and discussed, in order to make their presence more effective in the EC institutions responsible for consumer policies.

However, Spanish presence in the present EC institutions dealing with consumer issues, deserves to be mentioned. Thus, the Community

Consultative Council (CCC) bureau has one Spanish member from the Spanish Consumers Union (UCE); the sections have two Spanish members in Information and Education, one of them (from UCE) is its chairman; one Spanish member (from FEACU) in Health and Safety; one Spanish member (from UCE) in each one of the following sectors: Financial and Economic Services; Access to Justice; Standardization and Representation. Spain, even though its EC membership is recent, already is significantly present in the CCC. It is also important to underline the presence of a Spanish Vice-chairman (from ASGECO) and another Spanish member in the European Economic and Social Council, which covers Health, Consumption, Environment and Tourism. Three Spanish associations (UNAE, ASGECO and UCE) have offices in Brussels.

Repercussions of the EC consumer policy on Spain

Two well-defined stages may be established in the development of consumer protection within the EC: the first, covering up to October 1972, does not include a consumer protection policy in the EC scope of action, although it does recognize its importance, especially in connection with the Single Market concept, for the free movement of products and its subsequent repercussions on health, safety and economic interests. During this stage, there were General Action Programmes, with sectoral Directives oriented towards the harmonization of national legislation affecting consumers.

The second stage had a Preliminary Programme in 1972 and a second enlarged Programme in 1986. Its culmination included a bond between the defence of consumers' interests and the principles of free movement in the reformed Treaties of the Single Act. This situation means the formalization of consumer protection policy as an institutional right, raising it to the rank of a specific goal of EC legislative policy. The legislative process of harmonization was also strengthened.

Spain entered the EC during the period covered by the second stage, that is, when the EC policy programmes on consumer protection were already rather well developed. The legal foundation of this EC spirit is directly or indirectly revealed in constitutional imperatives. Thus, Article 51 of the 1987 Constitution established the rules of public action and other articles, especially 9,24.1,43.1 and, especially, 53.3, cover positive legislation, legal practices and public powers relevant to consumer protection.

The image of consumers, as passive receivers lacking the organized counterweight of demanding services or products, is anachronistic today, and is replaced by a balanced consumer policy, as long as three fundamental principles are respected: market transparency, product quality promotion and product competitivity. This basic idea implies the joint and coordinated action of public institutions and citizens, acting in a collective manner and organized under free associations. There can be no doubt that this policy answers to a long European tradition, as well as to EC policy in matters of consumer protection.

Spanish consumer rights

The expression of consumer rights did not exist in Spain as an integral political project until the Constitution took shape, giving positive regulation to the General Law for the Defence of Consumers.[4] This law establishes six basic rights, whose defence and promotion is carried out by public authorities. These rights are the following:

(1) Protection against risks affecting health or safety.
(2) Protection of legitimate economic and social rights.
(3) Compensation or repair of any damages or detriments suffered.
(4) Correct information about goods and services and about education.
(5) Hearing in consultation, participation in the preparation of the general provisions that affect them and representation of their interests through consumer associations.
(6) Legal, administrative and technical protection in situations of inferiority, subordination or helplessness.

The effective exercise of these rights, however, is through action programmes in priority areas. Spanish policy is to make good not only the late Spanish entry into the consumer society, but also the almost non-existence of consumer protection until the 1990s.

The Ministry of Health and Social Security has established the following areas of priority for its actions:[5]

(1) Building a legal framework to support consumer policy.
(2) Coordination between the different public administrations.
(3) Promotion of consumer associations.

Thus, the Government fully assumes the responsibility of a consumer policy, and is trying to consolidate it by giving effective realization to the rights of citizens, not only in relation to classic individual rights, but also to all other social rights, of which consumer protection is an important component; and also by the implementation of a consumer policy capable of contributing to a better system of production, making trading activities more transparent, improving the competitivity of Spanish products and the quality of goods and services offered in the market.

Spanish consumer planning

In the pre-constitutional period there were no logical and coordinated rules;

during this period, and especially in the 1960s, a variety of provisions appeared, which indirectly took account of consumers' interests.[6]. Of these, the following deserve mention:

The Advertising Statute, of 11 June 1964, required truthfulness and was aimed at consumer protection. However, it was not effectively applied until the arrival of Law 34/1988, 11 November 1988, called the General Advertising Law, which is the Spanish version of Directive 54/450/EC on misleading advertising.

Decree 3052/1966, 17 November 1966, on administrative infringements and penalties in matters of market discipline, compares the defence of tradesmen's interests with that of consumer interests in economic activities. Its updating was issued in the form of a Royal Decree 1945/83, 22 June 1983, which regulates infringements and penalties in consumer defence and agro-food production matters.

The first Spanish Alimentary Code was approved through Decree 2484/67, 21 September 1967, dealing with food, condiments, stimulants and beverages, their raw materials and, by extension, with products, materials, utensils and equipment used and consumed in the home. The origin of this Decree lies in the Interministerial Commission for Alimentary Planning, which is currently responsible to the Ministry of Health and Consumers. It should be emphasized that the Spanish Alimentary Code did not come into effect until 1975, and that each of the rules which govern it was promulgated between 1981 and 1982, as an answer to urgent consumer health protection measures approved in 1981 by the Congress.

To summarize, not only was consumer defence generally rather poor during this stage, but its application was not too effective.[7]

In the Constitutional and post-Constitutional period, Article 51 of the Constitution, which should be emphasized because it contains three chapters dealing with consumer protection, brought this matter forward in agreement with the declaration of fundamental consumers' rights, as shown in the 1975 Council of Europe Charter, in the EC Preliminary Programme of 1975, and in the second, enlarged EC Programme of 1981.

The Constitutional rule, in turn, was greatly developed under the General Law 26/1984, 19 July 1984, on Protection of Consumers and Users. This Law sets out goals and specific fields of action. However, the prescribed development was very difficult, both because of its innovative nature and because of its legal complexity; so much so that non-constitutionality appeals against 26 of the 41 articles presented by the Autonomous Communities of Catalonia, the Basque Country and Galicia had to be resolved by the Constitutional Court.

The following orders illustrate the development of this Law:

— On solvents, glues, bonding agents, paints, dyes, varnishes and other similar materials, relating to domestic use and children (Royal Decree 221/1985, 28 October.

- On packaging and labelling of hazardous substances and on declaration and classification of new substances (Royal Decree 221/1985, 28 October).
- On safety of toys, school materials and party-joke materials (Royal Decree 2330/1985, 6 November).
- On rules regulating industrial activities and the delivery of services in vehicle repair shops, their equipment and components (July 1986).
- Regulations governing cleaning, preservation and dyeing services of textile, leather, fur and synthetic products (November 1987).
- Safety standards for electrical materials (Royal Decree, July 1988).
- Protection of consumer rights in matters of domestic appliance repair services (Royal Decree, February 1988).

Some Ministerial Orders dealing with the promotion and support of national consumer and user associations were approved in 1988, as well as rules regulating the granting of aid to local corporations in matters of consumer interest. Royal Decree 825/1990, 22 June, deserves to be specially mentioned. It deals with consumer and user representation, consultation and participation, and regulates points of great importance, such as a user and consumer association register, the Council of Users and Consumers, requirements to obtain benefits granted by the law, and all prescribed and concordant provisions. Once this Royal Decree was implemented, the census of associations was closed and a new register book started, in order to update and control subsidies and, especially, to keep track of the real number of members and their territorial distribution.

Drafting new laws

The creation of a Consultative Consumer Council was planned for June 1991; and simultaneously Decree-Laws – dealing with labelling, presentation and advertising of industrial products; with a list of basic goods and services of common, and persistent general use; with consumer information offices and services; with comparative analysis; with information on housing; with customer services and guarantees; with special sales; with contests, games and gifts; with the amendment of the current infringements and penalties in consumer matters; and with the Insurance and Guarantee Fund – were drafted.

On the basis of this legal regulation of consumer protection, Spain started to implement the programme proposed during its six-month term as President of the EC; its four main points are the following:

- The integration of consumer protection policy within the remaining Community policies.

— A strengthening of safety and quality guarantees of all products available to consumers.
— Improvement of legal protection of consumers' rights, facilitating their access to justice.
— Promotion of directives and other actions to protect the economic interests of consumers.

This programme took shape under the Three-Year Action Plan, culminating at the end of 1992.

Spain has developed – and continues to develop – a wide programme of action within this context; some as important and in accord with the EC guidelines as: updating of the Spanish Alimentary Code; adaptation of technical and health regulations; regulations on safety of toys; coordinated control of safety of foodstuffs with local authorities, with a prompt exchange of information whenever there is danger to health at national or Autonomous Community levels; capacity to impose criminal or civil penalties for infringements which touch on the health and safety of consumers and users. The protection of economic and social consumer interests are also taken care of, as is compensation for any damage suffered, through the creation of a system of arbitrage.[8] The publication of correct product and services information and education in consumer matters are now valued in themselves, have their own advertising campaigns, and are promoted through the Municipal Offices of Consumer Information (OMICS), which cover over 70% of the Spanish population through the more than 600 existing offices.[9]

Users' and consumers' associations

The participation of citizens in consultation and through representation in political, economic and social life is a right that the 1978 Spanish Constitution upholds repeatedly. The exercise of this right, however, is subject to the promotion of associations, especially those linked with consumer policy.

Chapter IV of Law 26/1984 contains many references to users' and consumers' associations. However, the lack of a more specific and coordinated policy, together with other variables, such as lack of a tradition, low membership and financing problems, have not been conducive to the growth of Spanish consumers' associations. At the end of 1989, the Instituto Nacional de Consumo (National Consumer Institute) had recorded the existence of 118 associations in Spain, of which only seven had national coverage, encompassing all the others, in one form or another. It is significant to note that, three-quarters of the thirty-nine associations created in 1989–91, use federative models, breaking away from previous dispersion, and achieving more rational – and, therefore, more effective – forms.

Both institutions dealing with consumer policy and the associations themselves agree that an effective consumer viewpoint can only be achieved by:

— The integration of all existing associations in federative structures.
— Professionalization of users' and consumers' associations.
— Increased participation of users' and consumers' associations in consultative and executive organizations. For example, consumers are already represented, through their associations, in the Interministerial Commission for Alimentary Planning; the Insurance Compensation Pool; the Securities Market Commission; the High Board of Prices; the Consumer Sectoral Council and the Economic and Social Council.[10]

Association financing

The functional independence of associations is the argument used in favour of self-financing, an important complement in the mechanism of their economic financing. Aid and subsidies from public resources are regulated by the Ministerial Order of 8 March 1988. This order only considers *national* associations as candidates for subsidy and became effective in 1987.

In 1989, the budgetary funds for this purpose were Pts. 260 million distributed according to number of members and their location, and so that 25% was given for informative projects, such as pamphlets, 50% for training activities (courses, seminars, etc.) and to magazines. The regulations separated the programmes eligible for this subsidy into three well-defined parts:

— Ordinary programmes related to infrastructure, such as consulting, publishing, training and information offices.
— Programmes intended to strengthen consumer associations' presence and participation in institutional consulting organizations.
— Programmes agreed with the INC, especially those involving analysis and coordination. Generally, self-financing is carried out by collecting membership dues, subscription to and sales of publications and service fees.

Main Spanish user and consumer associations

The dispersion of Spanish associations has already been mentioned. At the end of 1989, there were 118 officially registered associations, although a clear trend towards federation was already noticeable. Out of the nearly one million members of user and consumer associations in Spain, only two (FEACCU and UCE) have more than 200,000 members. The main national associations, following the criteria of number of members, are:[11]

— Spanish Federation of Homemakers and Family Consumer Associations (FEACU), with 260,845 members, most of them homemakers.
— Spanish Consumer Union (UCE), with 158,612 members of every type.
— General Consumer Association (ASGECO), with 78,290 members, mostly cooperativists.
— Consumer and User Organization (OCU), with 72,960 members of every type.
— State Consumer and User Confederation (CECU), with 65,211 members of every type.
— Independent User and Consumer Federation (FUCI), with 48,181 members of every type.
— National Spanish Consumer and Homemaker Union (UNASI), with 22,733 members, most of them homemakers.

Costs and benefits to Spain of its adaptation to EC policy in consumer matters

It seems evident that in matters of consumer policy Spain is still in the development stage, if the EC average is taken as a reference. It is obvious, however, that Spain's membership in the EC has been a corrective to its long and embarrassing tradition of official 'forgetfulness' of the rights of citizens in their role as users and consumers. It still seems premature, and highly complex, to evaluate the advantages in economic and social terms; and this is for two reasons. First of all, it is still an expanding movement and, second, its consolidation is bound to be slow in imposing legal standards and, above all, in changing attitudes which have been positive in claiming rights, but not so much so in fulfilling the reciprocal duties.

It is impossible, from an overall point of view, to qualify and quantify in consumer terms the costs and advantages of Spanish membership in the EC. It is already possible, however, to evaluate certain important parts of it.

Among the advantages is the interest that this topic has raised among individuals and in the central, Autonomic and local administrations, since it has resulted in more legislation on consumers and their protection than in other EC Member States.[12] However, the legal regulation of consumption, which has reached a high degree of development in civil and trade law, is still deficient as regards penal, procedural and administrative law. There is still a long way to go, therefore, to fix the boundaries of legal consumer protection, and various administrations are working towards this, especially bearing in mind the Single Market of 1993. A certain administrative protection has been achieved, therefore, which may be summarized in several points: the creation of specialized organizations, institutional coordination, improvement of criteria and methods to inspect and develop them. The legal protection itself still has important gaps, from the viewpoint of complete regulation of consumer rights. Inferiority, or even helplessness, may be remedied through educative and informative campaigns, and with the promotion of serious, technically qualified associations.

In connection with associations, entry into the EC has created a very important launching point, although the situation is very deficient if compared to the EC average. One million members is a very small number, even though it was achieved in a mere five-year period. It is, indeed, a small number, but large when interpreted in terms of breaking away from a long tradition of no association at all.

To sum up, it may be said that there are important advantages in consumer matters, as a consequence of Spain's admittance to the EC, especially in connection with protection of food or public health, consumer protection, commercial transactions and environmental protection. In this area, the administration is developing a wide process of standardization which, as in the case of alimentary policy, presented 118 provisions between 1982 and 1989 and information on 111 standards. Effective mechanisms have been developed for control, through the Autonomous Communities and local authorities. The central government limits itself to the training of inspectors, laboratories and the development of an Early Alert Network, which reacts promptly to new risks, and further it expects to create a specialized group of inspectors within the Judiciary Police, with capacity to audit *ex officio* and not only at the request of one of the parties.

In connection with the prevention of environmental risk to consumers, the government acts in three different directions: guidance of negative consumer behaviour, in terms of environmental pollution; and prevention, supervision and control actions. In the case of water, these measures have been implemented in the shape of a Technical and Health Regulation for supply and control, a water chlorination plant and supervision and control instruments.

All the above advantages, however, should not let us forget the costs. In social matters, for instance, the individual and collective effort needed to adapt to the new situation of responsible performance of duties has meant breaking away from entrenched anarchic, cowboy behaviour. A great social effort is also being made to dissipate prejudices against associative activity. In the economy, even though it is premature to establish definite costs, consumption and its conformity with EC policy is having important effects on the Spanish economy, at two levels: First, the final price of products and services is experiencing a significant rise, as a consequence of the current rules. This circumstance has forced the modification of many production, manufacture and handling systems, as well as an improvement in the quality of raw materials or of service rendered. Although the relevant organizations do not yet have definite data, both the Spanish Federation of Entrepreneurial Organizations (CEOE) and the Ministry of Industry and Energy admit the effect of EC requirements on the rise of product and service prices during the last few years. Secondly, the repercussions of the present Spanish consumer situation on the foreign trade balance is perhaps more spectacular, since this has worsened. Higher product prices, as a consequence of the products' adaptation to the European consumer norms, have had a negative influence on Spanish market competitivity. It must not be forgotten, in conclusion, that enlarging the public services – those relevant to health and the Courts of Justice, for instance – to adapt them to European consumer policy rules, affects budgets and, therefore, creates a need for higher taxes.

Notes

1. Kennedy made this statement in a special message to the Congress on 5 March 1962, when he proclaimed the five basic consumer rights.
2. From the onset of the second decade of this century, there have been associative movements in Europe aimed at the protection of consumer rights. The first association in the EC countries was established in the Netherlands in 1926, although the first known regulations on matters of consumption were published in Denmark in 1902.
3. During the second quarter of 1988, when Spain occupied the Chair of the EC, an important step forward took place in consumer policy, when the Spanish government introduced an action programme to prepare the EC policy on consumer protection, which the Single Market would bring about. This programme was implemented in the so-called Plan de Acción Trienal (Three-Year Action Plan), which sought to harmonize and support more advanced national action.
4. The General Law for Consumer Protection is the foundation of this theme in Spain; it determines all political guidelines and regulations governing countless consumer-related aspects.
5. As may be deduced from the appearance of Julián García Vargas, Spanish Minister of Health and Consumer Affairs, before the Health and Social Security Commission on 7 June 1990.
6. Spanish isolationism, arising from a long authoritarian political regime, was not, however, totally impenetrable. Emigration and cultural osmosis helped to prepare rudimentary structures for the protection of user-consumers, which, in turn, were favoured by the demands of the foreign market.
7. In pp. 85–96 of his book *Europa y los Consumidores*, César Brana Pino gives us a complete and detailed list of the regulations developed in relation with these paragraphs and the following during each period.
8. Eighteen Arbitrage Boards had by June 1990 received 5,315 auditing requests, 63% of which have been solved. The mean cost of arbitrage is around Pts. 36,500 for each case. Two hundred and seven sectoral entrepreneurial organizations are members of these Arbitrage Boards, representing over 58,000 companies, as well as fifty-five user and consumer associations, apart from national organizations.
9. The OMICS cover 100% of the municipalities with over 50,000 inhabitants, and 50.5% of those of more than 10,000. The government is planning to increase this last block, to cover 100% of these smaller municipalities, and to launch a campaign to promote full coverage for those of less than 10,000 inhabitants; it is seeking joint means of management and cooperation with the provincial county councils.

10. The presence of four members, representing consumers, in the Economic and Social Council created by the government in December 1990, is an important proof that consumer policy is reaching high levels of interest in Spain, and of the influence which consumer associations are beginning to exert.
11. The activities of the central, Autonomous and local authorities are coordinated by the Commission for Cooperation which has already held over fifty-three meetings, since its creation in 1983. Its activity has been endorsed by the Sectoral Consumer Conference, which is an office for cooperation and collaboration between the various governments.
12. Sanctions, for instance, are very deficient, especially in local administrations or governments, whose maximum penalty is Pts. 25,000. The 1990 Budgetary Law, however, allows this to be increased up to a maximum of Pts. 2,500,000.

References

Braña Pinco, C. (1989) *Europa y los Consumidores*, Madrid, Fundación Universidad-Empresa.

Castillo, C.J. (1987) *Sociedad de Consumo a la Española*, Madrid, Eudema.

Diputación Provincial de Sevilla (1987) *Recopilación Legislativa de Consumo*, Sevilla, Area de Salud y Servicios Sociales.

Jensen, H.R. (1986), *La Educación del Consumidor en la Escuela*, Vitoria, Gobierno Vasco.

Ministerio de Sanidad y Consumo (1986) *Tres Años de Política de Consumo*, Madrid, Fondo General de Documentos del INC.

Ministerio de Sanidad y Consumo (1990) *Introducción a la Sociología Ambiental y del Consumo*, Madrid, INC.

Chapter 20

Education and training

Manuel Rodríguez Carrajo

The educational systems of the different EC countries constitute one of the best indicators of the European unity we are seeking to build. The construction of a united Europe is something which has been worked towards for years – not simply and solely based on economic matters, but also covering many other aspects, such as the political, social, educational and cultural fields.

In economic and political matters, European union will not be feasible unless it is based on a common patrimony, and an awareness and feeling is created among its inhabitants that makes them feel truly integrated within one common enterprise, which did exist in the Middle Ages, and which it would be convenient to recover in this modern era.

For this common awareness to be effective, people have to be brought close together, because the difficulty of mutual communications is one of the great obstacles that currently hinder this desired unity (Schneider, 1963, p. 62). Yet this is not an insoluble problem, although it is a very real one. One can certainly appreciate other people's cultures without understanding their language, but if what people truly want is to be able to speak to and understand each other, the only possible way to achieve it is to, at least, learn the languages of the neighbouring countries.

Thus, cooperation among the EC Member States in educational matters is part of this logic of building a united Europe, since it tends to bring people closer and to improve their living and working conditions. The different governments of the EC have realized this, and have therefore issued the 28 October 1988 European Parliament Resolution, on the need to promote the teaching and study of EC languages within the EC.[1] Total uniformity in each educational system would be self-defeating, since every country must maintain its own peculiarities. But, above certain idiosyncrasies, a greater unification of substantial issues should exist. The European Parliament itself introduced this idea when it asserted that the Community policy of cooperation in educational matters begun in 1974 aimed at preserving the originality of educational traditions and policies peculiar to each country, adding that no uniformity of the traditional teaching structure, methods or contents was being sought. The goal of this approach between the different educational systems of the EC Member States is, thus, quite clear. Uniformity is not the end being sought, but rather a greater closeness and a greater coherence between such systems.

This chapter analyses how much the Spanish educational system resembles the educational systems of the other EC Member States, using UNESCO methodology, terminology and data from 1985.

Pre-school education

According to the UNESCO, pre-school education is that which comes before the first grade and is not compulsory. It is known as kindergarten, nursery school or infant school attached to higher grade schools.

In Spain, pre-school education increased remarkably in the 1980s, due to various causes, among which the following may be mentioned (1) mothers working outside the home, which makes it necessary for them to find some place to leave their younger children; (2) the government's expansionist educational policy, which has brought about the creation of new centres; (3) Spanish society has become aware that children can be offered better socialization skills than they can obtain at home.

Total pre-school registration, which was 920,336 pupils in 1975, went up to 1,127,348 in 1985. In other words, the number of pupils registered for pre-school programmes increased by 207,012 in ten years, and this figure is far higher than in any other EC country, which, with rare exceptions, actually experienced a decrease in their pre-school populations, as a consequence of the low birth-rate prevalent in Europe. As in the majority of EC countries, most Spanish pre-school teachers are women. Denmark is almost the exception to this rule, where only 57% are women. In Spain, women teachers in these centres in 1985 formed 93%, a fall of 6% in comparison with 1975, when women teachers constituted around 99% of the total number. Quantitatively, the level of pre-school studies is very similar to that of the rest of the EC; however, the qualitative aspect shows many deficiencies. Bearing in mind that educational inequalities start from the first years of a child's life, these centres should be increased in those places where they are more necessary, such as rural areas and marginal areas in large cities. It is in those areas, however, where they are least provided. In these locations, parents cannot take proper care of their children, due to their multiple occupations or to their poor preparation.

Primary schooling

In UNESCO terminology, primary schooling covers what is known in Spain as Enseñanza General Básica (Basic General Schooling). This schooling is compulsory. Attendance at this first level is practically universal, as it is in the remaining EC countries (see Table 20.1).[2] Interregional differences in

Table 20.1 School attendance at each level*

Country	Year	Primary		Secondary		Higher level
		Gross	Net	Gross	Net	Gross
Belgium	1986	96	95	96	87	31.9
Denmark	1985	98	—	105	83	29.3
France	1986	112	100	95	86	30.2
German FR	1985	97	81	72	70	29.8
Greece	1984	106	92	88	79	23.5
Ireland	1984	100	—	96	—	21.6
Italy	1984	99	97	74	70	26.3
Netherlands	1984	95	87	102	87	31.0
Portugal	1984	127	—	52	38	12.6
Spain	1985	104	98	98	—	29.6
UK	1985	106	97	85	81	22.4
EC				85.9	75.6	26.95

* Gross rate is the relationship between the number of students of any age enrolled in any one level of schooling and the total population corresponding to that age group. Net rate is the relationship between the number of students enrolled in the schooling level and the population belonging to the age group of that level.

Source: *Anuario Estadístico* (UNESCO), 1988.

matters of primary schooling, which a few years ago were still noticeable, have disappeared.

The period of schooling dedicated to this primary level varies among the different countries of the EC, although those countries where compulsory schooling is shorter – Spain, Italy and Portugal – are seeking to increase the limits, to put them on the same level as the more advanced countries. In Spain, compulsory schooling used to end at the age of 14 years until recently. A new law extended this age to 16 years.

Concerning the pupil/teacher ratio, Spain, with 25 pupils per teacher, officially occupied the second last place, immediately above Ireland, which has 27 pupils per teacher. The Community average was around 18. Reality, however, was quite different. In the 1983–4 school year there were still 35.5 pupils per teacher in public primary schools, and 38.9 in the private sector, according to the study by the Commission des Communautés Européenes (EEC, 1987).

As reported by the OECD in 1985, Spain had poor school buildings and deficient equipment, which severely affected hundreds of thousands of schoolchildren in the compulsory schooling sector, especially in rural areas and on the periphery of large cities. And this is where, in fact, administrative efforts to repair these lacks should be concentrated, since citizens, on their own, are powerless to solve the problems. Experience has taught us, however, that the administration, too distant from weak and needy spots, does not always bear in mind the real lacks of individual school centres, but simply issues orders for every establishment, without taking care of specific problems. Our school system, therefore, must necessarily suffer from its low quality. Such a scenario was evidence of the low quality of primary schooling in Spain. The high rates of children leaving school after primary school confirmed this. Between 1975 and 1980 alone, some 770,000 school children between the ages of 10 and 14 years left the formal educational system.

Among the subjects that form the compulsory schooling programme, the LOGSE includes the study of modern languages. This is a new idea, in harmony with the subjects in the other EC countries, and very much in accord with the European unity that is being advocated.

Secondary schooling

Secondary schooling follows compulsory schooling: it prepares young people for different types of studies and its duration varies in different EC countries, depending on the length of the compulsory schooling period. According to UNESCO, secondary schooling covers second-level general schooling, normal schooling and technical and vocational training. Thus, when secondary schooling rates are mentioned, all three types of teaching have to be included.

Secondary schooling in Spain coincides nowadays with what is known as BUP and COU, and lasts for four years. With the new law, compulsory primary schooling will last until the age of 16, and secondary schooling will then only cover two years, from 16 to 18 years of age. As seen in Table 20.1, the schooling attendance ratio is significantly high in Spain, above 98% and higher than the EC average, which is 85.9%. This seems to indicate that secondary schooling in Spain is practically total, covering all young people between 14 and 19 years of age.

Vocational training experienced a greater proportional increase in the 1980s; 550,068 pupils were registered in 1975, and the figure rose to 1,160,987 in 1987. The number of women registered in this specialty also rose spectacularly. In 1975, the number of women doing vocational training represented 43% of the total, while in 1985 they already had gone up to 50%. In other words, as in the other secondary branches of teaching, the sexes were becoming more equal in vocational training.

Among the various reasons that might explain the high rate of Spanish young people in secondary schooling, an important one is the prohibition in Spain on employing young people under the age of 16. Faced with this fact, young people are forced to continue their studies, in BUP/COU, or in vocational training. This second option is very much devalued in Spain, and those choosing it are almost exclusively the ones who have failed the conventional baccalaureate, or have no economic means to continue with a university career. The administration has been criticized, and rightly, because it has not known how to organize vocational training. It has been overloaded with too many theoretical subjects, to the detriment of practical themes. It seems that the new reform of the educational system will give these studies, so popular in other countries, a new dignity.

Higher education

According to the UNESCO definition, the minimum requirement for higher education is that secondary schooling has been successfully completed, or that the possession of equivalent knowledge be proved. It may be taught in different kinds of establishments, such as universities, colleges, higher vocational schools, etc.

The number of Spanish students undertaking higher education grew faster than the EC average as a whole, during the period of time between 1975 and 1985; the figure for Spain increased by 908 during that time, followed by Belgium, with 764, and the Netherlands, with 704. In 1975, there were 1,518 university students per 100,000 Spanish inhabitants, which went up to 2,426 in 1985, an increase of over one third. In absolute numbers, in 1985, Spanish university students reached the figure of 935,126.

As seen in Table 20.1, the higher level attendance ratio represents 29.6 per cent in 1985, while in 1980 it was only of 22.8 per cent.[3] In comparison with the EC countries, Spain occupies the fifth place, above the UK, Ireland, Greece, Portugal, Luxembourg, etc. It is above the EC average, which is of 26.95%. The big increase in Spanish university undergraduates during the ten years analysed by this chapter was due to various causes, among which may be listed the birth-rate increase of the 1960s, the arrival of women in universities, the increased purchasing power of the Spanish population, a new awareness of the value of studies and the difficulty experienced by young people in finding their first job, which prolonged the years spent studying and led them to start new careers.

The addition of women to studies in general, and to the university in particular, may have been the most important factor in the spectacular increase in Spanish university undergraduates. Thus, during the decade in question male enrolment increased by 526 students per 100,000 inhabitants, while women quadrupled this figure, reaching the number of 2,171, the highest of any EC country.

The educational reform currently under way in Spain touches equally upon university studies, which are going to be in greater harmony with those around us, especially in the EC countries. This reform will mainly deal with the introduction of new careers, especially those with shorter cycles. The General Secretary of the Consejo de Universidades (Council of Universities) himself, when proposing the general guidelines for university reform, admitted the deficiencies of Spanish academic planning on the following points:

— An inadequate list of subjects to be taken at degree level.
— Few first or technical degrees.
— Curricula whose contents were frequently obsolete, too rigid and with little or no variation between centres.
— Study duration longer than the average in the EC countries.
— A rigid connection of each degree to the university centre which organizes its teaching, which means an inefficient use of the available teaching resources and high costs when a new degree is offered.
— Finally, an equally rigid connection between professional degrees and responsibilities, which makes it enormously difficult to add new degrees to the official catalogue.[4]

Public expenditure on education, in relation to the Gross National Product

One of the best indicators of the importance that a country gives to education is the amount invested in relation to its GNP. Authors agree in stating that the golden rule in this sense is that the State should invest 6% of its GNP in education. In 1986, Spain was investing 3.2% of its GNP in education, as seen in Table 20.2. This figure is very much below the average in the EC countries (which was around 5.1 per cent).[5] According to the journal *Coyuntura Económica* (1989), this percentage went up to 4 per cent in 1988, still very modest in relation with the EC average, which was around 6 per cent that year.

Table 20.2 Public expenditure on education in relation to GNP

		Total		Current expenditure		
Country	Year	Amount ('000)	GNP %	Amount ('000)	GNP %	Capital expenditure ('000)
Belgium (B. Frs)	1986	2,772,353,000	5.5	274,357,900	5.5	2,877,400
Denmark (Kr.)	1986	47,696,000	7.7	45,504,000	7.3	21,920,000
France (Frs)	1984	25,880,000	6.1	244,704,000	5.3	14,176,000
FRG (DM)	1985	83,691,000	4.6	75,566,000	4.1	8,125,000
Greece (Dr)	1984	100,293,421	2.6	96,314,851	2.5	3,978,670
Ireland (I£)	1986	1,057,530	6.7	962,795	6.1	94,735
Italy (L)	1986	35,112,000	4.0	—	—	—
Luxembourg (Frs)	1983	13,114,700	5.2	12,315,800	4.9	798,900
Netherlands (Fl.)	1984	27,375,000	6.9	24,168,000	6.1	3,207,000
Portugal (Esc.)	1986	181,841,000	4.4	159,867,000	3.8	21,974,000
Spain (Pts.)	1986	1,010,445	3.2	914,024	2.9	96,421
UK (£)	1984	16,678,000	5.2	16,007,000	5.0	671,000

Source: *Anuario Estadístico*, UNESCO, 1988.

Passing from the percentage of overall expenses in education in relationship with GNP to the percentage used on current expenditure, it is possible to see that these were 2.9 per cent in Spain, far from the Community average of 4.9 per cent.

Conclusions

All through this chapter, the fact has become very apparent that the educational system to be introduced in Spain had numerous points in common with the other EC countries. But analysing qualitative aspects, it is already possible to see substantial differences. In the first place, the LOGSE, Ley de Ordenación General del Sistema Educativo (Law for the General Planning of the Educational System), by which Spain is to be brought closer to Europe, has not yet developed nor has it been compulsorily introduced in our teaching centres. Thus, compulsory or primary schooling finishes at the age of 14. Those who wish to continue with secondary (baccalaureate) studies, will have to do so within the present curriculum, with three years of BUP and the useless COU. Students who start their academic life with the new law will not finish it until the twenty-first century arrives. That is the reason why it is believed that Spanish education will not be at the same level as the rest of Europe until the year 2002. But it is possible that, by then, the other EC countries will have improved their curricula once more, which would again leave Spain at the end of the EC line.

The introduction of new courses, especially technical ones of short duration, has not yet taken place, in spite of their importance for the development of the country, as recognized by the Secretary General of the Council of Universities. Thus, higher education will be disconnected from the real needs of today's society and, as such, it will also be very difficult for Spanish university students to compete in the European labour market when the Single Act comes into effect.

Vocational training is another subject pending resolution within the Spanish educational system, in relation to other EC Member States. This training is not valued as it should be, even within the new law for the reform of teaching.

The budget assigned by the government to education is well below the EC average, and that lack of investment results in a poor quality of teaching.

Notes

1. ES – DOC – DV – 71358.
2. The data offered by UNESCO refer to every primary school, both public and private. Adult schools and classes, and those for handicapped children are not

included. This must be taken into account in order to interpret the tables in this chapter.

3. To calculate higher education schooling rates, UNESCO took into account age groups between 20 and 24 years old.
4. Consejo de Universidades, 1987; pp. 16–17.
5. Table 20.2 presents the total of public expenditure, both current and capital, destined to education in the Gross National Product percentages. UNESCO understands that public expenditures in education are all those public expenses that the government assigns to public schooling, plus the subsidies destined to private schooling. Current and capital expenses are included, whether they are central or federal government expenditure, or from the state government, or the Autonomous Communities, provinces or regions, municipal or local authorities. Current expenses include administration costs, teaching and auxiliary staff salaries, school manuals and other teaching materials, study scholarships, social services and all other operative expenses arising from school establishments. Capital expenses include those relative to land, buildings, construction, equipment, etc.

References

Consejo de Universidades (1987) *Las Enseñanzas Universitarias en España y en la Comunidad Económica Europea*, Madrid.

Commission des Communautés Européenes (1987) *Les structures de l'enseignement dans les Etats membres de la Communauté Européene*, Brussels, Luxembourg.

Schneider, F. (1963) *Educación Europea*, Barcelona, Herder.

UNESCO (1988) *Anuario Estadístico*, Paris.

Chapter 21

Media policy

Emilio Rodríguez Lara

The death of General Franco in 1975 set up a new scenario, felt most especially in the areas of information and mass culture. During the first months of the following year, daily newspapers such as *El País* and *Avui* were born; one year later a Decree-Law on freedom of speech was published, and the Spanish Television (TVE) became an autonomous organization. The first democratic government chosen at the 15 June 1977 elections, abolished the Ministry of Information, a propaganda organization of the previous regime, and started the liberation of the chain of State daily newspapers, which were eventually privatized.

The Spanish Constitution of 1978 devoted Article 20 to the acknowledgement and protection of freedom of speech, in whose application several legal provisions, too numerous to list here, were issued in the course of the next few years.[1] The Constitution establishes regional autonomy and, as the Autonomous Community governments began to appear, the provisions dealing with the media subject to their jurisdiction were also published.

After the October 1982 elections, the Socialist party came into power, thus completing the last phase of the political transition. The status of the different communication media and political action relating to them will be discussed in the next few paragraphs, always from the point of view of integration within the EC. Audiovisual media are grouped together to take account of this sector's power to create European feeling,[2] although the author is conscious of its wide scope and of the fact that television would require a monograph all by itself. The written media are another group, to which information agencies have been added, although these might have been fitted in the former category, due to their multimedia function. In conclusion, this report will try to balance the costs and benefits that Spanish EC membership has brought to the field of mass media, and its prospects for the future.

Audiovisual media

The Law 10/1988, of 3 May, authorized the establishment of private television channels in Spain, although the three companies that were eventually selected did not start regular broadcasting until 1990. Thus ended the monopoly of public television, although the State TVE continues drawing the largest audience.

Article 18 of the Law establishes in its paragraph 3 that, the forecasts of Community law notwithstanding, licence-holding companies will have to be of Spanish nationality and be based in Spain. Article 19 establishes a maximum 25% share participation both for natural or legal persons and for foreign owned shares. However, in the necessary adaptation to the recommendations of the EC Commission, it would be possible for some of the licence-holding companies to have four or more EC owners, not of Spanish nationality, who would control the totality of capital.

One of the private channels, Canal Plus, 25% owned by its French namesake, broadcasts its main programmes in code and charges viewers a certain sum of money to see them. The other two channels, Antena 3 and Tele 5, obtain their income from advertising. Implementation of private TV is still short-lived in Spain, and a perspective is not yet available to show how public television will be affected, as to loss both of audience and of resources.

Television viewing in Spain is similar to that in France or Italy. Beside the three private channels and the two State channels, which are self-financed through advertising, the Autonomic Communities also run television as a third public channel of intermediate strength, grouped in a federation; most of them are in financial deficit.

Faced with the 1993 Single Market, measures aimed at preventing the dynamic expansion of the communication groups which would take the initiative away from law-makers, creating *de facto* situations under cover of regulatory vacuums, are necessary both in Spain and in the rest of the EC countries. Giuseppe Richeri warned of the uncertainty and confusion with which the EC is facing the problem of the European audiovisual industry, and the difficulties encountered in harmonizing interests.[3] There are various EC plans, still only projects, which are a testimony of what it would be necessary to do. Unification of television broadcasting is still far away, but coming closer (EUROPESAT, D2, MAC), as are standards and reception patterns (EUROCRYPT, EUREKA, HDTV) and the production of films and television programmes (MEDIA, EURIMAGES).

The EC is also producing more specific regulations, however, like the Council Directive of 3 October 1989 (89/552/EEC), on the coordination of specific legal, regulatory and administrative provisions of the Member States and relative to the exercise of television broadcasting. It deals with areas such as the promotion of programme distribution and production, advertising regulation, protection of minors, and the right to reply. The main goal is to establish the minimum necessary provisions to guarantee free television broadcasting throughout every EC country, which is the reason why this Directive has been called 'Television without Frontiers' and why it is considered one of the main instruments in the field of mass media to achieve European unity, due to the importance it generally granted to television as a vehicle of cultural dissemination.

Some think that the Council of Europe would be a better geographic framework in which to prepare a cultural media policy.[4] Convention CM 89/72 was signed in May 1989, dealing with cross-boundary dissemination of television. The matters with which it deals are very similar to those under the previously mentioned Directive, but the procedure for their application is more complex and requires ratification by all the Member States. Article 25 of Directive 89/552 EEC made it compulsory for Member States to adopt, before 3 October 1991, the legal, regulatory and administrative provisions necessary for its fulfilment. Spanish legislation is adapting itself to the Community regulations, as for example in the Resolution of the Dirección General de Medios de Comunicación Social, of 17 April 1990, which published the regulatory norms for advertising broadcasts on TVE. For advertising quotas within the daily programming, the 15% maximum established by the Directive has been set, while adopting more restrictive criteria, requiring advertising time not to exceed ten minutes per hour, instead of the 20% specified by the Directive, which would be the equivalent to twelve minutes per hour. The yearly calculation, of which the Directive makes no mention, was established at 10%. These same criteria had already been followed in the 1988 private television Law.

One section on which the TVE regulations almost literally duplicate those of the Directive, is that dealing with alcoholic beverage advertising. Rules for the protection of children with respect to television advertising not only duplicate the EC rules, but have also been enlarged to include toy advertising and children acting in publicity spots, which were not included in the Directive. The same happened with medical drug advertising, the scope of which now includes regulations on cosmetics and other health products. Regulations on how to insert advertising in the programmes, and on sponsored programmes, also follow the EC Directive. No mention is made in TVE advertising regulations of tobacco products, expressly forbidden in Article 13 of the Directive. In the previous TVE regulations, however, tobacco was given the same treatment as alcoholic beverages, and Article 8.5 of the General Advertising Law of 11 November 1988 forbade television advertising of tobacco and beverages with more than 20° alcoholic content, although the application of this rule was conditional on later regulatory planning. The declaration of motives for this Law begins with the express statement of the need to harmonize Spanish legislation with that of the EC, especially with Directive 84/450 EEC, of 10 September 1984, on misleading advertising.

Chapter III of Directive 89/552 EEC approaches one of the matters of greatest importance for the promotion of European industry competition in this sector. It is the establishment of quotas in programming reserved for broadcasting of EC origin. Article 4 establishes that the television broadcasting organizations shall reserve the majority of their broadcasting time for European programmes, although this proportion will have to be achieved progressively, and a series of mechanisms for EC action were established to this end. Article 5 reserves a minimum of 10% of broadcasting time or, as an alternative, and if the Member State so chooses, a minimum of 10% of its programming budget, for European works by producers independent of television broadcasting organizations. This is done in order to help other cultural industries, especially film-making.

For Spanish private television the Law set a minimum 40% quota for production originating in EC countries, and also demands that 15% be produced by the holder of the licence itself. It establishes as well that no less than 40% of commercial films shown every month be of EC origin. Although this regulation only refers to the three private channels, it should eventually be extended to the two State TVE channels. Autonomous Community stations would be outside the scope of the EC Directive which, for these purposes, excludes any television channels which are not part of a national network. The private television Law is in harmony with the Directive, especially if the fact is taken into account that the latter mentions quotas for 'European works', which are understood to be those originating in EC Member States or in bordering States which form part of the crossboundary Television Convention of the Council of Europe or third European countries, as long as certain requirements of majority EC participation in these works are met. The Spanish Law is more restrictive, demanding that they are productions originating in 'integrating countries of the European Community'.

Another provision of the private television Law which has to be interpreted as protection for the cinema industry is the one stating that in no case may commercial films be shown until two years after they were first seen in Spain, or until two years after their production, if they have not been shown in Spain. Films made to be shown exclusively on television, or those produced by the television company itself, are excluded.

TVE has made an effort to produce films, but the sums of money it has been granting to this endeavour are negligible when compared with those spent on purchasing foreign productions. Films are the television programmes with the highest audiences, and the consumption of films is growing, both on television and on videocassettes. According to data from the Instituto de la Cinematografía y de las Artes Visuales,[5] the number of spectators in Spanish cinemas has been decreasing throughout the 1980s, with the exception of 1989, the last one on which data are available, and where a slight recovery may be noticed. But the 1989 increase is due solely to the increase in those who viewed foreign films, since those who went to Spanish films continued to decrease. This increase in foreign-film viewers is the only positive aspect in the Spanish cinematographic scenario. The total number of cinemas continues to decrease, although some specialization has occurred, as well as the conversion of some large cinemas into several small ones. Spanish film production has also gone down during the last five years. Spain depends on North American distributors and productions, and in 1989 broke the world record for increased film purchasing from the United States, turning into its sixth customer at world level.

Spanish cinema has touched bottom, and its industrial structures are now almost non-existent. Its only salvation might be a joint effort with the EC countries, adapting its protection system to EC rules, since protection – as in the other European countries – is essential. Establishing quotas, as mentioned in Directive 89/552 EEC may be the way to maintain this cultural industry by means of television and video films.

Videocassette rental has decreased with the increased TV film offering, when private channels came into being, although their sale has increased, due to lower prices. The ownership rate of video sets in Spain is 145 per 1,000 inhabitants, while it is 200 in the rest of the EC, which probably means that some increase is to be expected.

Radio seems to complement the repertoire of audiovisual media. It is the first medium as far as credibility is concerned, the second in audience ratio, after television, and the last in advertising revenue, although it seems to be sufficient to maintain the sector's prosperity and a high level of income and profit. However, this prosperous era should be taken advantage of to fund future technological change. The EC EUREKA programme includes a land-radio network digitalization project for the year 2000, in order to be able to offer maximum quality.

Printed media and agencies

Paradoxically, the Spanish press is the leading media sector in terms of revenue while, at the same time, is has one of the lowest diffusion rates in Europe. In 1988, the diffusion rate (daily newspaper issues sold per thousand inhabitants) was 82.2, which goes down to 71.1 if we take into account only general information newspapers, excluding those dealing solely with sport.[6] Only Portugal has a lower rate of press diffusion among the EC countries. Advertising income, which has continuously grown, has turned the press into an expanding sector. Another characteristic is the ever-growing number of new papers on the market, although some are simply local issues of larger ones; entrepreneurial concentration is happening at the same time.

The influx of foreign capital in significant amounts has already begun in the daily press, most of it from EC countries, although its presence had already been felt in periodicals, where it already dominates half of the capital in magazines, has an important role in newspaper and periodical printers, and totally dominates distribution. The flexibility of restrictive rules in EC countries, due to the EC legislation, has given capital an opportunity to go international, as a way out of the concentration in the northern EC countries, where barriers of linguistic, institutional and other types have been putting a brake on expansion.[7] Capital diversification into different media is another method of concentration, which may eventually become overlapping monopolies, requiring regulating intervention from the EC.

In general terms, the non-daily press has much lower levels of diffusion in Spain than in the central Community countries, approximately one third of that registered in France or Germany, but it is an expanding sector, with a strong presence of foreign capital. Romantic magazines are a high proportion of sales, although general information magazines attract the highest percentage of advertising revenue.

The need to remove subsidies, with the Single Market of 1993 in mind, has been the cause of problems for the Spanish press. Even though advertising revenues have been high, and in most cases these earnings have been used to update technology, circulation is very low, and they depend almost exclusively on advertising; it is, therefore, a sector with little consolidation, which would succumb to competition from northern EC companies. Spain may well need a transition period of subsidies to allow it to fit in to the schedule of European unification. Before 1990, direct aid to the press had already been eliminated; it had been granted on the basis of circulation, newsprint consumption and the cost of technological conversion; at the end of that year, indirect aid, that is, reduction of postal, transport, telecommunication and taxation rates, was also removed. Since several EC countries are still applying such subsidies, Spanish newspapers would find themselves in a disadvantageous position.

A pluralist model of information agencies exists in Spain, as in other Latin countries; the dominant feature is one great national agency, linked to the State. The Agencia EFE is the most important one in the Spanish-speaking countries, and the Spanish State is its majority partner; it maintains a service contract with it, which is the company's main source of income. Integration in Europe has brought an effort to achieve greater competitivity, so that the proportion of income arising from sale of services in the market becomes larger, while State dependency decreases. EFE has started a process of technological updating, among which the use of the INTELSAT satellite may be mentioned. EFE, formerly a press agency, has now become a multimedia news agency, following the trend of the great world agencies. Its TV and radio departments, with information and programme production services, are acquiring increasing importance, and it has joined the European Photograph Agency (EPA), with headquarters in Frankfurt, which is formed by ten European national agencies. Among EFE's specialized services, the EFECOM, or economic information service, is domestically important. EFE's foreign projection is mainly aimed at the Hispanic American countries, and has achieved much in Central America, through the regional information cooperative ACAN-EFE It also offers English and Portuguese language services, however, and maintains links with media and agencies all over the world.

Europa Press is the main privately owned agency in Spain. It is financially linked to Opus Dei, a Roman Catholic organization widely implanted in the worlds of politics and business, which has given particular attention to the field of information and communications. There are several minor agencies, with specialist activities or working with regional daily newspapers, among which Colpisa, OTR and LID may be mentioned.

The balance

The implementation of the Single Market may represent an invasion by foreign (EC) capital of Spanish media companies and this, in principle, would be harmful for the autonomy of a sector which is not simply an economic entity, but a producer of culture as well. This invasion, however, is already happening and would have come about anyway, whether or not Spain had joined the EC. It cannot, thus, be counted on the negative side of the balance.

Community regulations on audiovisual media, on television especially, are not only going to be a means of achieving free movement of broadcasting, programmes, capital or workers, but will force the media of each of the Member States to follow regulations on advertising or for the protection of children, for instance, and this must be hailed as positive.

In the short run, the press may be the most harmed, although some Spanish companies are already applying strategies which will allow them to adapt smoothly. The idea of the press as a public service which has prevailed in the southern European countries may have contributed to this lack of preparation to face competition, but if the transition phase is overcome in gradual steps, the press may continue its social role as a public service and still become competitive.

On the whole, the balance is positive. Among other things, because not belonging to the EC would be much more harmful than the upheavals that its membership might cause.

Notes

1. Augustín Martínez de las Heras (1989), 'Las etapas españolas de la desreglamentación', in Alvarez, J.T. *et al.*, p. 429.
2. Georg-Michael Luyken (1990) 'Europa 1992: ¿También un mercado interior para los medios?', in Fundesco, p. 90.
3. Giuseppe Richeri (1990), 'El nuevo horizonte de la televisión en Europa', in Fundesco, pp. 197–8.
4. Fundesco (1989), *La Televisión europea del año 2000*, Informe del Grupo de Prospectiva de la Televisión Europea, Madrid, p. 82.
5. Bernardo Diaz Nosty (1990), 'El estado de la comunicación', in Fundesco, p. 54.
6. Ibid., p. 17.
7. Jean-Marie Charon (1990), 'Perspectivas de la prensa europea', in Fundesco, p. 115.

References

Alvarez, Jesús Timoteo *et al.*, (1989) *Historia de los medios de comunicación en España: Periodismo, imagen y publicidad (1900–1990)*, Barcelona, Ariel.

Banco de Bilbao Vizcaya (1990/1) *Informe sobre la Información: España 1990*, Bilbao.

Bustamante, E. and Zallo, R., (1988) *Las industrias culturales en España*. Madrid, Akal.

Fundesco (1989) *La televisión europea del año 2000: Informe del Grupo de Prospectiva de la Televisión Europea*, Madrid, Fundesco.

—— (1990) *Comunicación Social 1990/Tendencias Los medios ante el Mercado Unico Europeo: Informes Anuales de Fundesco*, Madrid.

Chapter 22

Tourism and cultural policy

Lorenzo Navarrete Moreno and Antonio Alvarez Sousa

Membership of the EC has meant changes to Spain's political, economic and sociocultural structures. These structures condition the movement of tourists, which gives rise to the assumption that there have been changes in Spanish international tourism[1] after its entry into the EC. These changes will be evaluated here in terms of costs or benefits.

Tourism and the theory of systems

Tourism is by no means an independent sector. The theory of systems states that it is a subsystem within a wider system (see Sessa, 1985), and its cultural, economic, political and social aspects are conditioned by the structure of society (Figuerola, 1985). Changes in the structure of society influence tourism and, in turn, changes in tourism will influence the structure of society, giving rise to costs and benefits (see AIEST, 1982).

Several authors have analysed the adaptation of the theory of systems to tourism (see Sessa, 1985). Retroaction effects happen inside an open system, such that changes in the general structure affect the subsystems, and their changes affect the general system. This is called 'retroaction' or the feed-back effect: the environment conditions the various systems, and they, in turn, have an effect on the environment.

Figure 22.1 is a summary of the effects of the different systems on tourism and their mutual relationships to shape the structure of society. The effects of tourism over the systems shown in Figure 22.1 which condition it are its costs or benefits. They affect elements of economic, social, cultural or political order,[2] indicating that analysis may not be carried out in simple quantifiable terms, since there are some aspects which are difficult, or impossible, to quantify (AIEST, 1982). Figure 22.2 summarizes these costs or benefits.

Tourism is an activity related to a large number of subsectors, independently of the organic structure in which it may be set, both in the EC and in the different Member States, and of the aspect from which it may be considered. In the Commission, tourism is located within GD XXIII,

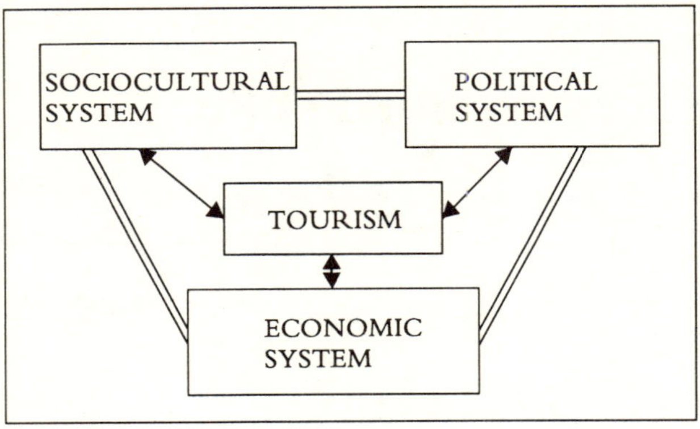

Figure 22.1 The feedback system between tourism and the structure of society

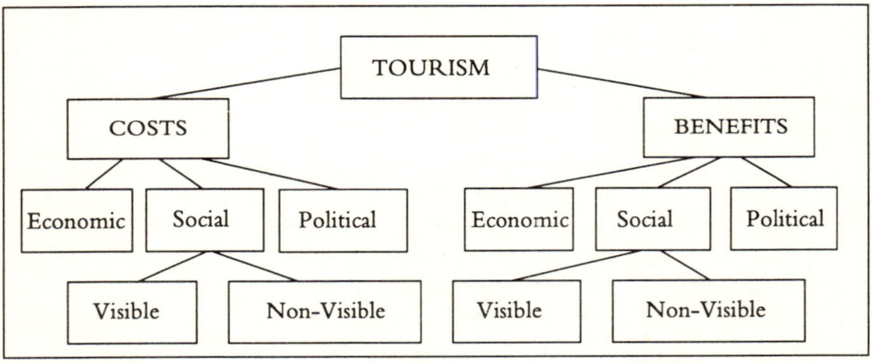

Figure 22.2 The EC and its influence on tourist structures

'Policy relating to enterprise, trade, tourism and social economy'. However, actions that influence tourism are to be found in other General Directives, as will be seen further on. In Spain[3] there is a General Secretariat for Tourism, under the Ministry of Transport, Tourism and Communications, but actions which affect tourism are also generated by the Ministries of Work and Social Security, of Social Affairs, etc. This is true again if we examine the various subjects under which studies on tourism have arisen: architecture, law, sociology, economics, anthropology, geography, etc. This adds an interdisciplinary dimension to its field, as well as the need to take into account the different aspects of EC policies that influence tourism, not only those within the Tourism Department of GD XXIII; perhaps the others might have a greater repercussion on tourism than those depending on GD XXIII.

To summarize, two types of EC action may be mentioned among those influencing tourism: (a) general actions – other than political ones – with

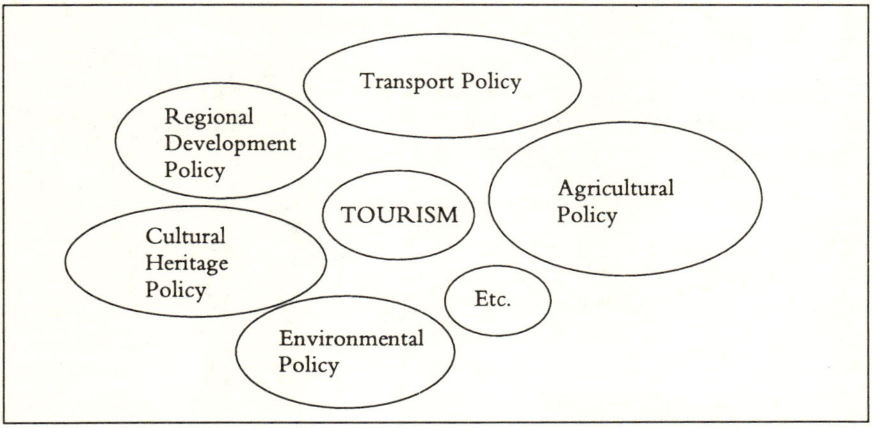

Figure 22.3 The policies which might affect tourism

important effects on the sector; and (b) specific actions. Figure 22.3 shows how other policies affect tourism, without completely encompassing it.

General actions that contribute to the development of tourism

Among general actions initiated by the EC which influence tourism, free movement of people between EC countries (the 1992 myth) may be mentioned, which for the time being involves the simplification of bureaucratic procedures and a diminution of Customs controls. This means easier travel, with shorter travelling times and, especially, shorter queuing times, which were a negative aspect for tourists.

The development of infrastructure such as communication networks, which greatly favour intercommunity relations, agricultural policy to improve farm dwellings, or environmental policy, also contribute positively to tourism. These policies become manifest as EC financial instruments through the European Regional Development Fund (ERDF), the European Agriculture Guidance and Guarantee Fund (EAGGF) and the European Social Fund (ESF). The purpose of the ERDF is to contribute to the reduction of imbalance between regions. Tourism is one of the factors which contributes to this end and, therefore, these funds should favour hotel building and any aspect related to tourist activities and communications infrastructures. The EAGGF, whose purpose is to develop rural areas, may contribute to the development of rural tourism, as the EEC Rules No. 4256/88 of the Council directly mention: 'Promotion of tourist and crafts investment, including the improvement of dwellings in rural operations', 'Environmental protection and the preservation of natural space'. The ESF's purpose is to foster employment and training. It serves as an application of the other two, since it contributes to training and recycling the human capital that will later implement the ERDF and EAGGF projects. It affects tourism directly, by providing vocational training for the sector.

Actions specific to the tourism sector

This policy includes two stages: one which covers the period of time between 1984 (Council Resolution on a Community Tourism Policy; DO No. 115) to 1986 (Council Resolution relative to improved seasonal and geographical distribution of tourism; DO No. C 340) and another, from 1988 (European Parliament Resolution on facilities for tourism, and its promotion and consolidation in the EC; DO No. C 49 and a Council Decision on a programme for the European Tourism Year, 1990; DO L 17) to the present time. A two-year gap appears in the middle – 1986–8.

These Decisions and Resolutions, as well as other proposals and reports related to this sector, may be summarized as follows:

— The distribution of tourism in space and time contributes to the correction of geographical and seasonal costs. This is made possible by means of guiding the provision of services and shaping demand towards social,[4] rural and cultural[5] tourism.
— Tourists may be influenced towards and given the legal means to demand safety and quality of service – this will result in an improvement in the provision of services.
– Increase knowledge and coordination in the sector, by harmonizing studies and surveys, as well as facilitating the cooperation of the various suppliers.
— Project financing (photography, cleanest city, etc.) for events such as the European Tourism Year. Advertising campaigns in countries such as the United States, Japan, etc., and the promotion of tourism within the EC, emphasizing the values of our common heritage – through the St. James's Route, for instance.

Consequences of community action on costs and benefits of tourism and its application to Spain

Tourism is a sector which satisfies certain positive economic, social, cultural and political functions – benefits, in other words. It is also accompanied by a series of handicaps or negative aspects – costs – which, although difficult to eliminate, may be modified by specific action. Let us now analyse these effects on Spain, following its EC membership.

Movement of travellers between the EC countries and Spain, after entry.[6]

To measure the implications for tourism in Spain after its entry into the EC, the movement of travellers is first considered, from entry to 1989, comparing it with a previous period of the same number of years. This is done both for Spanish travellers going abroad and for foreign travellers from the EC into Spain (see Table 22.1).

Table 22.1 Spanish visitors abroad, 1982 to 1989*

Year	Total ('000)	Previous year ('000)	Percentage change	Absolute change
1982	13,916	14,355	−3.1	−439
1983	14,245	13,916	2.4	329
1984	14,620	14,245	2.6	374
1985	15,651	14,620	7.1	1,032
1986	17,637	15,651	12.7	1,986
1987	18,228	17,367	3.3	590
1988	18,985	18,228	4.2	757
1989	23,306	18,985	22.8	4,321

* A yearly average of 40% left by Seo de Urgel-Andorra, for 24 hours.

Source: The authors, from data collected by the Secretaría General de Turismo del Ministerio de Transportes, Turismo y Comunicaciones.

An analysis of the data presented in Table 22.1 for 1982 to 1989, shows two time-periods: 1982–5 – prior to membership – and 1986–9 – following membership. Before membership, the cumulative yearly average increase of Spanish visitors abroad was of 2.25%. In the next period, following membership, this index rose to 10.75%. Figure 22.4 shows this increase.

As seen in Table 22.2, there has also been an increase in visitors from different EC countries into Spain. Against a cumulative yearly average growth of 1% during the first four years – prior to membership – the later period showed a 5.8% increase (see Figure 22.5).[7]

It may be said, to sum up, that the movement of travellers seems to indicate that Spain's entry into the EC has been accompanied by a very high increase in interrelations with other EC countries, and by a Spanish opening up towards the world in general.

Economic benefits of tourism

Travel has an important role in the economy. Table 22.3 presents an income and expenditure table for international tourism in the EC countries.[8] It may be stated that, as a general trend, there was a very strong increase from 1980

Table 22.2 Visitors to Spain, from the EC countries, 1981–9

EEC countries	1981 '000	1982 '000	Percentage change 1981/2	1983	Percentage change 1982/3	1984	Percentage change 1983/4	1985	Percentage change 1984/5	1986	Percentage change 1985/6	1987	Percentage change 1986/7	1988	Percentage change 1987/8	1989	Percentage change 1988/9
FRG	4,778	4,561	4.8	4,970	4.0	5,250	5.6	5,644	7.5	5,935	5.2	6,596	11.1	6,904	4.7	6,784	−1.7
Belgium	1,002	1,077	−7.0	1,023	2.1	1,002	−2.0	1,053	5.1	1,120	6.4	1,266	13.0	1,383	9.3	1,375	−0.6
Denmark	391	387	1.2	396	1.2	418	5.7	445	6.4	516	16.0	573	11.0	609	6.3	537	−11.8
France	10,872	10,659	2.0	10,331	−5.0	9,982	−3.3	11,001	10.2	11,280	2.5	11,671	3.5	12,086	3.5	11,994	−0.8
Greece	53	52	2.4	45	−14.9	48	5.8	52	8.6	48	−7.8	56	16.8	75	34.0	68	−9.5
Netherlands	1,356	1,381	−1.9	1,315	−3.0	1,385	5.3	1,417	2.3	1,557	9.8	1,685	8.2	2,004	19.0	2,035	1.5
Ireland	245	214	14.5	236	−4.0	240	1.7	207	−13.8	242	17.0	276	14.1	296	7.4	233	−21.5
Italy	658	559	17.7	669	1.8	814	21.6	1,022	25.5	1,090	6.6	1,193	9.4	1,333	11.8	1,512	13.4
Luxembourg	56	59	−4.2	56	−0.8	59	5.5	60	1.9	68	13.5	79	16.0	85	7.2	88	4.4
Portugal	9,235	9,377	−1.5	8,466	−8.3	8,352	−1.3	7,742	−7.3	9,524	23.0	8,969	−5.8	10,065	12.2	10,044	−0.2
UK	4,850	4,064	19.3	5,188	7.0	6,027	16.2	5,035	−16.5	6,429	27.7	7,550	17.4	7,646	1.3	7,346	−3.9
Total EC	33,496	32,390	3.4	32,695	−2.4	33,577	2.7	33,678	0.3	37,809	12.3	39,914	5.6	42,486	6.4	42,016	−1.1

Source: The authors, from data collected by the General Tourism Secretariat, Ministry of Transport, Tourism and Communications.

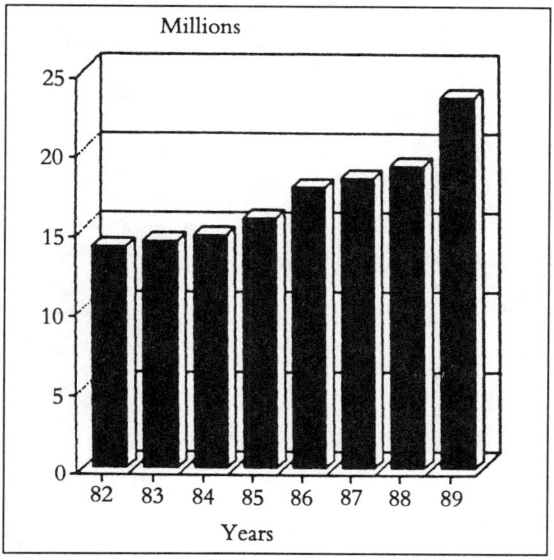

Figure 22.4 Spanish visitors going abroad

Source: Author, from data in Table 22.1.

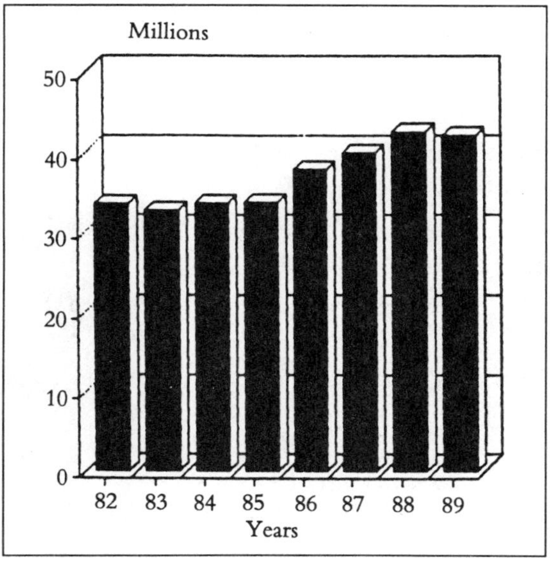

Figure 22.5 Visitors to Spain from the EC

Source: Authors, from data in Table 22.2.

Table 22.3 Travel: annual balance of payments data (ECU millions)

	1980	1981	1982	1983	1984	1985	1986	1987
Credit								
Benelux	1,304	1,469	1,605	1,927	2,117	2,195	2,316	2,615
Denmark	962	1,130	1,336	1,467	1,644	1,750	1,794	1,926
FRG	3,540	3,911	4,094	4,743	5,470	6,278	6,441	6,693
Greece	1,915	1,747	1,579	1,341	1,690	1,848	1,835	1,979
Spain	4,989	6,139	7,329	7,734	9,870	10,610	12,165	12,829
France	5,929	6,518	7,081	8,106	9,666	10,493	9,856	10,297
Ireland	412	446	515	543	608	726	669	725
Italy	5,986	6,566	8,210	9,690	10,454	10,966	10,055	10,540
Netherlands	1,197	1,480	1,582	1,657	2,156	2,195	2,279	2,343
Portugal	823	925	884	927	1,208	1,458	1,547	1,858
UK	4,957	5,351	5,705	6,874	7,799	9,321	8,262	8,884
Debit								
Benelux	2,369	2,604	2,236	2,357	2,486	2,706	2,947	3,426
Denmark	1,122	1,158	1,363	1,362	1,564	1,861	2,160	2,480
FRG	12,467	13,224	14,389	14,944	15,799	16,919	18,530	20,454
Greece	223	330	384	409	431	478	498	438
Spain	883	917	1,038	1,007	1,069	1,310	1,530	1,705
France	4,326	5,173	5,247	4,818	5,432	6,023	6,622	7,369
Ireland	442	462	503	505	521	560	695	705
Italy	1,371	1,267	1,473	1,586	2,191	2,471	2,971	3,928
Netherlands	3,361	3,208	3,492	3,705	4,168	4,515	5,009	5,572
Portugal	209	223	253	256	283	306	331	366
UK	4,590	5,888	6,536	7,032	7,891	8,341	8,961	10,341
Net								
Benelux	−1,065	−1,135	−631	−430	−369	−511	−629	−811
Denmark	−160	−28	−27	105	80	−111	−366	−554
FRG	−8,928	−9,313	−10,295	−10,201	−10,330	−10,643	−12,089	−13,761
Greece	1,691	1,417	1,194	932	1,258	1,370	1,337	1,541
Spain	4,106	5,223	6,292	6,727	8,802	9,300	10,635	11,125
France	1,603	1,345	1,834	3,288	4,233	4,471	3,264	2,929
Ireland	−30	−16	−12	38	87	166	−26	20
Italy	4,527	5,299	6,737	8,103	8,263	8,495	7,085	6,612
Netherlands	−2,614	−1,728	−1,910	−2,048	−2,012	−2,320	−2,730	−3,229
Portugal	614	702	631	670	925	1,151	1,216	1,492
UK	367	−537	−831	−158	−92	979	−700	−1,457

Source: Eurostat, 1990, p. 211.

to 1987, not just in nominal terms, but in real terms as well. If a positive balance is present in the EC as a whole, the importance is clear when analysing the balance per country: tourism serves as a balance sector, for income redistribution inside the EC, since it has favourable repercussions on the poorer countries. Spain and Portugal show the most favourable balances, with FRG and the Netherlands at the opposite extreme.

Table 22.4 Share of travel in the total balance of payments of each EC Member State (%)

Country	R/E*	1980	1981	1982	1983	1984	1985	1986	1987
Benelux	R	2.0	1.8	1.9	2.2	2.1	2.0	2.1	2.3
	E	3.4	3.1	2.6	2.7	2.5	2.5	2.9	3.2
Denmark	R	5.5	5.7	5.9	5.8	5.8	5.5	5.9	6.1
	E	5.9	5.4	5.5	5.2	5.1	5.3	6.3	7.3
FRG	R	2.7	2.7	2.5	2.6	2.6	2.1	2.1	2.2
	E	8.5	8.1	8.0	7.8	7.2	6.5	7.4	7.9
Greece	R	20.7	22.1	19.6	16.6	18.1	19.8	19.7	21.7
	E	2.6	3.0	3.3	3.4	3.1	3.0	3.9	3.5
Spain	R	20.5	20.8	20.6	21.1	21.1	21.0	25.9	26.1
	E	3.0	2.6	2.5	2.5	2.3	2.7	3.5	3.3
France	R	4.2	3.8	4.1	4.4	4.6	4.7	4.8	5.0
	E	3.1	3.0	2.9	2.6	2.6	2.7	3.3	3.6
Ireland	R	5.6	5.1	5.1	4.7	4.2	4.5	4.5	4.5
	E	4.2	3.9	3.9	3.7	3.1	3.1	4.1	4.1
Italy	R	8.5	7.2	8.1	8.8	8.2	8.1	7.7	7.8
	E	1.6	1.3	1.4	1.4	1.7	1.7	2.4	2.9
Netherlands	R	1.7	1.8	1.8	1.8	2.0	1.9	2.2	2.2
	E	4.8	4.1	4.1	4.2	4.2	4.3	5.1	5.4
Portugal	R	16.7	17.1	14.7	11.8	13.4	14.0	15.5	16.5
	E	2.7	2.2	2.1	2.3	2.3	2.4	2.9	2.5
UK	R	3.4	2.8	2.7	3.3	3.2	3.5	3.8	4.0
	E	3.4	3.4	3.3	3.5	3.3	3.3	4.2	4.7
EC-12	R	4.4	4.2	4.3	4.6	4.7	4.6	4.9	5.0
	E	4.3	4.1	4.0	4.0	3.8	3.7	4.5	4.9

* R = Revenue, E = Expenditure

Source: Eurostat, 1990, p. 213.

Tourism plays a very important role in the balance of payments of the EC countries. The relative importance of tourism in the balance of payments for goods and services of the Member States is shown in Table 22.4, from 1980 to 1987. A small positive balance is much more important in the balance of poorer Member States, such as Spain, Portugal or Greece.

In conclusion, it may be said that tourism is vitally important to the Spanish economy, as the most favoured EC country in terms of income

Table 22.5 Foreign currency income from tourism

Year	Total ($m.)	Change (%)
1981	6,715.9	—
1982	7,126.1	6.1
1983	6,386.1	−4.1
1984	7,716.7	12.9
1985	8,150.8	5.6
1986	12,058.4	47.9
1987	14,759.9	22.4
1988	16,686.3	13.0
1989	16,174.2	−3.1

Source: Secretaría General de Turismo, Ministerio de Transportes, Turismo y Comunicaciones.

generated by international tourism. After entry into the EC, a major increase in income was registered during the years 1986, 1987 and 1988.

However, 1989 and 1990 have shown a decreasing tendency: The diminishing trend of tourism and foreign currency receipts shown in Tables 22.2 and 22.3 for 1989, and which was repeated in 1990, is accompanied by the need for a new formulation of the specific items which affect tourist demands: the quality supplied (buildings, services, environment) and the marketing, which are considered to be the culprits. EC policy is positive in this respect and contributes to reducing the costs by granting funds (Comisión de las Comunidades Europeas, 1990). These subsidies funding specific action are accompanied by an environmental policy which also seeks to minimize earlier effects. This is a great improvement on the previous Spanish policy. Promotion of Spanish tourism in third countries is also a useful aid.

Economic costs of tourism

Activities related to mass tourism are centred around the sun, sea and sex; the best season to enjoy them is, of course, summer. As a result, demand is focused on these months, affecting the seasonality of the sector, and causing many centres to close for the rest of the year. All this, and the fact that tourist motives are not diversified and there is no promotion that would correct this, means that tourism is massed around very specific areas, from which it spreads to other sectors of the economy, even causing its destruction.[9]

These two problems – namely, seasonality and geographical concentration – have a high incidence in Spain. The Community Resolutions (Council Resolutions of 22 December 1986, relevant to a better seasonal and geographical distribution of tourism; DO No. C 340) are a very important step towards their resolution, aimed at causing a seasonal and geographical redistribution of tourism to solve the economic problems caused by these factors.

Sociocultural and political benefits of tourism

The economic benefits of tourism are even more important if its social repercussion is taken into account. Tourism gives jobs to a high percentage of the population. It is estimated that around 5% of total employment in direct jobs and over double that proportion in indirect ones in Spain comes from this sector.[10] This has alleviated Spanish unemployment.

At the cultural level, tourism has historically meant one of the most important means of communication and cultural exchange between European countries. In Spain, the pilgrimage to Santiago de Compostela has had enormous influence as a precursor to tourism, as a channel for communications and in allowing the penetration of cultural styles, giving its route a rich artistic-cultural heritage.

The first EC guidelines on tourism were published in 1984, and they already pointed to its cultural importance, arguing that 'Article 2 of the Treaty of Rome assigns to the EC the mission of promoting more direct relations between the nations which it unites. Tourism helps the EC to accomplish this mission. In putting into contact the nations of Europe, tourism constitutes an important aspect of European integration.' (DO, No. C 115, 1984:2).

One of Europe's goals is integration, not only at political and economic levels, but also culturally;[11] free movement of people is, therefore, one of the basic pillars of European integration, facilitating contacts between countries through tourism. Interrelation among people of different countries favours contacts and contributes to world peace and harmony,[12] strengthening the feeling of belonging to the same community of citizens.

The Council of Ministers of the EC agreed on action and aid to foster this, stating among other things that 'the integrating function of tourism can be taken advantage of to prepare for the implementation of the great 1993 space without frontiers', considering that tourism 'allows the promotion of a wider knowledge for the citizens of the cultures and life-styles of the other Member States' (Council Decision, 21 December 1988, relative to a programme of actions for the European Tourism Year, 1990; DO No. L 17, 1989: 53).

The incidence of this aspect is enormous in Spain. There has been a very important increase of people entering and leaving the country after entry into the EC, as reflected in Figures 22.4 and 22.5. If one remembers the historical isolation of Spain from Europe, and the need to integrate, then tourism is fulfilling a function of the first magnitude.

Sociocultural and political costs of tourism

There are several costs which may be put down to tourism. The most important ones are listed below:

— Social problems caused by unemployment, due to the seasonality of this sector.

— Impacts on the environment and cultural erosion, not only affecting monuments, but also to cultural peculiarities that are often turned into objects of tourism, and thus lose value and turn commercial, giving rise to an identity crisis and social conflicts.
— Drugs, prostitution, etc., since tourism has a liberalizing function or spring-board effect with respect to the destruction of daily life, habits, standards and roles, when everything is allowed for one month of the year, because 'I am on holiday'.
— Other problems have also appeared recently, such as laundering of money from illegal activities, refuge of delinquents, etc. These are made easier in tourist centres where social controls are low and police controls are difficult because of the excessive movement of people.

These are problems that stem from tourist activities themselves. EC membership and the subsequent protective measures brought forward their solution, bearing in mind that many problems would have been impossible for one single state to solve independently from the others, as the solutions required international measures. The EC rules and aid granted to the environment are very well known. The guidelines and protection relevant for maintenance of heritage items are also clear: integration does not mean destruction, but an understanding of diversity. Other problems, i.e. unemployment, are being fought on two fronts: one, by means of the European Social Fund; the other, through the promotion of tourism in other seasons of the year, thus helping to solve problems of traffic congestion and overloading of the environment, as well as favouring employment throughout the whole year.

Conclusion

The conclusion arising from all of this is that membership of the EC has meant a great step forward in tourism for Spain: positive aspects – benefits – have increased, and a solution to negative aspects – costs – is being sought.

In spite of the steps taken, however, EC action on tourism is still limited, although this sector is considered of vital importance. It is necessary to correct its total subordination to other policies; even though it is true that it must be connected with them, there are some aspects which may be only covered by a tourist policy, which could also benefit from action taken under other policies which might touch upon it (see Figure 22.3). This is why the creation of an independent Directorate General in charge of developing a continuous and coherent policy for tourism is necessary to coordinate the interests of the different Member States.

Notes

1. International tourism is understood as travelling to a country different from one's own, for a period of time exceeding 24 hours, for non-professional activities. (There are different definitions, which may be found in any manual relevant to the topic, i.e., Wackermann, 1988; Smith, 1989).
2. Besides these, the environment is an important sector of touristic impact. However, since its solution relies on political problems and decisions, it will be analysed within this field.
3. After the formation of the regional or Autonomous Community governments (Spanish Constitution, Title VIII, Article 148), some responsibility for tourism passed to the Autonomous Communities. Those relevant to international tourism, however, and some others, are still under the central government.
4. Senior citizens may travel free during the low season.
5. These two last types of tourism are increasingly valuable to the 'public', even though the 'masses' practise them less.
6. Data in this paragraph are relevant to movement of travellers in general. Since there is no control of the activities – touristic or professional – developed in most countries visited (none at all in the EC), it is difficult to evaluate who does what; in future, surveys will measure these factors. Data relevant to Spanish residents refer to travel to all countries of the world.
7. The decreasing trend of 1989 should be mentioned, however. This will be commented upon later.
8. This table, and the following, only contain data relevant to the time period 1980–7. The years 1988 and 1989 are not anlaysed because no data comparing countries were available for this period.
9. This destruction may become irreversible once tourism moves to a different geographic area.
10. Eurostat, 1987, reports that direct employment accounts for 579,400 jobs out of a total of 11,368,900 jobs in all economic sectors. However, because of its seasonal characteristics and because it sometimes is 'invisible' – this being one of the costs of tourism – it is hard to calculate all jobs generated in this sector.
11. We feel that economic and political integration needs a simultaneous cultural integration, which takes into account values and their differences.
12. See WTO, 1980.

References

Association Internationale d'Experts Scientifiques du Tourism (AIEST) (1982) *Interrelation between Benefits and Costs of Tourist Resources*, Vol. 23.
Comisión de las Comunidades Europeas (1990) Marco Comunitario de Apoyo

1989–1993, España, Luxembourg. Oficina de Publicaciones Oficiales de las Comunidades Europeas.

Eurostat (1990) *Tourisme 1987, Statistiques Annuelles*, Luxembourg, Office des Communautés Européennes.

Figuerola, M. (1985) *Teoría económica del turismo*, Madrid Alianza Universidad.

Sessa, A. (ed.) (1985) *La Scienza dei sistemi pero lo sviluppo del turismo*, Roma, Editrice Agnesotti.

Smith, Stephen L.J. (1989) *Tourism Analysis*, New York, Longman Scientific & Technical.

Wackerman, G., 1988, *Le tourisme international*, Paris, Armand Colin.

World Tourism Organization (WTO) (1980) *Actas de la Conferencia Mundial del Turismo de Manila*, Madrid.

Chapter 23

Social welfare policy and the fight against poverty

Isabel Ramírez de Mingo★

The final report on the first European Fight Against Poverty programme estimated that, half-way through the 1970s, there were approximately 30 million poor in the nine Member States. Poverty was defined as an income per consumer unit lower than half the average income of the relevant Member State. When this same definition is applied to the three new Member States, there are over 38 million poor among the twelve countries which constitute the enlarged EC. Using this definition once again, the first available estimate indicates that in 1985 there were nearly 44 million poor people in an EC formed by some 315 million persons; in other words, approximately 14% of the total population.

The Commission is conscious of the limitations of this estimate, which deals more with inequities than with the poverty in each of the countries. However, it has the advantage of allowing a comparison between the present situation and that of the 1970s. Another limitation of these estimates is that they refer to poverty in terms of income. There are no data which make it possible to know the trend in other forms of poverty: old or overcrowded housing, homelessness, interrupted or poor school-attendance, illiteracy, poor access to health services or bad quality of these same services, lack of other group services, unhealthy living or working environments. Nor is it possible to determine the more or less important number of people that suffer some type of social or cultural exclusion.

The number of poor in monetary terms increased in the nine first Member States, due fundamentally to the increase of unemployment, under-employment and casual and poorly paid jobs, as well as to the increase in single-parent families. It is estimated that there are around 16 million unemployed throughout the EC, and from one to two thirds of these have been jobless for at least one year in the seven countries where data

★ I wish to express my thanks to Professor Amparo Almarcha for her suggestions and remarks on the final draft of this chapter.

Table 23.1 Percentage of persons and families considered poor in the EC countries*

	Families		Persons		Children		Old People	
Countries	1980	1985	1980	1985	1980	1985	1980	1985
Belgium	2.0	1.5	2.2	1.7	2.4	1.7	3.8	3.1
Denmark	3.5	3.5	3.4	3.5	3.7	4.0	8.1	9.3
FRG	4.5	3.8	4.7	4.2	5.1	5.9	6.4	6.0
Greece	11.6	9.1	12.2	9.7	11.4	9.7	19.7	16.2
Spain	11.9	9.8	12.2	10.7	12.9	12.2	21.4	13.5
France	10.4	7.9	10.7	8.4	10.7	10.4	18.9	12.8
Ireland	10.2	9.0	10.1	10.5	12.6	15.7	17.8	7.2
Italy	7.8	8.7	9.2	9.3	10.5	9.0	12.2	12.0
Portugal	20.4	20.8	21.5	21.8	24.5	24.7	32.2	32.6
UK	6.3	10.6	6.5	9.8	9.0	14.0	11.0	13.0

* Poverty line: 40% of the national average income.

Source: Eurostat, *La pauvreté en chiffres*, Luxembourg, 1990; p. 34/3–35.

are available.[1] On the other hand, it is estimated that the number of unemployed among the poor population[2] is approximately 20% in the four States with reliable data. In connection with single-parent families, they form over 10% of families with children in the six countries whose data are known.[3]

The final report on the first programme stated that the differences between social security systems of the Member States were enormous. The group of needy people that has experienced greatest growth is that of the unemployed. And these are the very people that are offered less protection by social security, both as to the periods of time when they receive unemployment benefit and as to the requirements to receive benefits, as well as the level of assured protection. The last three Member States to have joined the EC – Greece, Spain and Portugal – have the least developed social protection systems, and their industrialization process is less advanced than those of the other Member States.

A quick comparison of the evolution of welfare levels between 1980 and 1985, taking into account the changes that have taken place in average incomes in the different EC countries, reveals that the incidence of poverty[4] among families has increased from 7.5 to 7.6%[5] and that poverty has experienced a more significant overall increase in the United Kingdom, Italy and Portugal, as seen in Table 23.1.

In the last few years, the EC has developed several stratagems against poverty. The first programme aimed to do research on an international level and was implemented from 1975 to 1980. A second programme in the fight against poverty focused on action-research and was developed between 1985 and 1989. A third programme of measures to promote the economic and social integration of groups of economically and socially less favoured people is being implemented, from 1989 to 1994.

In Spain, where underdevelopment has always existed, poverty has been tacitly accepted for a long time as an unavoidable feature of underdevelopment, rather than as a problem that can be dealt with as such. There are between 8 and 10 million people in Spain suffering from this problem[6]. In July 1987 (two years later than the other countries) Spain joined the Second Programme in the Fight against Poverty; it had sixteen projects, more than any other country: Great Britain came second, with fifteen; Portugal had ten, Ireland and Italy had nine and France and Greece seven each. These programmes were subsidized at three different levels: the EC contributed approximately 50%; the central government provided 25% and other public or private bodies contributed the rest. The following Spanish projects were approved: four projects for long-term unemployed people; one project for unemployed youth; two projects for elderly people; one project for immigrants and refugees; one action project in an urban area; five projects for marginalized people; two action projects in rural areas. These projects were located in Andalusia, Aragon, the Canary Islands, Cantabria, Castile-Leon, Catalonia, Extremadura, Galicia, Madrid, Navarre and Valencia. The Ministry of Health and Social Security participated in the financing of all the projects, with the exception of those in Cantabria and the Basque Country, through its Dirección General de Acción Social (General Directorate of Social Action). Furthermore, since the number of projects presented was far higher than expected, various Autonomous Communities and the above mentioned Ministry agreed to add nine further projects, outside the European programme, and located in Andalusia, the Canary Islands, Cantabria, Catalonia, Extremadura, Navarre and Valencia.

Analysis of the projects of the Second Programme, by sectors

The projects selected in 1986 and 1987 addressed a wide range of goals, which are summarized below:

Less-favoured urban areas: These fostered cooperation between urban populations and the different services, in order to establish more regular contacts; the improvement of the physical and social status of the less favoured districts and the reincorporation of 'marginalized' populations into urban society.

Impoverished rural areas: These projects were based on reports of local development, associating the official local services with the sociocultural development of the group. They promoted a model of EC development within the available resources, with the active participation of the affected population, as well as creating local structures or groups responsible for the promotion of regular contact with the authorities, encouraging cultural development, exploiting positive aspects of the local culture and trying to enrich it with new elements.

Long-term unemployed and unemployed youth: The existing services were developed, principally with information and guidance. New meeting and leisure places were created, allowing for mutual assistance and autonomy for the unemployed. At the same time, the creation of a new type of organization was promoted, to act in closer cooperation with the existing services, to facilitate the solution of day-to-day problems. The identification and promotion of new forms of integration in society were organized, not necessarily linked to professional status.

Old people: These projects were mainly addressed to the promotion of education and leisure, of home-care and the preservation and adaptation of their dwellings.

Single-parent families: New structures to house and care for children were offered, to allow their parents to participate in the creation of an environment that promotes self-help. These parents were given advice and guidance services to help them solve their problems, as well as group classes to teach them to live within their limited resources.

Second generation immigrants: They were offered information and guidance about their rights (particularly to social assistance), as well as the education of their children, especially the creation of kindergartens to improve their integration in Spanish society.

Refugees and returned emigrants: Unemployment is the most urgent problem affecting these groups, thus, the spirit of initiative is fostered here, to look for other working alternatives, and to increase education and information about the existing resources.

Marginalized groups: Gypsies, Bohemians, drifters, homeless people and all those who, voluntarily or otherwise, live outside social protection. The projects started for these groups are recent and experimental.

Evaluation of programmes in the Fight against Poverty

The EC programmes (1975–80 and 1985–9) yield some fundamental conclusions, both in matters of organization and of experiments:

(1) They have caused confrontation and exchange of experiences about certain methods of fighting against poverty from one Member State to the next.
(2) They have promoted studies and research, while raising the level of rational debate on the phenomenon of poverty.
(3) With the help of these programmes, some of the problems exposed by the establishment of comparative data in the twelve EC countries have begun to be identified.

The analysis of the results of these two programmes has also led to a series of methodological conclusions very valuable for later programmes:

(1) The importance of the *duration of the programme* has become manifest, demonstrating that a long programme, of at least four years, is essential to obtain positive structural results.
(2) It is necessary to focus resources, avoiding their dispersion.
(3) Not only should the evaluation of operations be performed at the end of the programme, but a follow-up task should be started from the moment the operation is launched. This follow-up may even lead, if necessary, to new guidelines for the projects.

We believe that these projects have sometimes originated a radical transformation in the methods of the traditional charitable organizations of the Member States, thanks to the governing principles of the programmes, according to which poverty is not simply a question of money or of access to traditional services, but is also linked to social and cultural segregation. The Second Programme encouraged public and private organizations to work together to solve a common problem, thus promoting the creation of a network of research specialists dedicated to the problems of the needy.

The structures of coordination have made it possible for different countries to cooperate on the projects, through the creation of international teams which have exchanged their experience and knowledge and, above all, have permitted the comparison of these projects around common concerns, which has already originated some efficient initial measures against poverty. After the initial results of the Second Programme's accumulated experience, it was pointed out that the most efficient strategies were a combination of government action and decentralized measures. Thus, the model of aid to people in situations of extreme poverty should be a combination of: (a) government measures (on a national scale) to take care of the most elementary needs, such as housing, food, health care, education and income; (b) local measures, which would tend to guarantee autonomy and give confidence to people without means, to help them fight against discouragement, powerlessness and social exclusion. Creativity has been encouraged through the decentralization of technical functions (management, etc.), although the Commission does exert more direct control over general organization.[7]

Conclusions of the Second Programme in the Fight against Poverty in Spain: positive and negative aspects

Conclusions are difficult to draw in the case of Spain, because of the great variety in conception, performance and evaluation of the projects. However, keeping this difficulty in mind, general agreement has been observed on the following points in most projects:

(a) The need to promote the existing social resources, especially in rural areas where they may not be utilized.
(b) Most projects expressed the wish to have a permanent interinstitutional commitment, and some of them had agreed to do so.
(c) The need to create permanent interinstitutional regional structures was formulated, and in some areas there could be a national organization.
(d) For those on the receiving end, mobilization of groups through associations and the creation of participatory structures, which gradually evolved towards self-management, helped them to solve their needs.

Personal contacts with several professionals who participated in the performance of these projects allowed us to receive the following complaints: the economic deadlines established at the beginning were not met; the various projects received little technical support; access to the funds available for the projects was hampered by excessive bureaucracy; coordination between various centres participating in the same project has been faulty; the documentation has not been centralized for easy reference, nor has it been correctly made available to all; finally, the workload has been excessive for those participating in the projects.

Future scenario of programmes against poverty

The Third Programme in the Fight against Poverty has two aspects: (a) measures to take care of needs originating in extreme poverty; (b) preventive strategies to help high-risk groups in crisis areas or economically depressed towns or regions. It is important to point out that this programme is not only the centre of exchange, stimulus and optimum use of resources, but will also produce strategic units, capable of being 'exported' whenever necessary, to be inserted in the local and national environment, which implies the cooperation of every actor in the territory in question. Preventive strategies for urban crisis areas or for very poor districts have to combine economic development policies decided at central level with local community development policies.

The need to have measures that integrate every dimension of the poverty phenomenon is emphasized. This integration has to be carried out through the coordination of policies and recommendation of the various public or private organizations, moving towards the development of autonomy, which is the basis for the rehabilitation of the needy.

The following recommendations are put forward:

(1) Specific measures should be implemented for job creation and vocational training to achieve the integration of the poorest sections of the population.
(2) Public and private services and institutions dedicated to the fight against poverty should evolve in accordance with the changing needs.

(3) Some kind of support has to be given to local families and groups to prevent their dependency on institutions.
(4) Any measures applied in the fight against poverty will be related to the economic and social trends in the State in which the project is developing.

It is essential that this Third Programme encourages optimum activity through decentralization of technical functions, while keeping a more direct control on the general organization.

As a summary, we believe that the following should be developed at Community level:[9] direct aid for the implementation of actual experiences; promotion of a coordination network, encouraging the exchange of experience; continuous evaluation throughout the whole programme; and information and help to exchange ideas.

Notes

1. Belgium, France, Germany, Ireland, the Netherlands, Spain and the United Kingdom (*Employment Outlook*, September, 1987, OECD).
2. Graham Room, *New Poverty in the European Community*, May 1987.
3. Belgium, France, Germany, Ireland, the Netherlands and the United Kingdom (Micheal O'Higgins, (*Lone Parent Families in the European Community: Numbers and Socioeconomic Characteristics*, April 1987).
4. The poverty concepts used here are in accordance with the definition adopted by the Council of Europe: 'Poor persons are understood to be those individuals, families and groups of persons whose resources (material, cultural and social) are so weak that they are excluded from the minimum acceptable life patterns, in each Member State [of the EC] in which they live' (EEC, 1985).
5. If the poverty line is taken as a percentage of families and persons whose average income is lower than 40% of the national average for 1980, we have an incidence of 8 million families that live in poverty, which would correspond to 26 million persons. If the 50% criteria is applied as the poverty line, these figures rise to 16 million people (Eurostat, *La pauvreté en chiffres*, pp. 31–2).
6. Thus, for instance, in the Community of Madrid there are around 160,000 people, slightly over 31,000 families, in a situation of extreme poverty; that is, their income is between Pts. 5,000 and 8,000 a month, according to the study *Pobreza y marginación* (Madrid, City Hall, 1989).
7. European Community Commission, *Informe sobre la Acción Comunitaria específica de lucha contra la probreza*, Brussels, November 1989.
8. Thus, for instance, the Proyecto de Red de Atencion a Transeuntes, Marginados e Indigentes (Project of Network of Care for Transients, Marginalized and Needy) has established the following in Madrid: institutional coordination of the whole network of care in this sector; projects of joint work at institutional level to achieve greater efficiency and profitability; coordination of public and private organizations to unify action and to plan future action for this sector; improvement of the care given, to increase the autonomy of the receivers; improvement, enrichment and motivation of the work carried out in this sector, to minimize the

harshness of the task and the low level of achievement (Indigentes de Madrid Project, 1988).

9. See *Boletín Comunidades Europeas*, 4/89.

References

Ayuntamiento de Madrid (1989a) *La pobreza en la españa de los 80*, Acebo, Madrid.

—— (1989b) *Las necesidades sociales en el municipio de Madrid*, Madrid.

Caritas (1988) *¿Sociedad dual? Pobreza y marginación en la sociedad de bienestar*, Madrid.

Comisión de las Comunidades Europeas (1984) *Decisión del Consejo relativa a la implantación de un programa a medio plazo de medidas para la integración económica y social de los grupos menos favorecidos*, Brussels.

Comunidades Europeas, Comité Económico y Social (1989) *Dictamen del Comité sobre la pobreza*, Brussels.

—— (1988) *Exchange* (Quarterly Information Bulletin of the European Community), Nos. 6,7,8,10,12 and 13, Koln.

Commission des Communautés Européenes (1989) Europe Sociale, *La lutte contre la pauvreté*, Supplement 3/89, Brussels.

—— (1990) *La situation sociale et économique des femmes agées en Europe*, Brussels.

Dirección General de Accion Social (1987) *Memoria. Programa por situaciones de necesidad*, Madrid.

Eurostat (1990) *La pauvreté en chiffres: L'Europe au début des anneés 80*, Luxembourg.

Muñoz de Bustillo, R. (1989) *Crisis y futuro del Estado de bienestar*, Madrid, Alianza Universidad.

EOCD (1987) *Employment Outlook*, Paris.

Ramirez de Mingo, I. (1990) 'Lucha contra la pobreza y la marginación', *Cambio social en Europa: su impacto sobre las mujeres* (edited by Amparo Almarcha), Madrid.

PART IV: POLITICAL AND LEGAL POLICIES

Coordinator: Miguel Angel Ruiz de Azúa Antón

Political systems
Miguel Angel Ruiz de Azúa Antón

Part III of this Spanish volume analyses eight aspects of European integration and their repercussions on Spain. It also considers the possible influence of Spain on the preparation of common European policies.

Chapter 24, by Professor Sánchez de Dios analyses the Spanish Parliament's control over the executive power which thus becomes a co-participant in European policy undertaken by the Spanish government. The chapter on the Spanish electoral system for the European Parliament emphasizes the internal problems revealed by the debate about this, as well as how it is used by nationalist parties, and the advantages that the system which has been adopted have for the representation of Spanish citizens in Strasbourg.

In his chapter on the formation of transnational parties and the party system, Professor Montero considers the costs and benefits of Spanish participation in the European political system, especially the impact which EC membership has had on the political actors. In cooperation with Professor Torcal, he underlines the achievements of Spanish citizens in view of their lack of a model of political participation, as well as what the possibility of electing European Members of Parliament has meant for the development of such a model.

The chapter on the protection of fundamental rights emphasizes the benefits of integration for cultural protection and links in with the issue of Spanish workers in other EC countries developed by Professor Izquierdo in Chapter 31, on migration policy and the costs that Spain will have to accept as the southern-most frontier of Europe.

In Chapters 29 and 30, Professors Rodríguez Caamaño, Almarcha and Morán analyse the loyalty towards 'Europe' felt by the Spanish people, and the benefits that EC membership has brought in the shape of educational reform.

Chapter 24

Executive parliamentary control

Manuel Sánchez de Dios

Spanish entry into the EC has meant a transfer of sovereignty to EC bodies. It is expressly recognized in Article 93 of the Spanish Constitution, which recognized the possibility of international treaties which transfer the exercise of competences derived from the Constitution to an international body or institution. Within the area of competences transferred to the EC, this power of transfer originated in a modification of the functions of the Spanish Cortes. As seen in the recent practice of both Houses, the main activity in relation to EC matters has been government control and legislative activity has been secondary. Furthermore, government control in EC bodies is ultimately based on the fact that, under Articles 93, 94 and 96.2 of the Spanish Constitution, only the Spanish Cortes has the power to ratify EC Treaties.

It cannot be stated, in principle, that the executive has had any material strengthening after entering the EC. What has mostly been done during this short span of time since Spain was admitted to the EC in January 1986 has been to build mechanisms for parliamentary control, using the earlier experience of the other Member States. These mechanisms, firstly, operate on the legislative process, to incorporate EC rules (Directives) into Spanish statues; secondly, through the control of Spanish government representatives in EC institutions; thirdly by the implementation of EC decisions by the public authorities for which the Spanish government is responsible. Out of these, the second is the most relevant, since it permits the exertion of influence on the negotiations carried out in Brussels between governments – and their respective administrations.

Characteristics of parliamentary control

The first thing to take into account is that, from the parliamentary perspective, the period considered in this chapter (the third legislature) is characterized by the existence of a Socialist majority government (Partido Socialista Obrero Español) and by a greatly divided opposition (six parliamentary groups and three groups of deputies). This meant the lack of a specific dialectical relationship between the government and the opposition, with the government complaining that it did not have a valid interlocutor, and the opposition complaining that the executive was trying to reduce the institutional and political relevance of Parliament. As a consequence, there was an important reduction in the efficiency of the parliamentary control then being constructed.

In reviewing the activity developed by the Spanish Cortes regarding the exercise of parliamentary control during the third legislature (between July 1986 and September 1989), it is possible to emphasize several characteristic traits. First of all, from a legislative perspective, the Spanish Parliament limited itself to debating and approving, always at the initiative of the government – in other words, by means of the introduction of a corresponding draft law – the regulatory measures needed to adapt internal law to the European ordinances. Approximately half a dozen laws were discussed and voted upon, without making any parliamentary modification. Second, it is remarkable that an annual debate on the EC was not established in the early years, though the general aspects of integration in the EC were considered among the topics dealt with in wider political debates. This happened in 1986 during the Government Investiture debate, in the 1987, 1988 and 1989 'State of the Nation' debates, and in that on the 'State of the Autonomies', held in 1987 in the Senate.

Yet none of the House sessions during the period under consideration had any general debate on problems and prospects of European integration, nor were sectoral discussions caused by questions or motions. That is, there was no parliamentary action that would have allowed parliamentary control of any general policy guidelines and decisions pursued by the executive, though the opposition tabled some such proposals in both Houses, which were rejected.

There were, however, an important number of oral and written questions, and interpellations and motions subsequent to interpellation, presented to the government, both in the plenary sessions and in the committees of both Houses. The fact that at least one third of these questions posed general or institutional problems should be underlined. As we shall see, the EC Mixed Committee predominates in the parliamentary control carried out by the committees.

Informative sessions were the most important parliamentary control activities. Indeed, the main base of parliamentary control has been the information given by the main players, whether on their own initiative or that of the Houses. The most important event was that when the President of the government informed the plenary meeting of the Congress of Deputies about the EC summit meeting for Heads of State, held at the end of the first Spanish term of Community Presidency. These events institutionalized control over an act which, owing to the importance of the decisions taken by it and to its influence on Spanish politics, has great public significance. Among other events, the informative sessions developed within the EC Mixed Committee were also important.

The EC Mixed Committee

The committee was created by the Law of 27 December 1985, on the basis of delegation by the government for the application of EC law (Article 5). It was conceived in accordance with the experience of some EC Member States, such as the UK and Denmark, where special committees had been established to follow-up on EC legislation. Following a proposal from the members of the opposition, a reform to the law was approved in July 1988, which reinforced its composition and functions.

The committee consists of a variable number of representatives, agreed upon by the Cortes, to guarantee the presence of all parliamentary groups. The President of the Congress of Deputies takes over the presidency of the committee, and normally delegates this function on the First Vice-President of the Congress. Voting is carried out by the weighted vote system, unlike other standing committees which use single votes.

The Congress of Deputies and the Senate have different material and formal powers; an example of this is the fact that only the lower House has powers to demand political responsibility of the government. This committee, however, has given equality to both Houses in EC affairs, and Deputies and Senators have the same powers and faculties. The only difference lies in the number of members assigned by each of the Houses (which, during the third legislature, was fifteen Deputies and ten Senators).

The committee was born through the need to establish a specific parliamentary mechanism to control the legislative activity of the government quickly and efficiently, in the form of short-term incorporation of all EC Directives in force at the moment of Spain's entry – bearing in mind that the process of entry compelled the government to do just that. For this reason, it was established that its functions were, basically, to consider, for the purposes of the provisions of Article 82.6 of the Constitution, the Royal Legislative Decrees issued in application of the derived (secondary) EC legislation. To fulfil this task, the committee prepared a report on fifteen Legislative Decrees, later approved by the plenary meetings of both Houses. Its competence was not considered as determinant or influential in the application of EC law. Rather it had an exclusively informative nature, following up on executive development of EC regulations.

The committee was also granted certain powers of control: thus, it must be informed by the government of draft EC legislation which might affect matters subject to reservations under Spanish law; the government must send any information on EC institutions relative to the application and implementation of Spanish membership of the EC; it must be informed by the government of the lines which inspire its policy within the EC; its function is also to translate any conclusions it prepares to the competent standing committee and, finally, at the beginning of each period of sessions, it must prepare a report of any actions carried out during its previous period.

At first, it seemed as if the major function of the Mixed Committee was the distribution or translation of government information to the relevant standing committees of each House, for parliamentary control to be exerted from there. It was not generally considered to be an important committee, in perpetual competition with the other parliamentary committees, especially with that for foreign relations. From its beginning, however, it was the centre of relations between the government and the Parliament in matters of EC policy, an instrument to generate parliamentary debate on every EC project. The Socialist government used it as its main means of communication with the Parliament. The opposition used it as its main device for government supervision. It has, in fact, taken the form of an atypical, and very important, committee, because its action encompasses the totality of government policies.

Because of its growing importance, there arose a need for reform, to increase its powers. It has, on one hand, been granted advisory functions (to the government), allowing it to prepare reports on draft legislation presented by the European Commission to the Council of Ministers, and it may, moreover, submit to the House any report it deems to be of special interest, in matters within its competence. This activity provides the committee with an *ex ante* control on European legislation. These powers, which it may exert at will, were not implemented during the third legislature. Furthermore the committee was granted powers in relation to the European Parliament and the national parliaments of the other EC countries, under the terms analysed below.

The committee held regular meetings. There was only a meeting of general information during the second legislature. During the third legislature, however, there were thirty sessions, averaging more than one meeting a month and, in the latter two years, a trend towards more frequent meetings.

Among the committee's activities, the most important is that of putting questions to the government. Over twenty-nine oral questions have been counted. They were all posed after 1988, and their contents have always been of a sectoral nature. The main activity of the committee, however, has been the holding of informative meetings (twenty-eight of them during the third legislature). As a rule, these meetings have given most of their attention to general issues, substantively because over one third of appearances have been from the Ministry of Foreign Affairs and the State Secretary for the EC, the two authorities with a more general and greater power in EC matters. With the exception of four appearances of administrative officers at their own request, and of the regular, institutionalized appearance of the Secretary of State for the EC, *every* appearance has taken place upon request from the opposition groups. It is also worthy of note, finally, that the Mixed Committee has experienced a growing interest in obtaining information from the government on current negotiations, or on the basic action lines of the Spanish government for future negotiations. In other words, the committee has been locating its field of action half-way between *ex post* and *ex ante* control of the executive action within the EC Council.

Faced with the loss of legislative function of the Houses in EC matters, the opposition has demanded that the committee becomes a body of advice prior to government adoption of decisions within the EC. The opposition also requested that the Mixed Committee be notified of EC draft legislation, before the Council approves it, and rejected the idea that the committee's main task should be, as it first was, one of *a posteriori* control on the basis of government-supplied information. The executive, in turn, has always maintained that the speed required by EC agreements made it impossible to seek parliamentary support or authorization for each decision that had to be taken, which would have resulted in paralysis. At any rate, this question has been determined by the majority nature of the Socialist government, which has allowed the implementation of *ex post* parliamentary control.

The Spanish parliamentary model, in any case, is framed within the general rule under which Assemblies, through the creation of specialized bodies, are endowed with the right to information on draft European legislation and allowed to make recommendations to the government. It is, really, a matter of capacity for influence, and it never has had a genuine power of veto or the obligation to make a decision in a specific sense. The influence may be politically important, but it can never block any negotiations which the executive may have entered into in Brussels.

On one hand, a shaping and strengthening of parliamentary control is under way, through the progressive institutionalization of general debates in the Chamber of Deputies and the implementation of a specialized follow-up committee for government action in EC matters. On the other hand, however, the capacity of the Spanish Cortes to condition the decision-taking capacity of the executive within the EC has not yet developed sufficiently to compensate for the decrease in its own legislative competence. Thus, Spain's entry into the EC has brought about a net loss of parliamentary control over the birth and adoption of decisions dealing with the transferred areas of power.

Control of competences transferred by the Autonomous Communities

One aspect to be particularly taken into account is that of parliamentary control of the exercise of competences transferred by the Autonomous Communities to the EC; that is, those competences which, according to the Spanish Constitution and the Autonomy Statutes belonged to the regional bodies prior to Spain's access to the EC.

It is well known that any power exerted by the EC means a correlative loss of power of the Member States. In States of a composite structure, within which there exist autonomous bodies, the loss of functions affects equally the central power and the autonomous powers; its measure depends on the internal distribution of power. Thus, in order to analyse parliamentary control in such States, it is necessary, before anything else, to determine to what extent the regional bodies participate in the shaping of EC-related decisions and their execution.

Under Title VIII, Article 149.1.3rd, the Spanish Constitution establishes that foreign relations are dealt with by the State, and Article 93 specifies that the government and the Cortes must guarantee the observance of international or supranational law. That is the reason why direct intervention of an Autonomous Community in international decisions or in the performance of international agreements is not possible, nor can their parliaments control EC policies. On the other hand, the Autonomy Statutes only establish the right of the Autonomous Communities to be informed of international treaty and agreement negotiations; they may also request the State to enter into treaties or conventions on matters of interest to the Autonomous Communities.

All of this leads to the conclusion that the central government has exclusive competence over State foreign relations, even though this does not prevent the participation of the Autonomous Communities in shaping its will. Besides, when taking part in EC decision-making processes, the general interest of Spain must always take priority over particular territorial interests. The incidence of EC integration on the distribution of competences between the State and the Autonomous Communities has been a constant concern in parliamentary debates. The Socialist executive has always maintained that integration should not affect the balance of decentralization, which the Spanish regional model has acquired with great difficulty.

A Resolution was approved in the 1987 'State of the Autonomies' debate, proposing the establishment of procedures to facilitate Autonomous Community participation in shaping the will of the State in matters bearing on the constitutional and statutory distribution of competences. Such procedures should allow, as well as guarantee, the necessary coordination between the State and the Autonomous Communities, so that the Spanish government may assure the fulfilment of some of Spain's international commitments. This topic was also mentioned in the 1988 and 1989 'State of the Nation' debates. The model of central government–Autonomous Community relations, however, has yet to be defined and, with it, the control of activities which affect territorial interests.

The activity developed by the Senate in controlling EC policies which affect territorial interests has not been very relevant. The way the Senate is organized nowadays, the House may not represent the Autonomous Community interests, even though the Constitution has defined it as a House of territorial representation. However, in matters of mediating between the State and the Autonomous Communities, the upper House has the advantage that it is the only one that bears the general representation of territorial interests, since there are representatives of different parties from each Autonomous Community. In the model of the 'central executive–regional executive' relationship, however, there is only a relationship between the government and the majority or governing party in each Autonomous Community. Thus, a reform of the Senate is proposed, for it to become a House of Autonomous Community participation. This reform should be centred on the reinforcement of Autonomous Community representation and an enlargement of the Senate legislative powers.

The incapacity of the Senate to channel the participation of the Autonomous Communities has led to an intensification of direct contacts between the national executive and the Autonomous Communities, although this relationship has not completely crystallized. All the parties have reached an agreement on several aspects. First of all, on the need to create a two-way information channel which allows the opinion of the Autonomous Communities about EC draft legislation which affects their interests to be heard; second, on the need to have a committee to organize relationships between the Autonomous Communities and the government, and of the Communities among themselves; third, on the fact that the State should defend the Autonomous Communities' points of view (and interests) in Brussels; and, finally, on the specification of terms in which the Autonomous Communities communicate with EC organizations and the establishment of channels of information between the EC committee and the Autonomous Communities, to prepare and present plans and projects to the latter.

Since 1986, a government proposal to sign an agreement between the State and the Autonomous Communities establishing cooperation procedures has existed. It is an agreement, not a law, because what is sought is to create an instrument without regulatory rank, based in consensus, which sets the rules of the game. Basically, procedures should consist of sectoral committees (already reflected in the Autonomous Process Law), formed by a meeting between the relevant minister and the corresponding councilman of each Autonomous Community, and in which the regions may express their opinions. A 'horizontal' cooperative body is also deemed necessary between the government and the Autonomous Communities, to complete the sectoral committees, because there are matters which they cannot reach. Finally, in accordance with the German model, the creation of an 'Autonomous Community Observer' is proposed. This would be a single person who acts before the EC Standing Representative Committee, taking care of the flow of information, and being, in effect, the Autonomous Communities' speaker; the virtue of such an observer, states the Government, is the unification of the positions of all the Autonomous Communities. The whole proposal is, thus, a question of generating a consultative mechanism to allow the Autonomous Communities to participate at domestic level in the drawing of general guidelines of the EC policies. This agreement was at first rejected by some of the Autonomous Communities, which would have preferred to establish a direct relationship with the EC institutions, notwithstanding the fact that relations in the EC are established between States (though some Autonomous Communities have found their own representation in Brussels through limited liability companies). The creation of the EC Regional Consultative Council has achieved some satisfaction for those Autonomous Communities which wished to have a personalized voice.

In practice, the Minister for Public Administration has been the one in charge of coordinating State and Autonomous Communities administrations. There also are some already established and operational sectoral conferences, where every Autonomous Community is represented. It is doubtful, however, whether these conferences give sufficient attention to the goal of participation of the Autonomous bodies in shaping the State will and in allowing the supervision of EC regulations by the Autonomous Communities. The national opposition has been pointing out that only consultation takes place at these conferences and no genuine negotiations are within their scope. Furthermore, EC regional policy for Spain is arranged around the Regional Development Plan (1989–93), which only affects the less developed regions. The government sends the plan to the EC after it has been examined by the Public Investment Committee of the Ministry of Internal Revenue (the most important sectoral conference). In other cases, the bases of the 'Community aid', provided by Article 92 of the Treaty of Rome, are the projects prepared by the Autonomous Communities, which the government simply transfers to the EC.

All of the foregoing shows that, first, Spain's entry to the EC has had an important effect on the framework of relations between the central government and the Autonomous Communities, due in large measure to the fact that the Spanish Senate is not able to represent territorial interests. Second, that the transference of competences from the Autonomous Communities to the EC has not yet been balanced by the appearance of procedures allowing the territorial bodies to particpate in the preparation of any EC decision which may affect them. As a result of this, it might be stated that Spain's entry into the EC has meant a reduction of parliamentary control over decisions affecting regional interests.

Supranational parliamentary control

It is obvious that national parliaments have little capacity to control EC institutions, although there is a very clear awareness that constant supervision is absolutely necessary. The traditional 'democratic deficit' refers to the fact that the members of the EC Council, which bears the real EC legislative power, are only subject to national parliamentary control as members of the cabinets. In other words, they are only controllable at individual levels, never collectively before the European Parliament or any other representative body. This has become worse through the Single European Act, which, by increasing the possibility of a majority decision being adopted, has reduced the individual importance of Ministers in the European Council of Ministers. This is the reason why new forms of control are proposed to complement those operating at the domestic level. These are based, first, on the European Parliament, because it is understood that it is only possible to control a supranational body from another organization of the same nature;

and, second, in the cooperation between national parliaments of the Member States.

Even though, originally, the European Parliament control activities were thought of in relation to the committee, in practice the Council has become their subject. The Council and, more specifically, the Foreign Affairs ministers, have been given the obligation to answer any oral and written questions addressed to them. Some oral questions, subject or not to a debate, allow for a resolution to be presented afterwards by a committee of five Delegates or by a political group. Another control instrument is the annual general report that should be submitted by the Council, after which oral questions may be debated. Furthermore, since the 1983 Stuttgart Summit, each Council Presidency must submit its programme at the beginning of the period of mandate and a report at the end.

At the EC level, the organization of parliamentary control is based on the European Parliament Resolution of 16 February 1989, adopted after the Seeler report. It proposes close institutional cooperation, supported on several elements, among which periodic contacts between national parliaments and MEPs might be mentioned, as well as the creation in each national parliament of a specialized committee or subcommittee on the EC, in charge of establishing relations with the European Parliament and with other national parliaments; and periodic contact between European Parliament Presidents and political groups, at national and EC levels.

Relationships between the Spanish Cortes and the European Parliament were not originally well founded, because there was no mandate compatibility between the European Parliament and the Spanish Parliament. The two groups of elected politicians became specialized and this, logically, led to a certain lack of communication between those groups. However, the need to narrow relationships between Spanish MEPs and national parliamentarians has already been made obvious and, according to criteria adopted by the European Parliament, it has already been implemented in the EC Mixed Committee.

Since the 1988 reform, not only has this Mixed Committee been granted the power to hold meetings with Spanish delegates to the European Parliament, but it may also establish cooperation with the European Parliament institutions. As a complement to these functions, the committee has also been empowered to maintain a relationship of mutual information and cooperation with the existing committees of national Parliaments of the other EC Member States corresponding to its own. During the third legislature, there have been several opportunities for this. Thus, since October 1988 working meetings between the committee and Spanish MEPs have been institutionalized. In October 1988 the committee held working meetings with the Spanish Community Committees and, in September, met with the Foreign Affairs Committee of the Second House of the Dutch Parliament (Tweede Kamer). In January 1989, the committee, chaired by the President of the Congress of Deputies, attended the monthly Plenary Session of the European Parliament in Strasbourg, on behalf of the Spanish Cortes.

During the third legislature, there were several contacts between Standing Committees of the Congress of Deputies with groups from other national parliaments of EC members and the European Parliament. Specifically, the Foreign Affairs Committees held three meetings, the Agriculture, Cattle and Fisheries Committees held one, the Defence Committees had one meeting, and the Community Affairs Committees held three.

Conclusion

To conclude, it is necessary to specify that parliamentary control in EC matters in Spain is as yet an unfinished process. This process is based on several pillars: first of all, on the complementarity between national parliamentary control and that generated by the relationship between the national parliaments of the Member States among themselves and with the European Parliament; second, and in connection with domestic parliamentary control, to foster greater consultative parliamentary intervention, prior to decision making; third, to promote the institutionalization of general debates in the lower House, which would enable important general policy agreements – taken at the highest EC level – to reach the maximum possible public audience; finally, to construct a new representative body for territorial interests, with consultative powers.

First steps have been taken to formulate an apparently complete control system, although it is not yet possible to state that the transfer of power from national representative bodies to EC institutions has been sufficiently or fairly compensated.

References

Cortes Generales (1990) *Conferencia de Presidentes de Estados miembros de la CE y del Parlamento Europeo.* (Madrid, 19 and 20 May 1989), Madrid, Congreso de los Diputados.

Medina, M. (1987) 'El Parlamento y la Recepción del Derecho Comunitario en el Derecho Español', *Revista de la Facultad de Derecho*, Universidad Complutense, Madrid, Vol. 72, pp. 403–8.

Montero Gibert, J.R. and García Morillo, J. (1984) *El Control Parlamentario*, Madrid, Tecnos.

Muñoz Machado, S. (1986) 'La Ordenación de las Relaciones de Estado y las Comunidades Autónomas con la Comunidad Europea', in E. García de Enterría, J.D. González Campos and S. Muñoz Machado (eds) *Tratado de Derecho Comunitario Europeo*, Madrid, Civitas.

European Parliament (1988) *Seeler Report*, Session Documents, Document PE DOC A2-0348/88/ parts A and B.

Pérez Tremps, P. (1990) 'Control Parlamentario de la Política Exterior', in A. Garrorena Morales (ed.), *El Parlamento y sus Transformaciones Actuales*, Madrid, Tecnos, pp. 271–86.

Chapter 25

The impact of the electoral system of the European Parliament on Spain

Francisco J. Vanaclocha Bellver and
Miguel Angel Ruiz de Azúa Antón

An electoral law for Europe

When Spain joined the European Community, Article 28.1 of its Membership Treaty stipulated that elections had to be held with direct universal suffrage to name the sixty Spanish representatives at the European Parliament. Since the Community had no regulations applicable to the case, Spain had to draw up its own legislation to regulate this new type of election, specifying the electoral system to be used.

In February 1987, the Government put forward a draft bill to Parliament for the reform of the 1985 Law on General Elections (LOREG – Ley Orgánica de Régimen Electoral General)[1] in order to regulate the elections to the Parliament in Strasbourg, adapting the 1985 Law by adding a new Title, no. VI: 'Special Dispositions for Elections to the European Parliament' and amending some common articles from the Law, 'insofar as this be strictly necessary'. These articles referred to the allocation of radio and television time during the election campaign; the order for counting the different ballot boxes at polling stations when there are various types of election at the same time; the State funding of part of election costs and limits on such expenditure. This chapter focuses on those aspects in which the Spanish election regulations took a new approach, even if in the end it was not put into practice.

Active and passive suffrage: a lost chance

There is no explicit reference to active (which has to be applied for) and passive (by right) suffrage for the European Parliamentary elections in the 1987 Law, so it is covered by the regulations drawn up in 1985. The chance to deal with the right to vote of citizens from other Community Member States resident in Spain was not taken up. Under LOREG, in order to vote one must be Spanish, of full age (18 years old), registered on the electoral census and not fall into any of the categories deemed by law unable to vote (sentenced prisoners deprived of the right to vote, those who have been deemed unfit to vote by judges and long-term patients in psychiatric hospitals, under judicial award). Those eligible for passive suffrage are Spaniards, of full age who are electors and not ineligible under the terms of Article 6 of LOREG.

There is no difference between the lower age limits set for active and passive suffrage, a situation that only holds in three of the twelve Community Member States: Germany, Spain and Portugal. In the rest of the countries – reflecting their domestic laws – the minimum age for candidates varies from 21 in Italy to 25 in the Netherlands. In 1988, one of the three youngest deputies in Strasbourg was the Spanish MEP, S. Garriga Polledo.

Active and passive suffrage, then, continue to be linked to the criterion of nationality, not residence. The residence criterion would be more appropriate to a Citizens' Europe in which the same rights are conferred on citizens regardless of place of residence. However, for municipal elections the 1978 Spanish Constitution recognizes the right of active suffrage for foreign residents where there is reciprocity (Article 13.2) according to practice applied in several Community countries. This right has been developed under Treaties covering the Dutch and Danes resident in Spain.[2]

By not reforming the eligibility requirements for voters and candidates to the European Parliament, nearly a quarter of a million Member-State citizens resident in Spain[3] have been deprived of the chance to participate in this important election. These Europeans can vote in the European elections of their own countries if these accept postal votes or delegated votes. The precepts of the Spanish Constitution on political participation in elections refer to national public affairs and do not prejudice those related to the Community, such that this issue remains open to Spanish legislation or to possible future European legislation. The loss of this chance has slowed the progress towards political integration and European citizenship, although in Spain residents' voting would have had little effect on the balances between different political forces.

The forbidden dual mandate

The Government's draft bill applied the same causes of ineligibility to MEPs as to Spanish Deputies and Senators. It also tried to prevent anyone simultaneously presenting their candidacy to the European Parliament and any other national or regional legislative Chamber. But this proposal did not survive and LOREG prevents only a dual mandate: no Spanish Deputy may simultaneously hold a seat in Strasbourg and in any of the Spanish legislative assemblies. This is positive in that it means that the Spanish MEPs can devote themselves full time to their supranational duties and thus help to put a stop to one of the European Parliament's problems, the absence of members at sittings. Moreover, the incompatibilities remain open to further provision of EC rules, which can be directly applied when passed.

The symbolic precedence of the European elections

Article 95.3 of LOREG establishes the order to be followed in counting ballots should various elections be held at the same time. This is a question of precedence, a subject that can sometimes cause grave conflict. The government's proposal was for the European parliamentary ballots to be counted after those of the Congress and the Senate, but the criterion finally accepted (suggested by the Basque Nationalist party, the PNV) was to count the European ballot sheets first, in a symbolic endeavour to concede a formal pre-eminence to elections to a supranational parliament over domestic ones.

A new electoral system

The political significance of an electoral system may vary but is always important. It is true that the very nature of the European Parliament means that the systems for electing MEPs, for the moment, have only a distant impact on the direction of Member-State politics. But, even in cases such as these, the design of a new electoral system is always problematic and uncomfortable for a country, because it tends to lead people to question the political equilibrium existing under the rules by which institutionalized power is achieved.[4]

It took scarcely two years to draw up the Spanish legislation to regulate elections to the European Parliament once the main political forces agreed to confirm the continuity of domestic electoral systems in essence, as established under the LOREG in June 1985. These new election regulations, required by the 1978 Constitution, had been the outcome of a broad-ranging parliamentary pact headed by the Socialist party (PSOE) and the Conservative formation, the Democratic Coalition (CD), sanctioning the legitimacy and efficiency of electoral systems drawn up in the initial stages of the transition which both these forces had formerly criticised harshly, albeit for opposite reasons.

The debate on the European electoral system took place in Spain in a different climate from that which had prevailed two years earlier. Public opinion polls showed that the political enthusiasm which had typified previous stages was cooling gradually. This was the outcome – more complex than contradictory – of three key events that occurred during 1986: the very strong polarization caused by the referendum on Spain remaining in the North Atlantic Alliance (March), the absolute majority with which voters returned the Socialists to both Congress and Senate (June) and the social impact of the mass student mobilization (December). Thus, the passage of the European Election Bill through Parliament in the early months of 1987 could have been a propitious occasion to question the essential elements of the electoral system in the most important legislative chamber, the Congress of Deputies, and the effects of these elements on the resulting political representation. However, quite the opposite occurred and, instead, its passage reaffirmed this representation. Let us now see how.

The dual objective of the new electoral system

As was made clear right from the start, when the draft Bill was presented to the Congress of Deputies, the electoral system for the European Parliament was to be based on two fundamental precepts. Firstly, insofar as possible, the main features of the system applied to Spanish parliamentary elections should be maintained so that European elections would fit in coherently with the general election regime. And secondly, the elections should be shaped in a manner in keeping with the singular nature of the European Parliament, for which it was deemed necessary to make the most of the system's possibilities for proportionality. The first precept led Spain to use the d'Hondt formula and a single vote on a closed, blocked list. The second determined the controversial choice of a single constituency and the refusal to establish any legal minimum for obtaining seats (see Table 25.1).

Table 25.1 Spanish electoral systems for the European Parliament and the Spanish Congress of Deputies

Electoral system for the European Parliament	Electoral system for the Congress of Deputies
– Direct universal suffrage	– Direct universal suffrage
– Number of deputies elected: 60	– Number of deputies elected: 350
– Single constituency	– 50 multi-member provincial constituencies and 2 single-member districts
– Single voted on closed, blocked list*	– Single vote on closed, blocked list†
– D'Hondt electoral formula	– D'Hondt electoral formula
– No legal minimums	– Legal minimum of 3% of valid votes issued in respective constituency

* There are two possible options for structuring the official ballot sheet: (a) showing complete candidacy for entire national constituency, or (b) showing list of candidates linked to the respective Autonomous Community included in the corresponding candidacy for the national list.

† Ballot sheet shows complete candidacy for the constituency.

The d'Hondt formula

Following the lead of nearly all the Community Member States – France being the only exception – Spain decided to use the same decision-making formula, i.e. proportional representation, as in domestic elections to the Congress, to regional parliaments and local councils. The fact that the d'Hondt formula had been used in four countries' elections to the European Parliament was also taken into account. Various documents and draft bills also assumed that it would probably be incorporated into the future standard electoral proceedings foreseen in Article 138.3 of the Treaty of Rome. Thus, the Spanish position was a statement in favour of this formula being employed throughout the EC when the time came.[5]

However, the d'Hondt formula is questioned in Spain. This is because it is often mistakenly held responsible for the low level of proportionality that the national parliamentary elections achieve (see Table 25.2), even though it

Table 25.2 Richard Rose Proportionality Indices for elections to the national Parliament and the European Parliament

		Proportionality Indices			
			European elections		
Country	Seats in the European Parliament	National elections*	1979/81	1984	1989
Italy	81	95	98	98	97
UK	81	85	81	88	86
France	81	79	94	93	95
FRG	81	98	96	95	97
Spain	60	84	—	93†	94
Netherlands	25	97	94	95	93
Belgium	24	94	93	93	91
Greece	24	88	96	97	96
Portugal	24	93	—	96†	93
Denmark	16	97	92	92	91
Ireland	15	97	89	87	85
Luxembourg	8	90	87	89	86

* The Rose index for the national elections covers the years following the Second World War until 1982.

† 1987 elections to the European Parliament in Spain and Portugal.

Source: The Richard Rose indices for the national elections are taken from J.R. Montero Gibert, 'Las elecciones legislativas' in R. Cotarelo, ed., *La transición en España*, Madrid, CIS (in press). The indices for European elections until 1984, in Lourdes Lopez Nieto and M.A. Ruiz de Azúa Antón, 'Elecciones nacionales y elecciones europeas, dos aspectos aplicables a España: la escisión de voto y la proporcionalidad' in L. Aguiar de Luque, ed., *Implicaciones constitucionales y políticas del ingreso de España en la C.E.E. y su incidencia en las Comunidades Autónomas*, Oñati, Instituto Vasco de Administración Pública, 1986, p. 106. The 1989 indices were drawn up by the authors from official election results.

has been proved that this is essentially due to the way the constituencies are divided. It is indeed true that it is not a paradigm of proportionality, but, as the analysts well know, it does produce a reasonably proportional ratio between votes and seats on its own.[6]

The debate on the European electoral system provided a golden opportunity to re-evaluate the d'Hondt formula as the electoral decision-making tool, and this was what finally occurred. The Izquierda Unida coalition (IU – United Left), led by the Communist party (PCE) was not against its application to European elections – provided it was within the framework of the entire Spanish territory – although the Communists had been its main opponents when the 1985 Election Law was being drawn up. Apart from this significant change of attitude, the lack of political consistency in the amendments that were put forward to substitute the d'Hondt formula with other more proportional ones was also of importance – formulae such as the Hare–Niemeyer formula, proposed by the Partido Nacionalista Vasco (PNV – Basque Nationalist party) and tried out for the first time a year before in the German parliamentary elections; or the Hare formula and the highest decimal fraction formula, proposed by the Partido Democrático Popular (PDP – Popular Democratic party) and by the Unió Valenciana (UV), a small, basically Conservative regionalist party.

Closed, blocked lists

Whenever people in Spain talk of some kind of crisis in the party system or the system of political representation, there is no shortage of support from all sorts of different sources for the idea that the electoral lists should be unblocked, thus providing citizens with the possibility of issuing a 'preference vote' in favour of some of the candidates on the party list for which they are voting. The debate on the pros and cons of blocked lists as compared with closed, non-blocked lists is therefore regularly reopened, examining the example given by countries such as Belgium, Denmark, the Netherlands and, above all, Italy, where the preference vote has been in force for some time.[7]

Given such circumstances, it could also have been controversial to keep the single vote on the closed, blocked list for the European elections because this was one of the keystones to the other Spanish proportional election systems. However, this was not so. Only the PDP put forward amendments to unblock the electoral lists, although during the parliamentary debate it was suggested that in the future it could really be a good idea to have open lists (*panachage*). The weakness of the positions contrary to blocked list candidates merely reflected the existence of an extremely broad political consensus in favour of reinforcing the role played by the parties in the electoral establishment of representation embodied by the European parliamentary institution.

The absence of legal minimums

It is usual in Spanish elections for the various lists to have to win a certain percentage of the valid votes in order to be able to be eligible for the adjudication of seats. This legal minimum can vary between 3% and 5%, usually depending on the size of the constituency, although it can also relate to the entire territory where the elections are held, irrespective of the number of constituencies into which it is divided (as has been the case in the regional elections in such places as Asturias, Murcia, Valencia and, in part, the Canary Islands).

Only the parliamentary group from Coalición Popular (the main opposition – focusing around Alianza Popular and, as such, heir to the old Coalición Democrática) advocated the introduction of a legal minimum, fixed at 5% of the valid votes issued (or, where applicable, 15% of those in the territorial area in which the presentation of lists was allowed). Their intention was to follow the models of France and the FRG. But it was not hard to see the exaggerated effect that such a minimum could have produced, so that the proposal was rejected after only a short debate (see Table 25.3).

Clearly, the proportionalist argument triumphed without much trouble with regard to the elements of the electoral system examined above. The main resistance to it – apart from the above-mentioned attempt to limit it by the right wing (CP) – came from the detractors of the single constituency.

The battle of the constituency: single constituency versus regional constituency

For some time, it had been clear that the thorniest problem to be dealt with in drawing up the Spanish electoral system for the European Parliament was going to be the choice between a single constituency and some alternative model of division into various constituencies adapted, totally or in part, to the regional organization of democratic Spain, i.e. to the dividing lines establishing the Autonomous Communities.[8] The provincial constituency used in domestic elections was rejected out of hand as too cumbersome.

The fact that Denmark, France, Greece, the Netherlands and Luxembourg – and later, Portugal – had a single constituency did not alter things especially, given the special features of the Spanish debate. What did was the search for a solution to obtain the levels of proportional representation considered impossible to renounce. At least, the defence of the single constituency revolved mainly around this argument, put forward by the Socialist majority, with the backing (on this point) of many of the other political forces at national level (Coalición Popular, Centro Democrático y Social (CDS) and Partido Demócrata Popular (PDP).

Meanwhile, all the nationalist and regionalist forces represented in the

Table 25.3 Potential effects of introducing legal minimums in European elections*

	On 1987 election results	On 1989 election results
With 5% minimum		
No. of votes required†	969,178	791,205
No. of parties which would continue to obtain parliamentary representation	4	4
No. of parties which would cease to obtain parliamentary representation	3 (5 seats)	7 (9 seats)
With 3% minimum		
No. of votes required‡	581,507	474,723
No. of parties which would continue to obtain parliamentary representation	5	5
No. of parties which would cease to obtain parliamentary representation	2 (2 seats)	5 (5 seats)

* Note that this simulation can be somewhat misleading in that the mere existence of legal minimums would probably have led to the formation of wider party coalitions and have led some voters to pay more attention to the tactical dimension of their votes. Thus, the election results would not have been exactly the same.

† The legal minimum is calculated on the total number of valid votes, which since 1985 in Spain would be equal to the sum of blank votes and votes for candidates.

‡ The number of seats that these parties would have ceased to win as a result of the legal minimum is shown between brackets.

Source: Drawn up by authors from official election results.

national Parliament were opposed to the single constituency. They wanted their respective territories to be turned into separate constituencies and thereby ensure that they would have specific representation in the supranational Parliament in Strasbourg. For the nationalist parties, in particular, it meant an exceptional opportunity to declare and project their national identity at European level: institutionalizing the direct election of their own representatives without State mediation and thus being able to operate under the fiction of acting on behalf of the constituency – for which, read 'nation' not 'State' – that had elected them before a parliamentary assembly called to represent the Peoples' Europe rather than a Europe made out of States.[9] From this angle, it was logical that the Basques and Catalans were the most vociferous in defending such positions.

The problem was how to make this aim fit with interregional equity and proportionality. This was hard to achieve, as could easily be seen in the proposals presented as amendments to the draft bill put forward by the Government.[10]

The representatives of the Agrupaciones Independientes de Canarias (AIC), Coalición Galega (CG), Unió Valenciana (UV), Parido Aragonés Regionalista (PAR) and Convergencia i Unió (CiU) were all in favour of basing constituencies on the Autonomous Communities. The last three even proposed a specific way of sharing out the seats between constituencies, initially allocating one seat to each Autonomous Community and distributing the rest according to their respective population with right to vote.

The Partido Nacionalista Vasco (PNV) proposed combining the Autonomous constituencies – including, at least, those of the Basque Country, Catalonia and Galicia – with others giving them 5 to 15 seats for each group, in keeping with what seemed to be suggested in the draft bills of the European Parliament itself. Their delimitation would be carried out 'taking into account the number of inhabitants, the administrative organization, geographical structure and historical tradition'. This proposal would have meant rewarding certain Autonomous Communities with seats, especially the Basque Country.

Eusko Alkartasuna (the radical bourgeois Basque nationalist party) proposed the generalization of the Autonomous constituency whilst allowing the possibility of bordering Autonomous Communities forming one single constituency. Their amendment in Congress – but not in the Senate – went so far as to advocate that the Basque Country and Navarre form a single constituency.

The deputy for Euskadiko Ezkerra (centre-left Basque nationalist party), Juan Maria Bandrés formulated the proposal that perhaps had most political impact: namely, to turn into electoral constituencies those Autonomous Communities whose parliament so agreed by absolute majority of its members, whilst the rest of the national territory should constitute one single constituency. One should bear in mind that the Autonomous Parliaments of Galicia and Catalonia had already made favourable pronouncements along these lines, later followed by the Basque Parliament but not by the Navarre Parliament, which rejected a similar proposal.

All the proposals mentioned and many others from nationalist and regionalist parties were made as part of a common stance opposing the single constituency, based on three main arguments: (a) that it was not in keeping with the territorial organization of the State; (b) that it did not respect the respective Autonomy Statutes, and (c) that it ignored the guidelines that the European Community itself had recommended to its Member States for settling electoral issues, in order that they should try to get their domestic legislation to reflect the different models of territorial organization.[11]

This was incisive criticism and consequently inflamed certain sensitivities. In diverse political and academic circles, people were aware that they had to find a system that could succeed in 'working out the use of Autonomous Communities as an electoral unit and the national territory as the framework for the allocation of seats, two requirements that were hard to reconcile'.[12] Along these lines and approaching the system in the FRG, two proposals worthy of special mention were put forward. One of them was advocated in the peculiar – and overriding – amendment put forward by two deputies from Coalición Popular, Sr Aizpún and Sr Medrano, that a big multi-member constituency be established, covering the whole country, in which 43 MEPs would be elected, and 17 single-member districts, corresponding to the 17 Spanish Autonomous Communities, i.e. demanding a dual voting system.

A second proposal, cannily presented by Izquierda Unida (IU-EC), established that the parties or coalitions could choose to present a single list of candidates at national level or else present specific lists for Autonomous Communities or groups of Autonomous Communities (lists whose number of candidates could not exceed the number of deputies in the Congress corresponding to the respective territory; they could include names, initials and symbols other than those by which the parties or coalitions to which they belonged were identified). The lists with a territorial scope would be formally linked (*emparentadas* or *apparentées*) prior to the elections for the purpose of counting the ballots. This and, therefore, the application of the electoral formula, would be carried out at national level, i.e. on the basis of the votes issued to each national list and the sum of the votes obtained by each set of linked lists. In this latter case, the allocation to each specific territorial list of seats won by the total of the lists linked together would be made by applying an electoral formula identical to that used previously.

The debate about the single constituency, both within and without the Spanish Parliament, contributed to a marked increase in the political tensions of the moment, more than anything because of pressure from national groups with a long history. The criticism against it reached such a hot point that during the annual 'Debate on the Nation' in Congress (February 1987), the President of the government put forward the exceptional offer that he would agree to amend the proposals of the government's draft bill if the opposition were able to come to an agreement and jointly present an alternative proposal.

As was only to be expected, such agreement proved impossible. Euskadiko Eskerra's proposal seemed to have certain possibilities of succeeding, but it had the disadvantage that in the not unlikely case of the way it suggested being followed, the Autonomous constituency could end up by being generalized as a result of the pronouncements of the majority or all the regional parliaments in a sort of chain reaction. Izquierda Unida's proposal offered an apparently satisfactory solution, by combining two territorial levels; but in practice, it was unworkable because the smaller Autonomous Communities would never manage to get any of their candidates elected (with seats shared out amongst the linked territorial lists). Thus, all in all, no proposal except that of the single constituency managed to avoid altering the interregional equilibrium in the kind of representation it produced.

Of course, the different parties' attitudes were not unrelated to the benefits or losses, calculated in seats, that each of the different proposals could entail for them. It was clear, for example, that for the smaller parties with a national spread (IU, CDS and PDP), anything other than counting ballots for the entire Spanish territory as a whole would be highly negative. This was precisely what inspired Izquierda Unida to make its imaginative proposal. But, in general, there were hardly any differences in the results obtained, either for Coalición Popular, the main opposition, or the best-established nationalist parties in Catalonia and the Basque Country (CiU, PNV and EA). Whereas, paradoxically, the great defendant of the single constituency, the PSOE, would have been the main beneficiary of the Autonomous constituencies.

One can extract an interesting conclusion from all this: that the election results that would be produced by each model did not carry most weight in forming the attitudes of at least the main actors in the fight over the constituency (whether single or Autonomous). Rather, the confrontation between different concepts about the criteria of articulation and integration of collective political identities in democratic Spain and how they should be represented in the supra-national framework of Europe predominated.

Electoral coalitions and 'polyhedral' lists

In an effort to bring down the temperature of the conflicts, an attempt was made to compensate the defeated defendants of the Autonomous constituency. This entailed a model which could well be called 'the polyhedral lists model'.[13] The electoral coalitions and parties could state when presenting their candidates to the Central Electoral Board, that they wished the ballot sheets used in some of the Autonomous Communities to bear only the names of candidates belonging to those territorial organizations or parties with a scope of activity statutorily limited to the said territory (the PNV in the Basque Country or the PSC in Catalonia, for example) and, where applicable, their own name, initials and symbol (Article 222 of LOREG). In this way, a single national list of candidates – closed and blocked – can be presented in a different manner, with different faces, in the official ballot sheets on which the voters identify and express their choice of vote (See Figures 25.1 and 25.2)

This means that, according to the criteria each party or coalition decide to adopt, they can make it clear on the ballot sheet so that the voters' eyes can immediately pick out which of the candidates on the national lists either belongs to a party from that Autonomous region (linked or federated with others at a national scale) or to the regional organization of a party with a wider orientation. The idea was to bring the candidates presented within the framework of the national constituency 'closer' to the electorate in territorial terms by offering a wide range of possibilities in drawing up the official ballot sheets and adapting the list of candidates they contain to each specific case.[14]

ELECCIONES AL PARLAMENTO EUROPEO 1989

DIPUTADOS

Doy mi voto a la candidatura presentada por:

POR LA EUROPA DE LOS PUEBLOS
(EA; ERC; PNG-PG)

CARLOS GARAIKOETXEA URRIZA *(Eusko Alkartasuna)*
HERIBERT BARRERA I COSTA *(Esquerra Republicana de Catalunya)*
ANTONIO OLIVES QUINTAS *(Partido Nacionalista Galego-P. Galegista)*
JOSEBA AZCARRAGA RODERO *(EA)*
PACA SEVILLA I GARCIA *(Ind.)*
JOAN BAPTISTA FONOLLOSA I GUARDIET *(ERC)*
JESUS MANUEL SUAREZ GARCIA *(PNG-PG)*
GREGORIO JAVIER MONREAL ZIA *(EA)*
JOAN MIR I OBRADOR *(ERC)*
OLEGARIO SOTELO BLANCO *(PNG-PG)*
M. ROSARIO AJURIAGUERRA OCHANDIANO *(EA)*
RAMON GARRIGA I MARQUES *(ERC)*
M. TERESA CASAL GARCIA *(PNG-PG)*
NESTOR BASTERRECHEA AZADUN *(EA)*
JOSEP RAHOLA I D'ESPONA *(ERC)*
MANUEL ELIAS PEREZ ALVAREZ *(PNG-PG)*
MARTIN UGALDE ORRADRE *(EA)*
OCTAVI MIARNAU I ROCA *(ERC)*
JOSE LUIS TEIJEIRO ALONSO *(PNG-PG)*
ROSA M. AGUDO HUICI *(EA)*
ERNEST BENACH I PASCUAL *(ERC)*
JOSE SUAREZ GARCIA *(PNG-PG)*
XABIER QUINTANA URTIAGA *(EA)*
CARLES FURRIOLS I SOLA *(ERC)*
JOSE PEDRO RIOL LOPEZ *(PNG-PG)*
JUAN IGNACIO RETEGUI PETRICORENA *(EA)*
JORDI MARTI I OLLER *(ERC)*
MANUEL JOSE GARCIA MONTEAGUDO *(PNG-PG)*
NIEVES ORMAOLEA LAUZIRIKA *(EA)*
FRANCESC CASES I MIANES *(ERC)*
ANDRES RODRIGUEZ PEREIRA *(PNG-PG)*
JUAN IGNACIO LORENTE ZUGAZA *(EA)*
FRANCESC XAVIER SIMO I ESPARRICH *(ERC)*
JOSE SOTELO BARROS *(PNG-PG)*
M. DOLORES IRUJO ELIZALDE *(EA)*
JAUME ALFONSO I BARCELO *(ERC)*
EMILIO ALONSO FERNANDEZ *(PNG-PG)*
JORGE KNORR BORRAS *(EA)*
BERNARDINA FITO I BESORA *(ERC)*
JOSE FRANCISCO EIRAS LEIS *(PNG-PG)*
M. ESTHER LARRAÑAGA GALDOS *(EA)*
JOSEP ROSILL I VIÑAS *(ERC)*
FERNANDO BARRO SAVIN *(PNG-PG)*
JUAN DANIEL BARANDIARAN JACA *(EA)*
JAUME OLIVER I ADROVER *(ERC)*
M. GORETTI SOBRINO MAROÑAS *(PNG-PG)*
JOSE LARREA ORMAZABAL *(EA)*
MARCEL.LI MARONES I FERRERA *(ERC)*
JOSE MANUEL PORTELA PAZOS *(PNG-PG)*
M. PETRA OYARZABAL IRIGOYEN *(EA)*
JOSEP BOLADERAS I FONT *(ERC)*
ABDON NUÑEZ FERNANDEZ *(PNG-PG)*
JOSE RAMON BERZOSA FERNANDEZ DE ARROLLABE *(EA)*
EMILI AYATS I PADROSA *(ERC)*
MANUEL ARIAS CARRAL *(PNG-PG)*
JOSE ALEJANDRO LIZASO MENDIZABAL *(EA)*
JAUME VIZCARRA I CLEMENTE *(ERC)*
JACOBO BARRAL OTERO *(PNG-PG)*
CARLOS SANTAMARIA ANSA *(EA)*
MANUEL BEIRAS GARCIA *(PNG-PG)*

Suplentes

JON MIRENA CASTAÑARES LARREATEGUI *(EA)*
JOSEP PONS I POCH *(ERC)*
MANUEL LOZANO CAMPO *(PNG-PG)*

ELECCIONES AL PARLAMENTO EUROPEO 1989
1989 EUROPAR LEGEBILTZARRERAKO HAUTESKUNDEAK

DIPUTADOS
DIPUTATUAK

Doy mi voto a la candidatura presentada por:
aurkeztutako hautagai-zerrendari neure botua ematen diot:

POR LA EUROPA DE LOS PUEBLOS-HERRIEN EUROPAREN ALDE
EUSKO ALKARTASUNA (E.A.)

CARLOS GARAIKOETXEA URRIZA *(Eusko Alkartasuna)*
HERIBERT BARRERA I COSTA *(Esquerra Republicana de Catalunya)*
ANTONIO OLIVES QUINTAS *(Partido Nacionalista Galego-P. Galegista)*
JOSEBA AZCARRAGA RODERO *(E.A.)*
GREGORIO JAVIER MONREAL ZIA *(E.A.)*
M. ROSARIO AJUARIAGUERRA OCHANDIANO *(E.A.)*
NESTOR BASTERRECHEA AZADUN *(E.A.)*
MARTIN UGALDE ORRADRE *(E.A.)*
ROSA M. AGUDO HUICI *(E.A.)*
XABIER QUINTANA URTIAGA *(E.A.)*
JUAN IGNACIO RETEGUI PETRICORENA *(E.A.)*
NIEVES ORMAOLEA LAUZIRIKA *(E.A.)*
JUAN IGNACIO LORENTE ZUGAZA *(E.A.)*
M. DOLORES IRUJO ELIZALDE *(E.A.)*
JORGE KNORR BORRAS *(E.A.)*
M. ESTHER LARRAÑAGA GALDOS *(E.A.)*
JUAN DANIEL BARANDIARAN JACA *(E.A.)*
JOSE LARREA ORMAZABAL *(E.A.)*
M. PETRA OYARZABAL IRIGOYEN *(E.A.)*
JOSE RAMON BERZOSA FERNANDEZ DE ARROYABE *(E.A.)*
JOSE ALEJANDRO LIZASO MENDIZABAL *(E.A.)*
CARLOS SANTAMARIA ANSA *(E.A.)*

Suplentes - *Ordezkoak*

JON CASTAÑARES LARREATEGUI *(E.A.)*

Figure 25.1

ELECCIONES AL PARLAMENTO EUROPEO 1989

DIPUTADOS

Doy mi voto a la candidatura presentada por:

IZQUIERDA DE LOS PUEBLOS
(I P)

JUAN Mª BANDRES MOLET *(EE)*
GONZALO VAZQUEZ POZO *(PSG-EG)*
VICENT VENTURA BELTRAN *(UPV)*
MARC PALMES GIRO *(ENE)*
MATEU MORRO MARCE *(PSM)*
ANTONIO RAMON GIL DIAZ *(AC)*
HERMINIO LAFOZ RABAZA *(UA-CHA)*
JUAN PONS MOLL *(PSM)*
JESUS CAÑEDO VALLE *(PAS)*
RAMON PEÑAGARIKANO GARMENDIA *(EE)*
ANA GANDON MENDUINA *(PSG-EG)*
ERNEST GARCIA GARCIA *(UPV)*
JOAQUIN VENTURA RUIZ *(ENE)*
ANTONI SANSO SERVERA *(PSM)*
LISARDO COLL BOTELLA *(AC)*
JOAQUIN HERRERO LORENTE *(UA-CHA)*
MARIA JUAN BENEJAM *(PSM)*
Mª ELENA MARGARITA GONZALEZ ELCORO *(PAS)*
Mª CORO AGOTE UGARTEMENDIA *(EE)*
FERNANDO MARTINEZ RANDULFE *(PSG-EG)*
ROBERT MIRALLES CEBRIA *(UPV)*
VICTORIA ALSINA KEITH *(ENE)*
CECILIO BUELE RAMIS *(PSM)*
Mª DE LOS REYES TARAJANO TABARES *(AC)*
ALFREDO JOAQUIN SANCHEZ UBEDA *(UA-CHA)*
JOSE RAMON FERNANDEZ GONZALEZ *(PAS)*
MIREN EDURNE IRIARTE AMIGOT *(EE)*
ANTON MARTINEZ ANEIROS *(PSG-EG)*
Mª GRACIA MOLES GARCIA *(UPV)*
JOSEP Mª VILARO VALLS *(ENE)*
Mª ROSARIO GALLARDO FERRER *(PSM)*
JOSE SUAREZ SANCHEZ *(AC)*
CHABIER MARIAS CONTE *(UA-CHA)*
Mª ANTONIA ANTON FERNANDEZ *(PAS)*
FERNANDO CAMPO ANTOÑANZAS *(EE)*
RAFAEL MARTINEZ CASTRO *(PSG-EG)*
CEBRIA MOLINERO LLORET *(UPV)*
JAUME SOLE MARTI *(ENE)*
FRANCISCO TROBAT GARCIAS *(PSM)*
JUAN FRANCISCO DELGADO GOMEZ *(AC)*
LUIS HORTAS TERRAZA *(UA-CHA)*
CARLOS RUBIERA TUYA *(PAS)*
TERESA CASANOVAS LLORENS *(EE)*
CARLOS VARELA GARCIA *(PSG-EG)*
ANTONI MURILLO PERIS *(UPV)*
JOAN CUSI FORCH *(ENE)*
JOSEFINA TUR MARI *(PSM)*
FRANCISCO MIGUEL ZUMAQUERO GARCIA *(AC)*
JORGE ESCARTIN GUILLEN *(UA-CHA)*
JULIAN FERNANDEZ MONTES *(PAS)*
KOLDO MARTINEZ URIONABARRENETXEA *(EE)*
GONZALO VAZQUEZ LOPEZ *(PSG-EG)*
JOSE LUIS GONZALEZ CUERVO *(UPV)*
ANDONI LLORET GISASOLA *(ENE)*
FREDERIC SEBASTIA MELIS FULLANA *(PSM)*
JESUS SALVADOR SUAREZ MENDOZA *(AC)*
MANUEL LOPEZ MARTINEZ *(PSG-EG)*
ROSA Mª COVADONGA CARVAJAL *(PAS)*
EMILIANO LOPEZ ATXURRA *(EE)*
XAN LOPEZ FACAL *(PSG-EG)*

Suplentes

SANTIAGO CABELLO SOLANAS *(UA-CHA)*
VICENT ALOS MORET *(UPV)*
ANTONIO MORRAL BERENGUER *(ENE)*

Figure 25.2

ELECCIONES AL PARLAMENTO EUROPEO 1989
ELECCIONS Ó PARLAMENTO EUROPEO 1989

DIPUTADOS
DIPUTADOS

Doy mi voto a la candidatura presentada por:
Dou o meu voto á candidatura presentada por:

PARTIDO SOCIALISTA GALEGO-ESQUERDA GALEGA
ESQUERDA DOS POBOS (P S G - E G / E.P.)

JUAN Mª BANDRES MOLET *(EE)*
GONZALO VAZQUEZ POZO *(PSG-EG)*
VICENT VENTURA BELTRAN *(UPV)*
MARC PALMES GIRO *(ENE)*
MATEU MORRO MARCE *(PSM)*
ANTONIO RAMON CIL DIAZ *(AC)*
HERMINIO LAFOZ RABAZA *(UA-CHA)*
JUAN PONS MOLL *(PSM)*
JESUS CAÑEDO VALLE *(PAS)*
RAMON PEÑAGARIKANO GARMENDIA *(EE)*
ANA GANDON MENDUINA *(PSG-EG)*
ERNEST GARCIA GARCIA *(UPV)*
JOAQUIN VENTURA RUIZ *(ENE)*
ANTONI SANSO SERVERA *(PSM)*
LISARDO COLL BOTELLA *(AC)*
JOAQUIN HERRERO LORENTE *(UA-CHA)*
MARIA JUAN BENEJAM *(PSM)*
Mª ELENA MARGARITA GONZALEZ ELCORO *(PAS)*
Mª CORO AGOTE UGARTEMENDIA *(EE)*
FERNANDO MARTINEZ RANDULFE *(PSG-EG)*
ROBERT MIRALLES CEBRIA *(UPV)*
VICTORIA ALSINA KEITH *(ENE)*
CECILIO BUELE RAMIS *(PSM)*
Mª DE LOS REYES TARAJANO TABARES *(AC)*
ALFREDO JOAQUIN SANCHEZ UBEDA *(UA-CHA)*
JOSE RAMON FERNANDEZ GONZALEZ *(PAS)*
MIREN EDURNE IRIARTE AMIGOT *(EE)*
ANTON MARTINEZ ANEIROS *(PSG-EG)*
Mª GRACIA MOLES GARCIA *(UPV)*
JOSEP Mª VILARO VALLS *(ENE)*
Mª ROSARIO GALLARDO FERRER *(PSM)*
JOSE SUAREZ SANCHEZ *(AC)*
CHABIER MARIAS CONTE *(UA-CHA)*
Mª ANTONIA ANTON FERNANDEZ *(PAS)*
FERNANDO CAMPO ANTONANZAS *(EE)*
RAFAEL MARTINEZ CASTRO *(PSG-EG)*
CEBRIA MOLINERO LLORET *(UPV)*
JAUME SOLE MARTI *(ENE)*
FRANCISCO TROBAT GARCIAS *(PSM)*
JUAN FRANCISCO DELGADO GOMEZ *(AC)*
LUIS HORTAS TERRAZA *(UA-CHA)*
CARLOS RUBIERA TUYA *(PAS)*
TERESA CASANOVAS LLORENS *(EE)*
CARLOS VARELA GARCIA *(PSG-EG)*
ANTONI MURILLO PERIS *(UPV)*
JOAN CUSI FORCH *(ENE)*
JOSEFINA TUR MARI *(PSM)*
FRANCISCO MIGUEL ZUMAQUERO GARCIA *(AC)*
JORGE ESCARTIN GUILLEN *(UA-CHA)*
JULIAN FERNANDEZ MONTES *(PAS)*
KOLDO MARTINEZ URIONABARRENETXEA *(EE)*
GONZALO VAZQUEZ LOPEZ *(PSG-EG)*
JOSE LUIS GONZALEZ CUERVO *(UPV)*
ANDONI LLORET GISASOLA *(ENE)*
FREDERIC SEBASTIA MELIS FULLANA *(PSM)*
JESUS SALVADOR SUAREZ MENDOZA *(AC)*
MANUEL LOPEZ MARTINEZ *(PSG-EG)*
ROSA Mª COVADONGA CARVAJAL *(PAS)*
EMILIANO LOPEZ ATXURRA *(EE)*
XAN LOPEZ FACAL *(PSG-EG)*

Suplentes - *Suplentes*

SANTIAGO CABELLO SOLANAS *(UA-CHA)*
VICENT ALOS MORET *(UPV)*
ANTONIO MORRAL BERENGUER *(ENE)*

The single constituency led to nationalist and regionalist political forces presenting themselves for European elections grouped together in big coalitions, determined by political proximity.[15] Very few parties of this sort presented themselves alone with any degree of success.[16] The 'polyhedral' lists contributed to these electoral coalitions appearing to be offering their voters 'linked' lists, which was positive for them and may also have stimulated electoral participation, albeit only in relative terms.

However, there are many criticisms of this type of list, because they show only one 'face' of the 'polyhedron', not showing the candidates by numbers indicating the place they hold on the national list. This misleads voters who are not experts in such matters, who cannot position their choice amongst all the candidates and therefore cannot calculate the probabilities of a specific candidate getting a seat.[17]

Political projection of the new electoral system

The new Spanish system for the European parliamentary elections clearly gave further political backing to the fundamental elements of the domestic systems for proportional representation: the d'Hondt formula and candidacies on closed, blocked lists. It also implicitly entailed a stand in favour of these in the standard electoral proceedings that the EC will one day adopt. In this way, Spain has made two pronouncements regarding the European Parliament, especially with respect to a future parliament with greater powers: firstly, that it is in favour of a proportional decision-making formula that will allow a reasonable margin of simplification in the parliamentary party system (depending on how the constituencies are divided up where it is applied); and, secondly, that it is in favour of reinforcing the role of the parties in the electoral set-up for European political representation.

There was something more important still. The final shape of the electoral system meant the overwhelming triumph of the proportionalist argument favoured by the government. It meant that sufficiently high levels of proportionality could be achieved even at the cost of the Autonomous articulation criterion that rules the way that Spanish territory is organized, or at the cost of failing to satisfy certain sectors that are especially sensitive about such issues. It was also observed that this line of argument went hand in hand with the desire that political representation be integrated in the framework of the nation-state. This was the reason behind the strong defence of the single constituency, which went beyond the debate on the technical (and very real) difficulties of finding an alternative model that did not threaten either the interregional equity or the proportionality of the representation.

It is true that the proportionality objectives were fully met, with a Richard Rose index of 93 in 1987, 94 in 1989: much higher than in the national elections whose index was 84 (see Table 25.2).[18]

Fortunately, the doubts that had been cast on the single constituency when it was being debated, i.e. that it would upset the system's legitimacy and vastly increase abstentionism, were not confirmed. The electoral system proved to work on the two occasions on which it was applied. It did not generate any politically significant exclusions and the abstention rate was perfectly normal for 'second-order' elections. This, however, does not mean that the Autonomous constituency argument has been dropped by nationalist parties, who continue to bring it up at key moments.[19] This can be seen as but one of the costs that the establishment of a single constituency entailed.

Nor should one ignore another aspect. Although bringing new co-ordinates and angles to bear on the issue, the debate reopened the old confrontation between different concepts about the equilibrium on which the European-level political representation of States with a complex national identity should be based. However harsh the debate and its consequences – which persisted for years in Spain – may have been, one can say in its favour that it provided a magnificent occasion to confirm that political integration in the European Community offers an ideal future background against which to dampen the nationalist tensions in the Member States by institutionalizing them. And at a time when Europe is sensitive to the rise of new nationalisms, it may be able to learn certain lessons from Spanish experience.

Notes

1. The Spanish Constitution requires election regulations to be established by a law known as Ley Orgánica, i.e. Organic Law. The passage, amendment and repeal of such laws must be approved by absolute majority in the Congress of Deputies in a vote on the whole bill (Art. 81 of the Spanish Constitution).
2. To date these agreements have been made with the Netherlands and recently with Denmark, published in the Official State Gazette, *BOE*, no. 287, 30 November 1990: 'Acuerdo entre España y Dinamarca, reconociendo el derecho a votar en las elecciones municipales a los nacionales daneses en España y a los españoles en Dinamarca'.
3. On 1 January 1990, there were 231,209 citizens of full age from European Community Member States legally resident in Spain, i.e. 60% of the total number of foreigners resident here.
4. Francisco J. Vanaclocha: 'Procesos y sistemas electorales' in M. Pastor, (ed.) *Ciencia Política*, McGraw-Hill, Madrid, 1988, p. 274.
5. Apart from in Belgium, Denmark, France, the Netherlands and Spain, the d'Hondt formula was also later used in Portugal.
6. Dieter Nohlen, *Wahlsysteme der Welt*, R. Piper & Co., Munich, 1978, p. 129.
7. See especially José Ramón Montero Gibert, *Listas "abiertas" y sistemas "cerrados". Sobre algunas propuestas de reforma electoral en España* (publication forthcoming).
8. Proof of this is Pablo Santolaya Machetti's comparative analysis of election

systems to the European Parliament: 'El sistema de las elecciones al Parlamento Europeo: un análisis comparado', paper given at the 5th Conference of the Asociación Española de Ciencia Política y Derecho Constitucional, San Sebastian, October 1985.

9. This formulation was covered by the concept expressed in Article 1 of the Act of 20 September 1976: that the European Parliament is the Assembly of the peoples of the States belonging to the Community, which was taken up word for word in the Preamble to the 1987 Organic Law amending the 1985 LOREG.
10. See María Victoria Garcia Atance, 'Crónica parlamentaria de la Ley Orgánica de modificación de la Ley Orgánica de Régimen Electoral General, para la regulación de las elecciones al Parlamento Europeo', *Revista de Derecho Político*, Madrid, no. 25, 1987, pp. 271–91.
11. The three arguments were summed up perfectly in amendment no. 1 presented in the Congress of Deputies by Deputy Juan María Bandrés (EE).
12. Pablo Santolaya Machetti, op. cit., p. 9.
13. Expression coined by M.A. Ruiz de Azúa Antón in the seminar, 'Jornadas sobre el Proyecto de Ley de Elecciones al Parlamento Europeo' at the University of Granada, April 1987.
14. See the ballot sheets reproduced in Figures 25.1 and 25.2.
15. See Chapter 26 by José Ramón Montero Gibert.
16. Only Convergencia i Unió and Herri Batasuna in 1987 and 1989 and the Partido Andalucista in 1989.
17. See the ballot sheets in Figure 25.1 in the 1989 elections, for Eusko Alkartasuna and the coalition in which Por la Europa de los Pueblos participated.
18. The Richard Rose proportionality index (PI) is calculated by $PI = 100 - (\Sigma[Ps - Pv/2])$ where Ps = Percentage of seats, and Pv = Percentage of votes. See R. Rose, 'Electoral Systems: A Question of Degree or of Principle?' in A. Lijphart and B. Grofman, eds., *Choosing an Electoral system: Issues and Alternatives*, New York, Praeger, 1984, p. 75.
19. An example of this were the failed negotiations between the PNV and the PSOE in an attempt to form a government for the Basque Country (November/December 1990), during which one of the demands of the Basque Nationalists was a Basque electoral constituency for the European Parliamentary elections. The President of the Junta de Galicia, the Conservative leader Manuel Fraga Iribarne, has also embraced the cause of the Autonomous constituency (February 1991).

References

García Atance, Maria Victoria (1987) 'Crónica parlamentaria de la Ley Orgánica de modificación de la Ley Orgánica de Régimen Electoral General, para la regulación de las elecciones al Parlamento Europeo' in *Revista de Derecho Político*, Madrid, no. 25, pp. 271–91.

López Nieto, L. and Ruíz de Azúa, M.A. (1986) 'Elecciones nacionales y elecciones europeas, dos aspectos aplicables a España: la escisión de voto y la proporcionalidad' in Aguiar de Luque, L. (ed.), *Implicaciones constitucionales y politicas del ingreso de España en la C.E.E. y su incidencia en las Comunidades Autónomas*, Oñati, Instituto Vasco de Administración Pública, pp. 99–109.

Montero Gibert, J.R. (1993, forthcoming) *Listas "abiertas" y sistemas "cerrados". Sobre algunas propuestas de reforma electoral en España* (publication forthcoming).

Pallares, Francesco (1988) 'Spain in Europe votes' *European Parliamentary Election Results*, No. 3, Dartmouth, T.T. Mackie, pp. 227–30.

Santolalla López, Fernando (1987) *Elección en España del Parlamento Europeo*, Madrid, Civitas.

Chapter 26

The formation of transnational parties and the party system in Spain

José Ramón Montero Gibert

Spanish politics has long been famous for its discontinuity. In little less than a century, Spaniards have lived through an enormous diversity of political regimes: two monarchic dynasties; two republics; two dictatorships (one of which lasted almost forty years) and one of the bloodiest civil wars in Europe. The political parties have sailed an equally stormy sea. Although universal suffrage (for males) was established in Spain in 1868, it was withdrawn on three occasions (1876–90, 1923–31 and 1936–77). And when people could vote, it was under anomalous conditions: firstly under the liberal monarchy at the turn of the twentieth century which was based on systematic falsification of the people's will, then under the Second Republic in the 1930s, condemned to sure demise by the political instability and electoral polarization that led to the Civil War and General Franco's dictatorship.

Since 1975, when the transition to democracy began, Spaniards have experienced the longest period of democratic normality in their entire history. The regularity and fairness of the many elections held since then have also been exceptional. For several reasons, the new political parties played a crucial role in this historical context. They made the transition possible by pacts cutting across almost all the political elites; they drew up a widely accepted Constitution by consensus; they managed to transform the old unitary State into a complex State of Autonomies and took part in its political and electoral life and in that of other Western democratic systems. Under what conditions did the new party system come into being? How have its electoral support bases evolved? How far are the parties involved in the Community organizations via their presence in the European Parliament?

Some of these questions lack the relatively straightforward answers that can be found with respect to other democratizing processes. As we shall see, the conditions under which the Spanish transition took place made the development of the parties as difficult as it was unequal. Ideological, organizational and leadership crises are still frequent. A governing party has disappeared and the negative consequences of schisms have affected parties of the left and right alike. In 1982, the party system was subjected to an extraordinary electoral realignment. And national and regional party systems have coexisted both under the system prior to this and under the current party system, making Spanish political life even more complex than that of most Western democracies.

Parties and election results

By any standard, Spanish political parties are outstandingly young. With very few exceptions, nearly all of them came into being after the death of General Franco in 1975 and prior to the first democratic elections of 1977. Under Franco, democratic parties were banned and persecuted. The only political outlet allowed was the inevitable single party which ended up as a bureaucratic structure with little influence. After the dictatorship, the parties had to create organization structures; groups of political elites; sources of funding; substantial political programmes and differentiating ideological labels *de novo*. As in other situations of blossoming democracy, the new parties could be counted in dozens: about 5,500 candidates belonging to over 150 parties and coalitions stood for the first legislative elections. Only a few of them had been able to participate in the initial negotiations with the government, via their leaders, to agree certain significant aspects of the transition. But all of them shared the uncertainty about the results that is so characteristic of initial elections.

To date, five parliamentary elections have been held for the Congress of Deputies and the Senate. They can be grouped into two periods: those of 1977 and 1979 in the first and those of 1982, 1986 and 1989 in the second (Montero, 1988). As can be seen in Table 26.1, there is an 'exceptional' election (1977 and 1982) and one or two 'normal' or 'ordinary' ones in each period. The 1977 elections brought in democratic mechanisms following the dictatorship and gave birth to a system of party competition; in 1982 there was a massive realignment in the party system, with the consolidation of democracy and the hand-over of the government to a moderate left-wing party after over forty years.[1]

In the first period, the two main parties, UCD and PSOE, representing centre-right and centre-left positions respectively, received more than 80% of the seats. Each of them was flanked by several parties (AP to the right and PCE to the left) with much lower support amongst the voters. The support for extremist parties was even lower: the extreme right obtained under 1% and the extreme left, although it received 3% of the votes, did not get any representative into Parliament. The electorate was divided almost down the middle between left and right (with slight bias towards the latter), with a symmetrical configuration in each block. This led to a strategy of searching for consensus between political elites to reach substantive agreements about the immediate steps to be taken in the transition, amongst which the initiation of a constituent process and the recognition of regional

Table 26.1 Votes and seats in Spanish parliamentary elections, 1977–89

	1977		1979		1982		1986		1989	
Party	Votes (%)	Seats	Votes (%)	Seats	Votes (%)	Seats	Votes (%)	Seats	Votes (%)	Seats
PCE	9.3	20	10.8	23	3.2	3	4.7	7	9.1	17
PSOE	29.3	118	30.5	121	47.3	202	44.1	184	39.6	175
UCD	34.8	167	35.1	168	6.2	11	(*)	(*)	(*)	(*)
AP	8.4	16	6.1	9	2.8	2	9.2	19	7.9	14
PNV	1.7	8	1.6	7	1.8	8	1.5	6	1.2	5
CiU	3.7	11	2.7	8	3.6	12	5.0	18	5.0	18
Others	12.7	10	13.2	14	9.2	5	9.2	11	11.4	14
Total	100.0	350	100.0	350	100.0	350	100.0	350	100.0	350

PCE Spanish Communist Party (left), since 1986 IU (United Left).
PSOE Spanish Socialist Workers' Party (left and centre left).
UCD Union of the Democratic Centre (centre and centre right).
AP Popular Alliance (right). Since 1989 PP (Popular Party).
PNV Basque Nationalist Party.
CiU Convergence and Union (Catalan centre-right coalition).
(*) Party ceased to exist.

Source: Montero and Torcal (1990: 122).

Autonomous Communities were perhaps the most important (Gunther *et al.*, 1986).

After the relatively few changes in the 1979 elections, those in 1982 were graphically and without too much exaggeration described as a 'cataclysm' (Caciagli, 1986: 149). These elections, also known as 'las del cambio' (the elections of the change) spectacularly altered the party map. Forty percent of voters changed votes: the volatility index was six times higher than in the previous election and five times higher than the European average since the 1940s. The UCD, which had been in government without a break since 1977, was punished for the factionalism of its party and the inefficiency of its governments. The PSOE managed to double its vote and achieve a sound absolute majority of seats, the first majority of its kind ever obtained in Spanish parliamentary history. To the left of the PSOE, the PCE put an end to a stage of internal divisions and crisis, breaking up into three parties and getting results similar to those of the Communist parties in Northern European countries. Meanwhile, the until then minority AP became the main opposition party, getting five times as many votes as in 1979, five times as many voters and twelve times as many seats in Parliament.

The effects of this massive electoral realignment radically altered the party system, the parliamentary decision-making mechanisms (which went from a stage of hung governments to another of governments with support from 57% of the seats) and the relations between competing parties (Linz and Montero, 1986). The previous equilibrium between the left and right-wing parties was broken, the left coming out on top; within the left wing, the PSOE's edge over the PCE went from 3 to 1 in 1979 to 12 to 1 in 1982. The disappearance of the UCD left the ideological space of the centre relatively open. And the growth of the AP raised certain questions about its ability to reduce its marked conservatism and become the UCD's substitute to the extent that it would be able to compete for government with the PSOE.

After 1982, the two following legislative elections have taken place against this background. And although some minor changes have occurred, the overall picture has not altered. The PSOE has lost more than two million of its 1982 voters and some percentage points, but continues to be the main party, with a considerable lead over the runner up, enjoying adequate parliamentary support and holding the government. Some of its old voters have shifted towards IU, a coalition dominated by the PCE; and another sector towards the CDs, a party born from the ashes of the UCD. But it is unlikely that either will be able to grow much beyond their current voting percentages in the future. And AP has continued to receive a similar number of votes and seats, its difficulties in attracting the centre vote becoming patent.

Since 1977, the lines of party interaction have been complicated by the presence of nationalist or regionalist parties at national level, principally the CiU and the PNV. These parties also occupy strategic positions in the systems of differentiated parties in their regions: the situations in the Basque Country, Catalonia, Navarre and the Canary Islands are unparalleled in the rest of Europe. Another exceptional characteristic is the instability of the party system. Indeed, reference has been made to 'volatile parties and stable voters' (Barnes *et al.*, 1986). In fact, it would be more appropriate to refer to the stability of certain basic attitudes and the volatility of the electorate as a function of the changing party programmes. Moreover, all the parties have suffered serious internal conflicts which some, such as the UCD, have been unable to survive. Both the instability and the internal conflicts have been especially severe in the centre and right-wing parties, which have undergone a considerable range of organizational forms and whose political articulation has yet to be crystallized.

Cleavages and party systems

The Spaniards' voting preferences have been marked by their moderation. Except in the Basque Country, extremist parties have lacked support. The parties getting into government have been broadly of the centre: in the first period, centre right – the UCD – and in the second, centre left – the PSOE. This is in keeping with the ideological moderation shown by the electorate since the transition began. Several indicators have shown that a substantial number of Spaniards rank themselves between centre and centre-left positions on left-to-right ideological scales and that their objectives in terms of social or political change fit into reformist options. The democratic system has also enjoyed a broad legitimacy which even held out during moments of greatest inefficiency under the UCD governments (Montero and Torcal, 1990). The continuity of these attitudes has acted as a counterweight to the instability shown by the parties and by the party system itself. Thus, the stability of the party system has not become – as in other transition processes – either a necessary requirement or consequence of democratic consolidation.

The establishment of relations between the parties and their voters has also developed along lines that present some outstanding features. During the Second Republic, religious, class and regional cleavages contributed decisively to the breakdown of the democratic system (Linz, 1967). This accounts for the widely felt fear that the restoration of political competition between parties could revive the cleavages that had been so extremely divisive and polarised in the 1930s. These fears, however, were not confirmed. Firstly, the Church hierarchy remained neutral in the first elections and the political elites then avoided maximalist positions whilst drawing up the new Constitution. Following the failure of the Christian Democratic parties in 1977 (when they obtained only 1.4% of the votes), the system did not have any confessional parties. UCD and AP, the two main conservative parties with a religious electorate did not manage to establish organizational links with the Church or with formal religious associations. The Church's protests on controversial questions (such as divorce, abortion or the funding of convent schools) were channelled through informal conversations with the government. They were further dampened by the high degree of secularization in Spanish society amongst the general public.

Secondly, all the parties adopted similar positions regarding the social groups they wished to attract. Social stratification obliged the parties to define themselves as cutting across class and to adopt catch-all strategies and aim at general targets. Despite the left-wing parties connections with the trade unions and the images of the conservative parties as having special links with the upper and middle classes, there was a general conviction that programmes based on social class arguments would have minimal electoral success. The weakness of class cleavages has been made evident by the low correlation between class identification and voting patterns and by the relatively varied social bases of the main parties' support.

Regional cleavages, however, (and thirdly) have been much more important and have led to the deepest splits between parties. Franco's dictatorship had aggravated the conflict surrounding Spanish national identity, a conflict that since the last century has repeatedly caused confrontations between those who defend the existence of a Nation State in Spain and those who declare the coexistence of a State with a pluri-national, pluri-cultural and multilinguistic reality. This historical conflict has been at the base of the appearance of peripheral nationalisms (especially in Catalonia and the Basque Country), of various nationalist parties in each region and, unlike that which occurs in other countries, electoral competition between different types of parties for general elections. Thus, there are differentiated kinds of electoral behaviour and some regions have their own party systems in which the majority presence of nationalist parties is an additional factor in their complexity. Although the Constitution contained this conflict by establishing a system of devolving powers over national territory through the Autonomous Communities, the confrontations of some Communities with the Government have continued to revolve around the traditional problems which are crystallized along left–right dimensions and the more exceptional problems which are related to the national dimension, nationalist identities, demands for greater self-government and aspirations for greater autonomy and/or independence (Linz, 1985).

There is, then, no single party system in Spain but several different systems, formed by the combination of a dominant system (which is spread out over most regions) with various peculiar systems (in the Basque Country, Catalonia, Navarre, Galicia and the Canary Islands). Both cases have, furthermore, undergone deep changes since the first democratic elections as a consequence of crises in the different parties and the effects of the massive realignment in 1982. This instability causes grave problems in typifying the Spanish case: by definition the party systems need time to establish a stable number of parties and patterns of interaction between them. Following the 1977 and 1979 elections, a moderate pluralist party system seemed to be emerging. Polarization levels were low. Unimodal distribution of voters along left–right scales (a dimension that structures interparty competition to a large degree) showed centripetal tendencies. The parties situated at the extremes – PCE and AP – could not be classified as anti-system parties. And although the bilateral competition in which they were involved was made more complex by the presence of nationalist parties, they did not manage to establish themselves in a two-party opposition.

The electoral realignment of 1982 altered these patterns. Thenceforth, these seemed to adjust themselves to those of a first-past-the-post party system: the PSOE has achieved three consecutive parliamentary majorities despite the fact that the system is formally described as proportional.[2] It has also managed to maintain its lead well ahead of the second biggest party, the AP, whose probability of taking over government is low for the moment. The disappearance of the UCD has led to increased polarization. But this has not been due to a sudden radicalization of voters' attitudes but to the already mentioned realignment in the party system: the partial substitution of the UCD by the AP has forced greater ideological distance between the PSOE and the AP. And the bipolar competition between them encourages the centripetal nature of the system, reinforced by the continuity of moderate voting preferences amongst Spaniards.

Some European dimensions of the parties

Whilst the Spanish political parties show signs of low social integration and weak organization on the domestic scene,[3] their levels of institutional integration in Europe are similar to those of other countries. The Spanish parties made quick contact with the main transnational European organizations. Indeed, the Liberal International, the Socialist International, the World Union of Christian Democrats and the International Communist Movement had already helped some Spanish parties during the initial stages of the transition. Albeit with rather diverse results, these organizations tried to spread new party images, promote their political leaders, provide technical aid and fund expenses at the first elections (Letamendia, 1978). Later, changes in the party map obliged the parties to alter their alignments with the transnational organizations. The most notable cases are of the centre and right-wing parties, which have tried to benefit from the names of organizations such as the European Union of Christian Democrats (the PP) and the Liberal International (the CDS).

The European elections provide a basic dimension in which the Spanish parties find their articulation in EC institutions. In general, the parties have contributed to the formation of EC policy with an extraordinarily high degree of consensus. Before Spain joined the EC in 1986, the parties faced the long negotiations together with positions verging on unanimity. The disagreements that have arisen since have always been kept relatively muted and directed towards specific issues. This approach also fits in with Spanish public opinion. According to data from numerous surveys, two out of three Spaniards are in favour of Spain's membership of the EC, think that things have gone better since then and believe that its effects are especially positive for Spain's role in the world, for the modernization of society, the smooth working of democracy and the development of the Spanish economy. Although only one in four considers him or herself a 'citizen of Europe', nearly 50% believe that the 'United States of Europe' could come into existence; 60% feel positively about the Single European Market of 1992 and over 70% declare themselves in favour of the endeavours to unify Western Europe (CIS, 1989).

The image of the European Parliament is somewhat less clear. As has tended to happen with other institutions, its public notoriety increased as the dates of the European elections drew nearer. About two thirds of Spaniards emphasized the good impression they have of the European Parliament and the importance it holds for Community life.[4] These proportions are higher than in other Community countries, something which may in part be due to the recent date of Spanish membership.

However, Spanish voters showed similar voting behaviour to that in other EC Member States. Both in 1987 and 1989, Spaniards also considered the European elections as 'second-order elections' (Schmitt and Mannheimer, 1991). As can be seen in Table 26.2, their results reaffirmed the PSOE's lead over the other parties and the PP's problems in increasing their number of votes. Perhaps the most outstanding peculiarity is the high number of political groupings that have won at least one seat: no less than eleven, a higher number even than from Belgium (ten) and only lower than Italy (thirteen). Many of them are coalitions of nationalist or regionalist parties trying to make the best of the election rules. The setting of a single constituency for all Spain and the application of the D'Hondt electoral formula increase the degree of proportionality in the results, which is clearly higher than in general elections. And the combination of this single constituency with the existence of many small regionalist parties makes it necessary to create *ad hoc* coalitions to group together the preferences of voters spread out over many provinces and Autonomous Communities

Finally, the majority of Spanish deputies have joined the parliamentary groups closest to their respective parties. Table 26.3 shows the composition of the European Parliament in 1987 and 1989 from this angle.

Conclusion

It is impossible to foresee the ways in which the European Parliament will contribute to the construction of a united Europe in the immediate future. Whatever they may be, the articulation of the parties through the groups in the European Parliament will definitely play an essential role. Likewise, in Spain, any forecasts are made on the one hand with the certainty that the party elites and organizations are of key importance for the democratic system and on the other with doubts about the exact form the party system and the interaction within it may take. As has been said with some irony, the Spanish parties are still 'in search of a system' (Vallés, 1987). Meanwhile, the

Table 26.2 European elections in Spain, 1987 and 1989

Party/List	European elections 1989 Votes (%)	1989 Seats	European elections 1987 Votes (%)	1987 Seats	National election, 1986: votes (%)
PSOE	40.2	27	39.1	28	44.3
PP*	21.7	15	24.7	17	26.1
CDS	7.2	5	10.3	7	9.3
IU	6.2	4	5.2	3	4.6
CiU	4.3	2	4.4	3	5.0
Ruiz-Mateos Group	3.9	2	—	—	—
PA	1.9	1	1.0	—	0.5
CN†	1.9	1	1.2	—	2.2
IP‡	1.8	1	1.3	—	0.5
HB	1.7	1	1.7	1	0.5
PEP§	1.5	1	1.7	1	0.5
Others	7.7	—	9.2	—	5.8

* 1986: Popular Coalition (PP and the small parties PL and PDP).

† Electoral alliance (EE only) of regional parties (PNV, CG, AIC); 1987: Unión Europesista (PNV, PGN).

‡ Electoral alliance (EE only) of left-wing regional parties (EE, ENE, PSG, UPV, PSM, AC, CA); 1987 without AC and CA; 1986 EE only.

§ Electoral alliance (EE only) of regional parties (EA, ERC, PNG); 1986 ERC only.

EE	European Elections
NE	National Elections
PSOE	Spanish Socialist Workers' Party
PP	Popular Party
CDS	Democratic and Social Centre
IU	United Left
CiU	Convergence and Union (Catalan centre-right coalition)
PA	Andalusian Party
CN	Nationalist Coalition
IP	Peoples' Left
HB	Herri Batasuna (Basque Nationalists)
PEP	Por la Europa de los Pueblos (For a Peoples' Europe)

Source: Schmitt and Mannheimer (1991: 154).

stability of the main ideological options of the electorate, the structural weakness of the parties, the regional imbalances in voting support and the erratic behaviour of some of the party leaders all seem to be confirmed. The mix by which these factors and the many other elements that they entail are combined together in the future will determine whether the parties 'find' a system that is both relatively stable and relatively predictable.

Table 26.3 European elections in Spain, 1987 and 1989

	1989		1987	
Political groups	Spain	Total	Spain	Total
Socialist	27	180	28	166
European People's Party (Christian Democratic)	16	121	17	114
Liberal, Democratic & Reformist	6	49	7	43
European Democratic	—	34	—	67
Green	1	29	—	—
European Unitarian Left	4	28	3	47
European Democratic Alliance	2	22	3	29
Technical of European Right	—	17	—	16
Left Unity	—	14	—	—
Rainbow	2	14	1	20
Non-attached	2	10	1	16
Total	60	518	60	518

Source: Schmitt and Mannheimer (1991).

Notes

1. This 'exceptional' dimension also affected an indicator that is usually sensitive to such circumstances, i.e. electoral participation: whereas in 1977 and 1982 the participation rate was 80%, in other other so-called 'normal' elections, this rate dropped to 70%.
2. However, the system acts as a first-past-the-post system in many constituencies due to a combination of factors, including the size of the districts and the population distribution. (See the chapter on the electoral system in this volume.)
3. The chapter on 'Patterns of Political Participation' covers some elements in this weakness.
4. These data come from different surveys carried out by the Centro de Investigaciones Sociológicas (CIS–Centre for Sociological Research) in 1987 and 1989 with representative samples of the Spanish population, surveys recorded in their data bank.

References

Barnes, S.H., McDonough, P., and López Pina, A. (1986) 'Volatile Parties and Stable Voters in Spain', *Government and Opposition*, no. 21, 56–75.

Caciagli, M. (1986) *Elecciones y Partidos en la Transición Española*, Madrid, Centro de Investigaciones Sociológicas/Siglo XXI.

CIS (Centro de Investigaciones Sociológicas) (1989) *La Opinión Pública Española ante Europa y los Europeos*, Estudios y Encuestas, Madrid.

Gunther, R., Sani, G. and Shabad, G. (1986) *Spain After Franco: The Making of a Competitive Party System*, Berkeley, University of California Press.

Letamendia, P. (1978) *L'Intervention des Organisations Partisanes, Transnationales dans le Processus de Democratisation Espagnol*, Université de Bordeaux I, Bordeaux.

Linz, J.J. (1967) 'The Party System in Spain: Past and Future' in S.M. Lipset and S. Rokkan (eds), *Party Systems and Voter Alignments*, New York, Free Press.

—— (1985) 'De la Crisis de un Estado Unitario al Estado de las Autonomías' in F. Fernández Rodríguez (ed.) *La España de las Autonomías*, Madrid, Instituto de Estudios de Administración Local.

—— and Montero, J.R. (eds), 1986, *Crisis y Cambio. Electores y Partidos en la España de los Años Ochenta*, Madrid, Centro de Estudios Constitucionales.

Montero, J.R., 1988, 'Elecciones y Ciclos Electorales en España, *Revista de Derecho Político*, no. 25, 11–34.

—— and Torcal, M., 1989 'Voters and Citizens in a New Democracy: Some Trend Data on Political Attitudes in Spain', *International Journal of Public Opinion Research*, no. 2, 116–40.

Schmitt, H. and Mannheimer, K., 1991, 'On Party Attachment in Western Europe and the Utility of Eurobarometer Data', *Western European Politics* No. 12, 122–139.

Vallés, J.M., 1987 'A la Busca de un Sistema: Los Partidos Políticos en España, *Razón y Fe*, no. 1060, 143–53.

Chapter 27

Patterns of political participation

José Ramón Montero Gibert and Mariano Torcal Loriente

In 1975, at the time of General Franco's death, Spain was one of the longest-standing dictatorships among those established in Europe during the 1930s. But, as in other authoritarian regimes, Francoism was not able to survive the death of its founder. A short time after, Spain was able to carry out a political change of spectacular scope. The transition process crystallized into a consolidated and stable democratic system, whose government took the shape of a monarchy and whose territorial structure is of regional or near-federal nature, presided over by a Constitution drafted by consensual mechanisms and approved by a majority.

This change was further reinforced after January 1986, when Spain joined the EC. Spanish membership put an end to a long period of coincidences and misencounters. In fact, during the last stage of Franco's regime, and during the first stages of transition, *Europe* had become a symbol of extraordinary wealth, the incarnation of freedom, democracy and economic development. Thus, the delayed Spanish adoption of European structures was partially balanced by the positive images of their symbols. These relationships have also been maintained in the strictly political field. Political participation patterns, which will be analysed in this chapter, have been subject to different degrees of conditioning by a set of attitudes, behaviours and images where those relative to Europe have had a relevant role.

After Spanish entry into the EC, this role has taken new expressions, but its importance continues. Although the profiles of Spanish participation are similar to those of most Western countries, they still present some distinct features. Some of them affect the decision-making process relevant to public policies; as a consequence, they also impinge on policies dealing with EC matters. Logically, political participation activities cannot be measured in strict terms of *cost* and *benefit* in connection with the EC. But they certainly are an essential factor, due to the fact that they condition the selection processes of political elites, channels of aggregation of interests and debates on policy consequences. The intervention of Spanish citizens in the European Parliament elections have also opened specific electoral participation possibilities, whose examination should be done in a manner integrated with all other participative activities.

Two interpretations of political change

Among others, some of the elements which characterize the political culture of the Spain of post-Franco times are its ideological moderation, its support of democratic principles and its political passivity (Montero and Torcal, 1989). This chapter is especially interested in the last aspect. As will be seen in this chapter, political information and interest levels of Spanish citizens are not large; their understanding of subjective competence and personal efficiency are also low, and their degree of political commitment, no matter by which indicator it is measured, is remarkably scarce. When this set of attitudes was detected at the end of the 1970s, many analysts related them with the 'disenchantment' caused by the lack of efficiency of the Democratic Center Union (UCD) governments and attributed them to the close temporal distance of Franco's times. It was then thought that the brevity of the democratic experience had conditioned the learning of participative attitudes, which would be feasible after the socialization process had been implemented for some time. Over ten years later, however, no substantial change seems to have come about: neither time nor the governmental difference introduced by the Spanish Socialist Workers Party (PSOE) have increased democratic performance or transformed the political passivity of Spanish citizens.

The co-existence of attitudes which support democracy with those of political non-involvement have given rise to two general interpretations of political changes (Botella, 1991: Gunther, 1988). One interpretation would underline the success of the processes of democratic transition and consolidation. The dismantling of the institutions of a long authoritarian regime, the creation of a widely accepted and reasonably efficient political system, the overcoming of historically polarizing cleavages, the governmental change to a moderate leftist party, and the full incorporation to the international scenario have been, *inter alia*, indubitable successes; so much so that they have turned the Spanish case into a mandatory reference point for other democratizing processes. In what might be termed a positive interpretation, these successes would imply a certain harmony between the political system and the political culture of Spanish citizens, in other words, between the democratic framework, their political attitudes and political activity patterns.

On the other hand, an alternative interpretation would emphasize political apathy and weak political commitment as the key definitive features. Both characteristics would be the product of a combination of historical factors, among which one might mention the tradition of political disorder and discontinuity of the two last centuries, the systematic vote manipulation when universal suffrage was implemented, the polarizing effects of the intense political mobilization of the Republic of the 1930s and the values of de-politicization, demobilization, apathy and anti-partyism which were instilled during the authoritarian regime. The demands of the political transition, which was carried out by means of consensual interparty agreements, virtually excluded the political participation of the masses at a time when an important readjustment of attitudes was being shaped. Thus, political passivity would simultaneously be a current manifestation of a dense historical tradition and one of the secondary effects of transition. Traditionally negative conceptions of political activity would also be combined with the lack of symbolic and instrumental stimuli under normal conditions. This, in turn, would affect the perception of political activity as a domain reserved practically to professional politicians.

Conceptions of politics and political interest

These interpretations are not mutually excluding. It is likely that one of the traits of the attitude of Spanish citizens is the integration of attitudes of support to democratic values with others of apathy and passivity. Numerous indicators show empirical evidence of this particular combination. Thus, for instance, since 1977, constant proportions of around 75% of Spanish citizens have been considering themselves slightly or not at all aware of what is going on in political matters. Among the feelings awakened by politics, lack of interest abounds more than attraction, and distancing is more prevalent than rejection. Some data which seem predominant since 1980 reveal that only around one quarter of Spanish citizens claim to have positive feelings towards politics, and that negative ones affect over one tenth of them. Furthermore, most conceive politics in terms of mistrust, indifference and boredom.[1] Even though these attitudes are not exclusive to Spain, the greater relative incidence of political non-involvement of Spanish citizens seems to stand out among other Europeans.

These conceptions are reflected in the classic indicator of interest in politics. In general, Spanish people are not different from other Western citizens in that politics assumes a secondary role in their lives. Politics is the subject that least interests Spanish citizens out of a list of ten topics, among which there are scientific, artistic, social and environmental subjects. Within the political field, the main areas of interest are, as might be expected, domestic and local politics, followed by regional politics and with international affairs occupying the last place. In spite of all the changes of the last twenty years, political interest has remained at really low levels. As may be seen in Figure 27.1, only one out of every four Spanish citizens manifests any type of interest in politics.

The only relative growth took place during the first transition years, and this diminished with the electoral victory of the PSOE, which meant the definite consolidation of the democratic system. Since then, around 40% of the Spanish people declare to have no interest whatsoever in politics, and between 70 and 80% have stated that they feel little or no interest in politics.

This lack of interest is considerably more profound than that of other countries. In 1990, the highest rates of apathy among the EC members, higher than the EC average of 53%, happened in Portugal, Italy, Belgium,

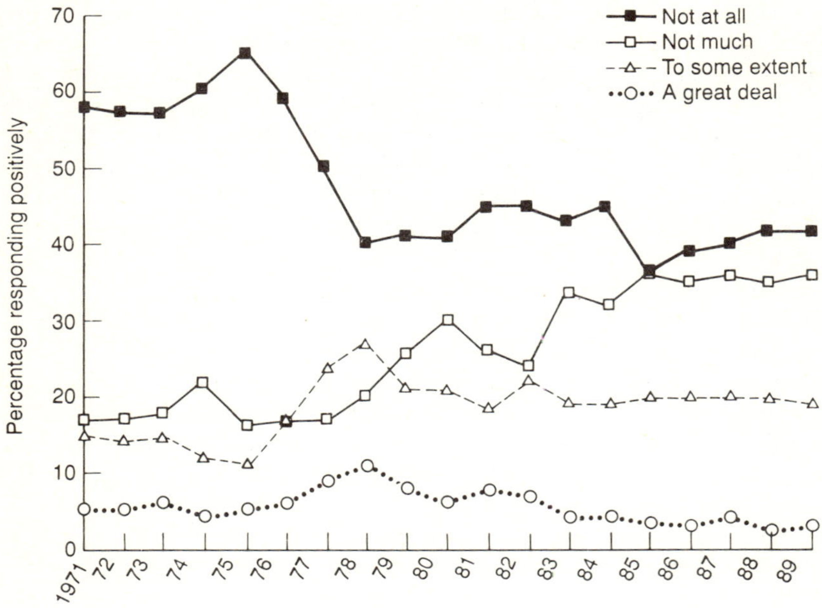

Figure 27.1 Interest in politics in Spain, 1971–89

Source: Data bank of Centro de Investigaciones Sociológicas (CIS).

Spain and Ireland; among those, complete lack of interest in politics was significantly greater in Portugal (43%) and Spain (42%).[2] A wider comparison, as may be the one shown in Figure 27.2, reveals the peculiarity of the Spanish attitude. Although, in some cases, perceptions of the importance of EC matters is high, interest in EC-related themes and political interest introduce considerable differences: only Portugal and Italy show lower interest rates for Community and politics than does Spain.

The basic lack of interest of Spanish citizens has important repercussions on their evaluation of politics and politicians. Political apathy is closely bound to feelings of powerlessness and confusion about political themes on one hand, and of personal inefficacy on the other. Two thirds of Spanish citizens agree with the statements that 'politics is such a complicated matter that people like me cannot understand what is going on', or 'in politics, the only thing that people like me can do is voting'. Thus, citizens project political inefficacy between two interrelated dimensions: perception of their incapacity to act politically and a belief in the lack of receptivity of the system as far as their demands are concerned.

These perceptions are accompanied by equally high ones of political cynicism. In the course of the last few years, there has been a decrease in

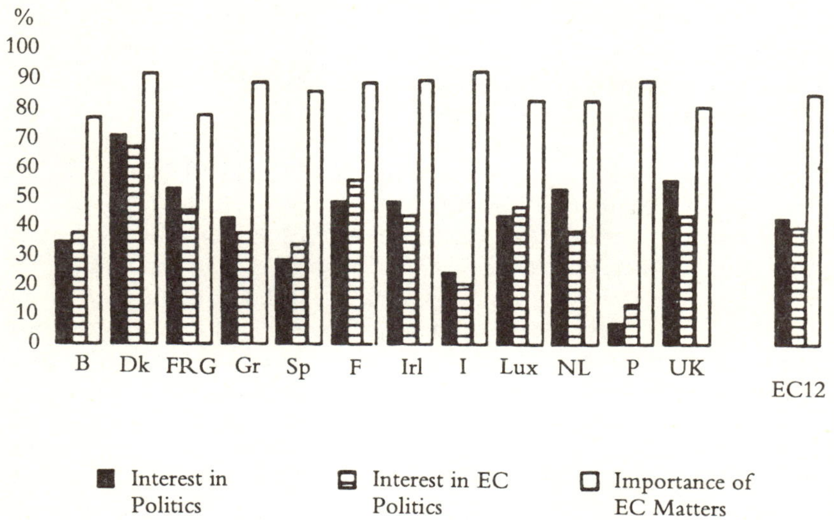

Figure 27.2 Interest in politics and in EC politics, 1988 (percentage of those responding)

Source: *Eurobarometer*, 30 December 1988, p. 6.

the proportion of those who keep positive opinions on professional politicians and their activities. Additionally, two thirds agree that politicians only act in defence of party or personal interests, do not believe what they say and are not very concerned with the opinion of the Spanish people.

The combination of this set of attitudes with positive conceptions on the legitimacy of democracy has been qualified as '*democratic cynicism*' (Maravall, 1982). Or, if this were linguistically feasible, as '*cynical democratism*' (Botella, 1991): this would refer to the mixture of democratic legitimacy, mistrust, scepticism, personal inefficacy and critical opinions on politicians' sincerity, honesty or motivations. Many of these attitudes owe their shape to the attitudes formed during Franco's times. But their persistence is explained through their inclusion in a wider attitude syndrome, formed by basic attitudes and beliefs: thus, for example, the low levels of interpersonal trust and of belief in one's inability to dominate the environment. Even though these levels may be similar to those in other European countries, their relevance is greater when combined with high doses of social anomie. The successive economic, political and social changes experienced by the Spanish people in the last two decades contribute to their perception of social and political reality as bewildering and inaccessible (López Pintor, 1982; Benedicto, 1989).

Political mobilization and participation

The political cultures of certain Western democracies share with Spain a similar distribution of political mistrust and cynicism. But they seem different through their greater readiness to mobilize and their greater levels of participation. There seem to be few resources in Spain allowing for action to be taken against rules perceived as unfair and harmful. Those feelings of inefficacy eventually lead to viewing political decisions as alien, and to a certain resignation towards their consequences. In 1980, this sort of fatalism could be seen in the fact that only 22% of Spanish citizens stated that they could do anything against an unfair or harmful local decision, and 20% said so with respect to a national decision. Although at that time the short democratic experience would justify the low levels of subjective political competence, the passage of time has not brought significant changes. In 1989, only 13% of the people thought they might influence the decisions adopted by the national government, 14% thought this of regional governments, and 18% of local authorities.[3]

Nor has the passage of time meant a change in the level of political participation of Spanish citizens. Involvement in political and social organizations and commitment in participative activities have continued at the same low levels as at the beginning of the transition. In 1981, Spain, with Italy and France, was one of the European countries whose citizens showed lowest membership of social organizations: only 31% of its citizens belonged to some organization, as compared to 50% of the Federal Republic of Germany, 52% in the United Kingdom and 62% in the Netherlands.[4] In 1989, not only did this weak membership continue in Spain, but it even increased in relative terms. An important sector of those who do belong to some organization are members of leisure, sports or cultural clubs. Trade union membership is, as in Italy, one of the lowest in Europe: in spite of their social visibility in collective bargaining, trade-union membership remains around 7%.

Membership of political parties is also very limited. Although it probably went up to 5–6% at the end of the 1970s, it has remained around 3% since then. Spanish political parties, born in a modern society, without the rigid class division of the 1940s, and in a time dominated by mass media, especially television, have not known how to establish significant bonds with social institutions and secondary organizations. The organizational weakness of parties is reflected in its scarce presence among voters, even in psychological terms. The level of party identification is very low. In accordance with data from the *European Values Survey*, Spain, Belgium, France and the United Kingdom shared minimum levels of party attachment: only 29% declared being close to some party, as compared with an average of 38% in the EC as a whole. And, among those who stated some degree of attachment, the weakness of Spanish respondents' links with the relevant parties stood out among the rest. According to *Eurobarometer* data, Spain is an EC country with a lower level of party attachment: it was

Table 27.1 Percentage of electors not voting at each election in Spain, 1977–90*

Type of election	'77	'79	'80	'81	'82	'83	'84	'85	'86	'87	'88	'89	'90
General election	21	32	—	—	20	—	—	—	29	—	—	30	—
Autonomic Basque Community	—	—	41	—	—	—	32	—	30	—	—	—	39
Catalonia	—	—	38	—	—	—	36	—	—	—	41	—	—
Galicia	—	—	—	55	—	—	—	43	—	—	—	41	—
Andalusia	—	—	—	—	34	—	—	—	28	—	—	—	44
13 Autonomous Communities	—	—	—	—	—	30	—	—	—	28	—	—	—
Municipal	—	40	—	—	—	34	—	—	—	30	—	—	—
European	—	—	—	—	—	—	—	—	—	31	—	45	—

* Percentages have been rounded to facilitate reading.

Table 27.2 Political participation activities in Spain, 1980–86, and in some European countries, 1974*

Activity	Spain 1980	Spain 1983	Spain 1986	European countries, 1974†
Reading newspapers' political section	25	28	26	65
Discussing politics with others	21	29	27	46
Trying to convince friends to vote like him/herself	7	9	8	15
Working with others to try to solve local problems	8	8	8	16
Attending political meetings	8	8	7	12

* Figures are percentages of those who perform each of these activities 'often' and 'sometimes'.

† Figures are mean averages in the Netherlands, United Kingdom, Federal Republic of Germany and Austria.

Source: For Spain: CIS Data Bank; for European countries: Barnes, Kaase *et al.* (1979: 541–542).

between 30 and 40%, while the average of the twelve European countries is between 60 and 70% (Schmitt, 1989).

Spanish participation in politics is, as may be expected, at a lower level than that of other democratic societies. The average electoral participation in the five general elections held up to 1989 was among the lowest in Europe. In fact, Spain occupied the last-but-one place among the mean electoral participation of the 18 European countries in 1979–90. Leaving the Swiss case aside, where participation levels were exceptionally low, the countries with a lower than average electoral participation were Spain, the United Kingdom, Ireland and France. Table 27.1 shows that, with only a few exceptions, non-voting percentages have not gone lower than 30% in the numerous elections held in Spain between 1977 and 1990. Voters assign a hierarchy to elections in their willingness to participate: needless to say, general elections are the most important to them, followed by autonomic, municipal and, at a certain distance, European elections.[5]

Finally, a comparison between some Spanish participatory activities and those of a selection of other European countries shows the consistency both in the participative behaviour of the former and in the difference between them. As may be seen in Table 27.2, there are considerable differences in political information and communications activities, which are linked to different levels of political efficacy and of subjective political competence. And, even though the activities requiring greater initiative and difficulty decrease, they nevertheless remain important. As in 1980, massive differences in participation still separate today's Spain from other democratic countries, though in selected activities these differences are considerably smaller. And a close linkage still appears between political inequality, implicit in participation mechanisms, and social inequality. It is true that these differences usually appear jointly in democratic systems; but in Spain they do so in an impressive manner (Maravall, 1982).

Conclusion

The basic restriction of political activities to those with higher social status produces a series of important consequences. In connection with political attitudes, it reinforces the already widespread feelings of political mistrust and inefficacy. And as far as the political system itself is concerned, it impedes its capacity to respond and prevents an effective aggregation of interests. Both aspects may continue to co-exist, but only if their commitment continues being very small: as a momentary, impulsive, short-term activity, with limited goals, mobilization lacks the achievements and awards of continuous political participation (Orizo, 1983). This lack gave rise to many examples in the course of the negotiations for Spain's entry to the EC and of its first years of membership: some of the most important Community policies were discussed and applied in processes characterized by sporadic mobilization of the affected groups. That is why, in general terms, their effectiveness is less than that achieved by those organizations which can give shape to their interests through institutionalized mechanisms.

The political passivity of Spanish citizens has a negative incidence both collectively in political decision making and individually in political efficacy. It also affects the very 'quality' of the democratic system. No matter how indeterminate this concept may be, it does seem obvious that it is linked to the critical, albeit articulate, indifference of the Spanish people towards many public questions, while, at the same time, it is also reflected in many dimensions of political, party and parliamentary life. And those relative to the EC are certainly no exception. Apathy, indifference, a lack of solidarity and inefficacy in relation to effective participation are hardly compatible with the efficient participation which institutionalizes a genuine and dynamic pluralism. As Linz has concluded (1990), Spanish society is in danger of becoming basically passive, more or less satisfied at individual level and, well-being aside, with no great collective – or even individual – ambitions; in other words, a rather grey society.

Notes

1. These data, and the majority of those quoted in this chapter, have been taken from surveys deposited in the Centro de Investigaciónes Sociológicas (Centre for Sociological Research, CIS) Data Base, in Madrid. Space constraints have

precluded specific descriptions of technical data, which may be found in Montero and Torcal (1990).

2. These data have been taken from *Eurobarometer*, 33, June 1990.
3. This situation is reinforced through the scarce recognition of political decisions adopted at different levels. Both in 1980 and 1989, the proportion of those who believed that measures taken by local authorities would affect their daily lives were 47% and 60% respectively, while the figures given at the same time in connection with the government, were of 48% and 50%, and 46% for regional governments (these last figures are only relevant to 1989).
4. These data have been taken from the European Values Survey, carried out in 1981 in the United Kingdom, Northern Ireland, Ireland, France, Belgium, Federal Republic of Germany, the Netherlands, Spain, Denmark and Italy.
5. The smaller rate of non-voting in the European Parliament elections of 1987 was due to the fact that thirteen of the seventeen existing Autonomous Communities held their local and regional elections simultaneously with them.

References

Barnes, S.H., Kaase, M. *et al.* (1979) *Political Action: Mass Participation in Five Western Democracies*, London, Sage.

Benedicto, J. (1989) 'Sistemas de Valores y Pautas de Cultura Política Predominantes en la Sociedad Española (1976–1985)', in J.F. Tezanos, R. Cotarelo y A. de Blas (eds), *La Transición Democrática Española*, Madrid, Sistema, pp. 645–78.

Botella, J. (1991) 'La Cultura Política en la España Democrática', in R. Cotarelo (ed.), *Transición y Democracia en España: Política*, Madrid, Centro de Investigaciones Sociológicas.

Gunther, R. (1988) *Politics and Culture in Spain*, Ann Arbor, Michigan, Center for Political Studies.

Linz, J.J. (1990) 'Reflexiones sobre la Sociedad Española', in S. Giner (ed.), *España: Sociedad y Política*, Madrid, Espasa-Calpe, pp. 657–87.

López Pintor, R. (1982) *La Opinión Pública Española del Franquismo a la Democracia*, Madrid, Centro de Investigaciones Sociológicas.

Maravall, J.M. (1982) *The Transition to Democracy in Spain*, London, Croom Helm.

Montero, J.R. and Torcal, M. (1989) 'Voters and Citizens in a new Democracy: Some Trend Data on Political Attitudes in Spain', *International Journal of Public Opinion Research*, No. 2, 116–40.

Orizo, F.A. (1983) *España entre la Apatía y el Cambio Social*, Madrid, MAPFRE.

Schmitt, H. and Mannheimer, K. (1991), 'On Party Attachment in Western Europe and the Utility of Eurobarometer Data', *Western European Politics*, no. 12, 122–39.

Chapter 28

Protection of fundamental rights

Carlos Bruquetas Galán

Protection of the system of human rights and freedoms becomes a reality by means, fundamentally, of two social systems. As Spanish citizens can verify, human rights need the protection of procedures anchored in the legal and cultural systems of a society. But there is an order of precedence between them: the establishment of rights and freedoms, their realization and materialization, always comes to the legal system through cultural channels. The implementation of the social system of cultural protection to human rights may be considered an essential condition for the implementation of the legal system, to achieve consolidated and permanent legal guarantees. The two systems, thus, are complementary.

These two systems may be provided with social structures to give different levels of shelter to the enjoyment of fundamental rights and liberties. The constitutional network forms the link between the two systems, taking cultural assets, the demands and convictions stemming from this culture, and giving them a legal format. In essence, the constitutional fabric describes what rights have to be protected and sets the basis for their legal guarantee, with inviolability proportionate to the cultural values with which that society has endowed them.

To talk about 'protection of rights', however, leads into some basic considerations, relative to the changing nature of protection and to the kind of protection granted, respectively. First, as the nature of human rights evolves, so is their content being reviewed, on the basis of the concept of 'human needs', which implies the evolution of societies in relation to changes and cultural relativity of values. It is not surprising that a trend has appeared, proposing the replacement of the terminology of *human rights* with a wider, more relaxed one of *human dimension*, which offers to overcome important evaluation and perception differences, such as the ones taking place between the northern and southern Mediterranean shores. This is an explanation of the present debate about the hierarchy of needs, that of values and fundamental rights: is it legitimate to establish a ranking among them, in order to give them some order of priority, or does the simple consideration of this possibility generate structure distortions which make it possible to violate some rights for the benefit of others?

The conceptual change on who must be the subject of human rights and what instances there are against which he must be protected is another element under revision. Next to individuals considered as equals in their circumstances, certain social categories acquire spatial prominence in their demand for protection; while, at the same time, other categories, factors and institutions are starting to stand out as generators of human rights violations and even of constraints that have been collected in legal systems under the shape of a permanent loss of some generally recognized guarantees. Vulnerable groups are introducing raw options, such as their demand for the right to euthanasia for terminal patients, freedom of thought for children, and their right to have a say in the choice of any teaching system, the right of the elderly not to be imprisoned in institutions, the right of ethnic minorities to be protected against plunder, ghettoization and even genocide by majorities, the right of less developed countries to be provided by international institutions with sufficient legal guarantees – *vis-à-vis* epidemics, deprivation of resources by others, starvation, war, etc.

Human rights also need protection sometimes. Both the legal and cultural systems of protection may be hampered by factors, social categories and circumstances which may limit these rights, or which could be used as instruments to legitimate certain constraints on their legal guarantees. Among these, the following may be mentioned:

- the non-recognition of cultural plurality, that is, of the right of minorities and historically immigrant communities to their own cultural identity;
- the application of military solutions to consolidation problems of ethnic, cultural or historical communities;
- terrorism and drug traffic, especially when some specific disproportionate 'fighting' systems are applied to solve these problems;
- the revitalizing of certain institutionalization processes (sects and religious groups, fundamentalist movements, groups formed around mass sports, certain powerful subsystems of a multinational nature, enterprise subcultures such as those originated in certain eastern countries, etc).
- a parallel growth of *fundamentalism* and *xenophobia* which, in times of economic recession, may be the consequence of a strong migratory avalanche towards prosperous areas, and of the subsequent economic-demographic polarization (welfare and birth-rate reduction vs. poverty and demographic growth), etc.

Thus, consideration of the correct protection of human rights is the very subject of this chapter. How should a plausible evaluation be approached, however, without making reference to the cultural system? Relativism in matters of culture, religion and values is the very factor that allows us to understand the reasons why some societies and individuals enjoy legal guarantees for their rights and freedoms, while, a few kilometres away, these same rights do not even achieve a definition. This is the reason why these social and cultural rights and, further, emerging rights relative to safety and development, form the best prevention and rights protection system; or perhaps even the beginning of a new system in agreement with the present international scenario. Because, while, for instance, underdevelopment beyond the borders of developed countries maintains misery and its consequences in a continuous centripetal movement towards the developed countries, recognition of the right to develop, cooperation of the more developed with lesser favoured parties and the introduction of the necessary elements to achieve it, is the equivalent of the development of the same human rights, that is, their establishment and enjoyment (Bruquetas, 1991).

Although the analysis of this topic cannot end here, a few thoughts about emerging human rights may be introduced here, and about their format, especially after the Declaration of the Right to Development. Some recent formulae on human rights, such as those dealing with security and development, may well impede the establishment and enjoyment of human rights in another area. The most refined cultural system of protection, the most pure legal guarantee system can turn into a simple piece of paper if war breaks out. The right to development is defined as inseparable from the right to cooperation for the lesser developed, without which, the enjoyment of freedom on the part of the more fortunate can be considered a system for the maintenance of caste, ethnic or racial privileges, especially in a Mediterranean European context in which countries outside the EC furnish it with a workforce essential to the upkeep of its welfare. As was mentioned before, however, this right is formulated along with others, inseparable from it: the right of people to enjoy international legal guarantees; in other words, the right of societies to develop in peace, to have systems which enable the peaceful resolution of conflicts, which protect the right to international peace and safety. The privileged position of the European communities in relation to emerging rights implies an equally privileged duty to consolidate and promote these new rights – which, from the beginning, have been seen as 'key rights' – at theoretical and practical levels.

These tendencies will probably be made manifest in the proliferation of centres for peaceful resolution of conflicts, in a multiplication of the relevant studies and in the implementation of cooperation strategies and of compensation funds addressed at the development and maintenance of peace and safety systems. These new structures, however, will not be free of stress, inherited from previous stages. Industrial sectors organized around expansive military projects or around technological development depending on armaments, and trade unions concerned about the growth of unemployment or their members' loss of purchasing power may get involved with other groups abroad to form a counterweight and to perform different functions where the signs of loss of balance in international security may appear. Or multinational organizations and security-related forums may develop tactics whose origin might be found in other previous stages of development, not suitable to the present situation, and under certain conditions may have to be recycled by the emerging forces, adapting their structures in genuine maturation processes (Prieto and Bruquetas, 1986). Any residual supporters of the former regime will not be able to avoid their decline, parallel to that of the economic schemes they supported; this development, however, will not be free from fluctuations and set-backs, which may occasionally be costly.

The key to an efficient system of cultural protection for human rights will, thus, lie in the contents and instruments given to these new structures. If the central role of some of these emerging rights is accepted, such as the right to peaceful and orderly development, emphasis may be placed particularly on compensation funds for development and security. Some policy may be imposed for the establishment of international compensation, cooperation and security, based on the preparation of statistical series to follow risk factors in different countries, regions and economic sectors. This will make it necessary to prepare plans for obtaining and incorporating funds and may imply the formulation of alternative criteria to be tested, leading to the definition of proportionality factors and of distribution systems, according to the defined risk factors. And it will tend to lead towards the practical application of policies, strategies and distribution systems in needy areas, creating cooperative structures and reducing contradictory stereotypes.

These introductory thoughts frame the nature of the subjects we are trying to evaluate. But the evaluation of costs and benefits of the cultural protection of human rights in Spain, on the basis of its EC membership, demands at least a brief look to the status of these rights, in the EC case and in the Spanish case. Let us first consider the case of the EC.

A new State is beginning to appear in Europe – some might define it as a new phase in State evolution, or as a new form of State – and its rules will reflect the framework of values which will rule in the new power aggregate. EC citizens will experience a lesser or greater degree of defencelessness, depending on the way these values are transferred from the cultural system to the legal system. One might wonder here whether the set of EC rules are being shaped as a paraconstitutional system or if, as has seemed the case in certain stages of the recent past, it was rather taking the shape of a trade and customs agreement. The answer to this is the key because, if it is so, the text which would ultimately result would not only express the initial economic expectations, but also the new legal guarantees of protection demanded by the new subjects. The real modernity of the EC design will be conditioned by the manner in which the rights of individuals and vulnerable groups are protected against factors which may constrain their enjoyment of these rights. In other words the creation of a European citizenship may be a fast way to achieve fully guaranteed rights, no longer subsidiary to other European institutions or to the national guarantees of each Member State. The Europe of the citizens and of historical and cultural communities is being proposed as a bid in favour of a better cultural and legal expression of human rights, in favour of a better future for them. The other bid is for the furtherance of economic prospects and contains the temptation to become a superpower, a new pole of world power capable of influencing the development of events in other regions of the globe. Growing or diminishing trends, such as the maturation of civil society or the sale of arms to Third World countries, may upset the balance in one or the other sense. Associative movements may, therefore, be the best instrument for new values and for the manifestation of the new demands for the protection of rights. Future protection of the right of coming generations to the preservation of the environment and of the European cultural heritage, within a framework of the right to sustainable development, cooperation, individual and collective safety, the peaceful resolution of conflicts and the enjoyment of international guarantees, may find in these movements some forms of postmaterialist ways through which the new human needs may be met.

This is the emerging framework in which the cultural protection of human rights in Spain within the EC context must be evaluated. The difficulties inherent in this evaluation stem from the uncertainty which surrounds the process of maturation of this emerging system which is now appearing in Europe. But it also stems from the peculiar Spanish process in which this cultural protection system has been shaped.

Human rights protection in Spain is not only interesting in itself, but also because of the consequences for third parties, given the apparent lack of cultural structures in which legal guarantees might take root. Spain is on the periphery, a bridging country destined to receive waves of immigrants in the centripetal movement mentioned earlier in this chapter, likely to suffer dramatic changes in its perceptions towards foreigners and, thus, destined to suffer a reversal in its values and attitudes, from those which were a response to the contempt in which it was lately held to a natural and increasing xenophobia. It is a society which runs the risk of being overwhelmed by its own power, faced with the sudden achievement of two age-old aims: to have a democratic system and to have put an end to its European isolationism. It might be stated that the departure of the ghost of underdevelopment leaves an empty place which could now be filled by the ghost of this lust for power. Spain is also a country which is struggling between the preservation of its new purity of European blood and its unwillingness to reject the erstwhile 'brother' countries in America or Africa.

In earlier centuries most of the present EC societies were creating a culture of freedom and advancing in the enjoyment of rights, but Spanish society moved at a slower pace and, in several areas, was stagnant. When the religious conflict that marked the birth of Spain was resolved into radical Christianity, its cultural system was subject to influences that caused a series of retrenchments, with some interspersed structural outbreaks, only to wither after a while. At last, during the Franco period a late consolidation of the Spanish bourgeoisie took place and a broad band of the middle classes emerged. This factor turned out to be the key to the birth of the cultural system furthering the protection of human rights. Concurrently, freedom of thought and choice was favoured in the new economic context, which fed on information that would probably not be provided by an authoritarian and autarchic system. So the State's survival was in the hands of managers who had not participated in its budgets; when savings and the incipient accumulation of capital were encouraged, the obscurantist tradition was finally buried and the emergence of a cultural system favouring the protection of freedom was fostered. Thus, in contrast to earlier upheavals, the end of Franco's era was calmly greeted by most Spanish institutions, under the decisive leadership of the monarchy. In the course of the last decades, they have become aware of that which was lacking under the authoritarian regime.

At the same time, the Spanish request to gain entry to the European institutions was emerging as a part of the new cultural system of protection. If some remnants of the former regime still existed in Spanish society, the emerging forces had found an essential support to overcome their own weakness. It was not simply a question of enlarging the market for Spanish products; after the appearance of the group known as the 'Munich collusion', it was clear that Spanish society was primarily seeking to secure liberty. The cultural protection system was thus coming to light again. Bonds with European institutions were a fundamental element in its consolidation and, later, in the emergence of a legal system of protection. A membership in these institutions was considered vital for the new organization of the State. Access to economic, legal and, to a lesser degree, security and defence institutions, was considered essential to go forward in the new cultural system, to raise barriers – walls if necessary – against any monopolistic, illegitimate or authoritarian proposals which might still linger. In the specific case of the European defence institutions, the doubts expressed were a reflection of the residual rejection of the power structures connected with the old regime, still live in Spanish memories.

The characteristics of consolidation in the European cultural system and the peculiarities of the Spanish system point up the difficulties of assessing costs and benefits arising from Spain's entry into the EC with respect to the protection of human rights. Three processes were crucial:

(a) Spain's transition to democracy, one of whose milestones is the 1978 Constitution.
(b) Spain's access to the European legal institutions, marked by its membership of the Council of Europe in 1977.
(c) Spain's entry into the EC in 1982.

It is not surprising that, in legal matters, the EC has been especially concerned with labour and economic aspects (Dekker, 1990), and has postponed a regulation on other human rights. This may well be one of the benefits of joining the EC, since many Spanish subjects have been able to leave aside their inferior immigrant status and to replace it with a higher one, of EC citizens with full rights. This benefit has been especially noticeable for its removal of job and salary discrimination for reasons of nationality or sex. It has also meant a high cost for Hispanics overseas, traditionally linked to Europe with ties of brotherhood and a lively social system, as well as dual-nationality agreements. It may also have costs in terms of increasing xenophobia in Spanish society, which, until recently was amongst the lowest in the EC, perhaps because of the low representation of other ethnic groups in Spain. It has been said that racism is to be expected as migration into the EC increases, due to the position of Spain as a bridge and to the xenophobic tradition in which the Spanish State was born (Christianity vs. Judaism or Islam). Even the Hispanic groups in Spain are beginning to experience this xenophobic trend, which materializes in a hitherto unknown loss of social consideration. African groups (both white and coloured), most of whom occupy marginal positions until now reserved for gypsies, are also beginning to be subject to it. In the short term, the recently issued legislation to regulate foreign presence in Spain has been interpreted as a real loss, when related to the Spanish tradition of hospitality, contrasting with religious xenophobia, but real nevertheless.

It may be thought, thus, that there is a certain EC imbalance in matters of legal protection to human rights, and that this imbalance may stem from the excessively economic environment into which EC institutions were born, unlike other European institutions. This institutional specialization, which leaves the protection and legal guarantees of these freedoms to the Council of Europe and to the European Court of Human Rights, may be considered as one of the sources of this imbalance, because both of them lack executive power and, at the same time, the EC is freed from the subsequent legal liabilities. These are the reasons why the EC signature of the European Human Rights Conventions is most essential for the legal protection system. Otherwise, the cultural system could suffer very important – perhaps even irreversible – impairment, as it would institute a tolerant attitude, making it possible to diminish the ruling and protecting authority, the national and Council of Europe authorities, and *de facto* legitimizing national situations contrary to – or in little agreement with – the spirit of human rights.

With reference to the Spanish process, several additional costs might be pointed out; in principle, they do not seem to be imputable to Community regulations or lack of them. I shall only mention here the costs due to the Spanish institutions responsible for the operation of the democratic system, and not those which may have originated in delays that may be blamed on the cultural system (i.e., a faulty application or flagrant violation of the regime of liberties by some law-enforcing officials – which, although not to be minimized, are not relevant to the Spanish social system). Certain areas of the constitutional system, however (Text of the 1978 Constitution, Jurisprudence of the Constitutional Court), give rise to additional costs. Among these, the following have been specifically mentioned (Prieto, 1990):

— the non-addition of *social rights* to the 1978 Constitution, which may only be pleaded before ordinary jurisdiction and lack the so-called *recurso de amparo* (appeal to the Constitutional Court for protection of fundamental rights and liberties).

— the weak protection of *fundamental rights in the private sector*, since the *recurso de amparo* to the Constitutional Court is only available to public powers, neglecting damage suffered by other emerging nucleii of social power. Their weakness renders the theoretical equality of the parties illusory in labour, trade and consumer relations and, especially in international or multinational relations.
— the loss of fundamental rights given to *conscientious objection* which, in 1987 and for administrative reasons, was lowered by the Constitutional Court jurisprudence to the right to apply for exemption from military service for moral reasons, thus excluding the right to object to compulsory military service.
— some *religious establishment* since there are ecclesiastical civil servants for the Catholic Church and important budgetary funds are directed to its religious orders.
— and the presence of a *permanent potential situation of deprivation of rights*, capable of affecting any citizen, which has stemmed from the individual temporary suspension of fundamental rights (in the anti-terrorist legislation, which is sometimes applied even to common offenders).

All these difficulties strongly suggest that the cultural system of rights protection is important, something which goes beyond the legal system and which still constitutes its very social matrix. The Spanish contribution to the cultural protection of rights and freedoms may be very valuable, as the sensibility generated by the lack of human rights may help the clear perception of some emerging human rights and the additional guarantees needed to complete the cultural system of protection. But the EC contribution to Spanish society, in spite of its legal vacuums and corresponding costs (which may legitimate situations when protection is lost) may be deemed of extreme importance for Spanish interests, lending them a superstructure to supplement the present deficiencies and allowing them to develop the necessary cultural system to guarantee correct operation of the legal protection system.

References

Bruquetas, C. (ed.) (1991) *Derecho al desarrollo o el desarrollo de los derechos*, Madrid, Instituto Ciencia y Sociedad Universidad Complutense.

Dekker, Ige F. (1990) 'The legal protection of human rights' in Memmo Wolters (ed.), *The Netherlands and EC Membership Evaluated*, London, Pinter.

Prieto, L. (1990) 'Los derechos fundamentales tras diez años de vida constitucional', *Revista Sistema de Ciencias Sociales*, May, 19–34.

—— and Bruquetas, C. (eds) (1986) *Libertades públicas y fuerzas armadas*, Madrid, Ministerio de Educación y Ciencia and Instituto de Derechos Humanos, Universidad Complutense.

Chapter 29

The consequences of EC membership for Spanish educational policy

Manuel J. Rodríguez Caamaño and Amparo Almarcha Barbado

This chapter cannot enter into questions of what sort of education might be optimal for all EC Member States, but neither can it stop at describing education in terms of economics and development because we would inexcusably lose the necessary perspective of what Europe is and what it should be.

In order to explain Tönnies' (1979) concepts of 'community' and 'association', we assume – as representatives of various institutions have stated – that we are not trying to attain either an associative (federal) Europe (material success and lack of solidarity) or a community Europe (spiritual success and little development), but rather an associative and, at the same time, communitarian Europe. On this basis, we define a type of education which will progressively abolish dysfunctions brought about by the strict application of a vocational or humanist education. And we believe this is necessary, because, among other reasons, 'young people are beginning to realize that they are the victims of a contradictory education. They are being trained to live in two different worlds: one is unreal, that of ethical values; the other is real and immediate, where ethical values are infringed, and this tolerance of infringement, through continuous acceptance, leads to the belief that the world of ethics is a chimera'.[1]

A vocational education means adapting to the material reality, which, as a consequence, implies dehumanization and, at this stage, the denial of European ideals. On the other hand, a humanist education, if one admits the existence of the 'two cultures', causes a distancing from material reality, resulting in the impossibility of achieving the ideals of equality, liberty and fraternity, and advancing towards their achievement.

To palliate the devastating effects that economics exerts over what is human and social, the suitability of an educational system is usually judged from the point of view of the complete training of individuals. They (*with no distinction for reasons of sex*) learn professional, human and civic aspects of those arts and values which will be beneficial to Europeans and to the human species. It is a question of training them as genuine European citizens, with everything this implies. In summary, it is a question of preparing people who are conscious of the wealth and well-being offered by developed capitalist societies and are less aware of the social costs this causes. Having recognized the part played by ideas and by materialism, we can better appreciate the role of education as a relevant and adequate means of mitigating the costs implicit in the material production mode on which we depend.

Education is the means which permits an understanding of the difficulties and needs of those who do not have a reasonable standard of living. If we start from the fact that developed capitalist societies make it possible to reduce the undesirable consequences of development, then it is a question of not producing and reproducing secretly what is not compatible with European ideals. Such an ideal can become a reality, existing as a buffer between the economic policy and educational policy of each and every one of the countries, breaking down the equation which subordinates human dimensions to mechanics. It is our opinion that EC educational policies, with some reservations, are those which provide the best solution to material, human and social interests of the various social organizations.

The Spanish educational system

Education plays a fundamental role in the maintenance of democratic order, because the essential premises of a system based in democracy demand a high level of training and civic culture. This is difficult to achieve if the educative system does not supply everyone with a suitable level of education. In a country like Spain, education is not only a function of social integration, which may be true of any other country in Europe, but it also plays a role in the reproduction of the inequities and privileges of society. Modern Spanish society, in fact, is focusing on achieving a teaching system which allows for an increase of equal opportunities and a better quality of life.

In the last few years, the relevant organizations and institutions have been trying to achieve goals which, according to the experts and education politicians, might eliminate the dangerous circle of self-generating social inequalities. These goals are: (1) democratic access for all citizens to the various levels of education; (2) a better quality of teaching; (3) improved status for the teaching profession, recognizing all trade-union, economic and academic rights; (4) a transformation of teaching centres into self-governing school communities; (5) a reform of educational administration, to make it more participative and efficient; (6) to finance teaching in a way that contributes to a redistribution of income; and (7) reform of research. All this implies a wide process of change at all levels, not least in the Ministry of Education and Science.

After the approval of the 1978 Constitution, teaching needed a new framework, not only because the constitutional text specifically required it, but because it was necessary to include the constitutionally granted rights and freedoms in the educational system. The education system's performance was no longer acceptable, because it was inequitable, inefficient and of poor quality.

So the first Socialist government had to face educational reform. As a legal answer, the LODE (Ley Orgánica sobre el Derecho a la Educación, or Organic Law for the Right to Education), of 3 July 1985, set out the lines along which a public service of basic teaching should settle. Fundamental to it is the improved quality of education and the promotion of educational equality. It also dealt with teaching staff, primary and secondary school curricula, special needs education and scholarships, etc. The LRU (Organic Law for University Reform) of 25 August 1983 gives the framework for university autonomy and for reform in favour of professionalism in research. This block of reforms, whose impact on Spanish education has been very deep, is only the first step in the change. The reform of Spanish teaching exists for two reasons: to achieve better quality and more equality for the educational system. The opportunities available to people in life depend mainly on the education received by them; the process of change in Spain also depends, to a high degree, on its level of education.

Educational activities, in accordance with the principles of the Constitution, recognize the following ends: (a) full development of the student's personality; (b) training on fundamental rights and freedoms; (c) the acquisition of intellectual rigour and good working habits; (d) qualification for the performance of professional activities; (e) training in the linguistic and cultural diversity of Spain; (f) preparation for participation in cultural and social life; and (g) training for peace, cooperation and solidarity among people.

It is necessary to add that the main area of concern in a country like Spain, is the quality of the teaching. In this sense, an effort has been made to improve results and the efficiency of the teaching. One of the indicators used in other countries is the number of pupils per teacher. In Spain, this remains one of the highest ratios in Europe, although it has been decreasing.

Integration in the EC

The CIS survey of Spanish public opinion on Europe and the Europeans (see Tables 29.1 and 29.2) shows a high level of acceptance of entry into Europe.[2] It also throws light on Spanish citizens' expectations of this process of integration (see Table 29.3).

Assessment of cost

Costs derive from a starting point weaker in resources and infrastructure or, what is the same, those resulting from adaptation to more developed societies. Most costs are relative, since investment in education can be seen

Table 29.1 Opinions on the consequences of Spanish EC membership (percentage of respondents)

	Things are better (somewhat, a lot)	Things are worse (somewhat, a lot)	Don't know/ No answer	Total
Total	61	19	20	(2,504)
Age				
18 to 25	68	15	17	(487)
26 to 40	68	17	15	(685)
41 to 50	59	24	17	(394)
51 to 60	55	23	22	(398)
Over 60	51	17	32	(533)
Schooling				
Less than primary	50	20	30	(694)
Primary	61	18	21	(899)
Secondary	69	16	15	(640)
Higher	67	20	13	(259)
Profession				
Entrepreneurs, managers	54	33	13	(620)
Small entrepreneurs, self-employed	66	18	16	(281)
Employees and intermediate staff	72	17	11	(204)
Farmers	53	26	22	(209)
Blue-collar workers	66	14	20	(662)
Vote in 1986				
PSOE	70	12	18	(853)
AP	51	30	14	(281)
CDS	64	21	15	(168)
IU	66	20	14	(88)

Table 29.2 Evaluation of the effects of Spanish EC membership on different fields

	Positve (v. good or rather good)	Negative (v. bad or rather bad)	Don't know/ No answer	Total
Spain's role in the world	73	6	21	100
Operation of democracy	68	6	26	100
Social modernization in Spain	69	9	22	100
Development of Spanish economy	57	20	23	100

Table 29.3 Expectations for future effects of EC membership

	It will be mostly beneficial for . . .	It will be most harmful for . . .	Don't know/ No answer	Total
Job possibilities	45	15	40	100
Family prosperity	41	18	41	100
Children's future	42	5	38	100

as 'deferred gratification'.[3] The aim is to achieve equality with the educational systems of the more developed countries. It is a profitable investment and it benefits Spanish society in particular and European society in general. The following is a list of situations which may be considered as 'costs'.

— Those originating from integration in a more competitive society which, no doubt, means increased effort from society and its institutions, in order not to be last in the queue.
— Selectivity increases by one or another means, with subsequent damage to economically, socially and culturally less-privileged groups.
— Although some corrective measures are being attempted in this field, it is obvious that, because of their greater specialization, private educational institutions play an important role, to the detriment of public ones.
— The perfecting of vocational training may possibly take the place of social location, that is, of schools passing social status from parents to children.
— It is possible that some languages will become more common, to the detriment of the indigenous ones, which may be considered a cost by the local population.
— The process of integration and adaptation to the new situation and circumstances may be considered a cost since it occasionally demands the same as Europe does, but lacks a European infrastructure. This is hardest for the less privileged groups, causing a disproportionate distribution of costs among the population.
— Even though complementary correctives exist, the development of competitivity and the individualism of Spanish students may be a social cost, bearing in mind that pragmatic logic demands the adaptation of individuals to the system and not vice versa, which may generate an inordinate increase of social fragmentation: the rationale is still that of the system.
— In the same way, the ever increasing specialization of individuals may also be considered as a high social cost, as it disconnects them from the wide reality of which they are a part.

— In terms of mental and physical health, the growing number of controls over individuals, which lead to constant stress from childhood to maturity, may also be considered a cost.
— Certain minorities might consider the disappearance of some authoritarian attitudes in teachers and the greater responsibility granted to pupils as a cost.
— Learning to adapt to a new 'situation' is considered a cost when the change is not accompanied by sufficient training to facilitate the transit. Thus, for part of the teaching staff, unaware of the new realities, the learning process very often means breaking away from previous mental patterns.
— There is no doubt that the impact of new technologies on education has introduced high costs at every educational level, from economic to cultural ones.
— The influence and participation of different sectors of society in education had demanded changes in control, attitudes, behaviour and values of the educational system. That is why everything has led towards one cost: the loss of the monopoly by those groups which used to control the system.
— It is possible that financing destined for common programmes with the rest of the EC countries, when subtracted from educational resources, may act to the detriment of teaching quality.
— It is probable that educational policies aimed at aiding those less economically favoured will never be sufficient, if the inequalities generated by the economic system are higher than the subsidies.
— If the long term future is forgotten and only the present is taken into account, benefits, in fact, are proportionate to the possibilities. Logically, the more resources are available, the better the training will be, and, therefore, the possibility of competing successfully will be greater. The minority benefits and the majority bears the costs. The costs are derived from the weaker economic starting position, which has less capacity to adapt. It must be stated, however, that costs would probably be greater in a situation outside the EC.
— It is necessary to point out that the costs affect: (a) the majority who, for the time being, are not beneficiaries of the goals of the education policy, since aid has not reached everyone; (b) some minority age groups, previously privileged groups with respect to status and mental ability; (c) to sum up, costs are the obvious result of the transition from a pre-modern educational system to a modern and up-to-date system.

In summary, this chapter argues that, for a variety of reasons, costs have been extremely low. In today's world, any educational system whose goal is to train the actors who shape its project so that, in due course, they will be able to replace the present active groups, must fulfil the demand required by social, economic, political and cultural realities of the national society, bearing in mind that it, in turn, forms part of a wider and more international society. It may be that what really is simply a condition inherent to developed societies – which demands constant adaptation from its members – is conceived as a 'cost'. Post-industrial societies are ruthless towards habits and beliefs they consider to be old-fashioned, and the educational systems we are testing, in a greater or lesser measure, try to increase the possibilities of developing freedom, equality, solidarity, peace and cooperation among mankind.

Measuring the benefits

Benefits are derived from inclusion in a more developed society and are irreversibly related to costs. Among the benefits, the following should be mentioned:

— rationalization of the educational system which, among others, includes these questions: reformation of the educational system; suitability of teaching to the needs of society; suitability of teaching to the needs of youth; suitability of teaching to the needs of the work market; suitability of teaching to the needs of the educational system itself.
— Equal opportunities became more efficient when it was understood and taken care of as equality of results. This special emphasis on aid may imply the breaking away from statistical anachronisms connected with the unequal representation of students according to their social class (richer ones, the minority, are better represented; poorer ones, the majority, are less well represented). Programmes of assistance for the economically less privileged have increased their participation in the benefits of the educational system quite remarkably.
— Equality of women, related to the gradual disappearance of insulting prejudices about women, which kept them in a defenceless, subordinate and undignified situation. It may well be argued [4] that this treatment is increasingly less discriminatory and a progressive tendency towards equality of treatment with men seems apparent.
— Quality of teaching continues as the main handicap of the Spanish educational system. The contribution of Joaquín Tena Artigas, Luis Cordero Pascual and José Luis Díaz Jares (1981) on the work of other EC countries is valuable and should be taken into account. It must also be added that rationalization of resources is bringing about a progressive increase of quality in our teaching system.
— In our opinion, a widening of perspectives is, so far, one of the greatest benefits of Spanish entry into the EC. A new horizon has been opened up, making our hopes more possible and our uncertainty easier to overcome, although the positive role played in our societies by this is normally not given great importance.

— Exchanges have increased relationships, bringing about greater enrichment for all those participating in them. The sector that has benefited most from this has been that of education.
— There are advantages, which are never sufficiently appreciated, derived from investment in human capital, through a higher budget for infrastructure and teaching staff, and this is advantageous to Spanish society.
— A definite consolidation of democracy as the political system that builds educational projects, translated into the active participation of every member in the educational system, in recognition of pluralism in all its aspects, and in respect for minorities.
— Another benefit is the effect on prejudice. Dogmatic, authoritarian or inquisitorial values, attitudes and behaviour have been seen as anachronistic and replaced by the fundamental values of democracy.
— Active participation in projects with other EC Member States means the reformation of certain aspects of our educational institutions and their teachers and researchers. Modernization is being sought in science, technology and research where, compared with the more advanced countries, Spain has been lagging.
— The abolition of assumptions that held the educational system captive has given it a new dynamism, removing barriers that prevented professional teachers from developing imagination, independence and freedom.
— The bureaucracy has become more flexible in dealing with validation of qualifications thus allowing free movement of workers.
— Greater legislative protection means greater protection for the rights of teachers and researchers.
— Unlike isolation, which brings deficiencies of every type, entry to the EC has brought a period of efficacy to the Spanish population, as old aspirations became a reality: to participate in the construction of a new Europe and, at the same time, to abandon our underdeveloped status and to enjoy modernity and its benefits.
— The advantages derived from a genuine education, that is, recognition of pluralism, acceptance of different concepts of reality, freedom to choose, and all other conditions which allow greater development to individuals.
— Activation of competitive systems, resulting in a more complete education.
— More emphasis on those areas of knowledge which until now, and with no explanation, had been marginalized in education.
— Greater opportunities for the children of immigrants.
— An enlargement of educational opportunities, by means of greater recognition of the role in society of women, of the aged and the young.
— Secularization of teaching.
— Greater connection between the educational system and Spanish and European social realities, the realities of domestic and foreign work

markets, the entrepreneurial and industrial worlds and cultural realities. In summary, there has been an increase in participation of different social forces in the educational system, by means of: updating curricula and the establishment of new bachelors' degrees, as an answer to the demands of today's realities; and participation in, among others, the ERASMUS, COMETT, EURYDICE, EURYCLES and LINGUA programmes.

Conclusions

The idea of Europe, and participation in it, has always been present in Spain and in Spanish citizens. However, it has been a historically gagged and unreachable idea. Bearing in mind that an account of the genesis and development of this Spanish affinity with Europe would go beyond the limits of this chapter, a summary would say that, under Franco's dictatorship, Europe represented the paradigm that would be followed by the opposition. Spain's geography and culture was located within Europe, so the Pyrenees or our culture were not what separated us from Old World societies, but rather the political power at that time dominant in Spain.

For education, once dictatorship was left behind and the new democratic regime launched, the transition gave rise to a series of changes pointing in the direction of a new educational model, one capable of equalling those in the rest of European countries. It should be pointed out that the greater thrust and attention that the Spanish democratic governments have given to the educational system *happened before Spain's access to the EC*. It is also necessary to underline the coincidence between the goals of the Spanish educational project and that of the remaining EC countries. Thus, it is to be assured that EC membership has meant a reinforcement of the domestic goals as far as education is concerned.

As previously stated, the rationalization of our educational system has tended towards the optimization of relations between the various components of the system and, as a bonus, has recognized and improved the position and functions that science and research must have in education and in society. The educational reform is producing a healthy and very recommendable reduction of the distance between formal ideas and reality. Some previously hidden and undesirable features of the old educational system are under control.

The majority acceptance of educational reforms by the population allows us to state that it was Spanish society itself which demanded this reformation and, later, adaptation and participation in European education structures. To conclude, in the comparative list established here in connection with costs and benefits caused by our entry into the EC, in educational matters, the sum of *benefits is greater*.

Notes

1. Enrique Tierno Galván (1972), *La Rebelión juvenil y el problema de la Universidad*, Madrid, Seminarios y Ediciones, p. 35.
2. CIS, 1989, *La opinión pública española ante Europa y los Europeos*, Estudios y Encuestas, No. 17, Tables 26, 27 and 29.
3. P.B. Horton and C. Hunt (1987), *Sociología*, Mexico, McGraw Hill.
4. See 'Equal Treatment of Women', C. González and A. Almarcha, Chaper 17, in this volume.

References

Calzada, Teresa-Eulalia and Gutierrez, Berta (eds) (1989) *Guía de la Educación en la Comunidad Europea*, Madrid, Centro de Publicaciones del Ministerio de Educación y Ciencia, ICE de la Universidad Autónoma de Barcelona.

CIS (1989) *La opinión pública española ante Europa y los europeos*, Madrid, Estudios y Encuestas, No. 17.

Ministerio de Educación y Ciencia (1989) *Libro Blanco, para la Reforma del Sistema Educativo*, Madrid.

SGT de Ministerio de Educación y Ciencia/Consejo de Universidades (1989) *Las enseñanzas Universitarias en España y en la Comunidad Europea*, Madrid.

Tena Artigas, Joaquín, Cordero Pascual, Luis and Díaz Jares, José Luis (1981) *La educación en España y en Comunidad Económica Europea*, Madrid, Ministerio de Educación y Ciencia – Secretaría General Técnica.

Tierno Galván, Enrique (1972) *La rebelión juvenil y el problema en la Universidad*, Madrid, Seminarios y Ediciones.

Tönnies, Ferdinand (1979) *Comunidad y Asociación*, Barcelona, Ediciones Península.

Chapter 30

Cultural policy and European identity in Spain

María Luz Morán

The concept of cultural policy, as it was expressed during the 1950s by American functionalist sociologists, deals with the set of beliefs, attitudes and values relative to the political system shared by most members of a given community. The main thesis postulated in those days by the first authors who started to work with those conceptual tools (the classic contribution is that of Almond and Verba),[1] is that a close relation exists between this ideological or cognitive dimension of the political system and some aspects of its shape and operation. The sociological analysis of this period, specifically, gives special emphasis to the bond that exists between a political culture of a 'civic' nature and the stability of democratic systems. Neither Almond nor Verba, in fact, nor most of the social scientists who made frequent use of this concept, specified the concrete meaning of the above mentioned bond, although this was no obstacle to a large number of empirical research projects which used the idea of political culture as a fruitful perspective for the analysis of political change and stability.

This chapter will not attempt a critique of the theoretical limitations of the political culture concept, which clearly goes well beyond its scope. It will simply analyse – bearing in mind the already mentioned theoretical framework – a concrete aspect of the formation of a new political culture in Spain, as a consequence of the transition from an authoritarian regime to a new democratic system. The concrete thesis it will try to prove is that the existence among large segments of population of a generalized feeling, which we shall agree to designate as 'European identity', has been an accelerating factor in the configuration of a political culture which, over a very short period of time, has adopted features very similar to those of the remaining Western European countries. This argument, however, has to be presented with two provisos: first, for the above-mentioned reasons, no attempt has been made to reach a general explanation of the specific modalities taken by this political change during the early years of the transition, nor during its later consolidation. Rigorous research in this field still has to be done to permit verifiable general hypotheses. Second, a warning that, although it will always be taken into account, this chapter will not go fully into the complex problem of what specific weight should be given to 'extra-national' factors when dealing with the political behaviour of citizens of a democratic society.

The already vast literature dealing with the Spanish process of political change published at the end of the Francoist authoritarian regime, does not, to date, include any work including an in-depth analysis of the construction of a new political culture in Spain during this period. This chapter will present some general thoughts which should be evaluated as a contribution to that line of work.

With no exceptions, all public opinion enquiries carried out in Spain at the end of the 1960s and during the first years of the 1970s,[2] reveal the existence among the population of a widespread wish for a moderate political change. In the days when Spanish society was being shaken by an undeniable economic boom and by drastic modernization of its social structure and general life, this feeling was not, however, compatible with the diffuse support not so much of Franco's regime as of the figure of the dictator. In fact, what could be noticed at all times was a feeling that belonging to the European sphere – understood as a complex framework which not only included economic and political aspects, but common life-styles and a shared cultural tradition, as well – was inevitable. Thus, while not forgetting the caution with which the available data have to be analysed, due to the constraints and difficulties encountered when performing opinion polls in an authoritarian society, a few years before the death of Franco, a transition to a 'European-style' democratic political system was perceived as something both unavoidable and desirable. This shared feeling was, no doubt, one of the binding elements between the forces of the traditional opposition to Franco, and the so-called technocrats of Franco's regime who, in the last years of his life, started a bid for change in that direction. During this period, and ignoring specific aspects that did generate political discussion (autonomic organization of the State, for example, just to mention one of the most important ones), the truth of the matter is that only a very small percentage of citizens took an 'anti-system' stance.[3]

Not only did the idea of Europe turn into a political model for a significant portion of the forces opposing Franco, but also, since the end of the Civil War, reference to the Europe 'outside' has been compulsory for Spanish artists and intellectuals. In any case, as has already been stated, at the end of the 1960s the ideal of an autarchy no longer seemed to be rooted in Spanish public opinion. As a consequence of all this, the reality of Spanish integration in Europe, which was embodied in the request for entry into the EC by the first democratic governments of the Democratic Centre Union,[4] has never been an element of political breakup, nor even of argument. Unlike other EC countries (as was the case of Denmark or even the UK), access to the EC and its foreseeable consequences for Spanish society (in connection, above all, with its economic structures) cannot be considered as a dividing line in Spanish public opinion or as a dividing force for the party system. Acceptance of the request for EC membership, thus, was one of the main political goals of every government during the 1977–85 period.

However, this basic consensus did not mean that the process of negotiation was not marked by controversies among the different political forces, but disagreements were always a matter of specific aspects of the process of integration, mostly those dealing with different evaluations of the consequences of membership on the main national economic sectors. Curiously, we have already seen that the European identity of Spanish citizens as a whole, never became the subject of political controversy. Yet, in parallel, the wider problem was being posed of how to combine the idea of Spanish identity with the maintenance of the 'national identities' of the so-called historic Autonomous Communities, together with what, through time, seems to have become a process of creating national identity feelings in regions which, until then, had never shown signs of wishing to vindicate this identity.

There is no doubt that it is hard to define the elements which form this idea of European identity. The empirical material used in this chapter is not sufficient to encompass such a complex reality, since resorting to opinion data does not include the psycho-social dimension of the concept itself and the more general idea of political culture which would be essential to reach any definite conclusions on the topic. Furthermore, even though the basic features of Spanish political culture are fundamentally comparable to those of the other EC Member States, the fact should be remembered that (if we agree to continue with the concept in its more classical, although limited, usage) this culture continues to exhibit constraints or deficiencies, particularly in connection with its associative-participative dimension.[5]

In spite of all this, the opinion data used in the second part of the chapter are not the only factor which will allow us to continue to consider the importance of the European dimension as an accelerating factor in the consolidation of the democratic beliefs and attitudes of the Spanish citizens. Electoral behaviour and, above all, the characteristics of the two campaigns for elections to the European Parliament (the last one especially, which took place in June 1989) also allow us to go into greater depth on those aspects. European election campaigns have been presented to the Spanish electorate as campaigns with a national theme (some parties have even used them as primary elections to test the popularity of their leaders), as no important differences existed in the positions of the various political parties with regards to European problems. The degree of consensus about the problems of the EC has been extremely high, even surprisingly high at times. As a sample, notice the fact that the most radical nationalistic groups (as is the case of Herri Batasuna in the Basque Country, a real anti-system coalition) accept the European supranational reality as something desirable, and look on it as a 'Europe of the nationalities'.

The very low degree of conflict which the European question rouses in Spain might be compared with the division and radical confrontation which erupted not only among the political forces, but among Spanish society itself

Table 30.1 Feelings towards the EC

	EC-12	Spain
Positive evaluation	31	38
Negative evaluation	19	11
Neutral descriptions	21	19
Aspects not linked to the EEC	1	—
Others	2	—
Does not know/Will not answer	25	33

Source: *Eurobarometer*, June 1988: 'What do you think when you hear about the EEC?'

as well, when the referendum about entrance to NATO was held. This conflict returns periodically when some specific topics of international policies arise. A good proof of this was seen in the debate about the Gulf War.

Let us analyse briefly some empirical data which support the statements made up to now. To begin with, some aspects of the evaluation of the European institutional dimension will be presented, with some comparative material. Throughout this chapter, we have seen that the general evaluation of the EC is very high in Spain, in spite of the short time since its entry. Furthermore, there are no significant variations in these positive attitudes, unless it is some increase in the favourable attitudes, and a smaller number of those who will not, or do not know how to, evaluate their attitude when questioned (it must be stated, however, that the percentage of those who 'Do not know/will not comment' is higher than in the rest of the EC (see Table 30.1)).

Thus, with higher levels than average in the EC, evaluation of it is highly positive. This is confirmed when we proceed to evaluate the perception of the impact of Spain's entry into the EC-12.

Not only is the optimism with which Spanish public opinion values the specific effects of Spanish membership to the EC relevant, but it increases as well with time, as shown by the data in Table 30.2. From the perspective adopted in this chapter, in any case, the most significant fact is the feeling that Spain has finally achieved its place in the Western world, and that this is frankly positive for the national life. These are consolidated elements in the new political culture of Spanish citizens. This is an important factor in the building of the legitimacy of the democratic system. Acceptance of this is widely present among the Spanish population, and no variable identifies sectors critical of this attitude. An interesting hypothesis which still remains to be verified is that this international dimension has played a very relevant role in the extremely high legitimacy achieved by the new political system in a short period of time. In fact, when the specific effects of the Spanish entry into the EC are taken into account as they appear to Spanish citizens as

Table 30.2 Spanish public opinion, 1986–88

Opinion about conditions in Spain	Nov. '86	Feb. '87	May '87	Nov. '88
A lot or somewhat improved	51	45	56	61
A lot or somewhat worse	20	34	30	19
Does not know/ will not answer	29	21	14	20

Source: Data Base at the Centro de Investigación Sociologica (CIS), Madrid.
'Would you say that things have improved a lot, are somewhat or slightly worse, or a lot worse in Spain after its entry into the EC (%)'.

Table 30.3 Percentage of respondents believing each item has benefited from Spain's entry into EC

Democracy in operation	68%
Economic development	57%
Social modernization in Spain	69%
Spanish role in the world	73%
Job opportunities for respondent	45%
Family welfare of respondent	41%
Children's future	52%

Source: CIS Data Bank, November 1988 Opinion Poll.

a whole, the idea that Spain's role in the world has noticeably improved with its EC membership immediately stands out. This idea is indissolubly associated to the perception of a social modernization process in Spain, and to the improved operation of democracy. However, symbolic or legitimacy factors are not the only ones that seem to be reinforced (and this is a very significant fact, which strengthens our hypothesis). When much more concrete proposals are made for the future (such as prospects for our children, or Spanish economic development), there is no significant fall in the support for Spanish adherence to the EC, although the percentages do diminish slightly, as seen in Table 30.3. Along the same lines, the prospect of European unification is accepted positively by nearly eight of every ten Spanish citizens, which, again, reinforces the depth of the European feelings in Spain.[6]

Every analysis prepared during this period by international relations experts concurred in pointing to the European dimension as a central point around which a good portion of the Spanish foreign policy pivots. Opinion poll data confirm that this is a generalized feeling among the Spanish population. However, the classical concept of political culture, as used in

Table 30.4 Frequency with which respondents consider themselves as Europeans

	% EC '87		% EC '88		Spain, '87		Spain, '88	
Often	14	48	16	53	21	59	17	53
Sometimes	34		37		38		36	
Never	49		44		36		42	
Does not know/ Will not answer	3		4		5		5	

Source: *Eurobarometer*, 1987–8: 'How often do you think that you are not only an inhabitant of your own country, but of Europe as well?'

this chapter and, to be more particular, the idea of 'a European identity' also include a variety of elements which are borderline to a psycho-social dimension which needs to be taken into account. A warning is necessary here: data on this matter, owing to the lack of a general study on the Spanish democratic political culture, are rather less abundant than those dealing with the perception of this new political-institutional reality in Spain. In spite of this and in order to be able to advance some hypothesis, some specific polls are taken into account other than the Eurobarometer data.

When only one year had gone by since full European integration in the EC and ten since the first democratic elections, more than half of the Spanish citizens (very or somewhat often) considered themselves European as well as Spanish. It must be pointed out that, even in 1987, the percentage is somewhat higher than the EC countries' average. Along those same lines, the number of those who never consider themselves as inhabitants of a supranational body, as is Europe, was slightly smaller in Spain than in all other nations considered, as a whole. This fully confirms that the element we have agreed to call 'European identity' is a very important element in the construction of new values and attitudes towards the democratic system. All of it is within the framework of a political culture in which, from the very beginning, the democratic system acquired high levels of legitimacy. In spite of everything, it must not be forgotten that a very considerable number of citizens admit that they hardly ever think about their identity as European citizens, which is also true of the other EC countries. To be specific, approximately four of each ten citizens do not include this idea among their attitudes or beliefs. In the Spanish case, and this is an important element for thought, the figures seem to indicate that, after a moment of great enthusiasm following adherence to the EC, positive percentages decreased somewhat in 1988, as the number of those adopting a negative attitude increases. We do not have later data to allow a verification of the idea that the initial European impetus has somewhat abated.

All this notwithstanding, it would appear that the high rates of approval for the EC will be maintained, while European feelings remain widely

Table 30.5 Feelings towards citizens of some EC countries (%)

	Germ.	Belg.	Franc.	UK	Gr.	It.	Port.
Very or rather favourable	66	61	62	56	61	71	67
Rather and very unfavourable	14	11	19	23	12	7	18
Does not know/ will not answer	20	28	20	21	27	22	20

Source: CIS Data Base, November 1988.

Table 30.6 Trends in feelings towards French and British citizens, 1983–8 (%)

	May '83	January '86	Nov. '88
France			
Very or rather favourable	39	43	62
Very or rather unfavourable	41	37	18
Does not know/ Will not answer	20	20	20
Great Britain			
Very or rather favourable	33	49	56
Very or rather unfavourable	45	28	23
Does not know/ will not answer	22	23	21

Source: CIS Data Bank, 1983–88.

spread among the population. The feelings of Spanish citizens towards those from the various EC countries are the last data which will be used to support the conviction that the Spanish population has positive feelings towards Europe (Table 30.5). Not only is there a frankly positive evaluation of the inhabitants of the other EC countries, with Italy as the one awakening the most positive feelings in Spanish citizens, but there is a surprising trend in this attitude. Check between 1983 and 1988 the cases of the two countries which, for historical reasons, cause a greater rejection: France and Great Britain (see Table 30.6). In both cases, there is a drastic inversion of the trend, and a majority negative evaluation is reversed, with a difference that goes up to 23 percentage points. Thus, Spanish *rapprochement* to Europe is not simply institutional, but those feelings of belonging to a common Europe are now joined with *rapproachement* to the countries that shape this new reality.

Notes

1. Almond and Verba (1970).
2. Readers are asked to refer to the CIS Data Base for surveys carried out during this period; but mention could also be made of, among others, the studies by R. López Pintor and J.M. Maravall, both in 1982.
3. An example of this might be found when considering the votes received by the extreme right formation, Fuerza Nueva, both in the 1977 and 1979 elections. In neither case did Fuerza Nueva get over 5% of the votes.
4. Although it must be remembered that during the last years of Franco's regime, the Spanish government issued a formal request for entry into the EEC.
5. This argument has been developed from the author's article 'Cultura Politica y Democracia en España' (1988).
6. The data on attitudes towards European unification come from a CIS survey of May 1987.

References

G. Almond and S. Verba (1970) *La Cultura Política*, Madrid, Euramérica.

López Pintor, R. (1982) *La opinión pública española: del Franquismo a la Democracia*, Madrid, CIS.

Maravall, J.M. (1982) *La política de la transición*, Madrid, Taurus.

Moran, M.L. (1988) 'Cultura política y democracia en España, *Documentación Social*, Special Issue 'Cambio Democrático y Cultura Política', October–December, pp. 9–25.

Chapter 31

The EC and Spanish immigration policy

Antonio Izquierdo Escribano

The 1980s qualified Spain to be regarded as an 'immigration' country – that is, a land experiencing the arrival and settling of people born in other countries. This does not mean that there was no positive international migration before 1981–90. During the second half of the 1970s, for instance, the number of people coming into Spain was greater than those leaving it. However, it was formed above all by returning Spanish emigrants and, to a lesser degree, by immigrants of other nationalities.

In 1981, there were over 215,000 foreigners residing in Spain, while at the end of 1990, they numbered more than 425,000 (see Figure 31.1). Also, during this same period, over 60,000 persons have acquired Spanish nationality and have therefore been removed from the statistics on foreign population prepared by the Ministry of Internal Affairs. Students, children under 16 years of age who do not have a residency permit and clandestine or illegal immigrants have to be added to these figures. At the end of 1990, the total number of foreigners (residents, students, those granted political asylum, or with temporary permits or no legal papers) was about 625,000; if the new Spanish citizens are added to this figure, it rises to close to 685,000.

This does not represent an excessive volume. Taking into account that the Spanish population exceeds 39 million inhabitants, the percentage of foreigners comes to around 1.6% of the total. The number and proportion of foreigners in Spain are still very far from those in other EC countries such as Germany, France, Belgium, the Netherlands and Italy, and especially so if only foreigners whose origin is from outside the EC are taken into consideration. In fact, the percentage of foreign population from countries outside the EC does not reach 0.8%, while in France, Belgium, the Netherlands and Germany it varies between 3 and 5 per cent. As a whole, the EC total is higher than 2.4 per cent, three times as much as in Spain.

In spite of all this, a rapid growth of the foreign population in Spain cannot be denied, as it doubled in the course of that decade. It was not only this volume, however, nor even the growth rate which accelerated Spain's

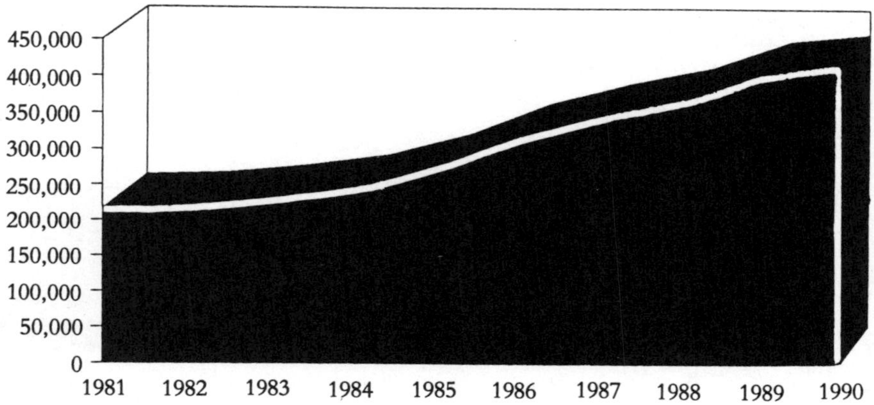

Figure 31.1 The trend in foreigners resident in Spain, 1981–90

Source: *Memorias Anuales de la DGP* (Ministerio del Interior).

awareness of itself as an immigration country. If possible, the broadcasting of news about the tragic cases reflecting the living and working conditions of clandestine immigrants has exerted a greater influence over public opinion and the government. That is why a cost and benefit balance of Spain's adherence to the EC is required as far as its repercussion on Spanish migration policy is concerned – including, of course, an analysis of the new Spanish reality as an immigration country.

The present trends and characteristics of 'illegal' immigration may be summarized as follows: 420,000 residents, just over 6,000 granted political asylum, 17,000 students and about 40,000 children and young people under 16 years of age. The distribution by nationalities shows the following results: 65% are European, 16% come from Latin America, 8% are Asians, 6.5% are Africans and 4.5% come from North America. By sexes, the presence of women reaches a remarkable 50.4%, and married persons amount to 58%, which suggests strong family immigration, already installed or in the process of re-grouping. The age pyramid confirms this last theory (9% are under 13 years of age) and adds another characteristic to Spain as an immigration country: the high presence of foreign pensioner residents (13% are over 60 years old.) All these data are drawn from the Documentation Service for Foreigners, at the Dirección General de Policía (Police Headquarters) and refer to the legal concept of a resident. The Population Census taken in March 1991 records the foreign population residing in Spain, independently of its legal situation.

To complete the scenario, the stock of legal foreign workers was around 95,000 in 1990, including self-employed workers from the EC, who do not need a working permit to perform their activities. The proportion of *working* foreigners with a current permit (excluding those in the process of renewing it, or in other intermediate procedures) – not *resident* foreigners – indicates that around one third of the legally authorized foreigners in Spain are working. Over 75% of them work in the tertiary sector; 14% in industry, and only 10% in construction and agriculture. Almost one half of working foreigners (48%) are European, most of them coming from the EC. The Spanish legal immigration map, finally, shows its deeper colours along the Mediterranean coast, Madrid and the Canary and Balearic Islands. This geographic distribution gives an indication of the proportion of non-working and retired residents, who spend their final years in the coastal and tourist areas of Spain. Let us also mention that the illegal immigration map, with only a few variations, is superimposed on the one described under legal immigration.

Illegal immigration: the regularization experience

The second temporary ordinance contained in the Ley Orgánica (Organic Law) of 1 July 1985, dealing with the rights and freedoms of foreigners in Spain, opened the possibility for foreigners with insufficient papers to regulate their status. The deadline for the presentation of documents and the necessary requirements proved to be insufficient and excessively rigid. Both criteria had to be extended and softened, in order to receive a greater number of the undocumented foreigners. The end result was still small (taking into account the estimations being then talked about of the number of foreigners of irregular status, which was supposed to be about 366,000) and the organization and publicity of the regularization process suffered from the lack of experience and the low political profile given to this operation by the government. In 1985, neither public opinion nor the authorities showed any concern about the influx of foreigners (both legal and illegal) into Spain. Data about this collective regularization, whose purpose was to encompass 'every one of the foreigners with insufficient papers' and not only clandestine workers, were as follows: some 38,000 applications were submitted, and, initially, 94% of the total were granted. These figures need to be analysed *externally* (whether the volume was significant in view of the total number without proper papers) and *internally* (what kind of immigrant was initially regularized).

The external analysis requires first an estimation of the number of irregular immigrants in July 1985. According to my own estimate, the number of foreigners with insufficient papers would be between a minimum of 51,000 and a maximum of 153,000. The intermediate number would be around 76,000 clandestine foreigners. According to these hypotheses, the applications submitted (38,000) represented 75, 25 and 50% respectively of the total foreign irregular immigrants. If we apply the rates of growth observed in regular (legal) immigration, an average hypothesis of the number of illegal immigrants on 1 January 1990 would be between 88,000 and 132,000. With the highest hypothesis, there would be 264,000 illegal immigrants in Spain at the beginning of this decade, and only 66,000 if we were to use the lowest hypothesis. I feel that the intermediate hypothesis is reasonable, and believe that the number of clandestine immigrants did not exceed 132,000 persons in January 1990.

The internal analysis – quantifying the profile of irregular immigration (from the scientific and political points of view) compared with those with insufficient papers – is more interesting. In order to foresee the future immigrant flows towards Spain, it is necessary to know their internal composition (sex, nationality and proportion of workers). Their origin and ethnic and cultural characteristics are important in predicting xenophobic stress between native and foreign populations. Spanish citizens are not concerned about 150,000 undocumented immigrants if most of them are European and Latin American. They are more concerned when they see Arab, black-African or Asian immigrants concentrated in the squares of villages and towns, looking for work, even though there may only be a few thousand of them.

In 1985, the distribution by continents of irregular immigrants who asked to have their situation regularized was: 30% European, 22% Latin Americans, 33% Africans, 12% Asians and 3% from the rest of the world (stateless persons, North Americans and from Oceania). According to my estimations, and to the intermediate hypothesis (132,000) at the beginning of 1990, the proportions would be the following: 25% Europeans, 17% Latin Americans, 46% Africans, 10% Asians and 2% from the rest of the world. This, in short, means a considerable growth of immigrants arriving from Africa. The distribution by continents (assuming that the total number of requests was representative of the whole) presented some surprises, such as the high number of European irregular immigrants and the scarce weight (in relation with what had been anticipated) of undocumented Latin Americans. Demographic characteristics (sex and age) of irregulars also turned out to be unexpected: 39% of the total number were women, 1% children under 14 and 6% people over 60 years of age. In summary: more women and pensioners than anticipated, and less family immigration than had been foreseen.

From the data on occupations given by some of those requesting regularization, it may be deduced that 37% of clandestine immigrants worked in services (mainly as waiters and hawkers); 23% in agriculture and construction; 11% in activities requiring high qualifications (professionals, teachers, office workers) and 28% are not in the work market (housewives and students). The occupational profile of immigrants lacking papers must be taken with a great deal of caution, since 64% of those requesting regularization did not declare any profession or trade.

What has, indeed, been proven is the intention to become settled in Spain for a certain amount of time. These immigrants have permanent characteristics, since only 9% of them asked for a short-term permit. The migration intentions of irregulars did not match the permissions granted. More short-term permits were granted (31%) than were requested (9%) and less residency and working permits than were requested by immigrants. In other words, immigration which sought to become permanent was given a deadline, and the undesired effect obtained was that, after one year, 53% of those initially regularized did not renew their permits, presumably returning to clandestine immigration.

In conclusion: to provide settlement for these illegal immigrants is as important as their regularization right from the beginning. Regularization must make it possible for the new legal status of immigrants to become a fact with a certain amount of continuity. At the time when decisions were taken, the division of conscience about immigration that dominates public opinion may have exerted an excessive weight on the Spanish administration. Things not sought by immigrants were granted without question, in order not to reject, with reasons, most requests submitted. Let us now deal with this hidden conscience of Spanish citizens.

The divided conscience of Spaniards towards immigrants

It would be a good idea to point out, before proceeding any further, that the total number of foreigners in Spain (both legal and clandestine) hardly represents 1.5% of the total population residing in the country. Not only is their volume small, but their composition by continents and nationalities shows a majority of Europeans who, together with North and South Americans, make up over three quarters of the total foreign population. With such a small proportion, it should not be odd that, according to a CIS (Centro de Investigaciones Sociológicas) survey of September 1990, 63% of those interviewed do not follow the news on immigrants, 49% feel that they have only a small amount of information, and 39% do not consider themselves at all informed about this topic: *In Spain, the 'immigrant problem' does not concern the people, who do not know anything about it.* Furthermore, 90% of those asked have not had any contact with foreign workers.

The attitudes of Spanish people towards immigrants must be interpreted within the context of a lack of information and of real contact. Their ideas are preconceived, mere ideologies with no experiences to sustain them, they are prejudices rather than formed opinions. Having said this, 29% of those interviewed believe that an ideologically racist political party might appear in the future, and 11% of them would be ready to vote for it if foreigners were to create serious problems. What would those serious problems be? Spanish people link foreigners with *unemployment* (64% believe that they are taking jobs that could be occupied by themselves, especially by the young), with *drug selling* (57%) and with *urban insecurity* (45%). In short: they are not necessary to replace native workers (74%) and they have a negative influence over the Spanish economy (38%). *In Spain, as in most EC countries, immigrants are seen above all as intruders who are taking something away from us.*

Given an image of immigrants in which negative aspects are dominant, it seems logical that a greater control over them is demanded and less permissive laws: 57% agree that the government should limit immigration; 63% believe that illegal residence of foreigners is little (46%) or not at all (17%) controlled. Half of the Spanish population believe that the situation of illegals should be settled and one third believe that they should be returned to their own countries. The condition they give to regularize clandestine immigrants is that they have a job and have resided at least two years in Spain.

The divided conscience of Spaniards towards immigrants is clearly manifest. On one hand, they admit (50%) that they live in worse conditions than Spanish citizens, crowded in living quarters in the worst districts, that they hold jobs that the Spaniards do not want and are paid smaller wages. They, therefore, should have the same rights (69%), receive government aid (68%) and their situation should be regulated. All these attitudes reflect *a memory of the recent past as a country of emigrants, and a feeling of guilt* about the situation of immigrants working in this country. On the other hand, *awareness of being a country integrated within the EC* leads those interviewed to demand stricter laws, to limit entry, to demand illegal immigrant control and expulsion, to protect the domestic work market. Such are the two sides of the coin: memories of being an emigration country and guilt feelings towards the living conditions of foreign workers; and awareness of being a European country, with attitudes of rejection towards immigrants, who are identified with drug peddling, lack of safety, unemployment and other social problems.

Immigrants from the EC enjoy a more positive image than those from the rest of Europe (with the exception of the Portuguese) and much more favour than those from any other part of the world. Only 7% of Spaniards think that the government should adopt harsh measures in connection with the arrival of workers from the EC, 29% think it should in connection with the Portuguese, and 78% in connection with Arabs. And this is so in spite of the fact that only 23% of Spaniards know any EC citizens personally (14% know some Portuguese) and hardly 11% have any kind of professional relationship with workers from the EC (6% with the Portuguese). Despite this, 85% of those interviewed would receive them well as neighbours and working colleagues and only 12% would try to prevent their children from marrying an EC European. There are, however, some black points in this favourable image. *The freedom that EC workers enjoy of working in Spain will be bad for Spanish workers*: 37% of those surveyed thought so, as opposed to 26% who believe that it will benefit them. This, in the opinion of the persons interviewed, is the cost than must be paid for a full EC integration, which will benefit rather than damage Spain.

An active immigration policy

In 1990, the public debate on irregular immigration into Spain burst forth in all the mass media: Spanish television, radio, newspapers and cinema reflected, widely and continuously, the exploitation and penury to which illegal immigrants were being subjected. On 26 June the Izquierda Unida (United Left) parliamentary group submitted a motion in the Congress of Deputies, urging the government to present a report on the situation of foreigners in Spain. It asked for regularization of the status of foreigners who had resided and worked in Spain for a sufficient length of time, that the right for families to reunite be granted, and that a draft immigration law be prepared.

As an answer to this motion, the PSOE government (Partido Socialista Obrero Español, Spanish Socialist Workers party) sent a communication to the Congress of Deputies, dealing with the situation of foreigners and with the basic guidelines of a policy. On 13 March 1991, all parliamentary groups (with the exception of Izquierda Unida) agreed on a draft resolution, which was passed by 219 votes in favour and 11 abstentions. This resolution covered eleven points, which may be summarized in four paragraphs:

(1) Organization of legal immigrants, depending on the labour needs of the economy and on the absorption capacity of Spanish society. In order to meet this goal, external measures include the modernizing of frontier installations and the use of visas as an instrument to orient immigration policy. Measures inside Spain include *the development of social integration programmes* for immigrants (employment, vocational training, housing, health and social protection) and *the reform of the administrative structure* responsible for the management of immigration policy (creation of Oficinas Unicas de Extranjeros (Foreigner's Offices), of an Immigration Service in the Ministry of Work and Social Security and an Interministerial Commission on Foreigners).

(2) Proposals connected with clandestine immigration: the regularization carried out in 1985 should be completed and the foreigners who have arrived since that time and now working in irregular situations should be made legal. Closer inspection and the imposition of larger penalties on those importing or employing illegal immigrants. And, finally, the reinforcing of the expulsion of illegal immigrants.

(3) Reducing the number of those seeking asylum and refuge, preventing the fraudulent use of the refugee protection system to promote illegal immigration, hastening the resolution of requests from persecuted persons and increasing the material means available to receive with dignity those seeking asylum.

(4) Promotion of aid for social and economic development of the areas that send illegal immigrants to Spain (the Maghreb, especially) orienting this aid towards the creation of jobs and the development of human resources. Finally, proceeding with the integration of Spain within the European space without frontiers, the Schengen Agreement and seeking common cause with all EC countries.

In summary, the policy proposed a gradual and orderly recruitment of legal immigrants, repairing the situation of clandestine immigrants, a reorganization of the means of access to the status of refugee and the development of concerted common migration policies within the EC. Criteria for the acceptance of legal immigrants, to legalize those lacking proper papers and to select the truly persecuted persons were not stipulated. In theory, the Spanish government opted for the intermediate way of *half opening the door to immigrants.* An impossible closure of frontiers or the impracticable opening of a single country to all the needy was not being postulated. Was this a policy agreed upon with or imposed by the EC? What are the costs and benefits of this policy? The next section will deal with these issues.

Final balance: costs and benefits for the immigration policy as a result of Spanish EC integration

Two ideas have seeped into Spanish public opinion: that *the government should fully respect the restrictive policy imposed by the EC* on matters of immigration (41% of those interviewed) and that *Spain is a 'bridge'* for immigrants who wish to go onto other EC countries (13%). On one hand, these two answers give us an idea of the high level of disinformation among the Spanish population on matters of immigration. On the other hand, *the 'half-open door' policy to immigration* implemented by the Spanish government has been fostered by public opinion.

Disinformation is quite obvious, since the EC has never imposed an active policy of legal immigration to Spain, nor has it agreed with the government the decision to regularize illegal foreigners who are able to show that they have work and a place in Spanish society. Even though the convenience of reaching agreement between the twelve Member States on matters of immigration and the need to coordinate migration policies were repeatedly mentioned in the course of the parliamentary debate of 13 March 1991, it is a known fact that every country decides for itself what, how and when to do about foreigners. This is so in general, although some decisions may be taken by a group of countries, or by the whole EC.

The entry visa requirement for Moroccan citizens, for instance, is a measure that the Spanish government would have taken anyway, and sooner rather than later, independently of the EC regulations. The main reason is that Morocco was the main source of illegal immigrants into Spain. The final thought which should be expressed is the following: there is no doubt that decisions taken by each EC Member State will have repercussions over the rest. We are, in a manner of speaking, walking towards a common domestic policy (the removal of frontiers) without having established a joint external policy. In the future, this factor will pose more than one contradiction, and, perhaps, some conflicts. Will Spanish and Italian regularization of immigrants, or the historical commitment of most EC countries to their former colonies not make their effect felt on the twelve Member States? In our own case, it may be stated that the Spanish Parliament has decided to maintain the traditional open door to the citizens of Spanish America. This is just one more case to add to others in other countries.

Spain, at any rate, has now become an immigration country, not simply a place of transit. The Spanish government understood this for a fact when it prepared the 1985 Ley de Extranjería, which was not a condition imposed by the EC either. This has been confirmed by a document sent in 1990 by the government to the Congress of Deputies, setting out immigration policy.

To summarize: as far as immigration matters are concerned, EC membership has not had tangible or important costs for Spain. Rather than a cost, ensuring stability and an increase in social benefits and services for EC workers is a product of the improvement experienced by the Spanish economy since 1985 as well as a necessary reciprocity for the benefits obtained by Spanish EC migrants regarding family welfare and benefits certain tax advantages. Neither aspect (costs and benefits) is very significant. Costs and benefits derived from the *European 'looking glass'* are something else, though. I am talking about the possibility of observing the experience of countries with a longer immigration tradition. This experience is present, sometimes explicitly and mostly implicitly in discussions, programmes, decisions and actions developed by the people, journalists, managers, experts and politicians over the future of immigration in the EC.

References

Codigo de Migraciones (1989), *Volume 1. Textos Legales*, p. 2.190, Madrid, Ministerio de Trabajo y Seguridad Social.

Izquierdo Escribano, A. (1990) *Immigration en Espagne et premiers résultats du programme de régularisation.* OECD Report by Working Group on Migration.

—— (1990 and 1991) *Réseau d'information dans le domaine des migrations d'états tiers*, Rapport par la Commission des Communautés Européenes.

—— (1991) *La imigración en España: legales y clandestinos*, Madrid, Ministerio de Trabajo y Seguridad Social.

Minutes of the parliamentary debate in the Congreso de los Diputados on the status of foreigners in Spain, March 1991.

Muñoz-Pérez, F. and Izquierdo Escribano, A. (1989) 'L'Espagne, pays d'immigration en revue', *Population*, No. 2.

IOE (1987) 'Los inmigrantes en España', *Documentación Social*, No. 66, Madrid.

Sopemi (1989, 1990) Analyse comparative des recentes experiences de regularisation en France, Espagne et aux Etats-Unis, Paris, OECD.

Index

Note: Page numbers in **bold** type refer to **figures**. Page numbers in *italic* type refer to *tables*. Page numbers followed by 'n' refer to notes.

90 0551537 8